PSALMS 1–72
A Commentary in the Wesleyan Tradition

*New Beacon Bible Commentary

PSALMS 1–72
A Commentary in the Wesleyan Tradition

David L. Thompson

BEACON HILL PRESS
OF KANSAS CITY

Copyright 2015
by Beacon Hill Press of Kansas City

ISBN 978-0-8341-3090-6

Cover Design: J.R. Caines
Interior Design: Sharon Page

Unless otherwise indicated all Scripture quotations are from the *Holy Bible, New International Version*® (NIV®). Copyright © 1973, 1978, 1984, 2011 by Biblica, Inc.™ Used by permission. All rights reserved worldwide.

The following versions of Scripture are in the public domain:

American Standard Version (ASV).

King James Version (KJV).

The following copyrighted versions of the Bible are used by permission:

The Holy Bible, English Standard Version (ESV), copyright © 2001 by Crossway Bibles, a division of Good News Publishers. All rights reserved.

The *New American Bible, revised edition* (NABRE), © 2010, 1991, 1986, 1970 Confraternity of Christian Doctrine, Washington, D.C. Used by permission of the copyright owner. All Rights Reserved. No part of the New American Bible may be reproduced in any form without permission in writing from the copyright owner.

The *New American Standard Bible*® (NASB®), © copyright The Lockman Foundation 1960, 1962, 1963, 1968, 1971, 1972, 1973, 1975, 1977, 1995.

The *New English Bible* (NEB), © the Delegates of the Oxford University Press and the Syndics of the Cambridge University Press 1961, 1970.

New JPS Hebrew-English Tanakh (NJPS), © 2000 by The Jewish Publication Society. All rights reserved.

The *New King James Version* (NKJV). Copyright © 1979, 1980, 1982 Thomas Nelson, Inc.

The *Holy Bible, New Living Translation* (NLT), copyright © 1996, 2004, 2007, 2013 by Tyndale House Foundation. Used by permission of Tyndale House Publishers, Inc., Carol Stream, IL 60188. All rights reserved.

The *New Revised Standard Version* (NRSV) of the Bible, copyright 1989 by the Division of Christian Education of the National Council of the Churches of Christ in the USA. All rights reserved.

The *Revised English Bible* (REB). Copyright © 1989 by Oxford University Press and Cambridge University Press.

The *Revised Standard Version* (RSV) of the Bible, copyright 1946, 1952, 1971 by the Division of Christian Education of the National Council of the Churches of Christ in the USA. All rights reserved.

Library of Congress Cataloging-in-Publication Data

Thompson, David L. (David Loren), 1940-
  Psalms 1-72 : a commentary in the Wesleyan tradition / David L. Thompson.
    pages cm
  Includes bibliographical references.
  ISBN 978-0-8341-3090-6 (pbk. : alk. paper)
 1. Bible. Psalms, I-LXXII—Commentaries. I. Title.
  BS1430.53.T49 2015
  223'.207—dc23

2015024597

DEDICATION

To
Dennis F. Kinlaw
and
to the memory of
Samuel Iwry,
beloved teachers and friends

COMMENTARY EDITORS

General Editors

Alex Varughese
    Ph.D., Drew University
    Professor of Biblical Literature
    Mount Vernon Nazarene University
    Mount Vernon, Ohio

Roger Hahn
    Ph.D., Duke University
    Dean of the Faculty
    Professor of New Testament
    Nazarene Theological Seminary
    Kansas City, Missouri

George Lyons
    Ph.D., Emory University
    Professor of New Testament
    Northwest Nazarene University
    Nampa, Idaho

Section Editors

Joseph Coleson
    Ph.D., Brandeis University
    Professor of Old Testament
    Nazarene Theological Seminary
    Kansas City, Missouri

Robert Branson
    Ph.D., Boston University
    Professor of Biblical Literature
        Emeritus
    Olivet Nazarene University
    Bourbonnais, Illinois

Alex Varughese
    Ph.D., Drew University
    Professor of Biblical Literature
    Mount Vernon Nazarene University
    Mount Vernon, Ohio

Jim Edlin
    Ph.D., Southern Baptist Theological
        Seminary
    Professor of Biblical Literature and
        Languages
    Chair, Division of Religion and
        Philosophy
    MidAmerica Nazarene University
    Olathe, Kansas

Kent Brower
    Ph.D., The University of Manchester
    Vice Principal
    Senior Lecturer in Biblical Studies
    Nazarene Theological College
    Manchester, England

George Lyons
    Ph.D., Emory University
    Professor of New Testament
    Northwest Nazarene University
    Nampa, Idaho

CONTENTS

General Editors' Preface   11
Acknowledgments   13
Abbreviations   15
Glossary   19
Bibliography   21

INTRODUCTION   25
   A. The Importance of the Biblical Psalter   25
   B. The Psalms as a Collection   27
   C. Psalm Superscriptions   30
      1. Attribution   30
      2. Instrumentation   32
      3. Tune or Song Titles   33
      4. Song/Psalm Types   34
      5. Uses   35
      6. Historical Notes   35
   D. The Psalms as Poetry   36
      1. Early Responses to Poetic Scripture   36
      2. Modern Approaches to Hebrew Poetic Rhythm   37
      3. Parallelism and Hebrew Poetry   39
      4. Hebrew Poetry and Terseness   41
      5. Significance of Poetic Scripture   42
   E. Recent Study of the Psalter   43
      1. Recent Study and Psalm Types   43
      2. The Psalms and Israel's Worship   48
      3. The Editorial Shape of the Psalter   50
   F. Authorship, Date, Audience, Provenance, Composition, and Occasion of the Psalter   52
      1. Authorship   53
      2. Date, Audience, Provenance, and Composition   54
      3. Occasion   55
   G. Hermeneutical Issues   56
   H. Theological Emphases in the Psalter   58
      1. The Lord Rules the Cosmos Faithfully and Mercifully   58
      2. Those Centered Wholly in the Will of God Have Abundant Life   60
      3. Worship Constitutes the Appropriate Human Response to God   61
   I. The Text of the Psalter   62

COMMENTARY	65
Book I: Psalms 1—41	65
The Two Ways: Torah and Destruction (1:1-6)	67
Yahweh's Royal Son (2:1-12)	74
Yahweh: Shield from Many Foes (3:1-8 [2-9 HB])	79
Who Can Show Us the Good Life? (4:1-8 [2-9 HB])	81
Prayer for Rescue from Lethal Lies (5:1-12 [2-13 HB])	84
Prayer in the Face of Discipline (6:1-10 [2-11 HB])	87
Prayer for Yahweh's Judgment (7:1-17 [2-18 HB])	90
Praise for Glorious Yahweh's Glorious Human (8:1-9 [2-10 HB])	93
Prayer for Yahweh's Rule over Haughty Humans (9:1-20 [2-21 HB])	96
Let the Hidden Yahweh Act (10:1-18)	99
Refuge at Yahweh's Throne (11:1-7)	101
Help in Yahweh's War of Words (12:1-8 [2-9 HB])	103
Prayer of the Distressed (13:1-6 [2-6 HB])	105
Prayer When Fools Prevail (14:1-7)	107
Who Inhabits Yahweh's Hill? (15:1-5)	108
Life in the Path of Life (16:1-11)	110
Prayer for Rescue and Vindication (17:1-15)	112
Song of Yahweh, the King's Rock and Refuge (18:1-50 [2-51 HB])	115
On Being Acceptable to God (19:1-14 [2-15 HB])	122
Affirmation of Yahweh's Blessing of the King (20:1-9 [2-10 HB])	127
The King's Trust in Yahweh (21:1-13 [2-14 HB])	129
Thanksgiving for Delivery from Desertion (22:1-31 [2-32 HB])	132
Praise Yahweh the Royal Shepherd (23:1-6)	136
Praise Yahweh the Glorious King (24:1-10)	139
Prayer for Rescue and Instruction (25:1-22)	143
Prayer for Vindication of a Blameless One (26:1-12)	147
Yahweh, My Light and Life (27:1-14)	150
Prayer for Yahweh to Shepherd His People (28:1-9)	154
Praise to the Enthroned One (29:1-11)	156
Thanksgiving for Wailing Turned to Dancing (30:1-12 [2-13 HB])	160
A Prayer for Refuge in Yahweh's Love (31:1-24 [2-25 HB])	163
A Witness: The Blessings of Forgiveness (32:1-11)	168
Praise for the Creator's Counsel (33:1-22)	170
Instruction in Yahweh's Goodness (34:1-22 [2-23 HB])	174
Prayer for Vindication and Rescue (35:1-28)	180
Prayer for Yahweh's Keeping Love (36:1-12 [2-13 HB])	183
A Teaching: Trust Yahweh; Don't Fret (37:1-40)	185
Prayer for Rescue from the Consequences of Sin (38:1-22 [2-23 HB])	192

Prayer of the Transient Sinner (39:1-13 [2-14 HB])	195
Prayer: Deliver from the Pit—Again! (40:1-17 [2-18 HB])	197
Prayer of the One Betrayed (41:1-13 [2-14 HB])	202
Book II: Psalms 42—72	**207**
Prayer for Vindication of the Downcast (42:1—43:5 [42:2—43:5 HB])	209
Prayer to the Sleeping God (44:1-26 [2-27 HB])	215
Verses for the King's Wedding (45:1-17 [2-18 HB])	220
Praise for the City of God (46:1-11 [2-12 HB])	225
A Song for the Great King Yahweh (47:1-9 [2-10 HB])	227
Praise for the City of the Great King (48:1-14 [2-15 HB])	229
A Poem for Dealing with Death (49:1-20 [2-21 HB])	232
Instruction on Feeding God (50:1-23)	236
Prayer of Confession and Recreation (51:1-19 [3-21 HB])	241
A Psalm against Betrayers (52:1-9 [3-11 HB])	248
The Godless Are Fools Still (53:1-6 [2-7 HB])	250
Prayer for Deliverance from Ruthless Attack (54:1-7 [3-9 HB])	251
Prayer for Rescue from an Erstwhile Friend (55:1-23 [2-24 HB])	253
Prayer of Trust for Deliverance (56:1-13 [2-14 HB])	256
Prayer for Rescue from Ravenous Lions (57:1-11 [2-12 HB])	258
Prayer for Deliverance from Uncharmed Snakes (58:1-11 [2-12 HB])	260
Prayer for Deliverance from Snarling Dogs (59:1-17 [2-18 HB])	262
A Prayer for Help from Neighbors (60:1-12 [3-14 HB])	265
A Prayer at the Paying of Vows (61:1-8 [2-9 HB])	269
A Song to God, My Only Hope (62:1-12 [2-13 HB])	272
Song of the King's Hunger for God (63:1-11 [2-12 HB])	274
Prayer for the Ambushed Innocent Ones (64:1-10 [2-11 HB])	279
Praise for the Creator, Zion's Savior (65:1-13 [2-14 HB])	282
Thanks for the One Who Answered Prayer (66:1-20)	287
A Prayer Song for All People (67:1-7 [2-8 HB])	291
A Song for God on the Move (68:1-35 [2-36 HB])	293
A Prayer from the Mire (69:1-36 [2-37 HB])	302
A Prayer of Petitions (70:1-5 [2-6 HB])	307
A Prayer for Approaching Old Age (71:1-24)	309
A Song for the King (72:1-20)	313

GENERAL EDITORS' PREFACE

The purpose of the New Beacon Bible Commentary is to make available to pastors and students in the twenty-first century a biblical commentary that reflects the best scholarship in the Wesleyan theological tradition. The commentary project aims to make this scholarship accessible to a wider audience to assist them in their understanding and proclamation of Scripture as God's Word.

Writers of the volumes in this series not only are scholars within the Wesleyan theological tradition and experts in their field but also have special interest in the books assigned to them. Their task is to communicate clearly the critical consensus and the full range of other credible voices who have commented on the Scriptures. Though scholarship and scholarly contribution to the understanding of the Scriptures are key concerns of this series, it is not intended as an academic dialogue within the scholarly community. Commentators of this series constantly aim to demonstrate in their work the significance of the Bible as the church's book and the contemporary relevance and application of the biblical message. The project's overall goal is to make available to the church and for her service the fruits of the labors of scholars who are committed to their Christian faith.

The *New International Version* (NIV) is the reference version of the Bible used in this series; however, the focus of exegetical study and comments is the biblical text in its original language. When the commentary uses the NIV, it is printed in bold. The text printed in bold italics is the translation of the author. Commentators also refer to other translations where the text may be difficult or ambiguous.

The structure and organization of the commentaries in this series seeks to facilitate the study of the biblical text in a systematic and methodical way. Study of each biblical book begins with an ***Introduction*** section that gives an overview of authorship, date, provenance, audience, occasion, purpose, sociological/cultural issues, textual history, literary features, hermeneutical issues, and theological themes necessary to understand the book. This section also includes a brief outline of the book and a list of general works and standard commentaries.

The commentary section for each biblical book follows the outline of the book presented in the introduction. In some volumes, readers will find section **overviews** of large portions of scripture with general comments on their overall literary structure and other literary features. A consistent feature of the commentary is the paragraph-by-paragraph study of biblical texts. This section has three parts: **Behind the Text**, **In the Text**, and **From the Text**.

The goal of the **Behind the Text** section is to provide the reader with all the relevant information necessary to understand the text. This includes specific historical situations reflected in the text, the literary context of the text, sociological and cultural issues, and literary features of the text.

In the Text explores what the text says, following its verse-by-verse structure. This section includes a discussion of grammatical details, word studies, and the connectedness of the text to other biblical books/passages or other parts of the book being studied (the canonical relationship). This section provides transliterations of key words in Hebrew and Greek and their literal meanings. The goal here is to explain what the author would have meant and/or what the audience would have understood as the meaning of the text. This is the largest section of the commentary.

The **From the Text** section examines the text in relation to the following areas: theological significance, intertextuality, the history of interpretation, use of the Old Testament scriptures in the New Testament, interpretation in later church history, actualization, and application.

The commentary provides **sidebars** on topics of interest that are important but not necessarily part of an explanation of the biblical text. These topics are informational items and may cover archaeological, historical, literary, cultural, and theological matters that have relevance to the biblical text. Occasionally, longer detailed discussions of special topics are included as **excurses**.

We offer this series with our hope and prayer that readers will find it a valuable resource for their understanding of God's Word and an indispensable tool for their critical engagement with the biblical texts.

Roger Hahn, Centennial Initiative General Editor
Alex Varughese, General Editor (Old Testament)
George Lyons, General Editor (New Testament)

ACKNOWLEDGMENTS

In the fall of 1962 I signed up for Dr. Dennis F. Kinlaw's first year Hebrew class at Asbury Theological Seminary. It changed my life. In that class and also in succeeding Hebrew and other ANE language classes God enlisted me in the ministry of teaching Bible to prospective pastors and teachers. Fellow classmates in those seminars were a room full of future OT scholars: John Hartley, John Oswalt, Victor Hamilton, Ken Gooden, Barry Ross. Time and again as I have worked on this commentary, memories of those life-changing times have invigorated me. Dr. Kinlaw remains a beloved mentor to this day.

I owe a debt of gratitude to the IT staff at Asbury Seminary: Brian Yeich, Robbie Danielson, and especially Gregory Sigountos. Without their repeated rescues and instruction this work would never have seen the light of day.

One of the special joys of participating in a project like the New Beacon Bible Commentary is the opportunity to form new professional and personal friendships. Working with editors Alex Varughese and Robert Branson has afforded me those opportunities. I am especially indebted to Dr. Branson for his incredible patience and his gentle guidance. Without his direction and encouragement this work would not have come to fruition. Working with him has been a particular delight.

Thanks be to God for his abounding mercies and for his gift of Scripture, including the Psalms. Time and again I have found myself caught up in worship as I pondered these songs. Of course the constant risk assumed by anyone who takes up the task of commenting on the Psalms is that one will "ruin" these priceless gifts from the Lord in the process of trying to expound them. My prayer is that the Lord of the Word will use my limited jottings to edify his people. To him be glory forever.

ABBREVIATIONS

With a few exceptions, these abbreviations follow those in *The SBL Handbook of Style* (Alexander 1999).

General

→	see the commentary at	
A.D.	anno Domini (precedes date) (equivalent to C.E.)	
ad loc.	at or to the cited place	
ANE	ancient Near East	
B.C.	before Christ (follows date) (equivalent to B.C.E.)	
ch	chapter	
chs	chapters	
CMn	construction marker/preposition with noun	
CMp	construction marker with pronoun	
e.g.	for example	
f(f).	and the following one(s)	
fs.	feminine singular	
Gk.	Greek	
HB	Hebrew Bible	
Heb.	Hebrew	
hl	*hapax legomenon*, occurs once (and hence often unclear for lack of contexts from which to ascertain a word's meaning)	
ibid.	*ibidem*, in the same place	
i.e.	that is	
lit.	literally	
LXX	Septuagint	
MS(S)	manuscript(s)	
ms.	masculine singular	
MT	Masoretic Text (of the OT)	
n.	note	
NT	New Testament	
On	object noun	
OT	Old Testament	
pl.	plural	
ptc.	participle	
repr.	reprint(ed)	
Sn	subject noun	
Sp	subject pronoun	
SS	superscription	
SSs	superscriptions	
Tg.	Targum	
v	verse	
Vg.	Vulgate	
Vptc.	verb participle	
vv	verses	

Modern English Versions

ASV	American Standard Version
ESV	English Standard Version
KJV	King James Version
NABRE	New American Bible, Revised Edition
NASB	New American Standard Bible
NEB	New English Bible
NJPS	Tanakh Translation
NKJV	New King James Version

NLT	New Living Translation	
NRSV	New Revised Standard Version	
REB	Revised English Bible	
RSV	Revised Standard Version	

Print Conventions for Translations

Bold font		NIV (bold without quotation marks in the text under study; elsewhere in the regular font, with quotation marks and no further identification)
Bold italic font		Author's translation (without quotation marks)

Behind the Text: Literary or historical background information average readers might not know from reading the biblical text alone

In the Text: Comments on the biblical text, words, phrases, grammar, and so forth

From the Text: The use of the text by later interpreters, contemporary relevance, theological and ethical implications of the text, with particular emphasis on Wesleyan concerns

Old Testament

Gen	Genesis
Exod	Exodus
Lev	Leviticus
Num	Numbers
Deut	Deuteronomy
Josh	Joshua
Judg	Judges
Ruth	Ruth
1—2 Sam	1—2 Samuel
1—2 Kgs	1—2 Kings
1—2 Chr	1—2 Chronicles
Ezra	Ezra
Neh	Nehemiah
Esth	Esther
Job	Job
Ps/Pss	Psalm/Psalms
Prov	Proverbs
Eccl	Ecclesiastes
Song	Song of Songs/ Song of Solomon
Isa	Isaiah
Jer	Jeremiah
Lam	Lamentations
Ezek	Ezekiel
Dan	Daniel
Hos	Hosea
Joel	Joel
Amos	Amos
Obad	Obadiah
Jonah	Jonah
Mic	Micah
Nah	Nahum
Hab	Habakkuk
Zeph	Zephaniah
Hag	Haggai
Zech	Zechariah
Mal	Malachi

(Note: Chapter and verse numbering in the MT and LXX often differ compared to those in English Bibles. To avoid confusion, all biblical references follow the chapter and verse numbering in English translations, even when the text in the MT and LXX is under discussion.)

New Testament

Matt	Matthew
Mark	Mark
Luke	Luke
John	John
Acts	Acts
Rom	Romans
1—2 Cor	1—2 Corinthians
Gal	Galatians
Eph	Ephesians
Phil	Philippians
Col	Colossians
1—2 Thess	1—2 Thessalonians
1—2 Tim	1—2 Timothy
Titus	Titus
Phlm	Philemon
Heb	Hebrews
Jas	James
1—2 Pet	1—2 Peter
1—2—3 John	1—2—3 John
Jude	Jude
Rev	Revelation

Secondary Sources: Journals, Series, and Reference Works

ANEP	*The Ancient Near East in Pictures Relating to the Old Testament.* Edited by J. B. Pritchard. Princeton, 1954.
ANET	*Ancient Near Eastern Texts Relating to the Old Testament.* Edited by J. B. Pritchard. 3d ed. Princeton, 1969.
BAR	*Biblical Archaeology Review*
BBHS	*Liber Psalmorum*, fascicle 11 of *Biblia Hebraica Stuttgartensia*. Prepared by H. Bardtke. Stuttgart, 1969.
BDAG	Bauer, W., F. W. Danker, W. F. Arndt, and F. W. Gingrich. *A Greek-English Lexicon of the New Testament and Other Early Christian Literature.* 3d ed. Chicago, 2000.
BDB	Brown, F., S. R. Driver, and C. A. Briggs. *A Hebrew and English Lexicon of the Old Testament.* Oxford, 1907.
BHS	*Biblia Hebraica Stuttgartensia.* Edited by K. Elliger and W. Rudolph. Stuttgart, 1983.
GELS	*Greek-English Lexicon of the Septuagint.* Rev. ed. Compiled by Johan Lust/Erik Eynikel, Katrin Hauspie. Peabody, MA, 2003.

GKC	*Gesenius' Hebrew Grammar.* Edited and Enlarged by E. Kautzsch. Translated by A. E. Cowley. 2d English ed. Oxford, 1910.
HALOT	*The Hebrew and Aramaic Lexicon of the Old Testament.* L. Koehler and W. Baumgartner, revised by W. Baumgartner and J. J. Stamm. Translated and edited by M. E. J. Richardson. 5 vols. Leiden: E. J. Brill, 1994-99.
IBHS	Waltke, Bruce K., and M. O'Connor. *An Introduction to Biblical Hebrew Syntax.* Winona Lake, IN: Eisenbrauns, 1990.
JBL	*Journal of Biblical Literature*
JNES	*Journal of Near Eastern Studies*
JSOT	*Journal for the Study of the Old Testament*
JSOTSup	Journal for the Study of the Old Testament: Supplement Series
KB3	Koehler, L., and W. Baumgartner. *Lexicon in Veteris Testamenti Libros*, 3d ed. Leiden, 1958.
SBLDS	Society of Biblical Literature Dissertation Series
UT	Gordon, C. H. *Ugaritic Textbook.* AnOr 38. Rome, 1965.

Greek Transliteration

Greek	Letter	English
α	alpha	a
β	bēta	b
γ	gamma	g
γ	gamma nasal	n (before γ, κ, ξ, χ)
δ	delta	d
ε	epsilon	e
ζ	zēta	z
η	ēta	ē
θ	thēta	th
ι	iōta	i
κ	kappa	k
λ	lambda	l
μ	mu	m
ν	nu	n
ξ	xi	x
ο	omicron	o
π	pi	p
ρ	rhō	r
ρ	initial rhō	rh
σ/ς	sigma	s
τ	tau	t
υ	upsilon	y
υ	upsilon	u (in diphthongs: au, eu, ēu, ou, ui)
φ	phi	ph
χ	chi	ch
ψ	psi	ps
ω	ōmega	ō
ʽ	rough breathing	h (before initial vowels or diphthongs)

Hebrew Consonant Transliteration

Hebrew/Aramaic	Letter	English
א	alef	ʼ
ב	bet	b
ג	gimel	g
ד	dalet	d
ה	he	h
ו	vav	v or w
ז	zayin	z
ח	khet	ḥ
ט	tet	ṭ
י	yod	y
כ/ך	kaf	k
ל	lamed	l
מ/ם	mem	m
נ/ן	nun	n
ס	samek	s
ע	ayin	ʽ
פ/ף	pe	p; f (spirant)
צ/ץ	tsade	ṣ
ק	qof	q
ר	resh	r
שׂ	sin	ś
שׁ	shin	š
ת	tav	t; th (spirant)

GLOSSARY

acrostic	a literary device in which consecutive lines of a poem begin with succeeding letters of the Hebrew alphabet, or some permutation thereof; also called an "abecedary"
bicolon	a line of poetic text composed of two usually parallel cola; also called a distich
catena	a linked or connected series of verses
chiasm	a literary device, named after the Greek letter chi, in which items are arranged in a reversing pattern as follows: a b c d c' b' a'
codicil	appended lines
cohortative	a Hebrew verb form that expresses a command, a wish, or strong desire in the first person, that is, "Let us . . ."
colon	a single line of poetic text (sometimes called a stich; plural, cola)
colophon	a note usually placed at the beginning of a document in order to improve the reader's understanding of it
dittography	a scribal error in which the eye returns to the beginning of a passage just copied and recopies that material, thus entering twice what should have appeared once
haplography	a scribal error in which the eye skips from one letter or word to the same letter(s), thus omitting the intervening materials
incipit	the first few words of a document by which the whole is identified
inclusio(n)	a literary device in which a unit begins and ends with the same vocabulary; also called a bracket
interchange	a literary device in which items are arranged in an alternating pattern as follows: a b a' b' a" b" etc.
jussive	a mood of the Hebrew verb system that expresses a command, an exhortation, or a strong desire in the third person, that is, "Let him . . . ," "May he . . ."
merism	a reference to a larger whole by naming extreme parts, for example, "heaven and earth" to refer to the whole creation
precative	identical in form to the preterite verb but like the jussive in meaning
tricolon	a line of poetic text composed of three, usually parallel cola; also called a tristich

BIBLIOGRAPHY

Albright, W. F. 1944. The Oracles of Balaam. *JBL* 63:207-33.
_____. 1969. *Archaeology and the Religion of Israel*. 5th ed. Garden City, NY: Anchor Books.
Alexander, Joseph Addison.1850-51. *The Psalms: Translated and Explained*. 3 vols. New York: Baker and Scribner.
Allen, Leslie. 1987. *Word Biblical Themes: Psalms*. Waco, TX: Word Books Publishers.
Alter, Robert. 1985. *The Art of Biblical Poetry*. New York: Basic Books.
_____. 2007. *The Book of Psalms: A Translation with Commentary*. New York: W. W. Norton.
Andersen, Francis I. 1970. *The Hebrew Verbless Clause in the Pentateuch*. No. XIV. Journal of Biblical Literature Monograph Series. Nashville: Abingdon.
Andersen, Francis I., and David Noel Freedman. 1989. *Amos: A New Translation with Introduction and Commentary*. Vol. 24A of The Anchor Bible. New York: Doubleday.
Anglim, Simon, Phyllis G. Jestice, Rob S. Rice, Scott M. Rusch, and John Serrati. 2002. *Fighting Techniques in the Ancient World 3000 BC-AD 500: Equipment, Combat Skills, and Tactics*. New York: St. Martin's Press.
Arnold, Bill T., and Bryan E. Beyer, eds. 2002. *Readings from the Ancient Near East*. Grand Rapids: Baker Academic.
Averbeck, R. E. 2003. Sacrifices and Offerings. Pages 706-33 in *Dictionary of the Old Testament: Pentateuch*. T. Desmond Alexander and David W. Baker, editors. Downers Grove, IL: InterVarsity Press.
Balentine, Samuel E., and John Barton, eds. 1994. *Language, Theology, and the Bible: Essays in Honour of James Barr*. Oxford: Clarendon Press.
Bauer, David R., and Robert A. Traina. 2011. *Inductive Bible Study: A Comprehensive Guide to the Practice of Hermeneutics*. Grand Rapids: Baker Academic.
Beale, G. K. 2004. *The Temple and the Church's Mission: A Biblical Theology of the Dwelling Place of God. New Studies in Biblical Theology*. Downers Grove, IL: InterVarsity Press.
Berlin, Adele. 1996. Introduction to Hebrew Poetry. Pages 301-15 in vol. IV of *The New Interpreter's Bible*. Nashville: Abingdon.
Boulding, Maria, O.S.B. 2000. Expositions of the Psalms 33-50, III/16. Vol. 2 of *The Works of Saint Augustine: A Translation for the 21st Century*. Edited by John E. Rotelle, O.S.A. Hyde Park, NY: New City Press.
Broyles, Craig C. 1999. *New International Biblical Commentary: Psalms*. Peabody, MA: Hendrickson.
Brueggemann, Walter. 1984. *The Message of the Psalms: A Theological Commentary*. Minneapolis: Augsburg.
Childs, Brevard S. 1979. *Introduction to the Old Testament as Scripture*. Philadelphia: Fortress.
Clines, David J. A. 1987. The Parallelism of Greater Precision. Pages 77-100 in *Directions in Biblical Hebrew Poetry*. JSOTSup, 40. Edited by Elaine R. Follis. Sheffield: Sheffield Academic Press.
Craigie, Peter C. 1983. *Psalms 1-50*. Vol. 19 of *Word Biblical Commentary*. Waco, TX: Word Books.
Crenshaw, James L. 2001. *The Psalms: An Introduction*. Grand Rapids: Eerdmans.
Cross, Frank Moore, Jr. 1950. *Studies in Ancient Yahwistic Poetry*. Baltimore: Ph.D. Dissertation, the Johns Hopkins University.
_____. 1973. *Canaanite Myth and Hebrew Epic: Essays in the History of the Religion of Israel*. Cambridge, MA: Harvard University Press.
Dahood, Mitchell. 1966. *Psalms I: 1-50*. 1966. Vol. 16 of The Anchor Bible. Edited by William Foxwell Albright et al. Garden City, NY: Doubleday.
_____. 1968. *Psalms II: 51-100*. Vol. 17 of The Anchor Bible. Edited by William Foxwell Albright et al. Garden City, NY: Doubleday.
_____. 1970. *Psalms III: 101-150*. Vol. 17A of The Anchor Bible. Edited by William Foxwell Albright et al. Garden City, NY: Doubleday.
Delitzsch, Franz. 1883. *Commentary on the Book of Psalms*. Revised by author and translated by David Eaton and James E. Duguid. New York: Funk and Wagnalls.
deVaux, Roland. 1965. *Ancient Israel*. 2 vols. New York: McGraw Hill.
Dietrich, Manfried, Oswald Loretz, and Joaquin Sanmartin. 1995. *The Cuneiform Alphabetic Texts from Ugarit, Ras Ibn Hani and Other Places*. KTU: 2d, enlarged ed. Band 8. Abhandlungen zur Literatur. Alt-Suyrien-Palastinas und Mesopotamiens. Edited by Manfried Dietrich and Oswald Loretz. Munster: Ugarit-Verlag.

Driver, G. R. 1931. Studies in the Vocabulary of the Old Testament, no. 2. Pages 250-57 in vol. 32 of *The Journal of Theological Studies*.

Enns, Peter. 1997. "*fpvm*." Pages 1142-44 in vol. 2 of *New International Dictionary of Old Testament Theology and Exegesis* (NIDOTTE). Edited by Willem A. VanGemeren. 5 vols. Grand Rapids: Zondervan.

Evans, Craig A. 2001. "The Dead Sea Scrolls and the Canon of Scripture in the Time of Jesus." Pages 67-79. *The Bible at Qumran: Text, Shape, and Interpretation*. Edited by Peter W. Flint. Studies in the Dead Sea Scrolls and Related Literature. Grand Rapids: Eerdmans.

First, Mitchell. 2012. Can Archaeology Help Date the Psalms? Pages 53-67 in *BAR* (July/August).

Flint, Peter W., ed. 2001. *The Bible at Qumran: Text, Shape, and Interpretation*. Studies in the Dead Sea Scrolls and Related Literature. Grand Rapids: Eerdmans.

Follis, Elaine R., ed. 1987. *Directions in Biblical Hebrew Poetry*. JSOTSup 40. Sheffield: Sheffield Academic Press.

Freedman, David Noel. 1987. "Another Look at Biblical Hebrew Poetry." Pages 11-28 in *Directions in Biblical Hebrew Poetry*. JSOTSup, 40. Edited by Elaine R. Follis. Sheffield: Sheffield Academic Press.

Gerstenberger, Erhard S. 1988. *Psalms Part 1 with an Introduction to Cultic Poetry*. Vol. XIV of *The Forms of the Old Testament Literature*. Edited by Rolf P. Knierim, Gene M. Tucker, and Marvin A. Sweeney. Grand Rapids: Eerdmans.

———. 2001a. *Psalms Part 2 and Lamentations*. Vol. XV of *The Forms of the Old Testament Literature*. Edited by Rolf P. Knierim, Gene M. Tucker, and Marvin A. Sweeney. Grand Rapids: Eerdmans.

———. 2001b. "*hna*." Pages 230-52 in vol. XI of *Theological Dictionary of the Old Testament*. Edited by G. Johannes Botterweck, et al. Grand Rapids: Eerdmans.

Goldingay, John. 2006. *Psalms: Vol. 1, Psalms 1-41*. Baker Commentary on the Old Testament: Wisdom and Psalms. Edited by Tremper Longman III. Grand Rapids: Baker.

———. 2007. *Psalms: Vol. 2, Psalms 42-89*. Baker Commentary on the Old Testament: Wisdom and Psalms. Edited by Tremper Longman III. Grand Rapids: Baker.

———. 2008. *Psalms: Vol. 3, Psalms 90-150*. Baker Commentary on the Old Testament: Wisdom and Psalms. Edited by Tremper Longman III. Grand Rapids: Baker.

Gordon, Cyrus. 1978. Pages 50-51 in "The Wine-Dark Sea." *JNES* 37.

Goulder, Michael D. 1996. *The Psalms of Asaph and the Pentateuch: Studies in the Psalter, III*. No. 223 in the JSOTSup. Sheffield: Sheffield Academic Press.

Gray, J. 1977. "A Cantata of the Autumn Festival: Psalm LXVIII." Pages 2-26 in no. 22 of *Journal of Semitic Studies*.

Greenfield, Jonas C. 1994. *'atta porarta be'ozka yam (Psalm 74:13a)*. Pages 113-19 in *Language, Theology, and the Bible: Essays in Honour of James Barr*. Edited by Samuel E. Balentine and John Barton. Oxford: Clarendon Press.

Gunkel, Hermann, and Joachim Begrich. 1998. *Introduction to Psalms: The Genres of the Religious Lyric of Israel*. Translated by James D. Nogalski. Mercer Library of Biblical Studies. Macon, GA: Mercer University Press. [Translation of *Einleitung in die psalmen: die Gattungen der religiosen Lyrik Israels*. Göttingen Handkommentar zum Alten Testament, 1933.]

Hartley, John E. 1992. *Leviticus*. Vol. 4 of *Word Biblical Commentary*. Edited by David A. Hubbard and Glenn W. Barker. Dallas: Word Books.

Hossfeld, Frank-Lothar, and Erich Zenger. 1993. *Die Psalmen I: Psalm 1-50*. Die Neue Echter Bibel: Kommentar zum Alten Testament mit der Einheitsubersetzung. Würzburg: Echter.

———. 2005. *Psalms 2: A Commentary on Psalms 51-100*. Edited by Klaus Baltzer. Hermeneia—A Critical and Historical Commentary on the Bible. Minneapolis: Fortress Press.

———. 2011. *Psalms 3: A Commentary on Psalms 101-150*. Edited by Klaus Baltzer. English Translation by Linda M. Maloney. *Hermeneia—A Critical and Historical Commentary on the Psalms*. Minneapolis: Fortress Press.

Howard, David M., Jr. 1993. "Editorial Activity in the Psalter: A State-of-the-Field Survey." Pages 52-70 in *The Shape and Shaping of the Psalter*. No. 159 in the JSOTsup, edited by J. Clinton McCann Jr. Sheffield: Sheffield Academic Press.

Hurtado, Larry W. 2003. *Lord Jesus Christ: Devotion to Jesus in Earliest Christianity*. Grand Rapids: Eerdmans.

Jastrow, Marcus. 1950. *A Dictionary of the Targumim, the Talmud Babli and Yerushalmi, and the Midrashic Literature*. 2 vols. New York: Pardes Publishing House.

Johnson, Terry, ed. and comp. 1994. *Trinity Psalter*. Pittsburgh: Crown & Covenant Publications.

Keel, Othmar. 1997. *The Symbolism of the Biblical World: Ancient Near Eastern Iconography and the Book of Psalms*. Translated by Timothy J. Hallett. Winona Lake, IN: Eisenbrauns.

Keel, Othmar, and Christoph Uehlinger. 1998. *Gods, Goddesses, and Images of God in Ancient Israel*. Translated by Henry Trapp. Minneapolis: Fortress Press.

Keener, Craig S. 2012. Introduction and 1:1—2:47. Vol. I of *Acts: An Exegetical Commentary*. Grand Rapids: Baker Academic.

Keil, C. F., and F. Delitzsch. 1989. *Psalms*. Vol. 5 of *Commentary on the Old Testament*. Repr. F. Delitzsch. *Commentar über den Psalter*. 2d ed. 1867. 2 vols. in 1. Peabody, MA: Hendrickson.

Kidner, Derek. 1973. Psalms 1-72: An Introduction and Commentary. Vol. 14a of *Tyndale Old Testament Commentary*. Edited by D. J. Wiseman. Downers Grove, IL: InterVarsity Press.

———. 1975. Psalms 73-150: An Introduction and Commentary. Vol. 14b of *Tyndale Old Testament Commentary*. Edited by D. J. Wiseman. Downers Grove, IL: InterVarsity Press.

Kinlaw, Dennis F., with John N. Oswalt. 2010. *Lectures in Old Testament Theology*. Anderson, IN: Francis Asbury Press.

Kraus, Hans-Joachim. 1988. *Psalms 1-59: A Commentary*. Translated by Hilton C. Oswald. *Biblischer Kommentar Psalmen*. Minneapolis: Augsburg.

———. 1989. *Psalms 60-150: A Commentary*. Translated by Hilton C. Oswald. *Biblischer Kommentar Psalmen*. Minneapolis: Augsburg.

Kugel, James L. 1981. *The Idea of Biblical Hebrew Poetry: Parallelism and Its History*. New Haven, CT: Yale University Press.

Lowth, Robert. 1835. *Lectures on the Sacred Poetry of the Hebrews*. London: T. Tegg & Son.

Lucas, E. C. 2008. "Poetics, Terminology of." Pages 520-25 in *Dictionary of Old Testament Wisdom, Poetry, and Writings*, edited by Tremper Longman III and Peter Enns. Downers Grove, IL: IVP Academic.

Lust, Johan, Erik Eynikel, and Katrin Hauspie. 2003. *Greek-English Lexicon of the Septuagint*. Rev. ed. Stuttgart: Deutsche Bibelgesellschaft.

Marcus, Joel. 2009. *Mark 8-16: A New Translation with Introduction and Commentary*. Vol. 27A of The Anchor Yale Bible. New Haven, CT: Yale University Press.

Mays, James Luther. 1994a. *The Lord Reigns: A Theological Handbook to the Psalms*. Louisville, KY: Westminster John Knox Press.

———. 1994b. *Psalms*. Interpretation: A Bible Commentary for Teaching and Preaching. Louisville, KY: John Knox.

McCann, J. Clinton, Jr., ed. 1993a. *The Shape and Shaping of the Psalter*. No. 159 in JSOTSup. Sheffield: Sheffield Academic Press.

———. 1993b. *A Theological Introduction to the Book of Psalms: The Psalms as Torah*. Nashville: Abingdon.

———. 1996. "Psalms." Pages 639-1280 in vol. IV of *The New Interpreter's Bible*. Nashville: Abingdon.

McCarter, P. Kyle, Jr. 1984. *II Samuel*. The Anchor Bible. New York: Doubleday.

Meek, Theophile J., trans. 1955. "The Code of Hammurabi," pages 163-80. *Ancient Near Eastern Texts Relating to the Old Testament*. Princeton, NJ: Princeton University Press.

Miller, Patrick D., Jr. 1985. "Israelite Religion." Pages 201-37 in *The Hebrew Bible and Its Modern Interpreters*. Edited by Douglas A. Knight and Gene M. Tucker. Minneapolis: Fortress Press.

———. 1986. *Interpreting the Psalms*. Philadelphia: Fortress.

———. 1994. *The Theological Significance of Biblical Poetry*. Pages 213-30 of *Language, Theology, and the Bible: Essays in Honour of James Barr*. Edited by Samuel E. Balentine and John Barton. Oxford: Clarendon Press.

Mowinckel, Sigmund. 1962. *The Psalms in Israel's Worship*. 2 vols. Translated by D. R. Ap-Thomas. Nashville: Abingdon. [Translation of *Offersang og Sangoffer*, 1951.]

O'Connor, M. 1980. *Hebrew Verse Structure*. Winona Lake, IN: Eisenbrauns.

Oppenheim, A. Leo. 1964. *Ancient Mesopotamia: Portrait of a Dead Civilization*. Chicago: University of Chicago Press.

Oswald, Hilton C., ed. 1974. *First Lectures on the Psalms I: Psalms 1-75*. Vol. 10 of Luther's Works. Saint Louis: Concordia Publishing House.

Pelikan, Jaroslav, ed. 1955. *Selected Psalms I*. Vol. 12 of Luther's Works. Saint Louis: Concordia Publishing House.

Pritchard, James B., ed. 1958. *The Ancient Near East: An Anthology of Texts and Pictures*. Vol. I. Princeton University Press.

_____. 1962. Ivory. Pages 773-75 in vol. 2 of *Interpreter's Dictionary of the Bible*. Edited by G. A. Buttrick. 4 vols. Nashville: Abingdon.

Rad, Gerhard von. 1962. *The Theology of Israel's Historical Traditions*. Vol. I of *Old Testament Theology*. Translated by D. M. G. Stalker. New York: Harper & Row.

Rainey, Anson F., and R. Steven Notley. 2006. *The Sacred Bridge: Carta's Atlas of the Biblical World*. Jerusalem: Carta.

Rasmussen, Carl G. 2010. *Zondervan Atlas of the Bible*. Grand Rapids: Zondervan.

Reimer, David J. 1997. "*qdx*." Page 744-69 in vol. 3 of *New International Dictionary of Old Testament Theology and Exegesis*. Edited by Willem A. VanGemeren. 5 vols. Grand Rapids: Zondervan.

Roberts, J. J. M. 2005. Pages 97-115 of "Mowinckel's Enthronement Festival: A Review." Edited by Peter W. Flint and Patrick D. Miller Jr. *The Book of Psalms: Composition and Reception*. Leiden: E. J. Brill.

Rotelle, John E., ed. 2000. Page 331 of *Expositions of Psalms 33-50*. Vol. 2 of *The Works of Saint Augustine: A Translation for the 21st Century*. Hyde Park, NY: New City Press.

Seybold, Klaus. 1990. *Introducing the Psalms*. Translated by R. Graeme Dunphy. Edinburgh: T & T Clark Ltd.

Stuart, Douglas K. 1976. *Studies in Early Hebrew Poetry*. No. 131 in Harvard Semitic Monograph Series. Edited by Frank Moore Cross Jr. Missoula, MT: Scholars Press.

Tate, Marvin E. 1990. *Psalms 51-100*. Vol. 20 of *Word Biblical Commentary*. Dallas, TX: Word Books, Publisher.

Thompson, David L. 1992. Psalms. Pages 504-63 of *Asbury Bible Commentary*. Edited by Eugene Carpenter and Wayne McCown. Grand Rapids: Zondervan.

_____. 1993. The Godly and the Good Life. Pages 246-66 in *Christian Scholar's Review* XII:3.

_____. 1994. *Bible Study That Works*. Rev. ed. Nappanee, IN: Evangel Press.

Tov, Emanuel. 1992. *Textual Criticism of the Hebrew Bible*. Minneapolis: Fortress Press.

_____. 1994. *Glosses, Interpolations, and Other Types of Scribal Additions in the Text of the Hebrew Bible*. Pages 40-66 of *Language, Theology, and the Bible: Essays in Honour of James Barr*. Edited by Samuel E. Balentine and John Barton. Oxford: Clarendon Press.

Van Der Toorn, Karel. 2007. *Scribal Culture and the Making of the Hebrew Bible*. Cambridge: Harvard University Press.

VanGemeren, Willem A., ed. 1997. *New International Dictionary of Old Testament Theology and Exegesis*. 5 vols. Grand Rapids: Zondervan.

Van Pelt, M. V., W. C. Kaiser, D. I. Block. 1997. "*hwr*." Pages 1073-78 in vol. 3 of *The Dictionary of Old Testament Theology and Exegesis*. Edited by Willem VanGemeren. 5 vols. Grand Rapids: Zondervan.

Vogt, E. The "Place in Life" of Ps. 23. *Biblica* 34 (1953), 195-211.

Waltke, Bruce K., and James M. Houston with Erika Moore. 2010. *The Psalms as Christian Worship: A Historical Commentary*. Grand Rapids: Eerdmans.

Watson, Wilfred G. E. 1994. *Traditional Techniques in Classical Hebrew Verse*. JSOTSup 170. Sheffield: Sheffield Academic Press.

Weiser, Artur. 1962. *The Psalms*. The Old Testament Library. Translated by Herbert Hartwell. Philadelphia: Westminster Press.

Whybray, Norman. 1996. *Reading the Psalms as a Book*. JSOTSup 222. Edited by David J. A. Clines and Philip R. Davies. Sheffield: Sheffield Academic Press.

Wiles, Maurice. 1994. *Newton and the Bible*. Pages 334-51 of *Language, Theology, and the Bible: Essays in Honour of James Barr*. Edited by Samuel E. Balentine and John Barton. Oxford: Clarendon Press.

Willis, John T. 1987. "Alternating (ABA'B') Parallelism in the Old Testament Psalms and Prophetic Literature." Pages 49-76 in *Directions in Biblical Hebrew Poetry*. JSOTSup, 40. Edited by Elaine R. Follis. Sheffield: Sheffield Academic Press.

Wilson, Gerald Henry. 1985. *The Editing of the Hebrew Psalter*. No. 76, SBLDS. Chico, CA: Scholars Press.

Wright, Christopher J. H. 1997. "*nḥl*." Pages 77-81 in vol. 3 of *The Dictionary of Old Testament Theology and Exegesis*. Edited by Willem A. VanGemeren. Grand Rapids: Zondervan.

Zenger, Erich. 2005. "Theophanien des Konigsgottes JHWH: Transformationen von Psalm 29 in den Teilkompositionen Ps 28-30 und Ps 93-100." Pages 407-42 in *The Book of Psalms: Composition and Reception*. Edited by Peter W. Flint and Patrick D. Miller Jr. Leiden: E. J. Brill.

INTRODUCTION

A. The Importance of the Biblical Psalter

Perhaps no other book of the OT is more beloved, more widely used, and more often interpreted than the Psalter. Several factors justify its broad appeal and import. It presents a veritable compendium of OT themes and theology, its horizons stretching from creation to consummation. And the Psalms do not simply *present* these themes; they *wrestle* with their validity and coherence for faith and practice.

Beyond Isaiah, no book of the OT apparently proved more formative in the self-understanding of Jesus of Nazareth than did the Psalter, judging from his appeals to Pss 22 and 110. When Jesus and the disciples sang a hymn at the "last supper" they most likely sang the Great Hallel, Pss 13—18, traditionally read at Passover.

New Testament writers pressed no OT book into service more than the Psalter in presenting and expounding the gospel of Christ. (See the "Index of Quotations" in the UBS Greek New Testament, pp. 906-9.) At Pentecost, at times of persecution, in theological reflection the earliest church turned to the Psalter for guidance (e.g., Acts 2:25 ff.; 4:25; 13:35). When modern congregants join in readings from the Psalter in public worship, they step in a line that reaches all the way back to the first churches, in which the singing of "psalms, hymns, and songs from the Spirit" occurred (Eph 5:19; Col 3:16).

From earliest days the Psalter exercised unrivaled influence on the Christian church. It provided the backbone for the church's liturgy by its presence in the liturgical offices—read, sung, and chanted at every turn throughout the day. Origen, Chrysostom, and Jerome, among others, preached and wrote extensively on the Psalms. It was Jerome's commitment to interpreting the Psalter that spurred him to learn Hebrew, which reintroduced that language into the church's exegetical resources from which it had disappeared because of the church's devotion to the LXX. Later the Reformers Luther and Calvin both featured the Psalms in their preaching and teaching, and the *Genevan Psalter* was a potent instrument in the spread and nurturing of reformed piety.

The strong European and American tradition of psalm singing carries a remarkable story of biblical influence via the Psalter. Reformed and Presbyterian churches, Congregationalists and Baptists on both sides of the Atlantic were exclusively psalm singing churches for over two hundred years, spanning the decades of the launching of the colonies in America. In the form of the old *Ainsworth Psalter* the psalms came to the new world on the Mayflower itself. And the *Bay Psalm Book* (1640) was the hymnal of American Puritans, reprinted seventy times through 1773(!), with the *Scottish Psalter* (1650) favored by Irish immigrants (Johnson 1994, v).

Over recent decades the church in the West has experienced a welcome revival of interest in singing the Psalter itself and in composing psalmlike music for worship. Believers ancient and modern have discovered the truth of claims on the Psalter's very first lines: those who give themselves to habitual recitation and reflection on the psalms will be extraordinarily happy (Ps 1:1-2)!

We may be surprised then to hear renowned Psalms scholar Hermann Gunkel opine that understanding the Psalter presents the modern reader with "extraordinary difficulties" (1998, 1). According to Gunkel, the poetic language that gives the Psalter its lyrical beauty also complicates its reading. The Hebrew poetry's brevity of expression, its economy in the use of syntactic markers, and each line's limited literary/historical context in its several brief poems all conspire to present an enigmatic text at points. Add to this the mysteries of its composition, and one may grant the claim.

B. The Psalms as a Collection

"The Psalter" names an anthology, a collection of diverse, discrete literary works. Each of its one hundred fifty psalms is a stand-alone poem in its own right. Understanding how we came to have the Psalter in its canonical form thus presents one of its puzzles, as does establishing the name of the collection.

The earliest attestation of the collection as a named book appears in Luke's writing where it is called "the Book of Psalms" (Luke 20:42; Acts 1:20). Here the Greek *psalmos*, "a song accompanied by a stringed instrument," apparently translates the Hebrew *mizmôr*, a term with roughly the same meaning that appears in the superscriptions (SS) of fifty-seven psalms.

The NT may reflect LXX practice at this point, since a premier, fourth-century A.D. LXX MS (Vaticanus) titles the collection simply *psalmoi*, "Psalms." A roughly contemporary LXX MS (Sinaiticus) lacks a title for the psalms, while a slightly later MS (Alexandrinus) calls this book *psaltērion*, the "Psalter," indicating fluidity in assigning a title to the work.

Interestingly, Luke also reflects the Jewish practice of naming the third section of the Hebrew scriptures "the Psalms," after that section's lead entry following "Moses" and "the Prophets" (Luke 24:44). References in Luke/Acts also assume a collection with numbered psalms (citing "the *second* psalm" in Acts 13:33, emphasis added) attributed to David (Luke 20:42).

The Hebrew tradition eventually settled on *tĕhillîm* or *sēpher tĕhillîm* ("Praises" or "Book of Praises") for a title, using a masculine plural form of the noun apparently reserved for this particular use (see GKC 87n, o). The singular form appears in 145:1 as the title of a single psalm (*tĕhillâ*), whose plural would ordinarily be *tĕhillôt*. Why this should have been the case we do not know, since "praises" or "hymns" does not describe many psalms well. At least one earlier collection of predominantly Davidic psalms carried the title *The Prayers of David son of Jesse* (Ps 72:20). This designation, "prayers/ *tĕphillôt*," suits many psalms in the early books of the Psalter but also is not comprehensive.

Indeed, it would be difficult to capture the diverse content and/or genre designations in a brief book title. Prayer psalms crying for deliverance dominate the early books of the Psalter, but more and more praise and thanksgiving songs appear toward the middle and final sections of the whole. This overall movement toward hymns and the fact that the Psalter ends in a flurry of extravagant praise in Pss 145—150 give the Psalter as a whole a positive cast, perhaps prompting the "Book of Praises/Hymns" as a title for the collection. Moreover, as James Luther Mays aptly put it, "Even psalms of prayer and instruction are, in effect, praise of the Lord." The prayers witness that "the Lord alone is God and savior of those who pray." The instructions testify that "the LORD is the pathway of life" (1994, 17).

Citations incorporated in narratives of Israel's early life suggest that even before and during the Davidic monarchy collections of poetry (or literature containing poetry) were at hand. Craigie notes reference to the *Book of the Wars of the Lord* (Num 21:14) and the *Book of Yashar* (2 Sam 1:18) (1983, 27). The fact that a song sung by David appears with minimal variation in both 2 Sam 22:1-51 and Ps 18:1-50 could indicate the presence of an archive or document from which both of these compositions (2 Samuel and the Psalter) could draw. The fact that both versions include the same SS (2 Sam 22:1-2a and Ps 18:1) would tend to imply the antiquity of at least some of the SSs in the Psalter.

As we have seen, the Psalter itself preserves some evidence of collections that preceded it and contributed to its final form. *The Prayers of David son of Jesse* in 72:20 apparently refers to Pss 3—70 predominantly attributed to David. Indeed, of the first seventy-two psalms only seven lack an SS of attribution (e.g., "for/by David" or "for/by Asaph"). And of the remaining sixty-five poems, fifty-six are Davidic. An additional eighteen of these "for/by David" psalms are scattered across the Psalter as a whole (86, 101, 103, 108—110, 122, 124, 131, 133, 138—145), giving the entire book a Davidic cast.

Evidence for an "Elohistic" editing of the songs now found in books two and three also sheds light on the formation of the Psalter. In this editing the name of Israel's covenant making God, "Yahweh" (written consonantally as YHWH), was replaced with the generic name of God, "Elohim." (See the chart below.)

Psalms	YHWH Appears	Elohim Appears	Psalms Without YHWH	Psalms Without Elohim
1—41	233	45	0	34
42—72	30	135	15	0
[73—83]	[10]	[35]	[3]	[0]
73—89	39	51	3	0
90—106	86	20	0	4
107—150	195	25	1	27

The editorial and collection work is especially obvious in poems that appear in both Yahwistic and Elohistic forms: 14 = 53; 40:13-17 [14-18 HB] = 70; and 58:7-11 [8-12 HB] with 60:7-12 [9-14 HB] = 108. Thus 14:2 reads "*Yahweh* looks down from heaven upon the children of men" (NKJV, RSV), while 53:2 [3 HB] has "*Elohim/God* looks down . . ." These doublets suggest the appearance of these psalms in diverse, smaller collections before they were incorporated into the Elohistic Psalter en route to inclusion in the present book.

The fact that we are unable satisfactorily to explain why and how such an Elohistic collection came to be does not warrant rejection of the idea (Goulder 1996, 18-19). In addition, contiguous psalms carrying attributive SSs "by/for/of the Sons of Korah" (Pss 42—49, 84—85, 87—88) and "by/for/of the Sons of Asaph" (Pss 73—83) likely indicate collections related to these temple singers and musicians. According to the Chronicler, under King David Heman, Asaph, Ethan, and their families were designated singers and musicians in the Lord's house (1 Chr 15:16-17, 19 ff.; 25:1-2).

The sons of Korah, on the other hand, were appointed keepers of the tabernacle service and gatekeepers (i.e., sanctuary guards) (1 Chr 9:19; 26:1 ff.). Although Korahites functioned as temple singers under Jehoshaphat (2 Chr 20:19), at the return from exile Ezra still has only the Asaphites as singers (Ezra 2:41 ff. = Neh 7:44 ff.). And now, by the time the Psalter reached its final form, it appears the sons of Korah had become temple musicians parallel to the sons of Asaph with songs attributed to each family. But this sketchy evidence does not allow us to write a history of these developments.

The SS, *šîr hammaʿălôt*/"*Song of Ascents*," found on Pss 120—134 could indicate another collection antedating the Psalter. But the SSs could as easily have been added in the final editing of the book.

The so-called *Egyptian Hallel*, Pss 113—118, could also present an earlier collection, marked as it is with the exhortation, "Praise Yah"/*halĕlû Yâh!* (*Yah* being a short form of the name Yahweh) at the beginning of Pss 113—114 and then at the end of Pss 115—117, with 118 ending in a bicolon doxology. Similarly Pss 146—150 all open with *halĕlû Yâh*, while Ps 150:6 concludes Ps 150 and the entire Psalter with this exhortation to "Praise Yah!" This "*Great Hallel*," which now concludes the Psalter with a flurry of praise, could also have been an earlier collection. It remains difficult to say.

Incorporation of material into the Psalter also made it available for broader use. We see this in the Chronicler's nearly verbatim use of Pss 105:1-15, 96:1-13, and 106:1, 47-48 to build his narrative of David's installation of the ark in Jerusalem in 1 Chr 16:8-36. Psalm 106:48 contains the doxology that marks the end of Book IV of the Psalter. Similar subscript doxologies also conclude the other books of the Psalter: 41:13 [14 HB] for Book I, 72:18-20 for Book II, 89:52 [53 HB] for Book III, and 106:47-48 for Book IV. Psalm 150 then closes Book V together with the Psalter as a whole. The fact that the Chronicler included the subscript doxology when he appropriated Psalter material for his narrative most likely indicates that the division of the Psalter into its five books had already occurred by the time of the Chronicler (ca. 400 B.C.).

C. Psalm Superscriptions

Perhaps the most obvious and often puzzling indicator of collection activity in the formation of the book of Psalms is its ubiquitous SSs. Only fifteen of the psalms carry no SS whatsoever (thirty-two if one does not regard *halĕlû Yâh* as a superscript or subscript in the *Hallel* collections). The SSs themselves are the most obvious indication that the majority of these poems have in some way been in the hands of temple personnel. These are the types of notations one encounters in the ancient world in connection with temple archives and the filing of materials there.

Since earliest times translators of the book of Psalms have included the SSs and where possible translated them (LXX, Tg.). Modern translators commonly do the same, with the exception of the NEB and REB, which omit the SSs altogether (but inconsistently include indications of the speakers in the Song of Songs). With the majority tradition we regard the notes as part of the canonical text. We have not been given this book without its SSs and subscripts. Although their meaning is at times uncertain, we are obliged to discern insofar as we can their contribution to understanding these poems.

The Psalter displays the following SSs.

I. Attribution

a. *lĕdāwîd*, "of David," appears on seventy-five psalms scattered across all five books of the Psalter (3—9, 11—32, 34—41, 51—65, 68—70, 86, 101, 103, 108—110, 122, 124, 131, 133, 138—145). The various meanings of the Hebrew preposition *l-* attached here to the name *dāwîd* open the phrase up to several possible meanings, none of which suits all its appearances.

It can indicate authorship, as for example, with Pss 3, 7, or 18, which carry notations suggesting an occasion for the poem, or with Pss 21 or 23, which simply could make sense as a song from David's pen. This understanding picks up the tradition that knows David as a poet and musician (2 Sam 23:1; 1 Chr 15:16-24; 16:7, 31; Amos 6:5). It also reflects the viewpoint registered often in the LXX renderings of *ldwd*, and the understanding generally assumed in the NT (e.g., Acts 2:34; 4:25). Although it was once fashionable and still possible to deny authorship of virtually any psalms to David (Seybold 1990, 37-38), there is no reason he cannot have written and even performed numerous psalms (Craigie 1983, 35).

At the same time we know that Ugaritic tablets of the Baal and the Kirtu myths were given the SSs *lb'l* and *lkrt* respectively. Clearly these SSs indicated not the author but the primary character in the works. One might also recall the common *lmlk*/"*belonging to the king*" impressions placed on large jars for wine and grain belonging to the crown. And a number of psalms carrying the *lĕdāwîd* SS sit awkwardly in his mouth, usually assuming a historical circumstance incompatible with Davidic authorship (e.g., Pss 138, 144, 147).

More likely then, in these cases we should translate "for the use of the Davidic kings" or "for inclusion in the Davidic collection." One could also conceive of a "Davidic" guild, similar to that of Asaph or Korah, but claiming David as their spiritual and professional ancestor (Seybold 1990, 37; see Broyles 1999, 26-31). We will usually use the descriptor "Davidic" in this more general sense.

b. *lamĕnaṣṣēaḥ*, "by/for the liturgical leader" or "archival director," appears on fifty-six psalms (4—6, 8—9, 11—14, 18—22, 31, 36, 39—42, 44—47, 48, 51—70, 75—77, 80—81, 84—85, 88, 109, 139—140). The verb on which this personal title is built (*nṣḥ*) has to do with leadership or supervisory tasks such as overseeing work on or in the temple (1 Chr 23:4; Ezra 3:8-9). Especially important for our purposes are persons charged with leading musicians with the musical instruments (1 Chr 15:21). This SS perhaps puts poems so tagged in the care of this temple leader.

c. "Of Asaph." We find this SS on twelve psalms (50, 73—83). The Chronicler ties Asaph and his descendants to musical and instrumental leadership in Israel's worship, beginning with appointment by David for worship centered in the ark (1 Chr 6:44 [6:24]; 15:17-22; 16:4-6) and continuing through the postexilic period (Ezra 2:41 = Neh 7:44).

d. "Of the sons of Korah." Eleven psalms carry this SS (42, 44—49, 84—85, 87—88). With one exception, the sons of Korah are known in Hebrew Scriptures as gatekeepers for worship facilities, from the time of the wilderness tabernacle to the pre-temple tent and then in the return from exile (1 Chr 9:19-22; 26:19; Ezra 2:42 = Neh 7:45). They are mentioned, however, as praising the Lord loudly in the worship assembly during the reign of Jehoshaphat (2 Chr 20:18-19). And the SS of attribution, parallel to that of Asaph, implies a status or role parallel to the Asaphites by the time of the final editing of the Psalter. A clear understanding of these matters eludes us.

e. "Of Moses" appears only on Ps 90. It is possible that themes in Pss 90—91 reminiscent of God's revelation of himself to Moses by the name Yahweh have drawn this attribution from the editors of the Psalter (Wilson 1985, 177-78).

f. "Of Solomon." Two psalms, 72 and 127, carry the *lišlōmôh* SS. Psalm 72 sits well either as "by Solomon" or "about Solomon," as does 127. Why the *lišlōmôh* attribution should appear where it does we do not know. Perhaps Wilson is correct that in Ps 72 the change of "authorial" attribution marks the seam between Books II and III, and that the 127 reference is frozen in the Song of Ascents group (1985, 156-58).

g. "Of Ethan" and "Of Heman." According to 1 Chr 15:17-18 under David these musicians were appointed to instrumental leadership in Israel's worship at the "House of God." Some have suggested the descriptor "Ezrahite" identified Ethan and Heman as natives of the land (i.e., Canaanites) and preserved memory of the influence of pre-Israelite traditions on the development of early Israel's worship guilds (Albright 1969, 121-25). The genealogical connections the Chronicler makes with Levitical roots would then be a literary device for expressing that influence. Ethan's name is attached to Ps 89 and Heman's to Ps 88 (1 Chr 2:6; 6:33, 39, 44 [6:18, 24, 29]).

h. "Of Jeduthun" (Pss 39, 62, 77). The inclusion of Jeduthun among David's chief musicians along with Heman and Asaph (1 Chr 9:16; 16:38) has led interpreters generally to see the Jeduthun attributions parallel to those with David, Asaph, and the sons of Korah, perhaps a by-form of Ethan. Not many have followed Mowinckel in understanding the noun not as a proper name but as a genre descriptor indicating a song of "confession" built on the root *ydh* (1962, II:213). The fact that the SS has the preposition *'al-*, "upon" or "according to," rather than *l-* in the other attributions has led to the suggestion that it may be a musical technical term, designating a tune or an instrument, rather than an authorial attribution.

2. Instrumentation

A number of the psalms carry notes that appear to designate an instrument with whose accompaniment a given psalm is to be sung or recited. As at other points in the superscriptional vocabulary, some of these terms remain unintelligible to us, although the form or syntax of the note may indicate that quite likely it is a musical notation. Translators often flag this uncertainty by simply transliterating the term, as does the NIV with "According to *sheminith*" on Ps 12, and as did the LXX translators centuries ago.

a. bingînôt or *'al něgînôt.* Built on the verb *ngn* "to play a stringed instrument," this SS indicates that a given song is to be performed "*with* a stringed instrument" (SS on Pss 4, 6, 54, 55, 67, 76) or "accompanied *by* a stringed instrument" (SS on Ps 61). So also the LXX, *en psalmois,* and most modern translations.

b. 'al šěmînît probably calls for accompaniment on an eight-stringed instrument (SS on Pss 6 and 12). The meaning is not clear, however, as most modern translations register by simply transliterating "According to *Sheminith.*" It could carry other meanings associated with the number eight, that is, "the eighth string" of an instrument (a lyre? [1 Chr 15:21]), or a particular octave (*HALOT,* 1562); thus NABRE the "upon the eighth."

c. 'el hanněḥîlôt. A (probably musical) technical term of uncertain meaning, occurring only in the SS of Ps 5, transliterated in the NJPS "On *neḥiloth.*"

Most related it to "flutes," *ḥălîlôt* (ESV, RSV, NJPS; see NABRE, "with wind instruments") or the root *ḥlh*, "to be ill," in which case it would be a topical not an instrumental designation. Appearance of the preposition *'el-* where we would expect *'al-*, is probably the result of *aleph/ayin* reduction common in later Hebrew.

d. *'al haggittît'*, "On/by the gittite," an uncertain musical term associated perhaps with the wine press (*haggat*) (8:1; 81:1; 84:1). Modern versions simply transliterate, "According to/On the Gittith."

See Othmar Keel (1997, 335-52) for fascinating images of the instruments and choreography of sacred music in Israel and the ANE.

3. Tune or Song Titles

As moderns sometimes do, biblical editors and worshippers at times referred to compositions by their opening words. Some psalm SSs reflect that custom. This *may* be reflected in Jesus' appeal to Ps 22:1 in the cry of dereliction (Mark 15:34).

a. *'al tašḥēt*, "Do Not Destroy." Probably a song referring to Moses' historic intercession with Yahweh for Israel (Pss 57—59, 75; see Deut 9:26). Thus most modern versions; but see NJPS, "*al tashḥeth*," simply transliterating, because of uncertainty regarding the note's meaning. An NABRE note ad loc. takes "Do not destroy!" as a scribal note urging retention of the psalm in a collection. This seems odd but does have support in the lack of prepositional phrase common to the other tune notations.

b. *'al yôna 'ēlîm rěḥôqîm*, "Sung to the Dove on the Distant Majestic Tree" (Ps 56) or the like appears in most versions with disagreement as to the specific tree involved. Note the NJPS transliteration, "on *yonath elem rehokim*," perhaps indicating overly cautious uncertainty in this case.

c. *'al 'ayyelet haššaḥar*, "Sung to the Doe of the Dawn" (Ps 22), as in most modern versions with variation, or perhaps "To the *Defense at Dawn*," reading *'ěyālût*, "defense, aid," with LXX (see 22:19 [20 HB]). The NJPS transliterates.

d. *'almût labbēn* (Ps 9) is of uncertain meaning. One should perhaps redivide the MT to *'al mût labbēn*, "Sung to 'Death to/for the Son,'" or read *'ălûmôt*, "Hidden things," with LXX. The RSV, NABRE, and NJPS transliterate. The NABRE in Ps 46:1 translates *'al 'ălāmôt* as "According to 'Virgins.'" Some suggest "for sopranos" or "in the style of young girls" (*HALOT*, 836).

e. *'al māḥălat*, a technical musical term of uncertain meaning. Most modern versions simply transliterate. Perhaps one should read *měḥôlat*, "a ring dance."

f. *'al šôšannîm* (Pss 45, 69), *'al šôšannîm 'ēdût* (80), and *'al šûšan 'ēdût* (60) may indicate accompaniment by a six-stringed instrument. Most take it as a tune designation, "Sung to 'the Lilies' [of the covenant in Pss 60 and 80]" (ESV, NABRE, NIV, RSV). As Koehler-Baumgartner concede (*HALOT*, 791 and 1455), "no certain meaning for this has yet been found," leading the NJPS to transliterate "On *shoshannim*" and "Shoshan eduth."

4. Song/Psalm Types

Scribes and worship leaders of the biblical period differentiated several types of compositions, in some cases song types.

a. mizmōr, a "psalm," appears on fifty-six psalms (3—6, 8—9, 12—13, 15, 19—24, 29—31, 38—41, 47—51, 62—68, 73, 75—77, 79, 80, 82, 83—85, 87, 88, 98, 100, 101, 108—110, 139—141, 143). This most common designation apparently indicates a composition written for stringed accompaniment, judging by the verb on which this noun is built, and by the LXX translation, *psalmos*, which carries the same meaning. Five times *mizmōr* appears also with the more general designation *shir*, "a song."

b. šîr/shir appears on numerous psalms, simply tagging the psalm as a "song" (45, 46, 48, 65—68, 75—76, 83, 87, 88, 92, 108, 120—134). The LXX translates *ōidē*, "an ode, a song" (usually of praise). If, as Mowinckel thinks, *šîr* (if it is not to be redundant) must have a more specific meaning than "a song," we do not know that meaning (1962, II:207-8).

c. maśkîl. Most modern versions indicate uncertainty as to meaning here by simply transliterating (e.g., NABRE, NIV, NJPS, RSV). The NKJV translates "A Contemplation," which may have support in LXX *suneseōs*, having to do with "intelligence." The Hebrew term itself may support this meaning, if it is related to the verb *lĕhaśkîl*, "to have success," especially with regard to insight, comprehension, and understanding. One is tempted to relate it to Israel's wisdom tradition, but it appears on few so-called wisdom psalms and is used as well more generally for singing praise (47:6 [7 HB]). See Pss 32, 42—45, 52—55, 74, 78, 88—89, 142.

d. miktām appears on Pss 16 and 56—60. Versions generally transliterate, indicating uncertainty. The LXX translated *stēlographia*, "an inscription" or "a title," which seems pointless; perhaps "an epigram"? The Vulgate understood it as a "lowly and simple" poem, perhaps "a plain song?" Check *HALOT* (583) for bibliography.

e. tĕpillâh. Found on Pss 17, 86, 90, and 142, all the versions understand this straightforward SS, as "a prayer." Since the majority of the psalms are in some sense prayers, one wonders what particular sense this SS carries, if any.

f. tĕhillâh. Found only on Ps 45 as an SS, the modern versions rightly translate as "a (song of) praise."

g. *šiggayôn*. Mowinckel may well have been right to relate this SS to an Akkadian cultic term meaning a "dirge" or a "lamentation" and also used in scribal colophons in worship materials (1962, II:209). The NABRE reflects this in its rendering as "Plaintiff song." Less likely, the NKJV has "a meditation." The fact that most modern versions simply transliterate indicates the uncertainty that prevails regarding the term's meaning (so also *HALOT*, 1414-15).

5. Uses

a. *lĕhazkîr*, "to make remember" or "for remembrance" or "to offer a memorial offering" is on Pss 38 and 70.

b. *lĕ'annôt* appears on Ps 88 and probably means "for singing" (see Exod 15:21). It could also mean "to answer" or "to respond," with the LXX, perhaps antiphonally, or even "to afflict" or "for affliction." The NABRE translates "for singing," following its meaning in Exod 15:21. Several modern translations link with the preceding *'al maḥălat* and transliterate (NIV, NJPS, RSV), perhaps surrendering prematurely.

c. *lĕlammēd*, "for instructing" marks Ps 60.

d. *lĕtôdâh*, "for giving thanks" or "for a thank offering" stands on Ps 100.

e. *šîr ḥănûkat habbayit* designates Ps 30 as a "song for the dedication of the house/temple."

f. *lĕyôm haššabbat*, "for the Sabbath day" marks Ps 92. See the SS for Ps 102 for more extended direction regarding use by the afflicted in pouring out their complaint before Yahweh.

6. Historical Notes

Thirteen psalms, all Davidic, carry notes tying the several poems to some historical circumstance. In Ps 7 the event is not known from the OT. The others reflect OT texts as follows.

a.	Ps 3	2 Sam 15:1—18:33; flight from Absalom
b.	Ps 18	e.g., 1 Sam 19:1 ff.; 24:1 ff.; 26:1 ff.; 2 Sam 5:17 ff.; deliverance from enemies such as Saul
c.	Ps 34	1 Sam 21:10 ff.; expulsion by Abimelech; 1 Samuel has Achish
d.	Ps 51	2 Sam 11:1 ff.; confrontation by Nathan
e.	Ps 52	1 Sam 22:6 ff.; betrayal to Saul by Doeg
f.	Ps 54	1 Sam 23:14 ff.; hiding in a cave from Saul
g.	Ps 56	1 Sam 21:10 ff.; 22:1 ff.; 27:1 ff.; in the hands of the Philistines
h.	Ps 57	1 Sam 24:1 ff.; hiding from Saul in a cave
i.	Ps 59	1 Sam 19:8 ff.; surveillance by Saul
j.	Ps 60	2 Sam 8:3 ff.; 10:15 ff.; battle against Aram Naharaim

    k. Ps 63   1 Sam 22:1 ff.; 24:1 ff.; in the Judean desert
    l. Ps 142   1 Sam 22:1 ff.; 24:1 ff.; hiding in a cave

Which of these notes, if any, were provided by the composer of the poems we can no longer say. All references to David here are in the third person, indicating an annotator's note *about* David, not David's note about himself. The LXX and Targum evidence suggests the continuing addition of these and other parts of the SSs in the course of copying and editing. Evidence cited earlier, though, supported the antiquity of at least some of these notes. In many cases the psalm itself, though compatible with the historical setting given, would not necessarily suggest the event noted. For example, the classic penitential prayer, Ps 51, has no explicit tie with David's sins with Bathsheba and his response to Nathan. Nevertheless, it remains eminently appropriate to that set of events and actually implies that the interpreter should at least initially read the psalm in the context provided. The SSs have become part of the canonical text and provide guidance for canonical reading, perhaps offering clues as to how all the psalms should be read.

D. The Psalms as Poetry

In a modern introduction to the Psalms as poetry we may expect to learn that Hebrew poetry is characterized especially by (1) a repetition of thought known as "parallelism," (2) a flexible but identifiable rhythm, perhaps even a meter, and (3) by a terseness entailed in the parallelism, rhythm, and vocabulary selection. But features of Hebrew poetry that seem so obvious to many contemporary readers have not always stood out as important for the interpretation of the psalms and continue to spark debate.

1. Early Responses to Poetic Scripture

First-century Jewish writers Philo and Josephus worked under the assumption that Hebrew poetry would operate by the metrical canons they knew from the Greek and Latin classics. Although they were aware of the phenomenon we call "parallelism," it did not capture their attention as did meter. Under the influence of Greco-Roman culture they scanned the psalms looking for classical meters (e.g., iambic pentameter). As an interpretive tool, this cultural imposition gave less than satisfactory results.

The Dead Sea scrolls similarly exhibit some possible awareness of the binary/bicolar structure we associate with parallelism, but give no sustained attention to it. 4QPs^c, for example, generally shows a small break for verse beginning, but random placement of the verse beginnings in the text columns. It generally indicates the bicolas' caesura but does not the second pause for a tricolon. 4QPs^e, however, indicates neither the start of its verses nor the caesurae of bicola. 4QPs^g separates the stanzas of Ps 119's acrostic and justifies each of the lines in the stanzas to the right, but shows no marking of the caesurae in its bicola. 11QPs^a shows random lineation, minimal if any break between verses, and no consistent indication of bicola. This manuscript treats Ps 119 as does 4QPs^q.

The Aleppo Codex, the prize Masoretic Text from the early tenth century A.D., shows a similar ambiguity toward parallelism. It justifies verse beginnings of Ps 119 to the right, separating succeeding stanzas in the acrostic, and indicating breaks either at the caesura or the athnach of its bicola. Psalms 34 and 111 are not scanned according to their acrostic structure, and show no interest in verses as bicola. Treatment of other poetic materials (Deut 32; Judg 5; Exod 15) shows no consistent interest in verses as bicola or in the structure of these lines as parallelistic.

The early Christian readers of the Psalter almost without exception proceeded with the same Hellenized assumptions as did Philo and Josephus. Although apparently aware of the parallelistic structure of these compositions, their interests lay in scanning these psalms with the classical meters. Origen, Eusebius, Jerome, and others all took this approach. The fathers occupied themselves with the search for uniquely Hebrew metrical schemes that might explain the psalms. They also pursued hermeneutical questions related to the use in inspired, sacred texts of tropes and stylistic conventions known already from pagan writers.

Jerome's opinion regarding Hebrew poetry influenced Christian reading of the psalms right on into the modern period. The result has been a continuing tendency to look to classical poetic canons for categories with which to understand Hebrew Scriptures. The classical meters named set patterns of alternating light and heavy stress (i.e., short and long duration of syllables) and line lengths. One iteration of the pattern was called a "foot." Short-long was an iambic foot (-/), long-short was a trochee foot (/-), long-long a spondee (//), long-short-short (/--) dactyl, and short-short-long (--/) anapest. A line of poetry is scanned in terms of the number of feet used. Thus a two foot line of iambic verse, "iambic dimeter," would scan -/-/. A four foot line of anapestic verse, "anapestic tetrameter," would scan --/--/--/--/. Recall of the accent distribution in almost any line from the Hebrew Psalter indicates why Hebrew poetry has resisted scanning in classical meters.

2. Modern Approaches to Hebrew Poetic Rhythm

Robert Lowth, in his *Sacra Poesi Hebraeorum* (1753), captured the attention of Psalms scholars for two centuries, prompting them to focus on poetic parallelism as a key to reading the Psalter. Unfortunately he retained and passed to his successors the assumption that Hebrew poetry would be scanned in classic metrics or in Hebrew adaptations thereof. Julius Ley, Eduard Sievers, H. Ewald, K. Budde, G. B. Gray, and others carried this program forward.

A failed attempt at this endeavor was Budde's discernment of a so-called qinah (i.e., lamentation) meter in the acrostic poems of the book of Lamentations. Budde claimed the qinah meter exhibited a 3+2 word stress pattern and was especially prominent in dirges. Succeeding research has not confirmed Budde's conclusions. The 3+2 bicola are not confined to dirges, and dirges beyond the book of Lamentations are not predominantly written in a 3+2 pattern. (Goldingay's resort to psychologizing the 3+2 pattern illustrates the problem well [2006, 40].)

But scholars have increasingly adopted the stressed syllable count of the sort Budde used to scan poetic lines. This boils down to counting words or word clusters as the "feet" by which lines are measured (e.g., 3+3 or 2+2). W. F. Albright and his students Frank Moore Cross Jr. and David Noel Freedman have made this approach to Hebrew metrics common currency in North American biblical scholarship (Cross 1950, 16-25).

Lack of consensus as to how a word count scan should proceed, however, has led Freedman, Cross, and others to adopt counting syllables as the most straightforward approach to Hebrew poetic structure (Freedman 1987; see p. 25 n. 14 for bibliography; Stuart 1976, 1-39). These scholars have discerned remarkable symmetry in the structure of some large units, supporting the considerable regularity of poetic lines. But syllable count has delivered little interpretive payoff for individual bicola. In Cross's hands, it has actually been more useful as a text-critical resource than as an interpretive tool. It achieves a product more obvious to the eye than to the ear, and still open to debate over syllables to be counted.

Thus no consensus exists regarding the meter or rhythm of Hebrew poetry, in spite of twenty centuries of inquiry into the matter. Increasingly students of these texts are taking this failure itself as evidence that Hebrew poetry simply has no meter! Its regularity cannot be explained as meter. (For an excellent survey of history of this research, consult pp. 3-67 of M. O'Connor's *Hebrew Verse Structure*.) For all practical purposes the repetition of the cola themselves, joined in parallelistic relationships and limited in length by the terseness also characteristic of this literature, provides the rhythm of Hebrew poetry, the cadence discernible even in translation. O'Connor's work, though so cumbersome as nearly to defy practical use, seems to support this understanding, with its insight that it is in the interplay of syntactic patterns that poetic constraints provide a regulation analogous to meter (O'Connor 1980, 67 ff., 73). But while O'Connor develops a catalog of clause types found in his corpus, he does not appear to uncover the system he was seeking.

3. Parallelism and Hebrew Poetry

Widespread consensus also supports the judgment that Robert Lowth erred when he described the connection between the cola in poetic bicola as "parallel," and when he classified these parallelisms as primarily synonymous, antithetical, or synthetic. The repetition of cola of similar length that dominates poetic passages gives the impression of lines in parallel. But upon further examination, "parallel" simply does not describe the relationship between the halves of many poetic bicola.

The distinctive bicolon graphs as follows: ____A____/ ___B____//, that is, a first line with a brief pause, then a second line with a longer pause. The pause after colon A differentiates B from A, but connects the two; the second pause is long enough to express the "relative disjunction" of colon B from following lines, making it separated from but "subjoined" to the preceding A, as James Kugel puts it (1981, 51). This "subjoined" colon B simply goes beyond A, extending it in any one of myriad relationships, "carrying it further, echoing it, defining it, restating it, contrasting with it, *it does not matter which*—has an emphatic, 'seconding' character'" about it (1981, 51). According to Kugel, this subjoining, this differentiation is the core of biblical parallelism. Without this sort of logic between succeeding lines, one does not have poetic bicola. Kugel has not succeeded in describing all possible parallelistic configurations (Watson 1994, 41), but his emphasis on the complexity and variety housed within "parallelism" yet distinguishable from prose has proved helpful. Research continues unabated, identifying more and more patterns covered by parallelistic expression. (See, e.g., the suggestions of Willis and Clines in Follis 1987.)

Lowth's classifications of parallelism as synonymous, antithetical, and synthetic focused attention on the semantic relationships between cola. "Parallelism" is actually a marvelously complex mode of expression that simultaneously engages semantic, syntactic, grammatical, phonological, morphological, and lexical features of the Hebrew language in a multileveled repetition or extension of thought.

While bicola of approximately similar length do dominate poetic passages, bicola whose parts are not of similar length frequently appear as well. They do so with such regularity that one should apparently conclude that, embedded in a sufficiently repetitive environment, this variety of line length, these "unparallel" lines, were also seen as poetic.

Because of these irregularities Kugel has concluded Hebrew "poetry" does not exist. The density of allegedly "poetic" features in a passage or the lack thereof is, he claims, instead a matter of style, not of genre (1981, 299-301). Whether this is true technically, trading stylistic descriptions of high and low for genre descriptions of poetry and prose seems an insignificant advance. Further, in spite of the fact that the term "parallel" does not precisely describe the relationship between the lines of many poetic bicola, its near universal currency in the study of Hebrew poetry and its usefulness in naming the almost indefinite variety of relationships known to serve the same functions in poetic discourse as clearly parallel lines do, these considerations lead us to continue to speak of poetic parallels and parallelism for this constitutive feature of Hebrew poetry.

Psalm 1 illustrates these matters well. Observe 1:1:

(A) Blessed is the one who
(B) does not walk in step with the wicked
(C) or stand in the way that sinners take
(D) or sit in the company of mockers.

Note first that cola B, C, and D particularize the opening colon (A) by specifying behaviors *not* characteristic of the blessed one. Note further that each term of colon B is paralleled in C and D: the negative, explicit in Hebrew and implied in English, the act (walk, stand, sit), the prepositional phrase of location (*in* step with, *in* the way, *in* the company), and the ungodly variously characterized (the wicked, sinners, mockers).

In the Hebrew text this "each term" parallelism is even more striking. The various ungodly are all named with masculine plural nouns: "the wicked" (*rĕšāʿîm*), "sinners" (*ḥaṭṭāʾîm*), and "mockers" (*lēṣîm*). The negated acts are all negated perfects, third masculine singular verbs: "not walk" (*lôʾ hālak*), "[not] stand" (*lôʾ ʿāmad*), or "[not] sit" (*lôʾ yāšab*).

The prepositional phrases all indicate location with the Hebrew preposition *b-*. And the specific locations are all indicated with a noun in a "construct" (English "of") relationship with the persons named: "in step with the wicked," "the way that sinners take," and "the company *of* mockers."

Finally the poet achieves an AB//B'A' chiastic array of the elements, in that in the Hebrew text cola B reads <negated verb + prepositional phrase>, <"not walk" + "in step with the wicked"> while cola C and D reverse this order reading <prepositional phrase + negated verb>, that is, <"in the way that sinners take" + "[not] stand"> and <"in the company of mockers" + "[not] sit,"> all of which ties these opening lines tightly together.

Verse 6 exhibits antithetic parallelism, putting the destiny and well-being of the righteous and the wicked in contrast:

(A) For the LORD watches over the way of the righteous,
(B) but the way of the wicked leads to destruction.

To be more precise, the bicolon deftly contrasts Yahweh's relationship to the life of righteous persons (he "watches over" it), with the future/consequences of the wicked ones' way (it perishes).

But it is not a simple, straightforward contrast, such as "Yahweh watches over the life of the righteous, but he ignores that of the wicked." Instead the B colon stands in contrast to the good life of the righteous described earlier in the psalm but now explained in colon A (that life not only does not perish but it flourishes, 1:2-3). And A stands explicitly in contrast with the dismal end of the way of the wicked, and implicitly with Yahweh's relationship to the wicked. So B emphasizes and elaborates A here by evoking a reality assumed by it as well as an explanation implied by it. One can graph the bicolon then as follows:

Yahweh watches over the way of the righteous
// [*Yahweh does not prosper the wicked*]
[*The way of the righteous prospers*]
// But the way of the wicked leads to destruction.

The poet closes the psalm with a chiastic array of the cola, beginning colon A and concluding B with a verb and placing construct phrases using the expression "the way of" around the caesura as follows:

<For watches over + Yahweh + the way of righteous> /
<but the way of the wicked + will perish> //
a + b + c / c' + a'.

But scattered throughout this poem with no obvious pattern are lines of significantly dissimilar length, which do not scan easily and which seem to lack parallel cola. Thus the opening line, "Blessed is the one who," seems to stand on its own, "metrically" outside the tight tricolon it introduces. Or perhaps it stands joined to the following tricolon *as a whole* as it would be to colon B if B stood by itself. "Not so the wicked!" in v 4 and "therefore" in v 5 likewise resist parallel scanning. Yet the whole composition should no doubt be thought of as poetic, if not as symmetrically penned as, for example, Ps 18.

Additionally, although vv 1, 2, 5, and 6 exhibit clearly Lowth's synonymous and antithetical parallelisms, other lines of the psalm present samples of the widely diverse patterns noted by Kugel and others that characterize a significant percentage of parallel lines.

So Hebrew poetry is dominated by bicola expressed in parallelistic lines of three or four words or word groups per colon. In these contexts tricola and "mono-cola" also appear. Hebrew poetry has no meter. But the balanced repetition exhibited in the interplay of syntactic patterns in the parallelism that dominates the genre provides a distinctive, rhythmic cadence.

4. Hebrew Poetry and Terseness

The balance and cadence discerned in Hebrew poetry depends in part on its terseness, which is expressed primarily in two ways. First, Hebrew poets regularly limited their use of select particles: the direct object indicator (*'et*), the definite article (*ha*), and the relative pronoun (*ăšer*) and various prepositions and conjunctions. The work of Francis Anderson and Dean Forbes has shown the usefulness of monitoring the presence of these words as one mark of poetic expression (Freedman 1987, 12-18). In addition to increasing brevity, the absence of these meaning markers contributes to the more implicit, cryptic nature of syntax in Hebrew poetry.

Second and especially in the B colon, ellipsis of terms assumed for the completion of the thought begun in colon A also shortens the line and renders it more ambiguous. Thus "Indeed our shield belongs to the LORD, our king [belongs] to the Holy One of Israel" (89:18) or "I will establish his line forever, [I will establish] his throne as long as the heavens endure" (v 29).

5. Significance of Poetic Scripture

What significance accrues from this pondering of the Psalter as poetry? First, we will not replicate the old rabbinic doctrine of "omnisignificance" in which "the slightest details of the biblical text," having been given by God, have a meaning that is both comprehensible and significant" and therefore to be identified and studied (Kugel 1981, 104). This invites us not to press over precisely the categories of "synonymous" or "antithetical" parallelism but to make room for the complex playfulness present in parallelistic expression.

Second, however, at the same time we will inquire as to how the B cola sharpen, elaborate, or otherwise carry forward the significance of the A cola. In addition our conclusion regarding the lack of meter and the acceptability of poetic lines of varying length supports our reluctance to emend the text for metrical causes.

Reflecting more theologically, readers who receive these biblical psalms as from the hand of God, inspired by his Spirit, know they deal here with a God who loves beauty. In addition to the attractive cadence of parallelism itself, many other features of Hebrew poetry simply heighten the beauty and symmetry, the attractiveness of the sounds of the words. Alliteration, assonance, rhyme, for example, primarily serve this aesthetic aim. God apparently loves beauty; surely he can appreciate our attempts to be and do beautifully.

It took centuries for the people of God to realize how extensive the corpus of inspired poetry actually was in the two testaments. Psalms, Job, Proverbs, Song of Songs, obviously; but also Exod 15, Judg 5, Gen 49, Deut 32, 2 Sam 22, Hab 3, and other famous pieces.

Then add extensive stretches of the prophets and from the NT the songs of Zechariah, Mary, Simeon in Luke 1 and 2, Phil 3:5-11, 2 Tim 2:11-13, and the songs of Revelation. Clearly a significant portion of God's Word comes to us in poetic form.

Use of this genre itself implies a certain openness in God. The ambiguity involved in its terseness and the increase in symbolism engages readers/listeners themselves in the communication process. God has apparently judged the heightened engagement worth the risk involved.

The use of poetry in Israel's sacred writings implies God's ability to, indeed, his delight in redeeming fallen culture. We have talked of Hebrew poetry. More precisely we might have talked of Northwest Semitic poetry or East Mediterranean or ancient Near Eastern poetry, for they share the same basic characteristics. The same poetic forms God's people used to praise him, the Canaanites used to worship Baal and other gods. Rejecting contamination by association Yahweh, as it were, staked a menorah in the midst of pagan culture, retrieving its beauty and unique power to communicate for Yahweh's own redemptive purposes.

E. Recent Study of the Psalter

Recent study of the Psalter has focused on three interrelated matters: psalm types found in the Psalter, the relationship of the psalms and the Psalter to Israel's worship (the temple and cult), and the editorial shape or structure of the book of Psalms.

I. Recent Study and Psalm Types

Two European scholars, Hermann Gunkel and Sigmund Mowinckel, have exercised dominant influence on the modern study of the Psalms since the early twentieth century. In numerous separate studies, then in a major commentary, and in an introduction to the Psalms completed in 1933 after his death by his student, J. Begrich, Gunkel pioneered the "form-critical" method in the study of the Psalms.

This approach takes its name from Gunkel's judgment that it was possible to discern basic literary types in the psalms, each having its own form (common structure and treasury of ideas) and each arising out of and shaped by its setting in the worship life of the community. He identified five main psalm types (*Gattungen*) or genres: (1) hymns, (2) communal laments, (3) royal psalms, (4) individual laments, and (5) individual songs of thanksgiving, along with several minor types.

Gunkel emphasized the study of the psalms within the context of the other OT songs and particularly within the literary and cultural context of the ancient Near East, most notably Egyptian and Babylonian materials. From such research Gunkel concluded that virtually the entire Psalter had its source in the cult, radically challenging traditional understandings of the settings of many psalms. The Davidic psalms of Book I, for example, in his judgment were individual complaints originally reflecting different specific rites or situations in the cult, such as incubation rites, prayers for healing, or exorcism of demons.

Psalms traditionally taken as messianic psalms Gunkel saw as spoken by and to the king, in songs analogous to the royal hymns of Babylon and Egypt and reflecting a view of divine kingship common to those cultures. These conclusions proved programmatic for following psalms studies.

Sigmund Mowinckel extended Gunkel's work in *The Psalms in Israel's Worship*, published in translation in 1967 but first published in six volumes from 1921 to 1924 as *Psalmenstudien* and later as *Offersang og Sangoffer* in Norwegian. He tied individual psalm types and the present psalms much more specifically to cultic settings. He attempted to reconstruct as fully as possible the liturgical contexts that produced the psalms and in which they were used.

Mowinckel concluded that an Israelite, autumn New Year festival was the major source of the psalms. Relying heavily on the Babylonian Akitu festival, he reconstructed a celebration in which Yahweh died and rose in conquest of the forces of chaos and was enthroned, confirming his kingship and continuation of the cosmic order for another year.

In his *Psalms* (1962) Artur Weiser carried Gunkel's work on much as Mowinckel had done, but he reconstructed an autumn covenant renewal ceremony rather than a divine enthronement festival. These scholars have enriched psalms study by identifying numerous passages in the Psalter that either assume or refer to worship occasions and liturgical acts (Mowinckel 1962, 1-22).

While subsequent scholars have worked under the influence of these pioneers, the findings of Gunkel and Mowinckel have attracted substantial critique as well. Scholars such as Roland deVaux have pressed the failure of the OT so much as to mention *explicitly* any of the major festivals or cultic events thought to have exercised pervasive influence on the Psalter and on the life of the people (1965, 502-6). Some have objected to the "myth and ritual" orientation they found in Mowinckel, especially rejecting a reading of Israel's kingship and Yahweh's rule through the lens of the dying and rising divine king in Babylon's Akitu festival.

Others, while refraining for lack of evidence from Mowinckel's extensive cultic reconstruction, nevertheless have supported his general approach. J. J. M. Roberts and P. D. Miller Jr. note that not only the enthronement psalms but also Israel's early poetry feature Yahweh's rule or kingship as a central element (Exod 15:18; Num 23:21; Deut 33:5; Pss 68:24 [25 HB]; 24:9). They grant Mowinckel's suggestion that Yahweh's kingship could well find emphasis in the fall Feast of Tabernacles, Israel's central festival. And they claim the expression *Yahweh mālak* should probably be translated "Yahweh has become king (and thus reigns)." They emphasize the exclamation "neither denies the eternal character of Yahweh's reign nor implies anything about a dying and rising god. The expression is more a proclamation of Yahweh's enthronement and rule than an actual royal investiture" (Miller 1985, 218-20; see Roberts 2005, 113-14).

In addition, though Gunkel's insight of psalm types with their common forms seems obvious, once pointed out, problems have arisen. Further research has demonstrated the difficulty, if not the actual inability of establishing clearly the common literary form assumed for each major type, such as the royal psalms or the hymns. Even though there are common rhetorical and structural features among the works grouped under a particular type, considerable variety also appears, at times stretching the forms beyond recognition. Not only so, but the types themselves prove open to question. The "laments of the individual," for example, turn out in many cases neither to be "laments" nor really to be tied to "individuals" standing apart from the community of Israel (e.g., Ps 130).

One reason for these difficulties is that Gunkel's literary categories derived as much from European literary studies as from the Bible. The task of discerning psalm types and forms should, upon further reflection, begin with an analysis of the categories identified by the psalmists themselves. The SSs of the psalms and other references in the poems together with their own subject matter should provide this data insofar as possible.

Hans-Joachim Kraus has made significant progress in this sort of research, attempting to discern and group psalm types/genres on the basis of the text's own awareness of these matters. His work is most accessible to English readers in his introduction and commentary of *Psalms 1-59* (1988, 38-61).

This work, a translation of the fifth (1978) edition, volume 1, of his German work, is particularly noteworthy. In it he departs significantly from his stance in the first four editions of that commentary. Kraus here works from a thoroughgoing critique of Gunkel's approach, emphasizing some of the questions noted above regarding Gunkel and Mowinckel's approach. This involves: identifying where possible the Psalter's own identification of psalm types; exercising restraint in appeal to cultic reconstruction for interpretation; and determining key psalm themes as an indispensable correlate of form criticism in this study (Kraus 1988, 38-41). The following presentation of psalm types reflects at many points this work by Kraus.

a. **Hymns of praise** (the *těhillâ*). Only Ps 145 is actually designated a "(song of) praise" in its SS. But numerous other references to the *těhillâ* in the psalms lead to the discernment of this general designation (Kraus 1988, 26, 43-47). The term appears frequently as the name of the songs of praise of individuals (e.g., Pss 22:25 [26 HB]; 65:1 [2 HB]) and the community (e.g., Pss 33:1; 100:4). The label highlights the distinctive yet general praise orientation of these songs. The "song of praise" can be a synonym for the "thanksgiving" (*tôdâh*) as in Ps 100:4 and can stand in parallel to the "new song" (40:3 [4 HB]; 149:1).

Other designations also appear for the song of praise, some of them included in the treatment of SSs above, for example, the cultic song (*šîr*) or the "psalm" (*mizmôr*). But these are not exclusively used for this song type and seem to call attention to other features of the song than its form and content, such as its accompaniment.

Four major themes find expression in the Psalter's songs of praise: praise of the Creator (Pss 8, 19, 33, 65, 100, 104, 121, 136, 148); Yahweh, the king (Pss 23, 47, 68, 93, 95—99, 145); Yahweh's sovereign activity in history (Pss 105—106, 114, 135, perhaps 78 and 136), with several themes sometimes woven together in a single song (Pss 68, 146—148). Then at times the theme is more generally the praise of God, his glory, or his works (Pss 67, 75—76, 103, 113, 117, 134, 146, 150).

b. Prayer songs (the *těpillâ*). The prayer song specifically designates the prayer for deliverance (Ps 80:3 [4 HB]) and the prayer of intercession (Ps 109:4), that is, prayer for another's deliverance (Kraus 1988, 26-27, 47-56). The song rises from deep distress (Ps 102:1; see 1 Kgs 8:38) and is at times uttered in a setting of sackcloth and fasting (Ps 35:13).

Often (with Gunkel) called "lament," or with others a "complaint," these are much more than lament or complaint. The worshippers here do not simply complain or bemoan their plight. They declare in faith their distress to God and cry to him for deliverance. The *těpillôt* (pl.) include prayer songs of the individual and of the people (i.e., community prayer songs; see Ps 80:5). Because of the arrangement of the book of Psalms achieved in its final editing, the prayer songs, which predominate in number, especially in Books I and II, do not in the end set the tone and overall impression gained from the Psalms.

Regarding themes expressed in these prayers, some few prayer songs are general prayers of distress (Pss 16, 82), but most not. The majority of the prayer songs of the individual carry the theme of deliverance from accusation and persecution (Pss 3—4, 7, 9—13, 17, 25, 27, 31, 35, 42—43, 54—59, 62, 64, 69—71, 86, 94, 109, 120, 139, 140—144). Others concern sickness and healing (Pss 6, 38—41, 88, 102, 130), closely related to the prayer song of the sinner (Pss 40, 51, 130).

The "prayers of the people" deal mainly with national defeat or distress and the need for restoration (Pss 44, 53, 60, 74, 79—80, 83, 85, 90, 106, 129), though other more general concerns appear as well (Pss 123, 125).

Several of these prayers cry for deliverance and vindication with such passion that they have come to be known as "imprecatory" psalms (Pss 5, 10, 17, 35, 58—59, 69—70, 79, 83, 109, 129, 137, 140). Prominent in many prayer songs are affirmations of deliverance or of God as Deliverer.

c. **Thanksgiving songs** (the *tôdâh*). The thanksgiving songs echo the themes from the prayer songs in the course of offering thanksgiving for rescue (Pss 22, 30, 66, 92, 107, 116, 118, 124, 138). On the one hand, they differ from the prayer songs in that deliverance sought has now come. On the other, they differ from the various praise songs in their frequent inclusion of narrative of their plight and deliverance in the thanksgiving and in their thanksgiving for specific deliverance experienced by the worshipper as opposed to praise for the various attributes and historic acts of Yahweh.

d. **Royal songs** (the *ma'ăšay lemelek*). The royal songs (Pss 2, 18, 20—21, 29, 45, 61, 63, 69, 72, 89, 101, 110, 132) include works of widely differing character but find their unity in their concern for the king—most likely David and his sons (Kraus 1988, 56-57). The king's relationship to Yahweh and the Davidic covenant, his enthronement, victory in battle, wedding, splendor, righteous rule, longevity, and salvation are important themes in these songs.

Changing speakers and form indicate liturgical use for several of these (e.g., Pss 2, 61, 72, 110, 132), though the exact nature of the celebration in which they would have been used is a matter of debate. Included here are songs that have come to be regarded as messianic.

e. **Songs of Zion** (*šîr ṣiyyôn*). Even the Babylonians knew of the "songs of Zion" (Ps 137:3), of which at least six have survived in the Psalter: 46, 48, 84, 87, 122, 126 (Kraus 1988, 58). Extolling Zion—her beauty, election, and sanctuary—the worshipper sang these songs, among other times, when entering the sanctuary after pilgrimage (Pss 84, 122).

f. **Didactic songs** (the *ḥokmâ*). The didactic songs may perhaps be a variety of prayer song and praise song, using the language and thoughts of Israel's instructional heritage, more than an independent psalms type (Kraus 1988, 58-60). Often called wisdom psalms, two traditions in Israel's life find expression here, the teachings of the wise and instruction from and in Yahweh's law/ Torah. One is familiar to us from Proverbs, Ecclesiastes, and Job. The other expresses instruction associated first with the priesthood (Mal 2:1-9). Psalm 1, a classic "wisdom psalm" focused in the blessings of Torah meditation, illustrates the merging of these two in what has come to be known as "Torah piety." ("Torah" here means not simply the law of Moses, but sacred instruction in general grounded in that Law.) Thus, these songs address the congregation in an instructional mode, some explicitly (e.g., Pss 34:11 [12 HB]; 78:1-2) and others implicitly (e.g., Ps 37). We take Pss 1, 32, 34, 37, 49, 50, 73, 78,

111—112, 119, 127—128, and perhaps 91, as didactic songs. Compare also Ps 19:7-11 [8-12 HB].

g. Festival songs and liturgical pieces (Pss 50, 81, 115, 121, 131, 133). Not surprising, several psalms (no doubt including some we have placed elsewhere) defy our ability to categorize with any confidence. If they constitute a grouping of their own, the indigenous name for it eludes the modern reader. Pss 121, 131, and 133 are all songs of ascent, but not the others. In some cases they related obviously to a specific festival, such as the New Moon (Ps 81).

The connection of the others is vague. Psalms 50 and 81 appear to provide settings for delivering divine oracles. Psalms 121, 131, and 133 are (perhaps benedictory) affirmations, with no obvious liturgical setting. Psalm 115 could perhaps be located in the praise songs but looks more like a liturgy of affirmation and response. Broyles has observed that Pss 5, 26, 28, 36, and 52 appear to be liturgies for entry to the temple, perhaps responding to the priestly instruction in Pss 15 and 24, which have long been recognized as such (1999, 10-11). Each of these mentions the temple. None has a specific affliction or direct threat to the pilgrim or a complaint element. Each contains indications of judgment in which some worshippers ("the wicked") are barred from entry, and others ("the righteous") are granted access to the temple.

2. The Psalms and Israel's Worship

Form-critical study of the Psalter has made abundantly clear the pervasive influence of Israel's temple worship upon the psalms we have, and vice versa. In spite of that fact, we are surprisingly uninformed regarding the actual content and breadth of worship in Israel's temples. Some speak of the Psalter as Israel's "song book." The designation is inappropriate, however, if by "song book" we mean an anthology, randomly arranged, from which selections are drawn for use without thought to the structure and purpose of the collection as a whole.

The Psalter then was not a comprehensive collection of works available in the temple library or archives for use in worship. Psalmlike compositions scattered throughout the OT, present in deuterocanonical writings and attested also at Qumran, argue for a temple corpus much larger than the Psalter. This means the Psalter represents a purposeful selection and collection of particular pieces from the larger temple holdings. This collection is purposefully ordered and arranged, with its own literary and theological structure and editorial goals, influenced by and influencing the temple cult.

Turning to the SSs in the Psalter, the *lack* of intelligible cultic information in them strikes us. Only eight of one hundred fifty psalms carry notes regarding their use in the temple (Pss 30, 38, 60, 70, 88, 92, 100, 102). And these are sufficiently vague and lacking in specifics as to allow the "cultic matrix from which they stemmed" to recede "into the distant past" (Wilson 1985, 169). Other superscriptional information that no doubt also related in some way to temple collections or liturgies early on had become puzzling, even to Jewish readers such as the translators of the LXX. This would seem to indicate minimal interest on the part of the final editors of the book of Psalms in the cultic setting as the key to understanding and appropriating the psalms.

Superscriptions that do speak of settings from which a given psalm should be heard take the reader not to the temple or its cult but to specific circumstances in the life of David, for example, "When he fled from his son Absalom" (Ps 3) or "When the prophet Nathan came to him after David had committed adultery with Bathsheba" (Ps 51) or, more generally, "A prayer of an afflicted person who had grown weak and pours out a lament before the LORD" (Ps 102).

Readers are directed by implication to find correspondences between their own lives and those of King David, the model psalmist, not usually to meditate on their participation in the temple liturgy. These notes loosen the psalms from cultic concerns, even obscure cultic ties, and free the poems to function on a personal level a la Ps 1:2 (see Wilson 1985, 143).

Clearly interpreters will be hampered if they ignore cultic information we can discern in the Psalter (e.g., the entry processional assumed by Pss 15 and 24). But the interpretive key to the whole apparently does not lie here. So much so that Goldingay considers the scholarly enterprise of reconstructing Israelite liturgy and worship as a meaningful part of Psalms interpretation a failure (2006, 54). We concur.

Nor do psalm types themselves (e.g., the prayers, the praises used in worship), form-critically and thematically discerned, provide the key to interpretation of the Psalter. The various psalm types appear scattered across the book. Even though prayers (the *tĕhillôt*) dominate the first two books of the Psalter, other song types appear frequently as well: wisdom songs, royal psalms, thanksgiving songs, praises, and even songs of Zion. The other books of the Psalter also are not structured by psalm type. Thus while the psalms arise from the world of the temple and the cult, study of this information has not provided the key to the corpus as it now stands.

The ubiquitous presence of SSs in the Psalter on the one hand coupled with their failure to provide sufficient cultic or literary information to unlock the collection on the other could well point to other possible functions of these notes in structuring the Psalter. Recent scholarship has pursued this possibility.

3. The Editorial Shape of the Psalter

In his 1981 Yale University Ph.D. dissertation, "The Editing of the Hebrew Psalter," Gerald H. Wilson proposed the most promising approach currently afoot toward understanding the Hebrew Psalter as we have it (1985). Wilson grounds his investigation of the Psalter in a meticulous analysis of Sumerian, Babylonian, and Qumran scribal practices for collecting and ordering hymnic materials (chs 1—5). Against this backdrop he then turns his attention to the SSs and postscripts of the psalms, looking for possible evidence of editorial shaping of the Hebrew Psalter (chs 6—7). Interestingly enough, his comparative studies uncovered several scribal techniques using SSs, postscripts, and colophons in the collecting and arranging of hymnic materials, but not along lines that form-critical investigations might have predicted.

Wilson argues convincingly for the Psalter's five book structure as an "editorially induced" framework by which the Psalter's overall impact is carried forward (1985, 191). Along with most he rejects the idea that individual psalms are meant to correspond to specific parts of Mosaic torah in this five-book scheme. But he shares the early rabbinical understanding that in some sense the five books given through David are parallel in significance to those given through Moses (199-203, 207-8). Within this five-book structure the Psalter has been organized around a twofold movement in which (much over-simplified) Books I to III present the theological problem of the fall of the Davidic dynasty and Books IV to V respond with an affirmation of the faithfulness and enduring reign of Yahweh. Different scribal strategies, all reflexes of those discovered in the Mesopotamian and Qumran corpuses, bind Books I-III and IV-V together.

According to Wilson, Pss 2, 41, 72, and 89 carry the backbone of the Psalter's first movement. Psalm 2 introduces the idea of the Davidic covenant and the rule of God through his anointed son, a theme that finds resonance with Ps 41, the concluding poem of the psalms' "most Davidic" book. Psalm 72, at the close of Book II, with its "Of Solomon" SS and its prayers for the king's son (72:1-2), extends the confidence in the continued blessing of Yahweh from David to his successors (1985, 210-11). Book III opens and closes with poems that raise question regarding God's faithfulness. Psalm 89 especially focuses on the anguished theological crisis triggered by the fall of Jerusalem, the accompanying demise of the Davidic monarchy, and the resulting question regarding Yahweh's faithfulness to his covenant with David (2 Sam 7:14).

Wilson considers Book IV to be the "editorial center" of the Psalter (1985, 214-19). Its striking set of "Yahweh Reigns" psalms (93, 95-99) answers the questions of Ps 89 with a resounding affirmation that the God who brought Israel out of Egypt would continue to be her refuge now as he was before the monarchy arose. The introduction of Moses into Book IV in SS (90) and content (105, 106) underscored the need now for the mercy shown to Israel under him (1985, 219). Book V closes the Psalter, apparently intending to present a "paradigmatic depiction of David in relation to his God" and "in response to the concerns of the pss which precede them" (ibid., 221). Psalm 119 dominates the landscape here, anchoring the entire Psalter in the love of Torah.

Integral to this understanding of the overall, editorial shape of the Psalter is the role of the psalms that open and close the Psalter. Lacking SSs, Pss 1 and 2 stand outside the psalms of Book I that, apart from Pss 10, 34, and 71, all carry SS. Several striking vocabulary links, including the blessings that bracket the two psalms with an inclusion (*'ašrê* in 1:1 and 2:12), tie the two together as an introduction to the Psalter. Psalm 1 pronounces the happiness of the righteous whose days and nights are filled with meditation upon the Torah of the Lord (1:2). The net effect is to present the "books of David" as Torah to be celebrated along with Torah given through Moses.

Psalm 2 raises the issue of the universal rule of Yahweh through his Anointed, the king whom he has installed in Zion. It broaches the claims of the Davidic covenant and the more fundamental issue of the rule of Yahweh, introducing this foundational question that will occupy the Psalter from beginning to end (see 145:1; 146:10; 149:2, 8). While Pss 1 and 2 introduce the Psalter by setting its basic agendas, Pss 145—150 conclude the collection with an extravaganza of praise known as the Great Hallel. "Let everything that has breath praise the LORD. Praise the LORD" (150:6). Walter Brueggemann suggests that in this reading the Psalter as a whole moves along the lines of the "orientation," "disorientation," "reorientation" experience (1984, 19).

Wilson's approach to the book of Psalms was inspired at least in part by Brevard Childs' call for renewed attention to the canonical shape of all biblical books, including the Psalter (Childs 1979, 504-25). James Luther Mays' brilliant work on the Psalter, also indebted to Childs, has in many ways run parallel to Wilson's, beginning with investigations on the role of Torah psalms in the shaping of the Psalter (1994b, 14-19, and 1994a, 119-27). J. Clinton McCann Jr. has built on Wilson's work in his work subtitled *The Psalms as Torah* (1993b, 25-50). Wilson's work has also drawn sharp criticism from scholars such as James Crenshaw, who regards his analyses as highly subjective with an overreliance on the final form of the text (2001, 98-101). Wilson's foundational work in comparative literature counters this critique quite well.

The "shape" of the Psalter speaks not only of the structure of the Psalter as a whole but also of the composition of smaller collections or units within the Psalter (e.g., Pss 28—30 or 93—100) and of the various textual references tying these contiguous psalms together. Redaction critical investigation that proved not to be markedly fruitful as an approach to the Psalter as a whole has seemed to be more efficacious when applied to smaller sets of psalms (see especially the work of Erich Zenger in Die Neue Echter Bibel, and in Zenger 2005).

Investigation of the textual references noted above, that is, the study of intertextuality or concatenation has also made an appreciable contribution to reading the Psalter. Study of these intertextual links was already taken up by the rabbis and early Christian scholars. Among nineteenth-century interpreters Franz Delitzsch (in his *Biblical Commentary*, 1:15-23) and J. A. Alexander (*The Psalms*, 3 vols.), both were attentive to catch key words, themes, grammatical connections, and so forth, drawing psalms together (cited in Howard 1993, 54-56).

These inter-psalm connections are especially obvious in contiguous psalm pairs (e.g., Pss 1 and 2, 50 and 51), inspiring W. Zimmerli's investigation of what he calls "twin psalms," his "Zwillingspsalmen" (Howard 1993, 66-67). But intertextual connections in the Psalter can connect more than two psalms (e.g., ʾěnôš in Pss 8, 9, and 10) and can draw pairs with considerable space between them into conversation (e.g., Pss 2 and 41, the beginning and end of Book I). These intertextual references do not appear to figure significantly in the macrostructure of the Psalter but do seem to contribute to lower level structuring and ordering of psalms in the collection.

Intertextual references in the Psalter produce all sorts of connections between the pieces involved, defying easy categorization. Some appear mainly to provide markers, bounding an editorial unit (e.g., the ties between Pss 2 and 41, marking Book I, and those tying Pss 1 and 2 together as introduction to the Psalter). Others develop or carry on a motif. Some appear simply to set up an open conversation between the poems involved, inviting reflection by the reader.

References comprised simply of topical similarity not controlled by closely related vocabulary or expressions are suspect, prone to proliferation much like topical chiasms. So Howard cautions, tongue in cheek, "if work at the lower level [this intertextuality] continues very long, soon every pair of adjacent psalms will be shown to have some significant—or logical—links between them" (1993, 68). Nevertheless, the study opens yet another fruitful path of reading for these fertile songs.

F. Authorship, Date, Audience, Provenance, Composition, and Occasion of the Psalter

Three preliminary comments are in order. First, in discussing all of these items we must distinguish between individual psalms and the Psalter as a book. Thus, in the question of authorship we are not talking here of the composer of Ps 1 but of the writer responsible for the Psalter. Second, because of the nature of the Psalter as a collection built over time, these matters are best discussed together. Third we have delayed consideration of these questions until we have put before the reader certain information regarding the Psalter germane to these matters.

1. Authorship

Probably the most important adjustment the modern reader has to make in considering authorship of the Psalter pertains to the nature of "book making," especially of literary works, in the ancient Near East and in Israel. The short of it is that literary production was more the work of scribes at temples and at the royal court than of individuals at home. And the copying/transmission of literary works was more likely than not to include editing and reshaping of works as they were handed down. (See Van Der Toorn 2007, 9-49.)

Dependence upon scribes was especially the case in societies that used syllabic cuneiform writing or Egyptian hieroglyph. Persons who wished to read and write there needed to master hundreds of signs/glyphs, limiting the pool of literate persons. In cultures with alphabetic scripts, writing and reading were more widely enjoyed, but the cultures were still highly scribal. Israel and Judah (along with many of their neighbors) used an alphabetic script, with only twenty-two consonants, much easier to learn and, we suspect therefore, more widely disseminated. Habakkuk apparently could write (Hab 2:2); Jeremiah worked through the scribe Baruch (Jer 36:1-4) but may well have been able to write.

As we have seen, the SSs of attribution on the psalms cover a variety of relationships between the piece and the person(s) named. The very presence of scribal SSs on many psalms tells us they have come to us through the scribal facilities either of the temple or the royal establishment. (See a similar notation of royal scribal participation in the shaping of the book of Proverbs [25:1].)

Some of these, we saw, indicated one or another of the musical guilds as responsible for the songs, for example, those from the sons of Korah (Pss 84—85, 87—88), a sort of corporate authorship. Some were attributed to David with an accompanying note clearly intending to convey authorship by David (Pss 3, 7). Others with a Davidic attribution assumed historical circumstances not possible or likely for David (Ps 138:2) and hence use *lĕdāwîd* differently.

Davidic attributions, however, dominate the Psalter, supporting the eventual association of the Psalter as a whole with David, in spite of the obvious attribution of a number of psalms to others or to no one. To locate a passage "in David" was to cite a psalm (Heb 4:7-8, quoting a non-Davidic Ps 95, though the LXX does carry a Davidic superscript here). The LXX, and even more the Targum, include SSs expanding the role of David in the Psalter. The Targum has David speaking in the Psalter "by the spirit of prophecy" (14:1; see Targum 79:1). This understanding that the psalmists speak prophetically by the Spirit surfaces in Peter's Pentecost speech (Acts 2:29-32; see also Heb 3:7-8). (See Broyles' helpful discussion of David and the Psalms for more detail [1999, 26-31].)

But as an answer to the question before us as to who wrote the Psalter, we have to confess our ignorance: "We do not know." We know neither the collectors nor editors responsible for the several smaller collections we encountered earlier, nor the person(s) who gave us the Psalter as we now have it.

2. Date, Audience, Provenance, and Composition

As for the date, audience, and provenance of the Psalter, as noted earlier, Jesus already referred to the third section of the Hebrew canon as "the Psalms" (Luke 24:44), naming the whole "writings" section by its lead book and assuming a book along the lines of what we have in our hands. And evidence from Qumran, especially from cave 11, shows the Essene community there copied versions of the Psalter apparently as sacred texts. But whereas the evidence indicates the presence of a book very close to the Psalter, it also shows that there were still varying textual traditions vying for acceptance, with entries in an order slightly different from the MT.

On the other end of the Psalter's development, around 200 B.C., ben Sirach probably has this third section of Hebrew canon in mind when he refers to truths handed down, "the law, the prophets, and *the later authors*" (emphasis added). Also, citation of psalms by the Chronicler could indicate that some form of the collection was already in circulation by ca. 400 B.C., or solidly into the postexilic period. But we lack text-critical or other information that could help us locate the place and the audience of the Psalter's first publication.

At this point a providential irony confronts us. On the one hand, the ubiquitous SSs indicate handling and probable production in the priestly, scribal community of the temple. But the psalms have been stripped of notations that would significantly inform readers of the significance of these worship/temple ties for interpreting the Psalter. On the other hand, most of the individual poems bear significant internal marks of composition for liturgy, for community worship.

Perhaps most obvious they are all poetic compositions. While occasionally an especially gifted worshipper may pray or sing spontaneously in lovely poetic lines, these prayers and songs bear the literary mark of professional liturgists, writing to elevate the language of worship for all worshippers.

In addition these psalms have been universalized through imagery and generalization. That mark frees them to function powerfully in nearly any setting—either in the temple or beyond it. The prayers for rescue describe enemies generally, speak of distress, of storms and miry pits, of snares and traps. As a result worshippers with myriad troubles locate their own situation, their own particular "trap," in these word pictures.

The songs speak generally of sins, transgressions, iniquities, without naming the specific sins of which the worshipper might be guilty. So persons with their own catalog of sins can speak the psalmists' words of confession as their very own. Similarly with the songs of thanksgiving and praise and other psalm types. This feature of the Psalter renders usual approaches to "audience" and "provenance" unhelpful. As Goldingay notes, the Psalter is simply of no help in portraying a history of Israelite religion and in locating the Psalter and various psalms in that history (2006, 31).

As a result, a distinctive feature of the Psalter is that by design it transcends particular times and places, particular "dates" and "audiences." Its history of composition and the origin of its several pieces are not determinative of its appropriation. The Psalter actually invites reading and appropriation by new readers who are able to see their own time and place in its timeless images, affirmations, and confessions.

An accident of translation has also assisted this process. One feature of the psalms that could impede its ability to speak cross-culturally is the name of Israel's covenant God, Yahweh. This is a particular deity from a particular people at a particular point in history. The translators of the LXX chose not to attempt a translation of the name "Yahweh," but used a translation convention using the Greek term *kyrios*, "Lord." This move opened the text to creative Christian use, since both the Lord God of Israel and the Lord Jesus Christ could be named by this term, depending on context.

Something of this convention remains in modern English versions that in some way flag the presence of the so-called Tetragrammaton (i.e., YHWH) in the text. A wide range of translation traditions use "Lord" (small caps) for this purpose: for example, the ESV, NABRE, NASB, NIV, NJPS, NRSV, REB, and RSV.

3. Occasion

Reflection on the "occasion" for the publication of the Psalter as we have it depends on previous conclusions regarding the theological shape and structure of the book as a whole. We know from other evidence that even after the dedication of the second temple the postexile community became increasingly people of a "book," the scrolls of Moses (the Pentateuch). With the grounding of the community in Mosaic torah, other historical, prophetic, and instructional writings congruent with that heritage were also collected and transmitted for use in worship and study.

Judging from the book itself, the "occasion" of the Psalter was the projection and support of a response to several of the restoration community's most significant questions. These theological challenges included: (1) the status of the Davidic covenant in view of the failure of the Davidic dynasty and the continuing lack of a king of any kind, let alone a Davidide; (2) the viability of the Mosaic covenant in view of the community's inconsistent experience of its blessings and curses; (3) the vindication of the rule of God in the world and of his character in view of events appearing to challenge both; (4) the validity of a reasonable hope for the community; and (5) the nature of daily life depending upon the responses to each of these matters.

The Psalter was edited to speak to the community in two ways. As we saw earlier, the Psalter was not exactly the "Temple Hymn Book," not its sole liturgical resource. Other worship resources were available in the temple. Nevertheless, the Psalter was used in the Second Temple period as a worship resource and thus impacted the life of all who worshipped at the temple. In addition, the Psalter's introductory psalm presented the collection to the reader as a form of Torah, a resource to be meditated upon day and night.

Of course we must not project modern literacy back into the postexilic community. Very few people would have had copies of this scroll. But some would have made copies from a master copy kept probably at the temple—scribes and priests from the temple and other sites. Through these persons the Psalter would have fed into the devotional, spiritual life of the people.

G. Hermeneutical Issues

The complex nature of the Psalter dictates a series of hermeneutical "moments" through which interpreters must pass in reading this "treasury of David." Because the individual psalms were apparently composed by liturgists for use in worship, we are compelled to ask in each case how this liturgical history informs the interpretation of each psalm. This is not the end but rather the beginning of the interpretive process, part of discerning the "plain" meaning of the text in its historical contexts, part of the first hermeneutic moment.

Because we now have these liturgical pieces lodged in certain literary contexts dictated by the literary and theological structure of the Psalter in its final form, we must also ask how each psalm's literary context informs our understanding of it. And we must ask how each individual psalm contributes to the structured Psalter as we have it. Both intertextual "conversations" and large-scale structural connections figure in this process.

Because we read the Psalter as Christians, we read informed by the NT's manifold appropriation of psalms to understand Jesus of Nazareth and to expound his person and his way. We are guided in that process by Jesus and the apostles themselves (e.g., Acts 2:25-28, 42). We do not read Christian interpretations anachronistically back into the historic text, stifling the text's earlier voice. First we hear that earlier voice. But we do follow the lead of Jesus and the apostolic community in unique appropriations that the historic text itself invited through its liturgical openness. They read the Psalter with interpretive strategies at home in first-century Judaism because they were first-century Jews! They heard the psalmist as David, inspired as a prophet who saw in advance Jesus and the birth of the church (Acts 2:29-30). While our reading strategies are not limited to those of Jesus and the apostles, we certainly read in continuity with their interpretive conclusions.

This involves recognizing that God in his wisdom has used even these culturally conditioned readings to convey his truth, as he has done throughout the entire history of revelation. The picture of David inspired as a solitary writer fits an understanding of inspiration somewhat akin to that of an apostle, inspired to write a particular biblical book, pacing about a prison as he dictates to an amanuensis and then signing the document in his own hand (see, e.g., Col 4:18). But the overall process by which God brings documents from liturgy and private experience through antecedent collections to their place in the final shape of the Psalter seems more a matter of guiding providence than specific inspiration. Paul calls this process God's "*ex*-spiration" of his Word: Scripture is "breathed out by God," *theopneustos* (2 Tim 3:16 ESV).

This hermeneutical move of reading the Psalter in congruence with Jesus and the apostles has already taken us past discernment of what the text "meant" to reading it in its canonical context. It has moved us toward the question of how the text, historically interpreted, speaks cross-culturally and cross-temporally. What has traditionally been called consulting the "whole counsel of God" or "interpreting Scripture by Scripture" proves more critical in discerning how the ancient text transcends its particular time and place, than in discernment of its historic meaning. In this process the text we are reading in the Psalter becomes the topic of discussion in the canonical dialogue.

Listening to the canonical dialogue's "discussion" of the Psalms text at issue, one hears, among other contributions, the "rereadings," the "redirections" mentioned earlier in the christological and ecclesiological readings noted, for example, from Luke and Acts. In addition one hears places in which the canonical dialogue essentially affirms the Psalter's claims (e.g., Ps 1 and its claims regarding the happiness, vitality, and well-being of those who center life in God's will). One also encounters texts in which the canonical dialogue critiques or corrects directions taken in the Psalter. One thinks here of Ps 137 and its approach to prayer for the enemy, an approach that must come under the scrutiny of Jesus and his word on this topic (Matt 5:43-48). These texts remind us that in Scripture God has given us the entire conversation, not simply the "last word" on many topics. The entire conversation has been "ek-spired." The whole conversation was inspired and remains God's Word (Thompson 1994, 65-84; Bauer and Traina 2011, 287-319).

The final hermeneutical moment we visit will be our appropriation of the text. Here we answer the question, "How should we then live?" or perhaps more adequately, "What should we be and do?" in light of the text we have interpreted and set in the canonical dialogue. We will not spend as much time on this as on the interpretation and canonical evaluation leading to it. We will prepare the ground for the readers' own work of appropriation based on their specific life situation. But we will often point the way in the "From the Text" section of the commentary.

H. Theological Emphases in the Psalter

1. The Lord Rules the Cosmos Faithfully and Mercifully

If, as Gerald Wilson claims, Book IV is the *"editorial* center" of the Psalter, then the issue of the reign of God is its *theological* center (1985, 215). The central claim, announced with emphatic repetition in Pss 93 and 95—99 of Book IV is that the Lord alone rules faithfully and mercifully his entire creation. Taken together these six songs do for God's kingship what Ps 119 does for the Lord's Torah, staking it as a major claim of the Psalter as a whole. This theme of the Lord's rule is pursued all the way to Ps 145. There the psalmist exalts God as King and worthy of great praise (vv 1-3), proclaims his gracious, compassionate ways with his creation (vv 7-9, 13-17), and calls every creature to praise him (v 21). This closing call puts the final songs of the Psalter structurally in the service of these themes.

These psalms in Book IV are the editorial center of the Psalter because they respond to the challenges posed to these claims in Book III. At the outset of Book III Ps 73 takes up again the challenge to the idea that the godly are actually blessed. Psalm 74 lays the claim that the Lord has been the poet's king from of old (v 12) beside a poignant telling of the destruction of the temple (vv 3-8) (see 77:7-9 [8-10 HB]; 79:1-5). Book III closes with unanswered questions regarding the status of God's promises to David in light of the catastrophic demise of the Judean monarchy (89:38-51). The Psalter does not so much argue God's faithful rule as it affirms it in the face of circumstances to the contrary.

God's faithful and compassionate rule of the cosmos, his status as great King over all (95:3; 99:4) is repeatedly linked to his role as Creator and Sustainer of that cosmos (15:1 ff.; 93:1; 95:4-5; 96:5; 104; 146:6). As Creator as the Lord has the wherewithal and the right to rule as he pleases. Who could possibly force his hand? So his habitual choice to rule faithfully and compassionately draws particularly joyful praise (103; 146:5-10).

The claim that Yahweh rules over all the gods (95:3; 96:4; 97:9) raises the question of the degree to which the Psalter grants the existence of other gods. On this question one may have to distinguish between the view implied by given psalms and the viewpoint of the Psalter as finally shaped and disseminated after the exile. Psalm 82, for example, may well come from a very early time in Israel's history, narrating the God of Israel's consignment of other gods to mortality (vv 1-2, 6-7). Psalms 86:8 and 138:1 appear to assume the reality of other gods, while worshipping Yahweh, God of Israel, alone. Psalms 96:4-5 and 97:7 clearly equate the gods of the nations with dumb idols, with no real existence.

At this point of God's faithful and compassionate rule, theology and life intersect directly for the psalmists. Beyond the psalmists' experience of God's faithfulness evident in the heavens, it is in their personal welfare or lack thereof that the Lord's rule is most immediately evident and at the same time most open to challenge (9:7-10; 10:1-18)! As King of all creation the Lord also functions as Judge, rendering and enforcing just verdicts throughout his entire realm (7:8-12; 96:10; 98:9; 146:7-10).

These profound convictions about the God of Israel as Creator and Sustainer, Judge and Deliverer, provide the theological foundation for the expectations and petitions permeating the prayers of the people. Because God has revealed himself as faithful, compassionate Ruler, Judge of all the earth, he can be counted on to hear the cry of the needy and to do something about their plight, no matter what the odds against them.

The second of the Psalter's introductory psalms links the Lord's rule of the nations with that of his royal Son, the Anointed (Ps 2). To rebel against one is to rebel against the other (vv 1-3). To serve the Lord is to serve the king he has installed in Zion (vv 11-12). By its designation of this anointed one as the Lord's "son," the psalm introduces God's historic covenant promise to David as a concern of the Psalter itself. God had assured David of a perpetual dynasty (2 Sam 7:4-11). The kingdom of God and the kingdom of David were not simply the same. God's sovereign rule extended to all Creation (Ps 103:19-22); David's clearly did not.

Nevertheless through the Davidic son God exercised his rule, as a comparison of the Davidic son's rule and responsibilities to those of King Yahweh in Pss 95—99 makes plain! Against this theological and literary backdrop the questions raised by Ps 89 at the end of Book III loom large indeed.

The Psalter "went to press," however, with God's promise of a Davidic son to rule on his behalf still dangling unfulfilled. This transformed royal psalms into messianic psalms. The Psalter retained songs of Yahweh's kingship and songs of the Davidic son's rule as statements of faith, not narratives of fulfillment. To this day, pious Jews who read these psalms do so in expectation. Christians have seen these expectations come to fruition in the person of Jesus, Son of David (Matt 1:1-17; Luke 1:67-79).

Briefly but significantly, one psalm sees that God exercises his will not only through the Davidic son but also through all human beings. Amazing as it is, the one who made the heavens has put the "works of [his] hands" under the rule of human beings whom he has also made (Ps 8:4-8 [5-9 HB]).

2. Those Centered Wholly in the Will of God Have Abundant Life

Psalm 1 introduces this cluster of rich theological claims already as a foundational theme of the Psalter. The psalmist effervesces over the profound well-being of those who occupy themselves with the Lord's "Torah" day and night (1:1-3). Quite likely this introductory psalm puts before us not only Mosaic torah but also the Psalter as a form of "Torah," that is, divine instruction. Much larger than simply "obeying God's law," this psalm presents the intense well-being of those who center all of life in discerning and doing the will of God.

This incorporation of the Psalter into Torah involves a remarkable transformation in which, as often noted, "the words of human beings to God have become the Word of God to human beings." The vast majority of the psalms obviously are prayers directed to God. Psalm 1 recognizes, however, that as persons read and sing these prayers they enter into worship. Meeting us in the Psalter he speaks his word through these prayers.

That we talk of "the will of God" is itself a tribute to the God of Israel (see Kinlaw 2010, 11-38). The pantheons of Israel's neighbors were populated with gods who either had no coherent will to reveal or for whatever reasons chose not to reveal their will to human beings. Their will was mainly divined by the reading of livers or the casting of lots (Ezek 21:21). Not so the God of Israel and of the Psalter. Instead the Psalter is replete with songs that trade in "the revealed will of God."

Some take up this issue straight on. God reveals himself, his glory, and his creative genius through the heavens (Ps 19:1-6 [2-7 HB]) and unveils his character and moral will through his Torah (vv 7-11 [vv 8-12 HB]). Because of this self-disclosure, the psalmist envisions the prospect of pleasing God his Redeemer in word, thought, and (presumably) deed (19:14 [15 HB]). Other psalms revel in the marvel and perfection of the Lord's self-revelation in Torah and in the bountiful life enjoyed by those who walk in his ways with integrity, who seek the Lord "with all their heart" (Ps 119:1-2).

Psalm 1 of course finds its theological home in the Mosaic covenantal tradition and in the standard teaching of Israel's sages. Those who obey God's covenant law will be blessed (Deut 27—29; Lev 26), as will those who live wisely in the fear of the Lord (Prov 1:8-33). The blessings envisioned here are immediate (in this life), concrete blessings (e.g., "peace" not simply as inner tranquillity but as absence of military invasion) (see Thompson 1993).

But these contentions of Ps 1 do not go uncontested in the Psalter. The fact that the Psalter's largest single psalm type is the *těpillâh*, prayers from deep distress, indicates life often at odds with the bounty celebrated in Ps 1. The failure of God's people at times to experience this "good life" is precisely the problem taken up by Ps 73. The wicked, carefree and prosperous as they are, contrary to what we would have expected from Torah and wisdom, are not only morally reprehensible but openly defiant of God (73:1-12).

Although now in hindsight the psalmist is able to see his discomfort for the envy that it was (vv 1, 21-22), and although he realized that not all the wicked have such enviable lives finally (vv 18-20, 27), and that in the end all he really needed was to be near to God (vv 23-28)—still the problem had been there and had to be faced. The challenge of the wicked that God either cannot actually see, is otherwise impotent, or is simply not in the picture at all surfaces repeatedly, to be rejected or denied or simply faced (e.g., 10:4-5, 13; 14:1; 22:8; 42:10; 53:1; 59:7; 64:9; 71:11; 94:7).

But Ps 1's confidence that the way of the Lord is the way of life abundant rises not from naïveté but from life experience and robust trust of the Lord. Most likely Ps 1 came to its present place after the exile in the later shaping of the Psalter as a whole. Or if it came to that place earlier, the final editors of the Psalms have let it stand. Either way, the editors who gave us the Psalter had been through the exile, through the difficulties of deportation and the disillusionment of the return community. These people knew "real life" and still insisted life with Yahweh was the way of profound well-being (see Deut 30:15-20). They breathe the same theological air as did Jesus in the Beatitudes pronouncing persecuted ones blessed (Matt 5:11-12).

3. Worship Constitutes the Appropriate Human Response to God

At the temple, along the way, or at home, the most appropriate response to life that persons can make is worship. Both the prehistory and the final shape of the Psalter point to this. Foundationally this involves carrying on one's entire life in the way of the Lord, informed by his Word. This espousing of Yahweh's way leads inevitably to trusting oneself to his kingship. It involves responding to the profoundest adversity in the confidence that Yahweh reigns.

These foundational orientations—"choosing life" by choosing Yahweh, and submitting to Yahweh's kingship—produce two prayer and worship foci especially. They issue in rich celebration of the Lord, his character, his historic mighty deeds, his glory, and more. They likewise open confession of sin and need, cries for all manner of deliverance for oneself and one's community.

I. The Text of the Psalter

The Hebrew text of the Psalter comes to us reasonably sound. Even so, a glance at the critical apparatus in the *BHS* shows that the text of a number of psalms has apparently suffered in transmission (e.g., Pss 9—10, 18, 49, 90). Nevertheless, we judge the MT to be the best preserved Hebrew text of the Psalter. The MT as published in the *BHS* serves as our base text, though we will give less regard to the Masoretic (Tiberian) pointing and notation than to the consonantal framework of the MT, which can be shown to be relatively intact from pre-Christian centuries (Tov 1992, 27-29). Where the MT appears to make little or no sense we will adopt other readings or offer emendations based on the ancient versions, with priority given to the LXX because of its demonstrated status as an independent witness. These occasions will often involve confusion of the *yod* and *waw*, easily confused in the early block or "Assyrian" script, and/or the *bet*, *dalet*, and *resh*, often confused in both the block script and paleo-Hebrew writing. In no case will we abandon the MT simply for "metrical" reasons.

A Note on a Reading Convention

Throughout the commentary I will refer to "the psalmist" as the one giving us the psalm at hand. Some who emphasize the liturgical origin of the psalms object to this as an overpersonalization of the compositional process. They see it as a throwback to a day when one imagined a uniquely inspired, shepherd bard on a hillside, writing out of his individual experience. Now, instead, we deal with a liturgical composer, a member of a temple guild or priestly family writing for the congregation.

Acknowledging this reality, my use of "the psalmist" prejudices no view of composition of psalms. I use it for convenience. But we must also push back a bit. True, the liturgical composers wrote generalizing in such a way that a wide range of readers/singers could see their own very particular situations in the world opened by any given psalm. But it also is true that the guild composer understood life sufficiently to fund the choice of vocabulary, metaphors, and similes capable of describing our particular plight or providence. This one whom God inspired to give us the psalm is "the psalmist."

Interaction with versions. First recourse for information regarding textual issues will be to the ancient versions, the Targums, the Vulgate, the Peshitta, but especially the LXX because of its chronological proximity to the MT. Citation of select English versions beginning with the KJV will not attempt to be exhaustive. Instead we will cite those versions that represent various translation options instructive for a given text.

COMMENTARY

BOOK I: PSALMS 1—41

The Two Ways: Torah and Destruction (1:1-6)

BEHIND THE TEXT

Psalms 1 and 2 comprise an introduction to the book of Psalms as a whole. Several features of the text point to this. First a lack of SSs sets them apart from the following poems. With the exception of Pss 10, 33, 43, and 71, all of the psalms in Books I through III carry SSs. Also several vocabulary links tie these two psalms together: *'ašrê*/**happy** (1:1; 2:12), *derek*/**way** (1:1, 6; 2:12), *'ābad*/**perish** (1:6; 2:12), and *hāgāh*/**meditate, plot** (1:2; 2:1). Finally, these two pieces introduce the two most important themes of the Psalter: the blessing of life centered in Yahweh's Torah, and the reign of Yahweh and the relationship of the king in Jerusalem to that reign.

The two psalms speak from different but related streams of tradition. Psalm 1 uses the language of Israel's wisdom community, especially as this community incorporated priestly concerns for instruction in Torah. It trades in distinctive contrasts known to us from the book of Proverbs (the righteous versus the wicked, the happy and "successful" versus the perishing). It reduces to two the ways open to human beings—the way of the righteous and the way of the wicked, with their two contrasting destinies. And it makes a person's response to Yahweh's Torah the point around which all of life turns.

Psalm 1's opening words place it among the "psalmic beatitudes" (e.g., Pss 32:1-2; 34:8 [9 HB]; 84:5 [6 HB], 12 [13 HB]), which Gerstenberger classifies as a "liturgical admonition" (1988, 40). If so, the admonitions are implicit, for a striking feature of this poem's adaptation of wisdom forms is its lack of direct admonition. The poem simply describes the contrasting dispositions and destinies of the righteous and the wicked, leaving readers to draw their own hortatory conclusions.

Psalm 2 is a royal psalm, devoted to issues related to the Davidic dynasty, specifically the coronation of Yahweh's anointed son. The relationship of the nations to this Son of Yahweh particularly occupies the poet. For more extensive treatment of these matters, see the Introduction.

While Psalm 2 may well be one of the older pieces in the Psalter, Psalm 1 has marks of later Hebrew poetry: terms that begin lines outside of meter, intrusion of the relative pronoun (*'ašer*), and the presence of unusually long lines. Although these features at points disrupt a crisp flow of balanced cola, tightly crafted lines at key points give the poem solid delivery of its far-reaching claims. The work hardly deserves the condescending assessment of "clumsy" (Gerstenberger 1988, 41). One can well imagine this first psalm being composed specifically to play this introductory role paired with Ps 2.

IN THE TEXT

1. The Fruitful Life of Those Who Delight in Torah (1:1-3)

■ 1 *O how happy the one . . . !* This exclamation launches Ps 1 and the Psalter as a whole, attributing profound gladness to the person this poem eventually calls "the righteous" (v 6). It can be translated as an English verbal clause: "Happy *is* the one who . . ." (so REB; compare NJPS, NRSV). But a verbless exclamation best conveys the cryptic syntax of the poem's opening word, caught well, for example, by the 1990 NAB ("Happy the man who . . .") and the NLT ("Oh, the joys of those who . . .").

The psalmist first describes this person negatively in three parallel denials (v 1*b*, *c*, and *d*) and then positively in a contrasting bicolon in v 2. The denials separate this profoundly glad person from three overlapping sectors of the population: wicked *persons* (v 1*b*), sinners (v 1*c*), and mockers (v 1*d*). Wicked designates persons generally by their character, "evil" as opposed to "godly." More specifically sinners names persons by their behaviors. They sin, breaking God's covenant with Israel (v 1*c*). Mockers assumes poor character and behavior contrary to the will of God but tags people by their toxic speech. Mockers and sinners "with an attitude," the wicked ready to belittle, to attack, to marginalize others.

But notice the denials themselves. Our truly happy one does ***not live*** [i.e., **walk**] ***by*** the advice of persons of evil character (v 1*b*). Such persons do ***not locate themselves*** (i.e., **stand**) in the lifestyle, the habits and attitudes (i.e., **the way**) of sinners (v 1*c*). They do ***not take up residence*** (i.e., **sit**) in the mockers' turf (v 1*d*). Whether there is a progression of identification with ungodly persons here is debatable. Carrying on life (**walk**), positioning oneself (**stand**), and continuing association with mockers (**sit in the company of** . . .) all present significant traffic with the values and behaviors of persons at odds with the God of Israel. The truly glad person of Ps 1 is known first of all by the persons, attitudes, and behaviors with which this one does *not* identify. In these preferences this person shares Yahweh's own disposition (Ps 5:5).

The only positive description of the person to this point in the psalm is that this one is truly happy. A Hebrew noun speaks the exclamation, describing the emotional and personal state of the person. Some translate the exclamation with **blessed** (e.g., ESV, NASB, NIV). The word **blessed** in Hebrew is a passive verb. **Blessed** assumes God has acted, bestowing some good upon a person. Recipients of these benevolent acts then are **blessed**. Such a translation is acceptable here, because the Psalter and this psalm explicitly assume the persons are profoundly happy *because* God has acted to save and to bless them. Their gladness is itself the gift of God. But, though this is assumed, the statement actually refers to the astounding happiness of persons known at least in part by their significant separation from the ungodly in Israel.

Meaning of the Word "Man"

The word **one** translates the Hebrew *'îš*, often rendered **man**, appropriate to the psalmist's culture but awkward in our own. Here, in the rest of the OT and in the NT as well, the word **man** is roughly equivalent to "person." **Man** stands for people in general, without significant focus on the gender (though *'îš* can make that distinction, e.g., Lev 13:29). This is not **man** as opposed to "woman," but **man** as opposed to some other creature or a thing. Although the four Hebrew words commonly used to designate a man/person (*'ādām*, *'îš*, *'ĕnôš*, and *geber*) can be differentiated in some contexts, any of the first three could have served to name this representative person (compare Hamilton 1997, NIDOTTE 1:262-66, 388-90, 453-55, 816-17).

■ **2** *But on the contrary*, *kî 'im*. In strong contrast to the three denials regarding truly happy persons in v 1, two positive claims in v 2 paint a very different picture. Having seen what does *not* command the attention of these happy souls, we now learn what *does* preoccupy these joyful ones—**Yahweh's law**. Their affections and their attention center in Yahweh's Torah. They have high regard for the content of Yahweh's instruction and profound appreciation for living that law and its place in defining Israelite culture (v 2*a*). They also devote energy and time to learning and pondering torah. **Meditate** refers to the subvocalization common in the ancient world in reading and also to the sort of "self-talk" involved in deeply preoccupied reflection. All their waking hours, all the affairs of life get considered in light of this law.

The law of the LORD here translates **the torah of Yahweh**. *Torah* in the Psalter and the OT at large generally refers to the five books of Moses or significant parts of it and especially to the law given at Mount Sinai (compare Exod 19:1-8). And, although Mosaic *torah* does include civil law, governing the nation and all persons in it, *torah* is larger than civil law and was viewed more as "binding instruction" and covenant content than as legal pronouncement. Hence we will often refer to this literature simply by its Hebrew name, *torah*, or as "instruction."

With this positive description of the happy one we can return to the opening claim that has governed the entire psalm to this point. Who has profound joy, according to this song? Persons known by their significant separation from the ungodly in Israel and also by their consuming appreciation for and continuing reflection on knowing and doing the will of God.

■ **3** Defined negatively in v 1 and positively in v 2, a protracted simile now pictures the truly happy one of v 1 as a lush and fruitful **tree**. The tree has been transplanted to a place of perpetual access to water—not a common place in Israel. *(Trans)planted/šātûl* generally designates planting slips (Ezek 17:22) or vines (Ezek 17:8-10) or trees that, unlike the planting of seeds (*nāṭa'*), actually involves *trans*planting. Someone has selected a prize location, calculated to support growth and fruitfulness. **Streams of water**/*palgê māyim* may refer to an abundant stream, if the metaphorical use of *palgê māyim* as a *flood of tears* in Lam 3:48 is a clue to its other uses.

Two results follow from this well-watered planting, timely fruit (v 3*c*) and perpetual vitality (v 3*d*). The last colon steps out of the simile and, perhaps interpreting the word picture, refers back to the person rather than the tree. The psalmist declares that everything this person tries **prospers**—turns out well, succeeds. The verb could be taken causatively, ***He makes everything he does prosper***, as in Ps 118:25 (Goldingay 2006, 84). But the simile assumes the tree's environment (***by the watercourse***) accounts for the foliage and fruit, not the tree itself. So the righteous person's immersion in Yahweh's teaching accounts for success in everything the person does, not some unusual effort toward success itself. Everything the person does? Of course it's hyperbole. Even so, this speaks unqualified good news. No wonder this person is profoundly happy!

2. Driven Life of the Wicked (1:4-5)

■ **4 Not so the wicked!** The brevity of this disclaimer packs it with meaning, because it invites the reader to fill in the interpretive blanks left open. It just asserts that none of the claims made of the truly happy person in vv 1-3 can be made of the wicked. The LXX emphasizes this by repeating the "Not so!" and adding "from the face of the earth" to the wind's driving away. The reader is supposed to think in terms of strong opposites. Not profoundly happy. Not able to resist the lure of the lifestyle, the haunts, the cynical speech of sinners. Not appreciative of Yahweh's instruction and not interested in its possible impact on personal or national life. And, consequently, not known for perennial freshness, productivity, or success across the spectrum of life's endeavors. These implications at the very least come to the surface.

A contrasting simile paints the explanatory picture. These persons are not like well-watered, lush, fruitful trees. **They are like chaff**! This picture jars the reader. In contrast to the transplanted tree of v 3 we might have expected a dry wilderness bush or a scraggly tree on the wall of a wadi. Instead we get *chaff*. One can scarcely think of a stronger contrast to the flourishing tree! In harvest the grain is brought to the threshing floor. Animals pulling sleds and walking on the grain knock seeds from stalks and chop the stalks to pieces. In winnowing harvesters toss forks full of stalks, seeds, and debris into the air so that the wind can carry off the lightest, throwaway material—the chaff. Seeds, stalks, and heavier debris fall back to the ground. Pouring this material through a sieve catches the foreign material and allows the grain to fall through into containers for collection and storage.

Chaff? It's the lightest, least significant, throwaway material from the whole harvest process. Driven away by the harvest wind—that describes the wicked! Windblown, not planted; dry and lifeless, not lush and alive; worthless, not valued.

■ **5** Now the poet draws conclusions (**therefore**) from his description of the wicked (v 4) and the truly happy one of vv 2-3. **Judgment**/*mišpaṭ* refers to various aspects of legal decision making—sometimes the legal decision or pronouncement itself (Deut 16:18), sometimes the legal claim being made (Jer 32:7-8), or the law upon which the case is based (Ps 89:14 [15 HB]). Here *mîšpaṭ* apparently refers to the litigation process itself where a decision will be rendered (Ezek 7:23; Job 9:32).

The assertion is that the wicked will not *yāqûmû . . . ba/***stand in the judgment**. Kraus points to similar wording in Ps 24:3, *Who will stand in/yāqûm . . . bi Yahweh's holy place.* He argues for a "sacral-juridical" gathering where persons were judged fit or unfit to enter the sanctuary and the worshipping assembly. Thus he translates, "Therefore the wicked will not enter the judgment court, nor sinners the congregation of the righteous" (Kraus 1988, 119-20). We know from Proverbs of the wicked finding themselves condemned by the community (Prov 5:14), and also of the relationship between Yahweh and his people pictured in the language of these community courts at the city gate.

The claim here about the fate of the wicked should perhaps be left in the context of an assembly of righteous persons in whose hands the decision regarding the wicked would rest (Goldingay 2006, 87). A programmatic introduction to the Psalter such as we have in Ps 1, however, invites the possibility that the writer refers to end-times judgment and life. The LXX points in that direction, reading "sinners will not rise again," as does the Targum, translating "The wicked will not be pure in the great day." Kraus ends up at this view, claiming these sacral-juridical structures were "spiritualized" by the time of this poem (1988, 120). Both construals make sense.

The two final verses of the psalm name the group to which the truly happy person of v 1 belongs—**the righteous**. The wicked have appeared as a group from the outset of the psalm, with the "truly happy man" as a representative individual, living faithfully in deliberate contrast to the masses. But now we discover the righteous person is no solitary believer, but a person living faithfully with the support and identity of a community of righteous persons.

3. Yahweh and the Two Ways (1:6)

■ 6 The closing bicolon provides the theological structure within which the preceding lines make sense, the theological rationale. Neither fate nor simple happenstance account for life as the righteous and the wicked experience it according to this psalm. The righteous, centered in and guided by Yahweh's Torah, have profound happiness and live vital, fruitful lives because **Yahweh knows** their way. He knows by active participation in their way. It is Yahweh's participation in the life of the righteous that accounts for life as they experience it. His knowledge of the affairs of the righteous cannot be confined to cognitive awareness, mastery of data about them. His knowledge must account for their lives.

The contrasting claim, that **the way of sinners perishes**, sounds on the surface as though this state of affairs simply is. The sinners' life appears to have in it the seeds of its own destruction. But the opening line (v 6a) suggests another conclusion. **The way of sinners perishes** because **Yahweh knows** it as well. His participation in the life of the wicked also accounts for their life as it is.

FROM THE TEXT

For post-holocaust readers Ps 1 seems like an incredibly naive description of life. Everything the righteous person does succeeds? Never so the wicked? Really? The cascades of complaint psalms that follow close on the heels of this poem raise obvious questions about these claims. But viewing Ps 1 as an intentional introduction to the Psalter leads to several insights.

For one thing this psalm, like the Psalter itself, is postexilic (either in its composition, its placement at the front of the Psalter, or both). This psalm meets us first in the Psalter by the design of scribal editors from the years after the exile. These saints and/or their immediate ancestors had been through the exile. They had heard stories of the destruction of the temple, the city of Jerusalem, and the land. They knew of children dashed against buildings, deportees with their eyes gouged out, and lonely years carving out a life in a foreign land. They had lived through the disappointing realization that life as a backwater province of the Persian Empire was not going to match the vision the prophets had proclaimed of life after the exile. If there was anything these postexilic believers definitely were not, it was naive. They had been through a deathly valley. And they had come through it convinced that life lived in the will of God as discerned through his Word was to be celebrated as a life of profound happiness and prosperity, *these traumatic realities notwithstanding*! This was firm conviction, not naïveté. The lens this psalm gives for reading the following psalms casts them as exceptions to the rule for God's people, not the full story of their lives.

The NT shares this understanding of the truly happy life. According to Jesus, in the kingdom of God truly happy persons include those who are persecuted because of their allegiance to him and the Gospel (Matt 5:10-12). The call to follow Jesus boils down to a call to deny oneself and to carry a cross (Mark 8:34—9:1). And God underscores his own brilliant glory by housing the light of his presence in our jars of clay, our "cracked pot" existence (2 Cor 4:5-12).

Further, this psalm makes Yahweh's Torah the center of the truly happy life. This happens also to be the truly righteous life. Profound gladness emerges from submitting human desires, indeed all of life to the will of God as discerned through study of Scripture. Persons who insist on forcing Yahweh's Word to endorse their own preferences will never find true happiness. This psalm does not advocate a legalistic version of Judaism (itself usually a caricature, against Gunkel). Instead it celebrates the vitality and gladness of those who trust Yahweh completely, who revel in his torah. Additionally, one suspects the editors of the book of Psalms intended to commend this book itself as Yahweh's instruction to be received with the same regard and submission as that given to the books of Moses.

Finally the rule of Yahweh to be introduced in Ps 2 surfaces already in our psalm. The "knowing" of Yahweh by which the righteous thrive speaks of Yahweh's providential entanglement in the lives of his people. Whether obviously present or thoroughly hidden, his knowing makes the difference.

Yahweh's Royal Son (2:1-12)

BEHIND THE TEXT

By its lack of SS, by several vocabulary links, and by the concluding blessing that brackets Ps 2 with Ps 1 (2:12 with 1:1) this poem is tied to Ps 1 as the second half of the Psalter's introduction (→ Ps 1, "Behind the Text" for specifics). The editors of the Psalter have raised here two themes programmatic for the book as a whole: life centered in the study and living of Torah (Yahweh's instruction) and the rule of Yahweh and its relationship to the Davidic dynasty.

Psalm 2 represents well the tantalizing situation readers of the Psalter encounter. On the one hand the poem evidences a probable place in temple liturgy or royal ceremony. Its abruptly changing voices/speakers argue for such a setting. A narrator opens with an incrimination of rebellious kings (vv 1-3), including their speech (v 3). The narration shifts to Yahweh's response (vv 4-6), including the words of Yahweh to the rebels (v 6). Yahweh's anointed king then speaks reporting Yahweh's coronation edict (vv 7-9). Finally the narrator urges enemies of the crown to serve Yahweh by submitting to the anointed son (vv 10-12). This sounds like remnants of a coronation liturgy.

On the other hand, when we attempt to penetrate the details of this probable ceremony for purposes of historical reconstruction or interpretation, we immediately hit a wall. We are sent back to the text not for purposes of reconstruction but to discern its theological contribution to the Psalter.

IN THE TEXT

1. Incrimination of Rebel Rulers (2:1-3)

■ **1-2** Why do the nations *rage* . . . and the peoples plot . . . ? (v 1). Not a question asking for information but a legal rhetorical device lodging an indictment of kings being arraigned for rebellion (see Gen 31:30; Jer 26:9; Job 7:19-20 et al.; Gerstenberger 1988, 45). Here we have the incrimination itself. The psalm assumes a configuration in which Yahweh rules as the great King over his domain, exercising his rule through his vice-regent. His realm includes nations over which he and his vice-regent also rule through local kings allied with him by covenant to rule locally on his behalf. The indictment may not have a particular rebellion in mind, but a world in which persons who should gratefully serve King Yahweh time and again rebel.

In this military context **the peoples** (*lĕʾummîm*) may well be "warriors" (Craigie 1983, 63, citing Hebrew and Ugaritic evidence). Their rebellious plotting (*hāgāh* [verb]) is **in vain**—doomed before it starts, at polar opposites from the meditation (also *hāgāh*) of the righteous on Yahweh's Torah (1:2).

Against Yahweh and . . . his **Anointed One** marks a critical conjunction between Yahweh and the Davidic king in Jerusalem. To rebel against one is to rebel against the other. Although the kingdom of Yahweh is not strictly equated with or limited to the kingdom of the Davidic ruler, Yahweh's rule is tied with sufficient clarity to that king that to plot against one is to plot against the other. Both Yahweh and the enemies understand this.

■ **3** Dramatically we are given the plot in a single bicolon. The rebels regard life loyal to Yahweh as **chains** and **shackles** to be snapped and cast off, a foolish and insolent assessment. They will risk breaking the covenant oaths they have sworn with king Yahweh and his anointed one.

2. Yahweh's Response to Rebellion (2:4-6)

■ **4** Yahweh "sits enthroned" (REB) translates the Hebrew *yôšēb* nicely, since in royal contexts the verb carries the notion of sitting on a throne or in a seat of judgment (compare 1 Kgs 8:25; Amos 1:5, 8). For the psalmists the heavens constituted Yahweh's cosmic dwelling. Yahweh also sat enthroned in the temple on the cherubim, the ark of the covenant being his footstool. The temple was the unique point of intersection between Yahweh's heavenly and earthly rule. Yahweh mocks the rebels, laughing in anger at the "boundless stupidity" of these "infinitely little" ones, as Delitzsch put it (Keil and Delitzsch 1989, 93).

■ **5** Yahweh's word proves sufficient to terrorize the rebels who find it one thing to plot rebellion, another to confront the king in person.

■ **6 I have installed my king on Zion.** The rebels' words conclude the first part of the psalm; Yahweh's words the second. King Yahweh's spoken response to the rebels focuses not on them but on the king whom he has installed to reign in his behalf from Zion. The response begins *wa'ănî nāsaktî*, to be taken either as emphatic, **As for me,** I have installed . . . or as circumstantial, **Meanwhile,** I have **already** installed. . . . Either is possible, but the emphasis on Yahweh as the actor answering the rebellion seems more fitting and direct and therefore preferred as the opening line of Yahweh's response. This reading is also preferable to the LXX, which reads these words as passive, "I have been installed as his king," and as words of the Anointed, assuming a slightly different pointing of the Hebrew consonants. Though possible, the pronoun I (*'ănî*) now lacks an antecedent, needlessly complicating the syntax.

My holy mountain, a particularizing parallel to Zion in v 5*a*, the mount on which both the temple and the royal palace stood, names the center of Yahweh's rule on earth.

3. Rehearsal of the Installation Edict (2:7-9)

■ **7-9** Now the anointed one speaks, eager (note cohortative *'ăsappĕrâ* and *BHS* 34.5.1) to **proclaim** [or *report concerning*] **the decree *of Yahweh*.** This **decree** the Deuteronomic historian calls a "covenant" in his description of the coronation of young Joash (2 Kgs 11:12). The proceedings involved: (1) crowning, (2) giving of the covenant document, (3) proclamation of kingship, (4) anointing, and (5) public acclamation ("Long live the king!"), several parts of which surface in our psalm. Judging from the quoted words that follow, the *ḥōq Yahweh*/**the LORD's decree** included reference to the foundational covenant with David (2 Sam 7:8-16, esp. v 14; Ps 89:27-28). This decree may include the declaration of sonship (2:7), the proclamation of dominion (v 8), and the publication of the royal mandate (v 9).

Now the anointed one quotes the declaration of covenantal sonship included in Yahweh's **decree:** . . . **"You are my son; today I have become your father."** In Egypt and perhaps in Canaan this royal sonship was ontological, the son being begotten by the patron god and sharing his deity (see Dahood 1966, 12, for bibliography). This was not the case in Israel. Among the many accusations leveled at Judah and Israel's kings, claiming deity does not appear. At this point the Davidic royal covenant uses father/son language at home in suzerainty treaties to formalize the dynastic promise Yahweh made with David and his offspring. See also related language in the Mosaic covenant (Deut 1:31).

After the declaration of royal sonship, Yahweh invites the new king to ask for all Yahweh is prepared to grant—worldwide dominion. This **inheritance** (as a share now of the "family's" holdings) is rightly his **possession** (inalienable property once received) as son of the great King, but he is urged to ask for it, underscoring the one to whom **the nations** and **the ends of the earth** finally belong (v 8; see Ps 146:5-6).

Concluding the decree of Yahweh he now publishes the mandate to guide the newly crowned king (v 9). **You will break them**, that is, the nations and the ends of the earth. This reading, **break them** (footnote) takes the MT *těrōʿēm* from *rʿʿII*, "to break, shatter" (*HALOT*, 1270, and most modern versions). Alternately, the NIV and NABRE, following the LXX, read the Hebrew *tirʿeh* from *rʿh*, "to shepherd." Either makes sense, and a possible wordplay between them may in any case bring both to mind. The contrast is striking indeed between the strength of the **rod of iron** and the fragility of the potter's clay jars smashed in v 9*b*. Closely related meanings of the Hebrew *šēbeṭ*—**scepter** or **rod** or "(shepherd's) staff"—only multiply possible construals. If the anointed **shepherds** (i.e., rules) these kings with a "staff of iron," a sobering irony stretches the shepherd metaphor usually used for more benign aspects of kingly rule (e.g., 23:1).

Perhaps more interesting here than the specific language, is the fact that the newly crowned king must win his inheritance in battle. He must take possession of his possession. That is his mandate.

4. Yahweh's Warning to the Rebels and Beyond (2:10-12)

■ **10-12** The narrator/liturgist now speaks the final lines of the psalm. **Therefore, you kings** catches well the force of the MT (*wĕʿattâ*) that signals both a climactic and a causal relationship between these lines and the preceding sections of the psalm. To this set of admonitions the incrimination, the coronation, and the dominion have been heading, perhaps signaled by a return to vocabulary of the early lines (**kings**, vv 10 and 2; **anger, be angry**, vv 5 and 12). The **or** in v 12 moves the admonitions to warnings.

The warnings urge kings and judges of the earth to wise action, sensible, practical, and open to counsel even in this tumultuous time. The warning calls for assessment of their situation in light of what they have heard of Yahweh and his anointed. **Serve the LORD with fear** (v 11) urges the rebels to the loyalty and submission they earlier thought to cast off (v 3). It implies the utter folly of their earlier plot.

Unfortunately the *b* colon in v 11 and the beginning of v 12 prove puzzling in the MT. **And celebrate his rule with trembling** translates the MT well enough (so LXX), but what does it mean? What sort of "rejoicing" is done with "trembling"? **Kiss his son** likewise translates the MT reasonably well and makes sense in light of the ancient custom of paying honor through a kiss of greeting (see 1 Sam 10:1). But this reads the MT *bar* as "son" and takes this term as an Aramaism. This is not so much impossible (see Prov 31:2) as simply very odd. Why suddenly and with no apparent benefit use Aramaic? The NJPS takes *bar* as Hebrew meaning "clean" or *bōr* meaning "purity" and translates "pay homage in good faith." An emendation that involves redivision and rearrangement of the MT consonants produces a line to be translated "Kiss his feet." Again this makes fine sense but lacks any real textual support beyond the fact of the difficult MT. The upshot is that several contemporary English versions stay with the MT (ESV, NRSV), some translating the MT idiomatically as "do homage" to the son (NASB).

The warning to the nations is buttressed by the threat of Yahweh's anger rising quickly and the rebels perishing **in [their] way**, even as they pursue rebellion. The NIV becomes virtually a paraphrase in this difficult line: **And your way will lead to your destruction.** The sense should perhaps be something like ***lest you perish en route to your rebellion.*** Known elsewhere for his compassion and forgiveness (compare Ps 103 among many), Yahweh's utter disdain for outright rebellion emerges clearly here.

The concluding colon implicitly offers another way to would-be rebels—taking refuge in Yahweh! On the unusual *ḥôsê bô* see GKC 116.h.

FROM THE TEXT

New Testament writers use Ps 2 to interpret Jesus and the earliest church especially at three points. First, in Acts 4:25-26 the first two verses of Ps 2 provide language for describing the wicked collusion of Herod, Pilate, and the crowds in the death of Jesus and the continuing hostility of the authorities to the fledgling messianic community. The citation may also anticipate the coming conquest of these rebels by the anointed son later in the psalm, which made John the Revelator's reference to this language in Rev 19:15 so apt.

Second, the coronation declaration of Ps 2:7 provides vocabulary for identifying Jesus of Nazareth as the royal Son of God at the outset of his ministry (Mark 1:11 and Luke 3:22). While it is likely that Mark may have understood Jesus already as the divine Son of God by the time of his writing (see Hurtado 2003, 283-316), Jesus' sonship first and foremost in the book of Mark itself is an expression of his messianic kingship. This is true not only at his baptism but also at the transfiguration of the Son and at the cross (Mark 9:7; 15:39). Even in John, who clearly presents Jesus as the divine Word and Son, Jesus' sonship is tied closely to his kingship (John 1:49). His sonship will finally be manifest in his universal rule. Elsewhere the writer of Hebrews quotes the whole coronation litany together with reference to the covenantal promise to David (2 Sam 7:14) in presenting the preeminence of the Son over all preceding modes of revelation (Heb 1:2, 5).

Third, the coming victory of Messiah over all foes finds expression in the royal mandate of 2:9. Revelation 12:5 and 19:15 see Messiah's rule over his foes with an "iron scepter" on the near horizon, linking Messiah's victory to the conquest of the gospel in 12:5 and Jesus' ultimate rule in 19:15.

Clearly the anticipations of Ps 2 have been and will be fulfilled in the life and death and coming reign of Jesus of Nazareth. All who take refuge in him are blessed. Christian readers of Ps 2 take heart in promise of the anointed one's universal dominion and victory over evil. The psalm and NT appropriations of it deliver the Christian from overly romantic views of a domesticated Jesus. They respond in trust and obedience to the psalm's call to live joyfully in the blessing of Messiah's kingdom (Rev 2:26-27).

Yahweh: Shield from Many Foes (3:1-8 [2-9 HB])

BEHIND THE TEXT

Psalm 3 is the first of many prayer songs for the individual, which will dominate Book I of the Psalter. The contextual note provided by the editors of the Psalter in the SS directs the reader to receive this poem as one of David's responses to the attempted coup by his son, Absalom. We know something of that dreadful time in David's life—dangerous, embarrassing, discouraging—from 2 Sam 15:1—18:33. With the 2 Samuel account in mind we think not only of a tragically fractured family and the multifaceted pain involved in it. We think also of political betrayal and cloak and dagger intrigue with lethal consequences on both sides. For more extended comment on the SS, see the Introduction, C.1.a, C.4.a, and C.6.

IN THE TEXT

I. The Psalmist's Many Foes (3:1-2 [2-3 HB])

■ **1-2 [2-3 HB]** Voiced to Yahweh, the song opens picturing the foes arrayed against the psalmist. He emphasizes the large number of his adversaries and the particular shape of their attack—**many** occurs three times in the first two verses! And his adversaries wage psychological-theological warfare claiming **God will not deliver him** (v 2 [3 HB]). They either insult the psalmist or God or both. Either the psalmist is so wicked that God will not help him, or his God is so inept that he cannot help. Oft repeated (note the participle, 'ōmĕrîm) by many, the verbal attacks make the assault on the psalmist particularly difficult. This attack also challenges the claim made in Ps 1 that the righteous are profoundly blessed because of the life-giving knowledge of Yahweh. It begins a conversation that will cover several psalms here early in Book I.

We take *selâh* and the change of person in v 3 [4 HB] as possible clues to the break in thought. (The NIV omits the *selâh*, an obscure liturgical note, whose contribution to the text is often uncertain. In some cases, as here, its meaning can perhaps be discerned.)

2. Yahweh the Proven Ally (3:3-6 [4-7 HB])

■ **3 [4 HB]** Over against this disclosure of his plight the psalmist lodges an emphatic contrast, **But you, LORD** . . . Contrary to the gainsaying of the adversaries, Yahweh represents the psalmist's nonnegotiable response to the slanderers. He scores three points. (1) Yahweh is his peculiar defense on every side, his **shield**. The obvious metaphor of protection, here sharpened by **around me**, is reserved mainly for deities and kings (see the parallel in 89:18 [19 HB]). (2) Yahweh is his **glory**, that is, the basis of his claim to honor (with LXX and most modern versions). (3) Yahweh is the one who **lifts *up his* head high**, that is, the one who time and again (note the ptc. again) shows support for the psalmist, vindicating him in the face of his enemies.

■ **4-6 [5-7 HB]** Alongside his claim regarding Yahweh as his saving ally, the poet posts testimony of his own experience of Yahweh. He has been answered when he called unto Yahweh (v 4 [5 HB]). He has rested in Yahweh's support (v 5 [6 HB]). And he anticipates no fear of his assailants (v 6 [7 HB]). Because of the fluidity of the temporal reference of both the preformative and sufformative tenses in biblical Hebrew, the need to emend the pointing of the temporal reference of the bicola is not clear. The poet may speak here of Yahweh's present help (so, e.g., NABRE, NIV, NRSV, REB, Craigie 1983) or perhaps of his past deliverance (ESV, LXX, NKJV, NLT, McKann in *NIB*). Either fits the form of the individual prayer for deliverance. I am inclined to read the MT as is and understand the lines as a testimony of what the prophet has already experienced. In v 4 [5 HB], then, *'eqrā'* (***I called***) is preterit (past reference).

The psalmist's claim to have slept well and safely sparks particular interest. He lived to awaken from sleep—Yahweh protected him! He was able upon lying down to find sleep—Yahweh gave him peace! He took this prayer to the temple—Yahweh answered there! During the whole affair Yahweh was sustaining him (*yismĕkēnî*)!

3. Plea for Yahweh's Rescue (3:7-8 [8-9 HB])

■ **7 [8 HB]** The logic of the brief poem focuses here on the plea for Yahweh to intervene forcefully to save him. The call for Yahweh to arise may picture him seated on his throne from which he rises to lead his forces into conflict. Cola 7 C and D may provide the rationale for the request—Yahweh has already proven his willingness and ability to vanquish the psalmist's enemies (then *kî* is causal and *hikkîtā*/**smite** and *šibbartā*/**smash** are perfects with indicative mood). Or 7 C and D may continue and heighten the psalmist's urging (the *kî* is then emphatic and the verbs are so-called precative perfects, expressing requests). The LXX and most contemporary versions read the former; so also Broyles in the New International Biblical Commentary and Goldingay in Baker Commentary on the Old Testament. The NLT, Dahood in the Anchor Bible 16, and Craigie in Word Biblical Commentary take as emphatic precatives. In spite of the balance of scholarship, I tend to think the context warrants the emphatic urging from the perfect verb (see *BHS* 30.5.4c).

■ **8 [9 HB]** A brief 2+2 line ends the prayer. Affirmation that salvation *does* come from Yahweh registers confidence and rejects the enemies' taunt from v 2 [3 HB]. A benediction gently strikes the petition chord once more with a verbless clause: ***Upon your people [be] your blessing.***

FROM THE TEXT

The challenge voiced in Ps 3 (v 2 [3 HB]) to the optimism of Ps 1 reminds readers that their faith will face challenge. Not every person and not every circumstance will support the notions that those who embrace Yahweh's way experience profound happiness and well-being (1:1-3) because of Yahweh's providential participation in their lives (1:6). Many will go another way. One legitimate response to such challenges includes continued calling upon Yahweh, rehearsing times of deliverance (3:3 [4 HB]) and flat-footed denial of the challenge (3:8 [9 HB]).

This psalm's two emphases expressed in vocabulary repetition are "the many" (various forms of *rbh* or *rbb* in vv 1, 2, 6 [2, 3, 7 HB]) and "salvation" (nouns and verb built on *yšʻ*, to save, in vv 2, 7, and 8 [3, 8, 9 HB]). They anchor two points of impact: (1) The many frequently err; head count does not establish truth. (2) God alone saves those who call upon him.

Who Can Show Us the Good Life? (4:1-8 [2-9 HB])

BEHIND THE TEXT

The liturgical background of this psalm can perhaps be seen in the fact that the psalmist, though praying as an individual, speaks perhaps also for a group in v 6*b* [7*b* HB]. Abrupt change of address in v 2 [3 HB] and v 6 [7 HB] could also indicate a worship setting for this piece.

For particulars of the SS see Introduction, C.1.b; C.2.a; C.4.a; and C.1.a.

IN THE TEXT

1. Prayer for Relief from Distress (4:1 [2 HB])

■ **1 [2 HB]** The song opens with a petition, *hear me* (most likely not a narrative, *he heard me* as the start of a prayer of distress). The psalmist addresses his God. Literally he calls on ***the God of my righteousness***, so translated by the ESV, LXX, NASB, and others. This renders the Hebrew well enough literally, but what does it mean? ***Righteousness*** (here *ṣedeq*) has to do with rights and right relationships. God's actions as related to one's righteousness would be to bring about justice or the rights or a right decision for a person. So the REB translates "the upholder of my right," and Dahood (1966) translates "of my vindication." This seems best as a follow-up to a petition.

Give me relief from my distress interprets the psalmist's metaphoric ***Give me room/space in my straights***. Context supports taking *hirḥabtā* with the NIV and NABRE as a precative (hortatory) perfect rather than a narrative (vs. LXX and most English versions). He stakes his case on God's mercy.

2. Admonition of the Compromised or Confused (4:2-6 [3-7 HB])

■ **2 [3 HB]** The psalmist turns from prayer to a rather surprising admonition and chiding of his adversaries. ***People*** (*bĕnê ʾîš*, lit. ***children of man***) probably indicates persons of means and station as opposed to lesser persons (see this distinction in 49:2 [3 HB] and 62:9 [10 HB]). ***How long*** is not a question to be answered with a time period but an indictment to be answered or rectified. Two concerns dominate. These well-off detractors tarnish his reputation and are infatuated with pointless falsehoods. Follow-up lines below lead one to think the empty lies these people follow have to do with more than general lack of integrity. They have given themselves to untruths about Yahweh (see vv 2, 6, 7 [3, 7, 8 HB]).

■ **3 [4 HB]** Judging from the admonitions here, the psalmist's protagonists claim Yahweh pays no special regard to those faithful to him and does not answer when they call to him. The psalmist counters their ignorance with experience to the contrary.

■ **4 [5 HB]** The precise meaning of this verse eludes us. It appears the psalmist exhorts the agitators to think more before they speak. The opening verb could have to do with anger, that is, ***be angry*** and do not sin *[in the process]* (so the LXX), but at whom and why? Or, it could simply refer to personal upheaval. The middle clause, ***speak in*** your hearts perhaps includes **on your beds**. But then a single verb is left for the final clause, making a very unbalanced tricolon. *Be troubled but do not sin; / talk to yourself upon your bed, / but be still.* It reminds us of Kugel's admonition against imposing balance in the name of parallelism (1981, 49-58).

■ **5 [6 HB]** **Offer the sacrifices of the righteous** probably focuses on the one to whom the sacrifices are offered as the point of rightness. Colon B supports this suspicion. Which deity is it to whom one should offer sacrifice? It speaks to the issue of trust and to the object of that trust. Instead of **trust in the LORD**, we might translate *put your trust upon Yahweh [not another]* or *direct your trust toward Yahweh [not Baal]*.

■ **6 [7 HB]** **Many, LORD, are asking, "Who will bring us prosperity?"** The **many** moan, wanting someone, some deity, to bring them **prosperity**. Judging from v 7 [8 HB], abundant harvest of grain and stock of new wine appear to be their concern. **Let the light of your face shine on us.** The NIV (with the LXX?) apparently reads the MT *něsâh*, "tempt," here as a corruption of *ns'*, "lift," and as the prayer of the psalmist (so also Craigie 1983, 77-78; Weiser 1962, 119; NABRE, NASB, NJPS, NKJV). It could also continue the words of the many people (ESV, REB, RSV). Some also read the MT as from *nws*, *The light of your countenance has fled from over us* (so Goldingay 2006, 117; Kraus 1988, 144). Since to this point it has been the psalmist who speaks to Yahweh, we cautiously take v 6b [7b HB] as the psalmist's words, asking God to demonstrate his ability to care for his people.

3. Testimony to Yahweh's Unique Provision (4:7-8 [8-9 HB])

■ **7-8 [8-9 HB]** Verse 7 [8 HB] could be a petition from the psalmist for joy in this crisis. Because, however, of the claim in v 8 [9 HB] we are reading this also as a claim, a testimony of Yahweh's intervention in the psalmist's plight. Yahweh has given him more joy than the abundant harvest brings to those dependent upon it for happiness.

Yahweh has given him such calm that, contrary to "the many" in v 6 [7 HB], he not only takes to his bed, but also (*yaḥdāw*) sleeps peacefully. Only Yahweh can have infused this sense of security into this troubled situation. Verse 8 [9 HB], understood thus, is read as a bicolon. Some also scan it as a tricolon: *In peace I both lay down and sleep; / for you alone are Yahweh; / you make me dwell securely.* Possible, but not as likely, since the point is not the singular identity of Yahweh but Yahweh's singular capacity to meet the psalmist's (and God's people's) needs.

FROM THE TEXT

James Luther Mays reminds us that in the psalmist's culture the attack on his character and honor by slanderous adversaries registered with the force of a physical attack on his person, if not more devastating (1994b, 55). The confidence and sense of tranquillity to which the psalm eventually leads the worshipper depends on the certainty that Yahweh does have special interest in those faithful to him (v 3 [4 HB]). Trust in him is not misplaced. Not the abundance of grain and wine but Yahweh's gift of radical calm grounds the psalmist's honor. This reminds us of the confusion caused by the worship of other gods as exposed by Hosea (2:2-13 [4-15 HB]) and Zephaniah (1:4-6).

Seven sets of identical or similar vocabulary along with unusual quotation of "the many" stitch Pss 3 and 4 together. With Ps 3's talk of awakening and Ps 4's testimony of going to sleep, the church has often found here prayers for morning and evening.

Prayer for Rescue from Lethal Lies (5:1-12 [2-13 HB])

BEHIND THE TEXT

Broyles concluded Ps 5 was best understood as a liturgy for temple entry, though it has generally been taken as an individual prayer of the distressed. A significant claim was that the prayer contained no direct, individual (or corporate) attack on the psalmist and that its particular concern was actual entry into the temple (1999, 11). Verse 8 [9 HB], however, seems to refer, albeit briefly, to enemies that the psalmist considers his own. And the prayer of the psalmist is not so much that he be rescued from the wicked as that the wicked be judged as a manifestation of Yahweh's character and a vindication of those faithful to him. The psalmist's central affirmation does deal with his entry to Yahweh's temple (v 7 [8 HB]).

On the SS see the Introduction, C.1.b; C.2.c; C.4.a; and C.1.a. On Ps 5 as a liturgy for temple entry see Introduction, E.1.g.

IN THE TEXT

1. For a Hearing with God (5:1-7 [2-8 HB])

■ **1-3 [2-4 HB]** In a series of requests emphatically stated the psalmist urges Yahweh to listen attentively to him. What others might dismiss as mutterings or sighing he wants Yahweh to understand.

In his muttering (*hĕgîgî*) the psalmist boldly addresses his petitions to **my King and my God**. With this address he assumes the position of grateful servant rejected by the rebels in Ps 2:1 in their futile plotting (*yehgû rîq*). His language evokes the mulling over Yahweh's Torah that occupied the righteous in 1:2 (*yehgeh*). The theme of Yahweh's kingship, raised first in Ps 2, the psalmist here makes personal. Yahweh is not only King of the nations, ruling through his Anointed King of Israel (Ps 2:4-7), but also the psalmist's own Divine King.

For to you I pray. Psalmists buttress both their petitions and their expressions of praise and thanksgiving with reasons. The poet has already implicitly grounded his prayer in the faithful relationship assumed by his address to Yahweh as his King and God. Now (taking the *kî* as **for** with most English versions) he appeals to the focus of his prayer—toward Yahweh, as opposed to other gods. The statement could also be emphatic (NABRE) or, less likely, a temporal clause ("When I pray . . ." [REB]). He also appeals to his practice of prayer: he lays out his offering morning by morning (Goldingay 2006, 128) and then waits expectantly for Yahweh's response. Psalm 5 as a morning prayer (5:3 [4 HB]) ties it, like Ps 3 (3:5 [6 HB]) to Ps 4 (4:8 [9 HB]), an evening prayer.

■ **4-5a [5-6a HB] For you are not a God who . . .** opens descriptions of Yahweh's relationships with wicked and arrogant persons that provide the most secure basis for the psalmist's prayers. Because of who God is, the psalmist's prayers are well placed (so most English versions). (Not taking the opening *kî* as a substantiating conjunction seems unhelpful [v 4 (5 HB)].) The sort of persons who please Yahweh, the persons whom Yahweh allows to keep company with himself, those who can stand under his penetrating gaze (v 5 [6 HB])—with regard to all of these Yahweh shows himself solidly on the side of the righteous and the humble.

■ **5b-6 [6b-7 HB] You hate . . . you destroy . . . you, LORD, detest.** Not just Yahweh's disposition toward the wicked but his actions toward those who live rejecting his ways buttress the psalmist's prayers (note the participles in vv 5c-6a [6c-7a HB]). **Hate** should probably be taken as covenant terminology. In ancient treaties hate described the suzerain's attitude toward an unfaithful vassal; love named the suzerain's faithfulness to his vassals and also the vassal's loyal relationship with his suzerain. Compare Yahweh's hatred of Esau and love of Jacob in Mal 1:2-3. See Amarna Letter 286 in Arnold and Beyer (2002, 166) and Deut 6:5.

■ **7 [8 HB]** Standing emphatically over against the arrogant wicked whom Yahweh rejects (***But as for me . . .***), the psalmist proceeds in the abundance of Yahweh's faithful mercy. In this mercy he makes bold to enter Yahweh's palace, that is, the temple from which Yahweh reigns. There, in appropriate awe and reverence he will prostrate himself toward Yahweh's temple in worship. If Broyles is correct in taking this as liturgy for entry to the temple, these claims regarding the psalmist's access to the temple are the center of the psalm, the point of the prayer.

2. For Direction and Deliverance (5:8-12 [9-13 HB])

■ **8 [9 HB]** In a second set of petitions, after those in vv 1-2 [2-3 HB], the psalmist pleads for Yahweh's leadership and instruction. The misdirection of persons opposed to or maliciously critical of the psalmist calls forth these requests for Yahweh to lead him in such ways that he finds himself in right relationship with Yahweh and Yahweh's purposes for him (i.e., in Yahweh's righteousness). The other request, for Yahweh to **make straight [his] path** evokes the picture of the king's road crew straightening and leveling the road to the temple. That road, that **way** of the Lord, is a life of obedience to him. Yahweh will make it straight by giving insight and instruction in worship.

■ **9 [10 HB]** As implied in the words used to name his adversaries the psalmist now supports these requests for direction by detailing their utter reliability. Their interior conceals destruction. Their speech, slippery and unreliable, spreads the stench of death, the accusation underscored by an unusual spelling of the concluding word in the line.

■ **10 [11 HB]** The requests for Yahweh to destroy these adversaries works from the theology seen already in Ps 1:6. The way of the ungodly perishes. By the providence of God, their habit of life has in it the seeds of its own destruction. So here, the psalmist asks for a judicial pronouncement—**Find them guilty, O God**—and also for an act of judgment by which they perish following their own advice and find no place in the temple. They are banished, a plight befitting rebels. They are not simply the psalmist's private enemies but are also conspirators against Yahweh. The writer marks out these lines from vv 7-10 [8-11 HB] with the repetition of the Hebrew *bĕrōb*, **in/by the abundance** of Yahweh's grace by which the psalmist enters the temple (v 7 [8 HB]) and of the adversaries' **many transgressions**.

■ **11-12 [12-13 HB]** The concluding verbs in these two verses have a hortatory force that registers more like a benediction than an exhortation. There is also a subtle causal force behind the aspirations. Thus implicitly, "As you respond to my prayer," **let all who take refuge in you be glad**. Additionally, this jubilance is the probable purpose of Yahweh's sheltering care: **Spread your protection over them, [so] that those who love your name may rejoice in you.** The final bicolon (v 12 [13 HB]) could either be a concluding support of the preceding pronouncements (with a substantiatory *kî*, so most English versions, LXX) or simply an emphatically stated conclusion.

Yahweh blesses **the righteous** (one) and like a shield, Yahweh **surround**[s] *him* (sg.) though **all who take refuge** and other references are plural. This "confusion" of singular and plural referents runs through the whole psalm. Editors and scholars often remedy "this deficiency" as a probable result of scribal confusion. One wonders if these "corrections" are well advised. Concordance of number may simply not be a concern of the writer. Perhaps the confusion plays off the simultaneous corporate and individual referent present in the "I" of the Psalter.

FROM THE TEXT

Whether Ps 5 was a liturgy for temple entry or simply a prayer of the distressed, it raises the problem of the response of the righteous to unwarranted attack by evildoers. The psalmist shares ground with other righteous suffers—Joseph, Job, Jeremiah, Jesus to name a few. The psalmist's response is so strident that this psalm is sometimes included among the so-called imprecatory psalms. Christian readers will already have thought of the teaching of the Master who has his disciples praying not against or at their enemies but for them.

At the same time they register an important aspect of biblical responses to evildoers. They are to be placed in the hands of Yahweh for judgment. Further, this psalm presses the notion that there are behaviors and attitudes that preclude one from entry to the temple. Worship of Yahweh is fundamentally incompatible with the loyalties expressed in the speech and behavior of the wicked. Though it is because of the powerful grace of God, still it is true that the psalmist speaks for those whose habits of work and worship are such that they do have entry to Yahweh's house of prayer.

Prayer in the Face of Discipline (6:1-10 [2-11 HB])

BEHIND THE TEXT

Psalm 6 presents a parade example of the individual's prayer song concerned with the need for healing and related distress. Its abrupt transitions perhaps indicate its use in temple liturgy.

On the SS see Introduction, C.1.b; C.2.a; C.2.b; C.4.a; and C.1.a. The SS has no specific, meaningful relationship with the content of the psalm, so far as we are now able to discern.

IN THE TEXT

1. Petitions for Mercy and Healing (6:1-5 [2-6 HB])

■ **1-3 [2-4 HB]** Taken together, the psalmist's opening petitions reveal his plight. He is ill, frail, and feeling traumatized. At his wits' end, twice mentioning his thoroughly rattled state, he cries out for healing (v 2*b* [3*b* HB]). Because he is sick, he concludes that Yahweh is angry with him. He presumes that Yahweh through his illness is seeking to **rebuke** or **discipline** him (v 1 [2 HB]). In his frailty he pleads for mercy. The staccato language of v 3*b* [4*b* HB] underscores his urgency: *And you, Yahweh—how long!*

■ **4-5 [5-6 HB]** **Turn, Lord** assumes Yahweh has turned away from him in his displeasure. In the psalmist's view, in order to rescue this saint the Lord will have to turn back toward him. At the moment he feels very much on his own as a target of Yahweh's anger. He bases his hope for healing upon Yahweh's demonstrated kindness (his *ḥesed*), the sort of faithful mercy exhibited throughout Israel's history.

In the Psalter Yahweh's *ḥesed* first appeared in 5:7 [8 HB]. There as here it provides the basis for the psalmist's prayer. Frequently functioning in this foundational role, the Lord's "lovingkindness" (as the KJV often translated it) permeates the Psalter. Here it supplies the *logical basis* for the psalmist's plea (i.e., **because of *your* mercy**). It could also give a *psychological* motive for Yahweh's response (i.e., act *for the sake of your loving kindness*).

It is this personal motive for Yahweh's action that the psalmist now pursues. He reminds Yahweh that in the realm of the dead, that is, in the grave there is neither memory nor praise of him. If Yahweh wishes to be remembered and even praised for delivering the psalmist, he will need to act soon, the reasoning goes.

2. The Psalmist's Anguish (6:6-7 [7-8 HB])

■ **6-7 [7-8 HB]** Back to the poet's anguish we are led, with a tightly stitched tricolon pouring out his heart. An impressive chiasm connects the B and C cola of v 6 [7 HB]: *'asheh bě . . . miṭṭātî/bědimʿātî ʿarśî ʾamseh*: vb + b- /b- + vb, pressing both sound and syntax into service to strengthen the lines. His **bed** is awash with **tears** (v 6 [7 HB]), so much so that his eyes grow weary from weeping (v 7 [8 HB]).

At this point another feature of the psalmist's problem appears—his **foes**. Verse 8 [9 HB] briefly identifies these adversaries by their behavior. They do evil. It is their habitual practice.

3. Rebuke and Testimony for Evildoers (6:8-10 [9-11 HB])

■ **8a [9a HB]** In an abrupt shift the psalmist now speaks directly to his foes. This direct address is unusual in a prayer for deliverance. **Away from me** assumes that these troublemakers are in some way focused on and gathered around the suffering one. These people are known by their life pattern of doing evil (*'āwen*). Although "those who do *'āwen*" is the most common descriptor of the wicked in the Psalter (appears twenty-nine times) precisely what evil they practice this vocabulary does not allow us to say. Quite likely it involves an abuse of power and malicious speech.

■ **8b-9 [9b-10 HB]** A second abrupt shift has the psalmist speaking *about* God in the third person (**the Lord has heard**) not *to* God in the second person as in vv 1-7 [2-8 HB]. And he voices an important claim. Testimony that Yahweh hears his people's prayers runs the length and breadth of the Psalter (4:3 [4 HB]; 5:3 [4 HB]; 17:6; 18:6 [7 HB]; 31:22 [23 HB]; 55:17 [18 HB], using the specific vocabulary of "hearing," with many other references using related vocabulary where Yahweh "answered" or "rescued" or otherwise responded to Israel's cry to the Lord). It generally presumes that God has already acted on behalf of the worshipper. That Yahweh has heard does not simply mean he has noted the petition for future reference, but that he has in fact acted to deliver—that's how the psalmist knows Yahweh has heard. He has recovered from his illness. Or, less likely, the past tense claim (**has heard**) makes a claim about the future as confidently as if it had already occurred.

These abrupt shifts are probably best explained as indications of liturgical direction, clues to the poem's previous life in temple worship. A temple liturgist now turns the worshipper away from the rehearsal of his profound distress to testimony of Yahweh's deliverance.

■ **10 [11 HB]** Translation of the closing bicolon of Ps 6 puzzles readers. Some construe it as a closing prayer: **May all my enemies be ashamed . . . ; may they turn back . . .** Kraus takes it as a present, general claim: "Shame and shock sorely assail all my enemies" (1988, 160). Some read the verbs as futures: "All my enemies shall be ashamed" (RSV, NRSV). The LXX takes it as a past tense claim: "My enemies have been ashamed." Either the present general claim or the future anticipation best reflect the MT. An inclusio via a flurry of similar sounding words punctuates the close of the psalm: *yēbōšû . . . yāšūbû yēbōšû*. Suddenly those who capitalized on the psalmist's plight find themselves exposed. To their shame, the disquiet experienced by the psalmist (twice noted in vv 2, 3 [3, 4 HB]) has now come upon his foes (v 10 [11 HB]), a serious blow in Israel's honor-shame culture.

Though mainly focused on a past trial in this poem, the psalmist's attention has been critically redirected by the community with whom he worshipped. Now his trial becomes the backdrop for testimony regarding Yahweh's intervention. He is healed; his foes are silenced.

FROM THE TEXT

This psalm lays bare the difficult situation afflicted persons found themselves in prior to the coming of Jesus. Common ANE theology and Mosaic covenant thought (Lev 26; Deut 28—29) both led the seriously ill to see their sickness as an expression of divine displeasure. Serious illness therefore could impugn one's character. It opened persons already distraught from their illness up to the slander of those seeking for one reason or another to abuse them.

God still uses adversity to discipline his people (Heb 12:4-11). But the NT clearly points to one place and one alone as the sure indicator of God's attitude toward us—the cross. In health or in illness we know God loves us because he gave his Son to die for us (e.g., Rom 8:31-39; 1 John 4:9; Thompson 1993). Confident of God's love for us, we are encouraged to cry out in our distress for his healing now (Jas 5:13-16). If sin should be a factor in the illness, forgiveness will still be part of the healing process.

Prayer for Yahweh's Judgment (7:1-17 [2-18 HB])

BEHIND THE TEXT

This prayer song of an individual (a *těpillâh*) pleads for rescue from unnamed, angry pursuers best likened to a marauding lion (v 2 [3 HB]). As usual in these songs, the accusations and the petitions come in the form of metaphor: a lion who stalks and tears. This veils from us the actual, specific threat confronting the psalmist, but also allows a diverse worshipping community to hear their various needs addressed in the word pictures and general statements. This mode of composition no doubt signals this song's use in temple worship at some point.

On the technical terms in the SS see Introduction, C.1.a; C.4.g. We are ill equipped to discern the relationship between these SS terms and Ps 7. The SS relates this song by David or about David to a certain Cush, a Benjamite. It is possible that David sings *about* things Cush has either said or written. Perhaps David sings this song *to* words Cush has written. We cannot tell. And unfortunately we have no other information on the connection between David, this poem, and this person. (See the Introduction, C.6.)

IN THE TEXT

1. Prayer for Rescue from Pursuers (7:1-2 [2-3 HB])

■ **1-2 [2-3 HB]** Before the petitions the psalmist lodges a declaration of trust: **LORD my God, I take refuge in you** (v 1 [2 HB]). This affirms the disposition called for already in 2:12 and declares the psalmist's core trust in Yahweh. This allegiance to Yahweh is implied repeatedly in the psalm with the address to "my God" (v 6 [7 HB]); LORD [*Yahweh*] **my God** (vv 1, 3 [2, 4 HB]), with LXX. From this faith base the petitions flow for rescue and deliverance. If Yahweh were not to act, the psalmist would stand alone, defenseless.

2. Denial of Charges with an Oath (7:3-5 [4-6 HB])

■ **3-5 [4-6 HB]** The psalmist denies that the slander of his adversaries has any basis in fact. Framing his denial as an oath emphasizes it. *Under no circumstances have I handled perversion*, or *By no means have I repaid my ally with evil*. The adversaries' accusations likely run along these lines. The question of the psalmist's character surfaces again in vv 8-11 (9-12 HB) as leverage hoping to prompt the desired response from Yahweh. His life and reputation are at stake. At the close of these denials (v 5 [6 HB]) and the transition to the psalmist's call.

3. Call for Justice (7:6-9 [7-10 HB])

■ **6-9 [7-10 HB]** The psalmist pictures now an international courtroom scene. He calls Yahweh to take the judge's seat. His claims and petitions trade on the fact that Yahweh's throne, guarded by the cherubim, was on the ark of the covenant, and that the ark itself was understood to be Yahweh's throne-chariot. Broyles is no doubt correct in hearing the psalmist's prayer against the backdrop of 1 Kgs 8:31-32.

Consistent with the parallelism and context, we should probably read v 6c (7c HB) as a hortatory perfect, **decree justice** rather than a past narrative, "thou has appointed judgment" (LXX and most English versions). In v 7b [8b HB] we should probably read an imperative from the root *yšb*, **to take a (judgment) seat**, rather than the MT *šwb*, **to return**.

Significantly here the psalmist stakes the outcome of the proposed judgment not only on Yahweh's character (see below, v 11 [12 HB]) but on his own as well. He asks for judgment according to his own righteousness and integrity (v 8 [9 HB]). He uses the language of the cases assumed in 1 Kgs 8:31-32, in which the accused is either "guilty"/wicked (*rš'*) or "righteous"/*ṣdq*. We should not think here of a presumptuous, Pharisaic attitude but of a response to a specific accusation in a civil court.

God who probes minds and hearts, reads literally ***who searches hearts and kidneys***. The psalmist speaks out of ancient physiology in which the Hebrew **heart** is roughly equivalent to the modern English mind. With the heart one thinks, judges, feels, commits. The ***kidneys*** for ancient Israelites were the seat of emotions, the locus of human feelings. Recall the (now) odd-sounding KJV translation of Phil 2:1, "If there be therefore . . . in Christ . . . *any bowels and mercies*"!? (emphasis added) reflecting the same idiom. A characteristic of Yahweh God is that, as an ongoing pattern (note the participle!) he knows what is hidden from others—thoughts and feelings—and can be depended on therefore to judge rightly.

4. Yahweh the Just Judge (7:10-13 [11-14 HB])

■ **10-13 [11-14 HB]** The psalmist first buttressed the initial call for help with strong denial of his guilt (vv 3-5 [4-6 HB]). Now he supports his prayer with appeal to the rightness, the justness of Yahweh the judge (v 11 [12 HB]) and his readiness to act in deliverance.

Military imagery dominates these lines. **God Most High** is a **shield about** the psalmist (reading the MT preposition *'al/about* as a short form of the divine name *'elyôn*). Well known from the literature of the ANE, this pictures Yahweh as shield bearer for the psalmist, a striking reversal of status. It reflects an intimate trust of Yahweh, like that between the king and his shield bearer. Upon this one the king depended for protection in the heat of battle (Keel 1997, 222-25).

In his righteous judgment, Yahweh is also **God who expresses anger**. The divine title, *'ēl zō'ēm* is parallel in form to other well-known divine titles such as *'ēl rōpēh* (**God who heals**) and *'ēl nōśē'* (**God who forgives**). This is an ongoing feature of his judgment, not reserved simply for catastrophic action.

If he [Yahweh] does not relent seems an unlikely use of the Hebrew. The line could refer to returning Yahweh's sword to its sheath (compare Ezek 21:5 [10 HB]). ***Yahweh will by no means resheath [his sword]; he will sharpen it.*** It could speak of a person's failure to repent (Goldingay 2006, 143)—***If one does not repent, Yahweh will sharpen his sword***. In any case he is armed to carry out decisive deliverance on behalf of his own. He sharpens his sword, draws his bow, and sets it for release (Ps 7:12 [13 HB]). His arsenal includes deadly weapons and flaming arrows ready for deployment.

5. Fate of the Enemy (7:14-16 [15-17 HB])

■ **14-16 [15-17 HB]** The well-known OT turn of thought that what the wicked devise comes back to trap them provides the final support for this prayer for deliverance. The wicked conceive evil and trouble; they will give **birth to disillusionment** (v 14 [15 HB]). The wicked dig a **pit** only to fall in it (v 15 [16

HB]). Verse 16 [17 HB] states the principle. God's rescue is, in some ways, built into human existence (hinted already in 1:6).

6. Promised Praise of Yahweh (Effect) (7:17 [18 HB])

■ **17 [18 HB]** I will give thanks to the LORD because of his righteousness. Several construals are possible. This could voice bold trust and clear hope that Yahweh will indeed deliver, prompting the thanks. It could imply that Yahweh has already delivered, in which case we have not so much a prayer for deliverance as a song of thanksgiving. It could be a standalone promise to praise Yahweh for his righteousness, a cause for praise in its own right, not related to an answer to this particular prayer.

The intent to praise the **name** [*the reputation and person*] **of the** LORD **Most High** (*YHWH 'elyôn*) provides some support for reading shortened forms of *'elyôn* in vv 8, 10 [9, 11 HB].

FROM THE TEXT

This prayer song voices the common cry of God's people for deliverance from their adversaries. The resilient confidence that the "Judge of all the earth" is thoroughly just, equipped to discern precisely the acts and motives of all parties. And he will intervene according to his purposes.

The NT appropriates a sobering line from this psalm to describe the capacities of the risen Christ. He warns the church at Thyatira that when he has judged her, all the churches will know that he **probes hearts and minds** (Ps 7:9 [10 HB]; see Rev 2:23). This presents one of those many places in the NT where OT Yahweh texts are directly appropriated by NT writers to describe Jesus Christ. That is, what could be said of Yahweh on this point could also be said of the Christ. One feature of biblical revelation that led the early church fathers to the doctrine of the Trinity surfaces here. This particular text provides corrective to a church at times inclined to romanticize gentle Jesus and distance him overly from his Father the God of Israel.

Praise for Glorious Yahweh's Glorious Human (8:1-9 [2-10 HB])

BEHIND THE TEXT

Only this song of praise of the Creator breaks the string of prayers for deliverance running from Pss 3 to 13. But modern readers will not appreciate the "magnificent condescension" celebrated in this psalm, as Broyles puts it (1999, 71), without an awareness of alternative views open to the psalmist regarding human origins. For example, the widely attested Atrahasis Epic has human beings created to relieve the lesser gods of the backbreaking work assigned them by the higher gods. Through the slaughter of one god, humanity is created to bear the disgusting yoke of divine labor (Arnold and Beyer 2002, 21-31, especially pp. 23-24). The *Enuma Elish*, another lengthy literary piece from Mesopotamia, takes a similar tack (31-50, especially pp. 40-42). Absolutely nothing of human glory and dignity applauded by the psalmist here finds expression in these cultural options. What a breakthrough of inspired insight Ps 8 presents over against the dismal estimate of human beings that dominated its cultural environment!

The SS's technical terms can be pursued in the Introduction, C.1.b, C.2.d, C.4.a, and C.1.a.

IN THE TEXT

1. Yahweh's Worldwide Glory (8:1-2 [2-3 HB])

■ **1-2 [2-3 HB]** The poem begins and ends with the identical exclamation, **LORD, our Lord, how majestic is your name in all the earth!** (vv 1, 9 [2, 10 HB]). This artistic bracket (inclusio) anchors the theological context in which celebration of human greatness can proceed. The exclamation states that celebration more energetically than would a simple declaration or claim. The direct address already affirms the Lordship of Yahweh in its opening words. But because of the ancient (since the LXX) translation convention of rendering the personal name of Israel's God, Yahweh, as LORD, the relatively uncommon appearance here of an explicit ascription of lordship by the Hebrew *ādôn*/ **Lord** is lost.

To speak of Yahweh's **name** is to speak of him via the words and deeds that reveal him. In this psalm Yahweh's creation deeds speak his splendor and glory. But, strangely, Yahweh has ordained that his strength will best be seen in **children and infants**. These are totally dependent upon others for their life and care. Through these little ones Yahweh chooses actually to halt the mighty (v 2 [3 HB]). We are not told how this works except that Yahweh ordains it. Luther sees here the proclamation of Christ's kingdom by "plain, simple, unsophisticated people, who are like infant children in that they set aside all reason, grasp and accept the Word with simple faith, and let themselves be led and directed by God like children" (Pelikan 1955, 108).

2. Surprising Glory Given to Humans (8:3-8 [4-9 HB])

■ **3-8 [4-9 HB]** The inclusio mentioned earlier features the exclamation **how majestic** (*māh 'addîr*) (vv 1, 9 [2, 10 HB]). A parallel exclamation, **what is mankind [*māh 'ĕnôš*] that you are mindful of them** in v 4 [5 HB]. The vocabulary underscores humans as frail and finite creatures (*'ĕnôš*). The psalmist's pondering of the heavens as made by Yahweh's fingers and ordered by his will prompts this outburst of insight. That the Maker and Sustainer of the heavenly bodies should occupy himself with such creatures and intervene on their behalf takes the poet off guard—*māh 'ĕnôš* indeed!

The song takes a surprising turn here (vv 3-5 [4-6 HB]). The psalmist could easily have pursued Yahweh's sovereignty over forces that their neighbors worshipped as deities—the sun, the moon, the stars (compare Zeph 1:4-5; Ezek 8:16). An anti-idolatry claim stands in the wings here. Instead, the psalmist uses God's creative work as the backdrop against which to celebrate the **glory and honor** of human beings. Even the celebration of human glory and honor turns out in this psalm to be theocentric, not anthropocentric. It traces the human spectacle not to human genius but to divine will. Yahweh himself, the Creator, made it so: human beings stand only **a little lower than the angels** (v 5 [6 HB]). Without this anchor in divine pleasure and purpose, celebrations of human glory tend to lose momentum, obscured by other, less appealing aspects of human beings.

Some debate arises over precisely what the poet claims here in the words **a little lower than (the)** *ĕlōhîm*. The term *ĕlōhîm*, a masculine plural noun, normally means "gods," or with a so-called plural of majesty, simply God. This is how Jesus read the word in Ps 82:6, at least in debate, according to John 10:34. In Job 1:6 the expression *bĕnê 'ĕlōhîm*/"sons of God" refers to parties in Yahweh's divine assembly. Though often translated **angels** (e.g., LXX, NIV), in this "outside of Israel" setting, it could mean (lesser) gods. In our passage *ĕlōhîm* should probably be taken as parallel to the expression in Job. The LXX took the term as referring to angels, as did the writer of Hebrews, quoting this passage in Heb 2:6-8. We should probably think similarly, though the NIV nicely opens the line up to a range of heavenly entities.

Not only do human beings have glory and honor because God made it so, but he made it so by naming them his vice-regents in the cosmos. He has **crowned** them, **made them rulers over** all God's **works** (vv 5-6 [6-7 HB]). The claim is sweeping in two ways. **Human beings** refers to, not just Israelites, but all of humanity. As a species we participate in the sovereignty of God and the rule of his world. Additionally, it is over **everything** that God has made humans are to rule. Conceptual and linguistic overlap suggests this psalm may well have been penned with Gen 1:26-28 and 2:19-20 in mind.

3. Yahweh's Worldwide Glory (Again) (8:9 [10 HB])

■ **9 [10 HB]** All of this is so shocking, so surprising—that human creatures, frail and finite as they are, should be given so much by their Maker. It constitutes an inverse, universal praise of Yahweh. The poet repeats again the praise implicit in the celebration of human glory.

FROM THE TEXT

The sad story line of Scripture as a whole, of course, details human squandering of the Creator's charge to rule. Inevitably we have chosen to rule such that stewardly dominion has become domination and exploitation. Especially in recent years the church has been saddled with this accusation. Indirectly this song calls human beings back to their created destiny as caring regents of all God's works.

Read through the eyes of persons reflecting on the crucified, risen, and exalted Jesus, these lines argued for the superiority of the second Adam even to angels (Heb 2:6-8).

Prayer for Yahweh's Rule over Haughty Humans (9:1-20 [2-21 HB])

BEHIND THE TEXT

Psalms 9 and 10 are remnants of what was once apparently a single poem. Together they present an acrostic poem. Every second line, it appears, began with a succeeding letter of the Hebrew alphabet. Hebrew "acrostics" in the Psalter rarely, if ever, spell something. Instead they simply run from the first to the last letter of the Hebrew alphabet. Hence these are usually called "alphabet" poems. Psalm 9 covers aleph to kaph; Ps 10 has vestiges of lines for letters lamed to tau. Additionally Ps 10 lacks an SS in a book dominated by psalms with SSs—another indication of earlier unity with Ps 9.

The LXX reflects this historic unity by treating Pss 9 and 10 as a single psalm (Ps 9). As a result the LXX's numbering is one song short of the MT until Ps 112. Because of further numbering disruption, the two textual traditions do not coincide again until Ps 147:12. Protestant translations have followed the MT in numbering.

But the unity of the original acrostic has long ago suffered disruption. The first seven verses of Ps 10 do not show an acrostic design, and the text as we have it defies emendation that would reconstruct the lost acrostic. Where the acrostic resumes, the placement of the lines reverses the normal alphabetic order.

Furthermore the two halves of the original poem (now Pss 9 and 10) exhibit different psalm types. Much of Ps 9 resembles a song of praise, while Ps 10 reads like a prayer of the distraught. These halves sit awkwardly together (compare 9:1 [2 HB] and 10:1). Meanwhile intertextual conversation *between* lines of a sort normally found between contiguous poems (compare 10:4 vs. 10:17). Our treatment will follow the MT and the traditional Protestant division.

IN THE TEXT

1. Praise of Yahweh, Righteous Judge (9:1-6 [2-7 HB])

■ **1-6 [2-7 HB]** The psalmist praises Yahweh for his mighty works (v 1 [2 HB]). Other psalms name these works specifically: creation, rescue from Egyptian bondage, the gift of the land, and the Davidic kingship. Yahweh's reputation as righteous Judge especially moves the psalmist here (vv 4, 7, 8, 19 [5, 8, 9, 20 HB]). Yahweh has upheld the psalmist's legal cause in court, rendering a just verdict. This praise pictures Yahweh as king. We should think of the psalmist as having brought his case to the temple, where Yahweh sits enthroned on the cherubim. The enemies in this case would be legal adversaries.

As Judge of all the earth Yahweh renders verdicts not just for the psalmist but also concerning **the nations** (v 5 [6 HB]). God not only renders verdicts but also carries out the sentence, erasing memory of the wicked.

2. Yahweh's Enduring Reign (9:7-9 [8-10 HB])

■ **7-9 [8-10 HB]** The LORD **reigns forever**, literally **sits [enthroned]**. The psalmist now makes explicit the picture assumed in the opening lines. He has secured his throne expressly for executing justice, and that for the whole world. The Lord is Judge not only of the psalmist's world but also of the entire world. In this legal context, where the poor so often suffer, with Yahweh the downtrodden find **refuge** (v 9 [10 HB]).

3. Song of the Poor (9:10-12 [11-13 HB])

■ **10-12 [11-13 HB]** Unlike thought of the wicked wiped out (v 5 [6 HB]), Yahweh's renown endures (v 10 [11 HB]). He has proven worthy of trust. Those who seek help from him are not forsaken. To the picture of Yahweh as King and royal Judge, the psalmist adds Zion as the seat of his throne (v 11 [12 HB]). Yahweh carries out the sentence of blood avenger. He does not forget the oppressed, nor is he distracted from executing his mission.

4. Plea for Mercy (9:13-14 [14-15 HB])

■ **13-14 [14-15 HB]** Here the psalm turns from praise to petition. The one to this point filled with praise now speaks under affliction. The needs of the acrostic pattern may have occasioned the surprising shift in thought here. Verse 13 [14 HB] actually opens with the call for Yahweh to *be merciful to me* (ḥānĕnēnî) filling the ḥet line.

The rearrangement and emendations of the MT assumed by the NIV do not seem necessary, as numerous versions ancient and modern show. Of course the psalmist's call for Yahweh to **see** his affliction at the hands of those who despise him is a prayer not simply for cognitive awareness on God's part but for rescue from these foes.

According to v 14 [15 HB] this deliverance will achieve its real purpose when in praise the psalmist recounts Yahweh's exploits on his behalf. The extended verb forms underscore the psalmist's eagerness publically to express his delight in Yahweh's intervention. Not only in the temple, which the prayer assumes, but in the concourse of Zion's gates he will offer praise.

5. Fate of Those Who Forget God (9:15-18 [16-19 HB])

■ **15-18 [16-19 HB]** Verse 17 [18 HB] carries the distinctive descriptor of the wicked in these verses, **all the nations that forget God**. It also tags the critical reputation of Yahweh here as one famous for executing justice. Here the wicked are caught in their own devices, dramatically portrayed in metaphors from hunting and warfare—pits, nets, traps. Yahweh at times works his justice through a "deeper magic" by which the way of the wicked carries within itself the seeds of its own destruction (compare 1:6).

The wicked are doomed to **return** to the realm of the dead (v 17 [18 HB]). Upon reflection, this sits oddly in biblical thought, because humans come not from the grave but from the word of God via the dust. One might "enter" the grave or "go to" the grave but not **return** there. Goldingay sees the problem but does not solve it (2006, 176-77). Keil and Delitzsch take this as roughly equivalent to returning to dust (1989, 171), but their explanation proves unconvincing. Kraus translates "to depart for" or "turn to" the grave (1988, 196), but recent reviews of lexical evidence have not favored leveling "return" to simply "turn" (*HALOT*, 1429). Perhaps Kidner sees through it by seeing in the wording "a revealing nuance"; though the wicked did not come from the grave, death has become "their native element" (1973, 70).

The destiny of the poor stands in stark contrast to the demise of the wicked. Yahweh will never forget the poor, nor fail to sustain the hope of the afflicted (v 18 [19 HB]).

6. Call for Control of Humans (9:19-20 [20-21 HB])

■ **19-20 [20-21 HB]** The poet turns now to cries for Yahweh to confront these God forgetters, **the nations**, and bring them into divine judgment. Especially the psalmist longs for Yahweh to put a stop to their parade of abusive power, a charade that leaves them confident that, unlike others, they are invincible and not accountable, not even to God.

Here the editors of the Psalter have set up an intertextual reference with Ps 8:4 [5 HB]. There the poet celebrates the glory with which Yahweh has crowned humans, the apex of his creation: "What is mankind [*māh 'ĕnôš*] that you are mindful of them?" Here the psalmists asks Yahweh to frustrate the parade of power by *ĕnôš* (v 19 [20 HB]) and to impress upon them that they are after all just human beings (*ĕnôš*; v 20 [21 HB]). Both realizations carry weight, the astounding glory of God's *ĕnôš* on the one hand and the need for *ĕnôš* to be reminded forcefully of the categorical difference between the most powerful *ĕnôš* and the terror-striking God of Israel. This inter-psalmic conversation is picked up again at 10:18, where the psalmist again asks Yahweh to reign in the terrifying and oppressive actions of *ĕnôš*. This intertextual reference could well account for the placement of these contiguous poems, ironically opening the door for fruitful reflection on Yahweh and his amazing human.

Let the Hidden Yahweh Act (10:1-18)

BEHIND THE TEXT

When we enter the second half of the garbled alphabetic poem we wade into troubled textual waters, challenging the interpretive skills even of the LXX translators. Signs abound of a text that has suffered considerably in transmission, including widely different renderings by various modern versions. We can treat only the most important of these.

The poem has two major movements. Verses 1-11 present the plight and vv 12-18 the psalmist's consequent appeal for Yahweh's intervention. After the opening query two paragraphs, vv 2-7 and 8-11, elaborate the apparently uncontested atrocities of the wicked, giving content to "times of trouble" (v 1).

IN THE TEXT

1. Yahweh's Absence in Troubled Times (10:1)

■ **I** The poet launches this prayer for rescue from the assaults of the wicked with a probing question: **Why do you stand aloof** from your people in the very times of trouble when they most obviously need divine deliverance? He asks not just about a particular time but about Yahweh's penchant for absence and hiddenness.

2. Arrogance of the Wicked (10:2-7)

■ **2-7** The poet concerns himself not simply with the despicable behaviors of the wicked, though these disturb him. They chase down the afflicted (v 2), congratulate violent oppressors (v 3). They propagate narcissistic values (v 3), with obviously no place for God in their world (v 4). They poison public discourse with their toxic and abusive speech (vv 6-7).

But beyond these reprehensible deeds the disgusting demeanor, the arrogance of the wicked magnifies both the impact of their deeds and the sting of the opening question regarding the absence of Yahweh. The wicked act in **arrogance** (v 2). They openly boast about their plans (v 3). They are vocal about their rejection of Yahweh (v 4) and their immunity to trouble (v 6).

The poet dramatizes this arrogance by repeatedly giving us the blasphemous words of these troublemakers. We should probably read v 4 as one such quote: **Yahweh will not avenge. . . . There is no God** (compare NABRE, NRSV). Then *I will never be shaken; I will live trouble free* (v 6). **God has forgotten, hidden his face. He will never find out** (v 11), and even directly to Yahweh himself, **You do not avenge** (v 13)! These boasts of the wicked directly deny the psalmist's faith claims—Yahweh *does* avenge (9:12 [13 HB]; 10:15), he seeks out (9:13 [14 HB]; 10:14), he does not forget (9:12 [13 HB], compare 9:18 [19 HB]; 10:12). Repetition of several Hebrew words draws these lines tightly together: *dāraš*/**to seek out**, *to avenge*; *rā'â*/**to see**, *find out*; *šākaḥ*/**to forget**, along with the less common negative, *bal*. These two psalms do open battle over the introductory promises of Ps 1.

3. Violence of the Boastful (10:8-11)

■ **8-11** Language from the hunt and from experience with man-eating beasts pictures the violence of the boastful. **Like a lion** lurking in his lair or in ambush outside the village, he kills the hapless (vv 8-9). Like a hunter taking his prey, he drags off his victim (v 10). The ongoing threat of encounter with lions and bears in Israel's hill country and especially in the valley of the Jordan made these potent images for the psalmist's readers (compare Keel 1997, 85-94).

Just what we should think of these pictures is not clear. On the one hand, assuming that for the most part we should not think of the wicked literally crouching in the thicket outside the village as the metaphors picture, we do not know specifically what the wicked have done to the psalmist and those for whom he speaks. On the other hand, the pictures are full of violence, some of it lethal. If the psalmist did not include actual violence in the reality he deplores, other less violent images could have been chosen. We should think of serious attacks by these arrogant ones who consider themselves even above God's law.

4. Call for Yahweh to Act (10:12-18)

■ **12-15** All of this leads to a series of petitions for the God who does not forget, not to **forget** (v 12), for the God who does see to **see** (v 14), for the God who does call to account to hold **the wicked** accountable (v 15). The call for Yahweh to arise and **lift his hand** (v 12) trades on the faith that he sits enthroned on the ark and its cherubim. He rises and lifts his hand (with its weapons) to do battle (Keel 1997, 218-21).

■ **16-18** **The LORD is King for ever and ever** (v 16). This confidence in King Yahweh underwrites the claims and petitions of the entire alphabetic poem.

The psalmist's vision widens again from solitary cases of distress to the national scene and Yahweh's **land** (v 16). The fact that the nations no longer possess Yahweh's land demonstrates his sovereignty. His pursuit of justice for **the fatherless and the oppressed** (v 18), for all who have inadequate resources to defend themselves, also speaks of his kingship, of his compassionate sovereignty.

As a result, in King Yahweh's realm frail humans (the *ĕnôš*) will no longer terrorize in their pretentious exercise of power. This lexical clue (*ĕnôš*) takes readers back to 9:20 [21 HB] and 8:4 [5 HB] and prompts them to reflect, among other things, on the role of Yahweh's kingship in bringing about the potential envisioned for the promising human.

FROM THE TEXT OF PSALMS 9 AND 10

Taken as a whole, this broken acrostic eloquently proclaims the kingship of Yahweh the Most High, who rules from Zion. Its two voices first praise and then argue the themes of Yahweh's dominion, his righteous judgment, and his deliverance of the oppressed. Paul uses the language of 10:7 to describe the moral corruption of the wicked, but now with the shocking insight that all humans, without the grace of God, are "the wicked" (Rom 3:14)! Moreover he preached to pagans the psalmist's claim that Yahweh rules the nations and claimed the resurrection of Jesus Messiah from the dead settled the argument about this matter (Acts 17:31). At the same time John the Revelator acknowledges that the full expression of the rule of Yahweh and his Messiah will only appear finally in the eschaton (Rev 11:15).

Refuge at Yahweh's Throne (11:1-7)

BEHIND THE TEXT

Scholars puzzle over the form and genre of this little poem. Unless, contrary to many, we take v 6 to be an imprecatory wish, the psalm contains prayerful meditation on the proper response to adversaries. But it has no petitions. Even if, as below, we take v 6 as petition, there is no direct address to Yahweh in the song. Pondering the bases of refuge from the wicked preoccupies the poet here.

For treatment of SS elements, see C.1.a and C.1.b in the Introduction.

IN THE TEXT

1. Refuge in the Face of Mean Advice (11:1-3)

■ **1-3** At the outset the psalmist points in the only direction to which one might usefully flee from ill-intentioned naysayers—to Yahweh, God of Israel.

"He says, in fact: Here I stand" (Weiser 1962, 155). Then he confronts his antagonists head on. **How dare you say!** conveys the indignation with which he resists the advice thrown at him (Gerstenberger 1988, 77). The intensity of the experience gets flagged in the vocabulary used: **How then can you say to me!**, literally **to my soul** (*nepeš*) with reference to the person as a flesh-and-blood creature with feelings, tastes, and embodied identity.

Flee like a bird to your mountain translates the MT well (already in the LXX; recently ESV, NASB, NKJV) but is generally washed out to "flee like a bird to the mountains," comparing Ps 121 or Ps 55:6. But the comparisons fail: 55:6 has the fleeing bird but no reference to mountains; 121 has the mountains but no fleeing bird. More likely **your mountain**, a very specific mountain associated with refuge, must be in mind. This, one suspects, would be the Temple Mount. The faithless jab at the supplicant mocks his confidence in refuge to be had in encountering Yahweh in his temple and thus finding refuge in worship.

Having quoted the spurious advice (v 1*b*), the psalmist continues describing the relational meltdown that threatens him (vv 2-3). Hunting metaphors similar to those at the close of Ps 10 describe his plight, indeed the human plight (v 2). Bows drawn, arrows set, ambush from the shadows set the scene. Cultural, relational foundations crumble, leaving the righteous wondering what they can possibly do (v 3).

2. King Yahweh Tests the Righteous (11:4-7)

■ **4-7** The poet returns to his core response; King Yahweh is his refuge and Yahweh remains unshaken (v 4). Emphatic by word position and repetition, Yahweh is the focus. In this case the light shines on Yahweh as royal judge. He is enthroned in his holy palace, that is, the Jerusalem temple (extending the royal theme of 2:6). His throne, from which he pronounces and executes just decisions, is in heaven. But Broyles' warning is well taken that we must not drive much of a wedge between the earthly temple and the heavenly throne (1999, 80). The ark and cherubim in the Jerusalem temple were thought to be Yahweh's throne-chariot, and the link between the earthly palace and the heavenly one was thought to be real and direct. From there his gaze calls the entire race to account (v 4).

Verse 5 could be scanned several ways: **Yahweh examines the righteous, but the wicked *and the ones* who love violence he hates**, or **Yahweh examines the righteous *and* those who love violence, *but the wicked he hates***. The LXX favors the former. Either makes sense, especially if one recalls Yahweh's examination (*bāḥan*) is not necessarily negative, his *bḥn* of the righteous being a sign of his loving attention. On the other hand, **with all his being** he stands against those **devoted to violence** (Goldingay 2006, 188). Goldingay catches well the appearance again of *nepeš* referring to Yahweh himself (MT: **his soul hates** and his **whole person loathing** of the wicked).

Built upon the faith claims of vv 4 and 5 a solitary petition (v 6) calls for Yahweh's intervention. **Let him [Yahweh] rain fiery coals upon the wicked** probably intends to bring Gen 19:24 and the judgment of Sodom to mind. The dire consequences pictured here indicate the seriousness of the attack upon the psalmist's trust in Yahweh. Even though the LXX already took the Hebrew as a future (**He will rain**) we would expect this meditation to include a petition. Hence, with the MT's jussive we translate **Let Yahweh rain fiery coals on the wicked** (so ESV against most recent interpreters).

FROM THE TEXT

Rarely do God's people assert their trust in him without having to deal with voices to the contrary. Confidence that God knows their plight and all human affairs grounds their trust in him. The prayer that the Lord might openly and decisively judge their faithless adversaries is understandable but rarely actually witnessed. Perhaps this explains the fact that the NT sees the prayer of v 6 not in the NT or early church but in the eschaton. God's people can pray for fiery coals and scorching winds upon the wicked and the forces of evil, but they need not expect these to occur decisively until the consumation (Rev 14:10; 20:10; 21:8).

Help in Yahweh's War of Words (12:1-8 [2-9 HB])

BEHIND THE TEXT

Psalm 12 offers another prayer for deliverance either for an individual or the community, a prayer of the sort that dominates Books I and II of the Psalter.

For information on the technical terms in the SS, see C.1.a, C.1.b, C.2.b, and C.4.a in the Introduction.

IN THE TEXT

I. Call for Rescue (12:1 [2 HB])

■ **I [2 HB]** The psalm opens with an urgent call for rescue but delays disclosing the problem. First the reason for the plea appears—the demise of the godly and those dependable in the faith. The situation from which the poet wants deliverance is so severe he is convinced such people of integrity are completely dying out.

2. Lies of the Arrogant (12:2-3 [3-4 HB])

■ **2-3 [3-4 HB]** Specifically the psalmist is weighed down by the triviality and duplicity rampant around him in public discourse. Toxic speech poisons the social environment. Little can be taken at face value. Of course these worthless words reveal the more intractable and deeper problem of deceptive hearts.

The crisis of integrity prompts a petition that the Lord would **silence all flattering lips and every boastful tongue** (v 3 [4 HB]). Cutting off lips and tongue probably refers not to actual mutilation but by metonymy to removing *persons* who speak falsely (a device by which a whole is named by reference to one of its parts). At the same time, we recall that in some ancient Near Eastern law the literal cutting lips off and cutting tongues out was mandated punishment for certain crimes (Arnold and Beyer 2002, 115). It is not beyond possibility that the psalmist has this action by God in mind.

3. Yahweh Rises at the Groan of the Poor (12:4-5 [5-6 HB])

■ **4-5 [5-6 HB]** Now we hear the actual words of the wicked. They speak as a group specifically responding to assumed attempts to chastise or instruct them in the use of their tongues. Their retort boils down to boasting, **We, and no one else—including God—have control of our speech. We will speak as we please**. One is hard-pressed to think of more arrogant speech in the Bible. This talk expresses the rebellious stance of those who set themselves directly against Yahweh and his anointed son (Ps 2:1-3).

The words of Yahweh's decision to act in response to the psalmist's prayer match the arrogant boast of self-sovereignty in v 5 [6 HB]. In response to the groanings of the poor and afflicted, Yahweh will spring into action. **I will now arise** trades on the picture of King Yahweh rising from his throne to stand, leading his forces in battle.

Yahweh will **protect them from those who malign them** (v 5 [6 HB]). Literally and most likely Yahweh **will put the supplicant in a safe place/in deliverance for which he has longed**. Or perhaps the wicked do the longing, that is, negatively pursuing, raging, or hard-pressing (NIV, Kraus 1988, 206). Others, with the LXX, have Yahweh "shining forth" for the psalmist, which requires unnecessary alteration of the text (so Craigie 1983, 136).

4. Confidence in Yahweh's Promises (12:6-8 [7-9 HB])

■ **6-8 [7-9 HB]** Commendation of Yahweh's words supports the promises just made (v 5 [6 HB]). Reference to Yahweh's Word as Torah could pick up the opening claim of Ps 1:2 and also anticipate talk of Yahweh's word multiplied in Ps 119. More likely the unusual reference to **Yahweh's words** (plural!)

refers not so much to his word in general as to the immediately preceding promises. Unlike the foul and deceptive word of the wicked, Yahweh's word is **flawless**, likened to **silver** thoroughly **purified**. And faithful Yahweh himself underwrites these words.

The psalm closes (v 8 [9 HB]) with an inclusion that brackets the poem with reference to the dire situation *among the whole race* (compare v 1 [2 HB]). The sober reference to the predatory prowling of the wicked and the corrupt values that lead people to elevate truly vile behavior—these references underscore the difficulty of the plight from which the poet seeks deliverance.

FROM THE TEXT

Psalm 12 sets two patterns of speech in sharp contrast: the corrupting lies and self-justifications of the wicked, and the encouraging promises of Yahweh. Both of these themes recur in Scripture start to finish, elaborating the creative power of words. Finally we are invited by God's grace to be done with corrupt talk of all kinds and to join God's own creative project by ministering grace through our words (e.g., Eph 4:29—5:2).

Prayer of the Distressed (13:1-6 [2-6 HB])

BEHIND THE TEXT

Students of the literary forms of the psalms have seen this poem as a model of the prayer of a severely distressed individual. In its repetitive use of **How long?** it also features one of the stock expressions of ancient Near Eastern psalmography. Compare the similar prayer, for example, to the Mesopotamian goddess Ishtar:

How long, O my Lady, shall my adversaries be looking upon me,
In lying and untruth shall they plan evil against me. . . .
How long, O my Lady, wilt thou be angered so that thy face is turned away? (Gerstenberger 1988, 84, citing *ANET*, 384-85)

See the Introduction, C.1.a, C.1.b; and C.4.a, for treatment of elements of the SS.

IN THE TEXT

I. The "How Long?" Questions (13:1-2 [2-3 HB])

■ **1-2 [2-3 HB]** The most striking feature of this brief poem is the series of four **How long?** questions asking **How long?** the supplicant must wait for Yahweh to act on his behalf. There is a certain impertinence to the questions. Gerstenberger notes the use of this **How long?** expression in Exod 10:3;

16:28; Num 14:11, 27; Josh 18:3; 1 Sam 1:14; Job 8:2, and discerns them all to be introducing reproachful speech (1988, 84). This is strong language to be aimed at Yahweh, even in prayer. In addition to the plight itself, the psalmist bears the pain of "the unfathomable affliction of abandonment by God" (Kraus 1988, 216).

The themes of Yahweh's forgetting (*šḥk*) and hiding/being hidden (*str*) surface again here. Psalm 9 made much of the fact that Yahweh does *not* forget the cry of the oppressed; he *does* remember and avenge wrongs done (Ps 9:12 [13 HB]). In Ps 10 both *šḥk* and *str* occur again. The arrogant claims **God has forgotten, he hides his face, he never sees!** Against this the psalmist pleads for Yahweh to rise and not forget (10:11-12). This song leans hard on these issues again.

The third question is problematic. The NIV has **How long must I wrestle with my thoughts?** with the MT, ESV, NASB, and Goldingay translating similarly. The LXX either emended or had a different text asking for Yahweh to "shine forth," perhaps referring to the Aaronic blessing (Num 6:25) (Broyles 1999, 89). Others take it to involve the psalmist's "pain" (NRSV, RSV) or "cares" (NJPS). In my judgment there is insufficient evidence to leave the MT.

2. Plea for Yahweh's Answer and Illumination (13:3-4 [4-5 HB])

■ **3-4 [4-5 HB]** The questions lead straight into the petitions, where the psalmist pleads for Yahweh now to see and act on his behalf. The direct address, **my God**, both acknowledges the psalmist's loyalty to God even through adversity and strengthens the expectation that Yahweh should be obliged to answer.

Give light to my eyes, or . . . strengthens the psalmist's petitions by casting them in an either/or situation in which Yahweh becomes fully responsible for the outcome. Either Yahweh responds positively to the psalmist's plea and goes into action on his behalf or dire consequences will follow. The word *lest* (*pen*) is explicit in 13:3*b* [4*b* HB] (**lest I** sleep), v 4*a* [5*a* HB] (**lest my enemy**), and should be assumed also as implicit in v 4*b* [5*b* HB].

Should Yahweh remain hidden and forgetful, the poet will **sleep in death** and will **fall**. In view particularly of the reference to death, one should probably infer that chronic, serious illness is the psalmist's plight. Death itself may be his enemy (compare Ps 88). The affirmations and confidence of 3:8 [9 HB] and 4:8 [9 HB] are here taken up, with a bit of irony. The **fall** he fears involves being shaken to the core (compare 10:10).

3. Anticipating a Song (13:5-6 [6 HB])

■ **5-6 [6 HB]** In stark contrast (**but I**) to the fate that threatens the psalmist, he stakes out his unshaken foundation in the faithful mercy of Yahweh (his *ḥesed*)—and anticipates his praise of Yahweh's deliverance. He refers back either to his history (*I have put my trust*) or his habit (*I put my trust*). Then he looks ahead to the song he will raise—indeed has already begun to intone. The anticipation already foreshadows deliverance and transforms the plight he now inhabits.

FROM THE TEXT

The concluding anticipation of song focuses the readers' attention not on the change of circumstance but on the saving grace of God who alone holds promise of deliverance. Calvin allows as how the poet is "already as a man without life, unless God breathe into him new vigor," and that "although the world threaten us with a thousand deaths, yet God is possessed of numberless means of restoring us to life" (quoted in Kraus 1988, 216).

Prayer When Fools Prevail (14:1-7)

BEHIND THE TEXT

Psalm 14's form is so "mixed" as to render form-critical analysis pointless; its place in Israel's worship is sufficiently lost as to block insight from cultic reconstructions. A nearly duplicate version of this poem edited for the so-called Elohistic Psalter appears in Ps 53. The fact that the poem appeared in two collections prior to inclusion in the present Psalter could argue for an earlier composition, with Psalm 14 being the older of the two.

For SS terms see the Introduction, C.1.a and C.1.b.

IN THE TEXT

1. The Fool and Company (14:1-4)

■ **1-4** We should not take the fool's claim that **"There is no God"** (v 1) as the metaphysical conclusion of a formal atheist. **Fool** here, as elsewhere in the OT, does not primarily give an intellectual assessment. Instead the **fool** (*nābāl*) names a moral ignoramus, lacking insight into life in general (LXX, the unthinking one). The *nābāl* is the kind of person who rapes his half-sister (2 Sam 13:13) and dishonors the community (Isa 32:5) (compare Goldingay 2006, 212). These (we should think here of a group, the text moving back and forth between collective singular and plural) are practical atheists who think God is irrelevant.

This practical theology inevitably produces corrupt behavior (Ps 14:1-4). No one with this approach to life characteristically does good—not one (emphasized by verbatim repetition in vv 1*d* and 3*c*). This may be hyperbole, but the point is clear. A significant sector of persons in the psalmist's world figure God out of life, and others suffer for it. These fools don't get it. **They devour** God's **people** as easily as though they were having a good meal (v 4).

2. Indictment of the Fools (14:5-6)

■ **5-6 There**, that is, in their situation of ignoring God, terror overtakes them, **for** or rather *but* (adversative *kî*) **God is**, as a matter of fact, among **the righteous**. They attempt to thwart the plans of the needy, **but** (*kî* again) Yahweh proves to be **their refuge**.

3. Salvation from Zion (14:7)

■ **7** The sketch of the fool's attempts to evade God and of Yahweh's engagement in the life of his people nevertheless issues in the prayerful wish for salvation from **Zion** (v 7*a*) and anticipation of Israel's joy at that turn of events (v 7*b*). *From* **Zion** must have in mind the temple and the palace as sources of Yahweh's deliverance. Through the king and God's people gathered to worship Yahweh will bring a new day for Israel. If reference is made in v 7 to the returning of the Judah's captivity (LXX, NASB, NKJV), then we should think of an exilic or postexilic prayer. More likely (most English versions; compare *HALOT*, 1385-87), reference is generally to a reversal of the fortunes of God's people. The prayer anticipates their joy when God confutes the fools who lead the community astray and prey on the helpless.

FROM THE TEXT

Paul mines the opening lines of this song for words to describe humanity's pervasive wickedness (Ps 14:1-3 in Rom 3:11-12). His reading sends us back to our psalm, realizing it makes little difference whether the poet is Davidic, preexilic, or much later. The prayer invites God's people prayerfully to meditate on human sin as much or more than on deliverance from that foolishness.

Who Inhabits Yahweh's Hill? (15:1-5)

BEHIND THE TEXT

By this liturgical piece instruction in preparation for worship occupied the liturgy itself. Perhaps we should think we have here a meditation for persons being installed in their course of priestly duties in the temple. It could also have figured in the entry of ordinary worshippers. It easily moves from that liturgy to a place of general prayer and meditation. The concluding promise shows its broader concern with instruction in the will of Yahweh (i.e., in Torah).

See Introduction, C.1.a and C.4.a, for SS terms. See Othmar Keel (1997, 120-27) on the whole business of safeguarding temples and their sacred space from profanation.

IN THE TEXT

1. Who Inhabits Yahweh's Sanctuary? (15:1)

■ **1** The piece starts with a question regarding the identity of persons who are permitted to *sojourn* or **dwell** in Yahweh's **tent** (*'ōhel*) (compare 24:1). As noted above, the question may relate to screening persons for their course of temple service. More likely one can see this language being used affectionately by the faithful referring to occasions of pilgrimage and protracted worship at their beloved temple.

If **tent** is used precisely, this could be an old song from David's reign prior to Solomon's building of the temple (2 Sam 6:1-19). Alternately the poet may evoke those ancient days by reference to the temple using metaphoric language of tent and dwelling in place of more precise vocabulary (compare Pss 24:3; 27:4-6; 61:4). Yahweh's **holy mountain** refers to the elevated area immediately above the ancient city of David in Jerusalem (recall 2:6), where the temple was eventually built.

2. Criteria for Abode (15:2-5b)

■ **2-5b** The psalmist answers the question of identity by reference to the candidate's character and righteous life, rather than by reference to tribe, age, gender, or other qualifications. "Who can dwell . . . ?" (v 1). **The one whose walk is blameless, who does what is righteous, who speaks truth from their heart** (v 2). **Blameless** describes especially a person of authenticity and transparency (compare Gen 17:1), not perfection by a moral checklist. **Righteous** names a behavior deemed right by agreed upon standards with emphasis on right relationships. Ongoing, long-haul demonstration of integrity and godliness is the concern here. (Note the Hebrew participles.)

This platform of general uprightness the poet elaborates primarily by the person's habits of communication (Ps 15:2c-4). Positively, the one cleared for dwelling in Yahweh's tent **speaks the truth**, thoughts matching words (v 2c), keeps commitments made under oath (v 4c; compare 24:4), **honors those who fear Yahweh** (v 4b). Negatively, this one does not gossip (v 3a), doesn't bring reproach on neighbors (v 3c; compare 24:3), does not respect reprobates (v 4a), does not deceive (v 4d). More generally, then, this one does no ill to a neighbor, does not lend **money** at interest, and does not take a **bribe** (vv 3b,

5a, b). This interesting concern about edifying speech and the heart source of words ties this poem to contiguous psalms. Recall the fool's speech (14:1), the slippery lips and worthless talk of 12:3, Ps 10's repeated attention to the words of the wicked (10:6, 11, 13), as well as the liars and mockers in 3:2 [3 HB]; 4:6 [7 HB]; and 5:6 [7 HB].

3. Promise of Perseverance (15:5c-d)

■ **5c-d** The concluding assurance does not match the opening direction of the psalm. We would have expected "The one who does these will dwell on Yahweh's holy hill," answering v 1. Instead a promise of personal and spiritual stability and perseverance appropriate to Yahweh's sacred mountain appears. To **be shaken** here would involve serious, earthshaking disruption and destruction (compare 10:6; 13:4 [5 HB]).

FROM THE TEXT

Psalm 15 contributes to a significant stream of biblical insight regarding acceptable worship. Worship of the God of Israel is from start to finish a personal, spiritual transaction. The mechanics of worship, though not to be ignored, are strictly secondary (compare 50:7-23; 51:16-19 [18-21 HB]). Jesus' anticipation of persons who worship in spirit and truth trades in this insight (compare John 4:23; Matt 12:33-37).

Life in the Path of Life (16:1-11)

BEHIND THE TEXT

After its opening petition this psalm delivers a statement of trust and confidence in Yahweh, probably in the face of death. See the Introduction, C.1.a and C.4.d, for the SS's technical terms.

IN THE TEXT

1. Prayer for Safekeeping (16:1)

■ **1** The prayer for God to guard the psalmist indicates no specific threat. The later testimony and praise seem to indicate some serious, perhaps even lethal danger.

2. Confirmation of Loyalty to Yahweh (16:2-4)

■ **2-4** Textual difficulties here preclude certainty in interpretation. (Kraus, perhaps wisely, just "translates" v 4a with dots [1988, 233]!) The supplicant has made parallel claims to two parties, to Yahweh (*lyhwh* [v 2]) and to the saints of the land (*lqdšym* [v 3]). To Yahweh he has affirmed Yahweh's lordship, by implication his own status as Yahweh's servant, and his conviction that his well-being is to be found nowhere but in Yahweh.

Regrettably, it is difficult to say just what he speaks to the godly of the land. But it appears to involve a clear repudiation of persons who look to other gods for their welfare (v 4a). The psalmist will not participate in their worship. Libations of blood were not in themselves necessarily forbidden; but sacrifice to other gods and trust in them for life's goods would have been the issue. These would be persons, like those castigated by Hosea (2:5-9 [7-11 HB]), who were convinced their well-being depended on their worship of Baal or other rivals of Yahweh. They would have regarded faithful Yahwists and their refusal to participate in such worship as a threat to life and fertility (compare Jer 44:15-23).

3. Testimony of a Pleasant Heritage (16:5-6)

■ **5-6** Using language from the ancient distribution of the land—**portion, lot, boundary lines, inheritance** (compare Num 26:55; Josh 14:1-4)—the poet celebrates his situation. Yahweh has given him a good, **pleasant, delightful** life and rebuts those who multiply trouble in their errant faith. Beyond that, Yahweh has given himself as the supplicant's portion. Perhaps a Levite from the tribe that received Yahweh himself, not a portion of land, as their inheritance here celebrates this good life (compare Num 18:20; Deut 10:9). Or just as likely a non-Levitical worshipper claims the Levites' blessing as his own spiritual reality. Yahweh has made it so.

4. Life Worship Brings Security (16:7-9)

■ **7-9** The poet's commitment to Yahweh as his Lord and sole good (v 2) leads to a life of blessed reciprocity. The psalmist focuses continually upon Yahweh, while Yahweh guides him, even through his dreams. This engages his whole person (his **heart** [v 9], literally his **kidneys** [v 7], and his **liver**, along with his **body** [v 9]) in joyful security.

5. Confidence in Rescue from Death (16:10-11)

■ **10-11** Hebrew death language is known to Scripture readers, but also presents surprises. **The realm of the dead** or **sheol** (*šĕ'ôl*) here is simply the grave/underworld everyone enters at death, not hell. That Yahweh will not abandon his **soul** to **sheol** refers not to some nonphysical aspect of his person but instead to his whole embodied self (his *nepeš*). Then a homonym complicates matters. Hebrew *šāḥat* can mean either **corruption**, decay (so LXX, and, e.g., ESV, NASB, NIV) or "pit" (NABRE, NRSV, REB) or **Netherworld**, depending on its derivation. Parallelism in 16:10 argues for **sheol // pit** more likely than **sheol //** corruption.

Confidence that Yahweh will not abandon his own to a premature death provides the basis for the preceding celebration of life. Simply being rescued from death would have provided little cause for celebration. Old Testament saints expected death and looked forward eventually to their timely demise—"old and full of years" (2 Chr 24:15; see Gen 25:8). But premature death, early entry to the normal ravages of the grave, presented no blessing. It was a cause for fear and regret. From this the psalmist has found refuge (Ps 16:1). He will experience joy now in the life-giving presence of Yahweh.

FROM THE TEXT

The *šaḥat* homonym of 16:10*b* cited above opened the way for the NT's most important appropriation of this psalm. Following the LXX the early church found here a prophecy of the resurrection of Jesus, that is, of the fact God did not leave his holy one, Jesus, to experience the corruption of permanent burial (compare Acts 2:31; 13:35). Although this interpretation probably did not capture the original sense, it was in continuity with Ps 16's celebration of God as the sole and victorious source of unending, abundant life. Indeed, the resurrection of Jesus provided full and complete warrant for this celebration.

Prayer for Rescue and Vindication (17:1-15)

BEHIND THE TEXT

The SS presents this psalm to us as a **prayer of David**, a *tĕpillâ*. Psalm 102 (SS [1 HB]) identifies the *tĕpillâ* as the song to be used when needy worshippers in their weakness pour out their ardent plea to Yahweh. We have here a technical term, an indigenous designation for the poem form critics have called the individual lament. See the Introduction, C.1.b and C.4.e, for more on the SS.

IN THE TEXT

1. Prayer for a Just Hearing (17:1-2)

■ **1-2** Already in the petition itself, the psalmist supports the legitimacy of his prayer. He states that his **plea is just** (v 1*a*), a "just cause" (ESV, NASB), and claims his **lips** utter no deceit (v 1*b*). He strengthens his prayer by resting it in the character of Yahweh himself. From Yahweh himself he anticipates a right verdict. Yahweh will have seen aright and will judge accordingly. These statements lead us to think the psalmist faces assaults on his character.

2. Psalmist's Faithfulness (17:3-5)

■ **3-5** What follows elaborates the decision-rendering process and also buttresses his appeal. The verbs of v 3 clarify Yahweh's dispensation of justice.

Yahweh examines and does an "on site" evaluation during the night. He assays, as happens in the smelting process, though he will find no devious scheme in the psalmist. This sounds like a so-called incubation rite in which the accused spends the night in the temple before Yahweh and expects to receive a verdict on his case from Yahweh.

Then a series of claims regarding the psalmist's uprightness strengthen his case. Questions regarding verse division and the meaning of the text as we have it preclude certainty at several points. A reasonable read would be as follows. He claims speech above reproach (v 3d). Guided by Yahweh's word he has taken care regarding the way of the rapacious, presumably to avoid it (v 4). He treads steadily in Yahweh's ways (v 5).

3. Prayer for Demonstration of Yahweh's Love (17:6-12)

■ **6-12** The preceding claims commending the psalmist's character lead logically to a renewal of his petitions to be heard (v 6). He seeks a demonstration of Yahweh's faithful mercy, saving those who rely on him from rebels against God's will (v 7).

He asks to be kept **as the apple of [*Yahweh's*] eye** (v 8). By now a set expression in English, in Hebrew this presents a puzzle. The MT reads: *'îšôn bat 'ayin*, **little man of the daughter of the eye** (no **apple** present). The diminutive *'îšôn*, **little man**, apparently refers to the tiny reflection of oneself seen when one looks into another's eyes at close range. The Targum reads "(little) circle," that is, the pupil of the eye. The LXX has "apple," perhaps a reference to the circular pupil. Hebrew *bābâ* would be ***pupil***. One suspects *bat* as a corruption of *babat*, found only in Zech 2:12. How the tender **little man in the pupil of one's eye** came to get lost in translation for apples remains a question. The psalmist wants protection as one close to, treasured by Yahweh (compare Keil and Delitzsch 1989, 231).

The shadows of [*Yahweh's*] wings (Ps 17:9) picks up the protection of holy things symbolized by the ancient cherubim. They stood guard over the ark in the tabernacle (Exod 37:6-9) and later in Solomon's temple (1 Kgs 6:23-28).

The psalmist elaborates those from whom he seeks protection, first in a series of relative clauses and then a set of independent claims. Though the MT is again a bit muddled, it appears these are persons who devastate, who hound him (Ps 17:9), surround and glower at him (v 11). Their opulence and **arrogance** close them off (v 10). Then, with a clear text again, he pictures them as hungry lions on the prowl (v 12). All of this about his adversaries in order to emphasize the seriousness of his plight and to support his cry for deliverance.

4. Prayer for Confrontation of the Wicked (17:13-14)

■ **13-14** The prayer uses images from Yahweh's life as divine warrior: **Rise up . . . confront them . . . with your sword rescue me.** The seriousness of the verbal attack can be inferred from this language. Unfortunately textual and lexical puzzles in v 14 resist confident interpretation. We should probably think of v 14*a* and 14*b* as an extension of the description of the wicked from whom deliverance is sought in v 13*b*.

Handling the MT *mmtym* that appears twice is critical. Is it a form of *mĕtîm*, **men** or **people** (hence "save me from such men" [most English versions]) or *mimĕtîm*, **one who slays them**, or some other form having to do with bringing death, *mwt* (LXX; Kraus 1988, 244) or something else? Then v 14*c* and 14*d* may either continue this elaboration of Yahweh's treatment of the wicked (ESV, NABRE, NKJV, NRSV, RSV)—satisfying but limited to the earthly level of full bellies, perhaps even ultimately toxic (Weiser 1962, 181-82)—or may treat Yahweh's contrasting provision for his treasured ones (Craigie 1983, 160; NJPS, REB). In striking contrast to all of these, the psalmist will "see [Yahweh's] face" (v 15).

5. Concluding Affirmations (17:15)

■ **15** The Hebrew *ṣedeq*, translated "my plea is just" in v 1 and **vindicated** in v 15 brackets the poem, focusing once again on the innocence of the one praying. **Seeing, beholding Yahweh's face** in this context has most likely to do with meeting God in worship at the temple (compare 11:7; 42:2). Although our context tempts us to construe **when I awake** as resurrection, the immediate context leads us to expect reference to the psalmist's experience in the temple. He has spent the night there under Yahweh's scrutiny (v 3), hoping in his sleep to receive a revelation from Yahweh (the so-called incubation rite). Awaking from that slumber he will be satisfied, indeed vindicated and sated by the sight of tokens of Yahweh's presence.

FROM THE TEXT

Delitzsch pens fascinating lines on 17:15. Having noted Luther's and the tradition's interpretation of 17:15 as referring to resurrection hope and Calvin's rejection of that idea, Delitzsch opines that the postexile hope that all in the grave will one day hear "the voice of Him who wakes the dead" was "surely not known to David" (1989, 244).

But then he proceeds to ask why this truth toward which divine revelation had advanced may not have been "already heard . . . as a bold demand of faith and as a hope that has struggled forth . . . out of the comfortless conception of Sheol David did possess" (ibid.). Why, except for God's timing, we do not know. But that resurrection faith dawned upon Israel only later seems to be the case (compare Mowinckel 1962, 251-53).

John the Revelator finally claims that in the new Jerusalem, where no temple other than God himself exists, God's servants in worship will see his face as the pinnacle of human hope (Rev 22:4).

Song of Yahweh, the King's Rock and Refuge (18:1-50 [2-51 HB])

BEHIND THE TEXT

This royal song comes to us from David, servant of Yahweh. According to the SS it was sung upon the occasion of David's rescue from his many enemies, particularly from Saul. Although not every song connected to David with the *lĕdāwid* attribution was from him, there is no textual reason this poem cannot have been his. Cross and Freedman showed that numerous textual difficulties in Ps 18 and its double in 2 Sam 22 could be resolved by appeal to orthographic features ancient enough to have been misunderstood in the biblical period (Cross 1950, 58-71). And, in the case of this particular text, the SS—identical for both editions—also argues for a very old composition. I see no reason to push it late.

On the other hand, the psalm nowhere expressly claims to have been penned by David. Some of the boasts of the psalm sit better as testimony written about David than as boasts made by David himself. It is quite possible that the *lĕdāwid* attribution in the SS is to be **for David** or **about David** or the Davidic king.

Only Pss 78 and 119 are longer than our song. From the perspective of genre, this length allowed incorporation of a variety of psalm types. Although the resulting piece is complex, it manages a powerful unity. It is the longest testimony in the Psalter to the way Yahweh repeatedly turned catastrophe into triumph. See the Introduction C.1, C.4 for more on the SS.

IN THE TEXT

1. Yahweh Answers the King's Call (18:1-2 [2-3 HB])

■ **1-2 [2-3 HB]** Just as Ps 51 carries a rich vocabulary for sin and sinfulness, this psalm starts with an exciting parade of appellations for Yahweh, with the poet tapping several different scenes to describe his God (v 2 [3 HB]), most of them natural images. Yahweh is David's strength, his unreachable cliff, his safe crag in the **rock**, his **refuge** (from the hunt), his **deliverer** (providing escape), his **God** (the basic commitment), his **shield** (from the dangers of battle), his saving **horn** (as of the mighty bull seen as a beast pressed into battle), and his **fortress** (fortified and high up the tel). All of these commend Yahweh as one in whom to seek refuge.

One select picture, Yahweh as the king's **shield**, deserves additional comment. Yahweh is that impenetrable barrier that guarded David from blows and projectiles hurled down on the servant of God. But from ancient iconography Othmar Keel has shown that the **shield** quite likely refers not simply to a shield but to the shield bearer at the officer's side. He was the one *holding the shield* that protected the officer from incoming missiles. Strictly speaking, says Keel, "'shield bearer' implies a subordinate position." He holds the shield for the king or the general. Keel continues, "To summon Yahweh as 'shield bearer' presupposes that intimacy which permits one to ask a friend to perform a lowly service without in any way offending him" (1997, 222).

This is the God whom David will exalt (v 1 HB). The king could be said to **love** (<*rḥm*) Yahweh in covenant terms, but this would be different vocabulary (<*'hb*). The term used here according to the MT is not usually addressed to superiors. More likely we should read *exalt* (<*rwm*), as suggested by Bardtke (*BBHS*).

2. Rescued from the Snares of Death (18:3-6 [4-7 HB])

■ **3-6 [4-7 HB]** Briefly the king notes his cry to Yahweh for deliverance (v 3 [4 HB]) and the life-threatening crisis in which he found himself (vv 4-6 [5-7 HB]). **Cords** entangling him, dragging him down to the grave and **torrents of destruction** terrified him. Yahweh from his *palace* attended to the king's cry (v 6 [7 HB]). *Palace* here would be the **temple**, if this song is from later than David. If Davidic, it would be a reference to Yahweh's heavenly palace and throne.

The high drama of Yahweh's answer will be elaborated in the following lines. In preparation for this shift, the language intensifies. Verse 3 [4 HB] had the psalmist calling on Yahweh. Now he **cried** out to the Lord; his **cry came** to Yahweh (v 6 [7 HB]).

3. Drama of Yahweh's Intervention (18:7-15 [8-16 HB])

■ **7-15 [8-16 HB]** Yahweh's passionate response to the psalmist's cry triggered a sympathetic reverberation in the creation order. Language fit for describing a volcanic eruption with attending earthquakes and thunderstorms were needed to describe this answer of Yahweh. A tricolon full of sound play opens the description of Yahweh's response: *wattigʿaš wattirʿaš . . . wayyitgaʿăšû*, **trembled and quaked . . . trembled** (v 7 [8 HB]).

What follows is a collage of scenes picturing this divine eruption. The complexity of the picture emerges when one attempts analysis to discern what the poet may actually have had in mind and how this specifically related to

Yahweh. The imagery resembles language we have seen describing Baal's doings in Canaanite religious texts.

At points natural phenomenon are directly related to Yahweh. In v 8 [9 HB] **smoke** ascended **from his nostrils** or *in his anger*; fire or lightning devoured **from his mouth**; **burning coals blazed** from him. In other places Yahweh acted upon aspects of the storm or the eruption. **He parted the heavens and came down** (v 9 [10 HB]). He rode on a cherub, flying as on the **wings of the wind** (v 10 [11 HB]). Yahweh used the dark rolling clouds as his hiding place (v 11 [12 HB]). On the other hand, the banks of clouds were also set ablaze with hail and fiery coals as they passed by (v 12 [13 HB]). Yahweh Most High **thundered from heaven**, as though raising his **voice** (v 13 [14 HB]). He let his **arrows** fly (i.e., **lightning**), scattering **the enemy** everywhere (v 14 [15 HB]). At other points phenomena occurred as a result of Yahweh's acts. The primal streams at the footings of the mounts were **laid bare** by Yahweh's **rebuke** and the **breath** [*wind*] **from** his **nostrils** (v 15 [16 HB]).

We recall that all of this has been in the service of introducing the specific deliverances Yahweh accomplished for the psalmist (still to come in vv 16-19 [17-20 HB]) in response to his desperate prayer (vv 3, 6 [4, 7 HB]). The language does not attempt a clear picture of what Yahweh did to deliver the king. Rather it aims to stress in a most dramatic fashion the awesome might of Yahweh. When Yahweh appeared it was like an earthquake, a volcanic eruption and a hailstorm and thunderstorm unfolding simultaneously. He was absolutely uncontrollable and unmanageable. Blessed indeed are those upon whom Yahweh looks with favor.

4. Further Testimony to Rescue (18:16-19 [17-20 HB])

■ **16-19 [17-20 HB]** The plea for deliverance also trades in picture language. Yahweh reached down from a high, safe place and pulled the psalmist from raging **waters**. We are told the plight involved enemies that were **too strong** for the psalmist on his own (v 17 [18 HB]). They confronted him in the worst possible time, a time of calamity and **disaster**. But God provided critical support that brought the psalmist through these pressing circumstances. It was like being brought through a narrow ravine where snipers harassed him out into a safe, broad field (vv 18-19 [19-20 HB]). If we want more specific information, we will need to rely on the SS and its reference to armed, political conflict, such as the time Yahweh snatched David from Saul's hands (compare 1 Sam 19—24).

The final colon of this paragraph explains why Yahweh should have troubled himself to act on behalf of the psalmist—because God **delighted** in him! At the same time this line anticipates the next part of the song in which the poet attributes Yahweh's deliverance to his own devotion to Yahweh, a move that jars some modern interpreters.

5. Rescue as Response to the King's Righteousness (18:20-30 [21-31 HB])

■ **20-30 [21-31 HB]** What the poet claimed generally from Yahweh's perspective in v 19 [20 HB]—that Yahweh delighted in him—he now states specifically in terms of his own character and faithfulness to Yahweh (v 20 [21 HB]). Yahweh **rewarded** the king according to the king's **righteousness** (v 20 [21 HB]).

The psalmist pursued this theme in terms of Yahweh's choices. Yahweh **dealt** (v 20*a*), **rewarded** (vv 20*b*, 24*a* [21*b*, 25*a* HB]), showed himself **faithful** and full of integrity (v 25 [26 HB]). He exhibits purity with the **pure** (v 26 [27 HB]). The poet also speaks from the perspective of his own character and behaviors. He has carefully held to Yahweh's ways (v 22 [23 HB]). He has kept focused on the written/revealed articulations of Yahweh's will, not turning aside from them. As Yahweh demonstrates integrity with the psalmist (v 25 [26 HB]), so the psalmist has acted in good faith with Yahweh, refraining from iniquity (v 23 [24 HB]).

In vv 27-29 [28-30 HB], addressing Yahweh directly, the psalmist accented these claims. He did so either with three statements laying out the causes that underwrite the claims, or with three bicola beginning with their own emphatic particle—*yeah* or **surely** or *indeed*, or some combination thereof. The Hebrew particle *kî* presents this ambiguity. The NIV unhappily leaves the *kî* untranslated. The RSV takes the first as substantiation ("For thou dost deliver . . .") and the last two emphatically ("Yea, thou dost light . . ." and "Yea, by thee I can crush . . ."). The ESV takes all three as substantiation.

Here are the accented claims. Yahweh not only delivers those faithful to him but also responds shrewdly to the perverse who forsake him (v 26 [27 HB]). Although he saves an afflicted people, he brings down the arrogant (v 27 [28 HB]). His God lights his **lamp** and dispels his **darkness** (v 28 [29 HB]). **My lamp** sounds like a metaphor for the psalmist's life and vitality, which Yahweh here preserved. By his God he found himself able to "rush a barrier" (NJPS) or *defeat a squad of soldiers* (*gĕdûd* could mean either) and **scale a wall** (pictures from a successful raid) (v 29 [30 HB]). All this the psalmist based on the fact that his God participated as an active agent in his life (v 29 [30 HB]).

These celebrations of Yahweh's deliverance of the psalmist conclude with a tricolon applauding God's impeccable way, the purity of Yahweh's word, and his role as the out-in-front Deliverer for **all who take refuge in him** (v 30 [31 HB]). This response, taking refuge, echoes the trust sought for Yahweh's anointed at the outset of the Psalter (2:12).

6. Yahweh's Unique Deliverance (18:31-36 [32-37 HB])

■ **31-36 [32-37 HB]** The poet substantiated (*kî*) his celebration of Yahweh's response to the king by appeal to Yahweh's utter incomparability. Then follows a tightly knit set of lines elaborating the manifestations of this uniqueness. The paragraph's opening tricolon stakes out Yahweh's unique status as a deity and as Deliverer—**the Rock**. Among the many pictures of their God, Yahweh as Israel's Rock takes the reader straight back to ancient poetry devoted to founding events of the nation (compare Gen 49:24; Deut 32:4, 15, 18, 30, 31).

Now the specifics. God **arms** the king **with strength**, that is, with ***competence*** or ***skill*** (Ps 18:32 [33 HB]). He makes this warrior's **way secure**, that is, makes his performance in battle flawless, reflecting Yahweh's own flawless way (Deut 32:4). Psalm 18:33*b* [34*b* HB] interprets v 33*a*: **feet like the feet of a deer** are surefooted feet, ***able*** to stand ***secure on a rocky ledge.*** The point is not swiftness, which one might think of, but rather salvation, stability in a chaotic and troubled time (compare Hab 3:19). Similarly Ps 18:34 [35 HB]: **trains . . . for battle** (colon A) is specified in **bend a bow of bronze** (colon B). As Assur, god of war and storm, presented his bow to the Assyrian king, Yahweh arms the king of Judah with his own strong bow (Keel 1997, 215).

Bronze bow/*qešet nĕḥûšâ* (v 34*b* [35*b* HB]) occurs only here and in Job 20:24 and is puzzling in both places. On the surface a bronze bow, stiff by virtue of its construction from metal, would be useless in battle. Bows not only must be strong but also must be pliable. Even ancient composite bows were strengthened by adding various types of wood and strips of bone, not with metal components. Some have taken this to mean bronze-tipped bows, but although we have evidence of bronze-tipped arrows, no evidence of bronze bows possessed by warriors or used in battle has surfaced. (On all of this see Anglim 2002, 8-17.)

Perhaps the fact that we have a bronze bow from the ancient world attested only in a weapon given by the gods to a king (see figure 297 in Keel 1997, 217) is a clue. Only a god or a king trained by a god can draw this superbow! Here by hyperbole it emphasizes Yahweh's arming of the king for victory in battle. Dahood takes *nĕḥûšâ* as from *nḥš*, "to practice divination, charm, enchant," and understands our expression as a "magic bow." He compares a tale from Canaanite lore involving a magic bow made by the gods and decisive for the hero Aqhat (Dahood 1966, 115). This is possible but not as apt a parallel to v 34a [35a HB] as one would like. Solutions appealing to "bow" as "(el)bow" and the arms also leave behind the battle context of v 34a.

Your saving help my shield is *your shield that gives me victory* (v 35a [36a HB]). Or perhaps better, we should take the MT *māgēn* as **gift** instead of shield, yielding **You gave (me) your victory as a gift.** The **right hand** (v 35b [36b HB]) with which Yahweh supports the king is always the strong hand, the skilled hand.

What it is that made the psalmist great, however, depends on our reading of the MT *'nwtk* (v 35c [36c HB]). Homophonic roots take the meaning in diverse directions. *'nh-I **to answer*** indicates Yahweh's response, his aid (RSV). The parallel text in 2 Sam 22 probably indicates this *reading*. *'nh-II **to be bowed down*** could underwrite **your help** or the ESV "your gentleness." The NJPS offers "Your care has made me great," from *'nh-III*. Dahood may be right to insist on a meaning from the same root but parallel to "victory" in Ps 18:35a [36a HB]: "Your *conquest* made me great" (McCarter 1984, 471, following Dahood [1966, 116]).

7. Yahweh and the King's Exploits (18:37-45 [38-46 HB])

■ **37-45 [38-46 HB]** Exaltation of Yahweh now proceeds through celebration of the king's exploits. These lines probably give us the clearest insight into the situation from which Yahweh actually delivered David. God gave him dramatic military victory. First person verbs with the king narrating his triumphs increase. Focus shifts to include the devastating effects on the king's enemies. The first two bicola of the section include these emphases:

> I pursued my enemies and overtook them;
>> I did not turn back till they were destroyed.
> I crushed them so that they could not rise;
>> they fell beneath my feet. (Vv 37-38 [38-39 HB])

This first person celebration of victories catches one's eye. We are accustomed to hearing Yahweh himself speaking in first person narratives like this. One thinks of Josh 24:2-13. Theologically the poet has not driven a wedge between the king's doings and Yahweh's through him, as Ps 18:39, 40, and 42 make clear [40, 41, 43 HB]. The king's successes are themselves gifts of Yahweh. The first person emphasis does register, however, that Yahweh has not acted unilaterally in elevating the king.

Numbered among the king's enemies are Yahweh's people who call on him, if to no avail (v 41 [42 HB]). Included also are foreign adversaries who surrender to the king and come cringing to serve him, some insincerely (vv 42-45 [43-46 HB]). Although these claims could simply be royal hyperbole, it is lines like these that incline one to see behind them to the turmoil and ultimate consolidation that saw David come to kingship in Israel.

8. Yahweh and David's Exploits (18:46-50 [47-51 HB])

■ **46-50 [47-51 HB]** As it began, this majestic song ends in a climactic exultation of Yahweh. **The LORD lives! Praise be to my Rock! Exalted be God my Savior!** A possible toehold for interpreting this line appears in the second clause. Word order indicates a probable precative: "Blessed be my Rock!" (Andersen 1970, 49). Most versions follow the LXX for the last clause: "Let God my Savior *be* exalted!" The first clause can also be a precative, "May Yahweh live!" as Dahood has demonstrated (1966, 118). But what does it mean to wish the living God to live!? Perhaps this is why the versions regularly settle for the exclamation, **The LORD lives! Rock** and *my salvation* tie these concluding verses to the psalm's opening in v 2 [3 HB]—a poetic inclusio. Two modifying bicola further extol the psalmist's God—**the God who avenges me . . . who saves me from my enemies** (vv 47-48 [48-49 HB], tied closely to v 46 [47 HB] with participles). **Saves** and **enemies** add two more vocabulary ties of the psalm's opening verses with this concluding paragraph (compare vv 48 [49 HB] and 3 [4 HB]).

Verses 48 and 49 [49 and 50 HB] turn to address Yahweh directly. They portray the king relatively as a man of peace, this song notwithstanding. His enemies are those who take the initiative in war—*they* rise up. It is violent men from whom God delivers the poet.

The psalm's final tricolon (v 50 [51 HB]) shifts again to third person praise of Yahweh. It puts the song not on the lips of the king himself but on the tongue of someone writing for the king or about the king (a court poet?). Stress falls again on the king's close relationship with Yahweh. The king belongs to Yahweh. It is Yahweh who has anointed his choice for the throne (i.e., Yahweh's anointed one). These words bring forward the introductory concern of Ps 2 for God's anointed. Before the readers hear the agonizing questions of Ps 89, they sing of Yahweh's great commitment to and historic deliverance of David and his dynasty.

FROM THE TEXT

Paul used the language of Ps 18:49 [50 HB] to express his mission to the Gentiles (Rom 15:9). Likewise with Ps 18 we celebrate astounding victories wrought and granted by God.

But for the editors of the Psalter and for nearly every reader since the earliest this song of the king has been sung in the absence of a Davidic king. This has prompted three responses. Lacking a king, readers have read this song as directed to them, positioning the king's celebration of Yahweh and his deliverance as the congregants' own words, the so-called democratization of the royal psalms. Alternatively (or also) the song has been read eschatologically, anticipating God's restoration of the king announced by the prophets (e.g., Jer 23:5-6; Ezek 34:20-24). Additionally Christians have concluded that the resurrection of the crucified Jesus from the dead has demonstrated him to be both Lord and Christ (Rom 1:1-4; Acts 2:36). He proved to be the heir to the praise and promise of royal songs such as Ps 18.

On Being Acceptable to God (19:1-14 [2-15 HB])

BEHIND THE TEXT

This delightful poem shows well the benefits of concentrating the interpreter's attention on the final form of the text and not simply on questions of compositional history or form-critical issues. At least two clearly defined genres surface here. The first five verses present us with a beautiful praise of the Creator (19:1-6 [2-7 HB]). The next three verses contain a tightly structured celebration of Yahweh's Torah (vv 7-9 [8-10 HB]). The final five verses (10-14 [11-15 HB]) continue attention to Torah but focus on its significance for the psalmist himself. The first two sections, of very different genres and each quite complete in itself, may well have been discrete compositions aimed at two different types of worshippers or different congregational needs.

But the canonical poem as it stands directs our attention away from these matters of compositional history to the significance of the work forged by setting these pieces together. The resulting work, if achieved by nothing more than bringing these pieces together, now probes the issue of knowing God and the significance thereof. For the SS terms see the Introduction, C.1.b, C.1.a, and C.4.a.

IN THE TEXT

1. Heavens Declare the Glory of God (19:1-6 [2-7 HB])

■ **1-6 [2-7 HB]** A beautiful, chiastic bicolon launches the poem. **The heavens + declare + the glory of God // work of his hands + proclaim +** *the firmament*, that is, Sn + Vptc. + On // On + Vptc. + Sn (v 1 [2 HB]). Two things **the heavens declare**—God's glory and the fact that the **skies**, that is, the heavenly dome in which the luminaries of day and night appear, are handmade by him.

The psalmist writes carefully. The heavens—by virtue of their gigantic array, their variety, and their dependability across long periods of time—speak of the fact that they are "hand made." Considering the heavens, one easily concludes someone or something very large and very awesome, very old and very creative made them. The mind moves quickly to God. Beyond the apparent dependability of the heavens, from which one might conclude the dependability, perhaps even the faithfulness of its Maker, the heavens speak relatively little about God's character. But it does easily register its Maker's divinity and majesty. This is itself a significant message.

Verses 2 and 4 [3 and 5 HB] take up the nature of the celestial proclamation. It is unceasing. Day and night the heavens percolate the message. The verbs hint at the nonverbal nature of the communication, but the direct objects make the message character of the transaction clear ("message" and "knowledge"). Verses 3 and 4 [4 and 5 HB] clarify; no audible words are actually heard. Nevertheless their **voice/line** goes out in all the earth; their ***utterances*** clear to the end of world. The psalmist has in mind a universal message.

Their measuring line (*qawwām*) carries a critical implication. The term names a line used by builders to measure their work. As a metaphor it regularly implies accountability, something by which someone will be judged. The psalmist is clear that, although the celestial message is limited, it is critical. It generates universal accountability to the Creator of the heavens. The NIV—with the LXX, the Vulgate, and most English versions—"corrects" the MT, reading *qôlām*, "voice," for *qawwān*, "line." The change is not necessary and surrenders important interpretive ground. (The KJV, ESV, and NASB follow the MT.)

God has pitched a heavenly **tent** for Sun (vv 4*c*-7 [5*c*-8 HB]). Abruptly but clearly linked to the preceding lines (***in them***) the poet claims the God whose glory the heavens declare has put a tent in the sky for Sun (not "the sun"). "*The* sun" would be modern speak. "Sun" acknowledges that for nearly everyone in the biblical world "sun" was a god or goddess—"Shamshu"/"Shamash" in Mesopotamia, "Shapshu" at Ugarit, "Re" in Egypt, and eventually "Shemesh" to Israelites.

The metaphors—a **bridegroom** stepping young and vigorous from his wedding **chamber**, a youth in his prime eager to start a race—emphasize Sun's strength (v 6 [7 HB]). From one extremity of the heavens to the other his heat finds everyone without exception. Ancient theological reflection built on the universally pervasive light and heat of the sun, so that Sun was revered for his capacities for discernment and illumination. A long hymn to Shamshu expresses this well.

> O Shamash, all the world longs for your light.
> If a man practices usury, you destroy his owner,
> if a man acts maliciously, an end is made to him.
> You yourself make the unjust judge discover prison,
> lay punishment on the one who accepts a bribe and commits injustice,

but the one who rejects a bribe and intercedes for the weak
is well pleasing to Shamash, and he will lengthen his life. (Arnold and Beyer 2002, 199)

Sun attracted devotees in Israel, also. Manasseh actually installed Sun paraphernalia in the Jerusalem temple (2 Kgs 21:5 and 2 Chr 33:5 state that "he built altars to all the starry hosts"). And Ezekiel's visionary tour of Yahweh's temple exposed elders kneeling down with their backs to Yahweh's temple, their faces toward Sun (Ezek 8:16)! Since this was still thought of as Yahweh's temple, one suspects these elders were accommodated Yahwists, expressing a "solarized" Yahwism. Read through these eyes, "The Lord is Sun" (not "A Sun") would be confusing. This sort of syncretism or accommodation to Shamshu worship would have been thoroughly subversive of Mosaic faith.

The psalmist's few lines regarding Sun, then, are not randomly selected material for mere illustrative purposes. Instead he levels a strong polemic at one of the strongest and most attractive deities of the nations, strips it of its divinity, and presents it as Yahweh's creation, at its best extolling the glory of God! In the process he calls into question all man-made arbiters of truth and right that do not find their source in God.

2. Torah Revives the Soul (19:7-11 [8-12 HB])

■ **7-11 [8-12 HB]** Abruptly the poet turns from God's declaration via the heavens to his Torah, its characteristics and its impact. His style marks the change as clearly as does the content. Longer lines of varying lengths give way to six bicola of nearly identical length, syntax, and cadence. Tight, parallel, compact, their very form suggests the stability of Yahweh's law. And this *is* about Yahweh's law. Whereas the name Yahweh was conspicuous by its absence in the first five verses, every line now names this as Yahweh's Torah, Yahweh's testimony!

I do not discern a particular order in this series of lines, though the concluding line is general like the first. Similarly the series of adjectives that describe each facet of Yahweh's Torah do not seem to be in a necessary order. Each one could modify any of the Torah aspects listed. But, though the particular order of the characterizations does not seem critical, their exposition of Torah is significant.

The paragraph begins (v 7 [8 HB]) with the OT's most general term for Yahweh's historic word, his **law**, better his ***Torah*** (***Instruction***). The following five nouns are not synonymous, but they do overlap. Perhaps the general claim that Yahweh's Torah **refreshes** **the soul** is detailed in the following lines. Yahweh's **statutes** (v 7 [8 HB]), instructions derived from inspection, Yahweh's **precepts**, Yahweh's **commands** (v 8 [9 HB]), and his **decrees** (v 9 [10 HB]) name the aspects of his **law** celebrated here. Although **the fear of the** LORD as a name for Torah has no precedent, it should probably be taken as just that, perhaps a name of endearment.

These bicola explore traits of Yahweh's Torah and the effects it has on those who live it. Yahweh's **law . . . is perfect**, seamless and uncontaminated. Guiding those who keep it away from dissolution and destruction, it actually restores their vigor (v 8 [9 HB]). Its guidance is trustworthy, dependable, a steadfast source of enlightenment for the simple who are so easily confused. Yahweh's law teaches uprightness on all subjects it addresses, gladdening the **heart** of all who look to it for guidance in the ways of the Lord (v 8 [9 HB]). Yahweh commands purity, ennobling the desires of those who embrace Torah. This reading prefers ***pure*** (so ESV, REB) to **radiant** (LXX) as a description of Yahweh's command. As a text that both prescribes and produces **the fear of the** LORD (v 9 [10 HB]) Yahweh's Torah is "unsullied" (REB) and permanent. As instruction that both contains the record of Yahweh's just decisions and guides life by them, every one of his **decrees** are true and right.

As Ps 1 already claimed, those who continually delight themselves in Yahweh's Torah find themselves immensely blessed. They live refreshed. Their aspirations mirror God's will. Their moral and spiritual sense does not fail them. This life proves very desirable, as captivating as fine **gold** and as delicious as fresh **honey** (v 10 [11 HB]).

3. Petitions for Acceptance by Yahweh (19:12-14 [13-15 HB])

■ **12-14 [13-15 HB]** At this point the poem resists clear demarcation of a literary boundary. A transition seems obvious, from celebration of Yahweh's Torah to petitions based on the psalm to this point. But the poet has sewn the two paragraphs together by placing the Hebrew word *rāb* (***much, great***) as the final word in three bicola that straddle this transition, literally ***fine gold much*** (v 10 [11 HB]), **great reward** (v 11 [12 HB]), and **great transgression** (v 13 [14 HB]). The move from contemplation of Yahweh's character and will to awareness of the psalmist's need proves close at hand.

To this point the poet has spoken as a celebrant. Now he positions himself as Yahweh's servant (v 11 [12 HB]), needy and deferential, aware of his own debt to Yahweh's instruction. He testifies to the cautionary force of Yahweh's laws—they warn him; and to their significance in determining his circumstances—keeping them carries significant consequences (**great reward**). Moreover they enable awareness of *inadvertent* sins that would remain hidden without their instruction (v 12 [13 HB]). The petition for Yahweh to clear him of *hidden faults* (presumably hidden sins) should be taken in connection with Torah in the immediate context. Through Torah Yahweh will clear him.

The psalmist now prays either to be restrained from insolent sins or from arrogant people (v 13 [14 HB]). Although the noun in question (*zēdîm*) usually refers to arrogant persons, one wonders about the sense then of v 13*b* [14*b* HB] and his desire that these arrogant not rule over him. The prayer that Yahweh would restrain him from arrogant deeds and keep him from being dominated by such sins on the surface at least seems to make better sense. When this happens he will also be innocent of **great transgression** (v 13 [14 HB]), that is, outright rebellion versus inadvertent sins mentioned earlier.

The concluding line of the psalm could be either a statement (1) of present reality, **My words and my thoughts are acceptable in your sight**, (2) of future aspiration, **My words and my thoughts will be acceptable in your sight**, or (3) of prayerful desire, **Let/may my words and my thoughts be acceptable in your sight**. The latter two seem most likely. As a continuation of the result of Yahweh's restraining influence seen in v 13*c* [14*c* HB], **Then . . . my words and my thoughts will be acceptable in your sight.** More likely v 14 [15 HB] is a continuation of the prayer begun in v 11 [12 HB].

In any case the psalmist's testimony or prayer anticipates congruity between his inner being and his outer life, between thoughts and behavior. No more words at odds with secrets of the heart. No more longing of the heart unrealized in deeds. The poet rises to lofty spirituality indeed, his inner and outer life in concert and acceptable to Yahweh.

How this marvelous situation of integrity will come about the psalmist hints in his selection of names for Yahweh—his **Rock** and his **Redeemer**. As his **Rock** Yahweh will provide him a place to stand while the torrent rushes by. As his **Redeemer**, Yahweh will liberate him from bondage to sin from which he could never extricate himself.

FROM THE TEXT

The Apostle Paul concurs with the psalmist's claim that creation, in Ps 19 the heavens, implies the majesty and divinity of the one who made it (Rom 1:18 ff.). They do so with sufficient clarity that human beings can legitimately be held accountable for their response to this proclamation of the cosmos. Recall that in Romans, human beings stand condemned not because of their rejection of Jesus Christ but because of their rejection and corruption of what might be inferred about God from the cosmos. Still, the heavens' revelation of the Creator's "eternal power and divine nature," as Paul puts it (Rom 1:20), is a limited disclosure, ambiguous and silent concerning the moral character and personal disposition of this God. The heavens sing of God but the music lacks words. It is as though the heavenly choir hums its song. God's world tells his glory!

Both the psalmist and Christians long after him rejoice that God has told us more about himself than can be inferred from the heavens. He has spoken his word, inspired much of it to be written, and has finally spoken of himself in the living Word, Jesus (John 1:1-18; Heb 1:1-2). Here at last we learn unambiguously that the Creator is holy love, through and through (John 3:16-19; Rom 5:8; 1 John 3:16; 4:7-12). Being just, righteous, completely truthful, wise, and dependable, Yahweh's Torah implies that he himself is of the same character. The ambiguity is gone. God's Word tells his way. It is as though the heavenly choir has now begun to sing the words of the Creator's song.

But the psalmist moves beyond the Creator's self-disclosure in the world and his Word. He prays for Yahweh's entanglement in his life, forgiving him, restraining him, shaping him so that he lives pleasing to the Creator, inside and out. Yahweh's work shapes his people. The composer of the song has taken the baton and is directing the performance of the symphony he himself wrote. It pleases him through and through.

Affirmation of Yahweh's Blessing of the King (20:1-9 [2-10 HB])

BEHIND THE TEXT

One of the Psalter's songs for the king, Ps 20 probably comes from the early days of the temple (Seybold 1990, 131). The final bicolon contains petitions. The rest of the poem presents affirmations that, if directed to God, would be petitions. Here, however, directed to the object of the prayers, the wishes become statements of blessing for the king. Verses 1-5 [2-6 HB] have a group speaking to a person we later discover to be the king. Perhaps a priest speaks for this company of worshippers. In v 6 [7 HB] the king himself testifies to divine deliverance. In the final verses (7-9 [8-10 HB]) the group again declares its trust in Yahweh en route to concluding petitions (v 9 [10 HB]).

A recently published Aramaic prayer to Horus, an Egyptian deity, and written in Demotic (late Egyptian) script bears striking resemblance to some lines of Ps 20, especially vv 2, 5, and 6 [3, 6, 7 HB] (see Goldingay 2006, 302-3). Of uncertain date, its relationship to Ps 20 is a matter of debate. In spite of its interest, at this point it does not advance our understanding of Ps 20.

For specifics of the SS, see the Introduction, C.1.a, C.1.b, and C.4.a.

IN THE TEXT

■ **1-2 [2-3 HB]** **May the LORD answer you.** The first verb's jussive mood sets the stance of the first five verses. We have a series of blessings addressed to someone whose identity remains to be determined: **May the LORD answer you . . . ; may the name . . . protect you. May he send you help** and so on (vv 2-3). **Answer** assumes a prayer to which Yahweh responds. **Protect** here carries the idea of being lifted above trouble.

The name as subject of the verb **protect** trades on the notion that one's name represents one's person. So in v 7 worshippers exult "in the name of the LORD our God," that is, in God himself. **The God of Jacob** (v 1) in this song ties royal and Zion theology traditions to patriarchal traditions from which these streams of thought are sometimes unnecessarily separated.

When Yahweh answers he will dispatch **help from** his **sanctuary,** the temple in **Zion** (v 2). Yahweh's presence was by no means confined to the Jerusalem temple. He dwelt in heaven (v 6 [7 HB]) and made himself known in the far corners of the cosmos (139:7-12). Still he was uniquely associated with this sacred place, his palace, where heaven and earth met.

■ **3-5 [4-6 HB]** The addressee turns out probably to be the king (vv 6, 9 [7, 10 HB]) who will have provided numerous **sacrifices and . . . burnt offerings** (v 3 [4 HB]). **Sacrifices** (*minḥôt*), literally **cereal offerings** or simply **tributes**. The *minḥâh* was often thought to be the burnt offering of the poor (compare Lev 2:1-16). But if this is the king's offering, then it would be functioning on its own as a gift. The blessing is that Yahweh might **remember,** that is, *favorably regard* and *count as meritorious*.

Although neither the LXX nor most English versions reflect it, the use of the same verb ties these two verses together asking for Yahweh to bring to fruition all the king's plans and desires. **May he *grant* [*yiten*] the desire of your heart . . . May the LORD *fulfill* [*yĕmallē'*] all your requests** (Ps 20:4a, 5c [5a, 6c HB]). Sandwiched between these requests is the desire to have cause to shout for joy at the king's victory and to march in celebration under banners (*ndgl*) emblazoned with the name of the worshippers' God. The LXX reads the Hebrew *ngdl*, "We will rejoice over the name" (so Kraus 1988, 277-78, with *BHS*). Either makes sense. The MT, the more difficult reading, is to be preferred. These lines express the consistent faith of Israel that human plans—even the king's—are futile without the engagement of God in the process. **May we shout** (v 5 [6 HB]) signals for the first time that the poet speaks for a group.

■ **6 [7 HB]** Now this I know: **The LORD gives victory to his anointed.** The king speaks with a confidence perhaps grounded in a favorable response to the preceding blessings, though as readers we are given no clear sign of this. Various renderings—**gives victory** or ***saves***, ***has saved***, ***will save*** rise from the ambiguity of the verb's perfect tense, *hôšîa'*. All of these are possible, but the context favors renderings that express conviction as to what Yahweh *will* do over recitations of what he has done.

The reference to ***his anointed*** anchors the construal of this poem as a royal psalm. This title carries on the Psalter's fundamental interest in the well-being and role of Israel's king (2:2; 18:51 to this point). The king is *Yahweh's* anointed. Yahweh has a particular stake in his well-being and in all circumstances where he is put in jeopardy. Verse 6c [7c HB] carries on the jussives, even if spoken by the king: ***Let him [Yahweh] answer***.

■ **7-8 [8-9 HB]** Two lines drawn together by emphatic identification of the speakers with the pronoun **we** declare **trust** in Yahweh. When the king goes to battle some put their trust in military equipment (war horses, chariots). **But we** [over against these] **trust in the name of the LORD our God.** Then again, **They are brought to their knees and fall, but we** [again in strong contrast] **rise up and strand firm.** This declaration of trust was difficult to maintain, as we know already from the reign of Solomon (1 Kgs 10:26; compare Deut 17:16).

■ **9 [10 HB]** Now we hear the only direct petitions in the psalm. They focus on the king, who has been the implied center of attention all along and on the worshippers who have blessed the king in anticipation of adversity.

FROM THE TEXT

In all the royal psalms the question arises regarding the point of their preservation. At the time of the final collection and editing of the Psalter as a book, the Davidic dynasty had long since disappeared. Preservation for historical memory hardly warrants including them and would only have complicated faith. More likely their inclusion expresses the confidence that Yahweh will in his own time yet keep his word. This confidence God vindicated when he raised Jesus of Nazareth from the dead. Bursting virtually all expectations as to who and what the promised "David" would be, God made the crucified Jesus both Lord and Anointed One (i.e., Messiah) in his resurrection from the dead (compare Jer 30:1-9; Ezek 34:20-24; Acts 2:29-36; Rom 1:1-4).

The King's Trust in Yahweh (21:1-13 [2-14 HB])

BEHIND THE TEXT

This royal song, like Ps 20, shows signs of composition for liturgical use. Both its focus on the king and its apparent references to 2 Sam 7 and Yahweh's covenantal promises there to the Davidic dynasty point to an occasion renewing that covenant. This is probable, even though there is no scholarly consensus on precisely when such a ceremony would have occurred in Israel (compare Craigie 1983, 188-90; Mays 1994b, 103; and our Introduction, E.1 on Recent Study and Psalm Types). The poem features several key aspects of Israel's understanding of kingship.

Psalm 21 is a good example of a work attributed to David/*lĕdāwîd* but probably best understood as either **for the Davidide/the Davidic king** or simply **for David** rather than **of David**. For more on the SS, see the Introduction, C.1.a, C.1.b, and C.4.a.

IN THE TEXT

After the SS, the psalm divides easily into two parts: vv 1-6 [2-7 HB] with a supporting affirmation regarding the king (v 7 [8 HB]) and vv 8-12 [9-13 HB] with a concluding prayer (v 13 [14 HB]). The opening lines address Yahweh directly regarding his history of blessing and preservation of the king. The second movement (vv 7-12 [8-13 HB]) speaks directly to the king regarding the king's coming exploits under the blessing of Yahweh. Because the first half of the psalm seems anchored in the past, the *yqtl* verb forms should be taken as general presents (is doing), noting what the king or Yahweh does, rather than futures (will do).

■ **1 [2 HB]** The first verse of the psalm stakes out the reality upon which the whole psalm depends. What reality? It is Yahweh's strength and his alone by which the king accomplishes the marvels celebrated in this poem and in which he revels. **In your strength** (*be'ozzĕkā*) appears in the first and last lines of the song, emphasizing this focus by inclusion and infusing the whole poem with this anchor.

■ **2-3 [3-4 HB]** The prayer of Ps 20:4 that Yahweh would grant the desires of the king's heart has now been answered. Verse 3 [4 HB] claims Yahweh **came to greet him** [the king] **with rich blessings**. Yahweh met the king with the intent to give gifts and bestowed upon him "enhancement of life" as promised to David in 2 Sam 7:13-29. Kraus emphasizes the comprehensive nature of Yahweh's beneficence to the king (1988, 286). Calvin summarizes: "The king shall want nothing which is requisite to make his life in every way happy, since God or his good *pleasure* will anticipate his wishes, and enrich him with an abundance of all good things" (Kraus 1988, 188, 286 n. 1 citing Calvin's commentary on Psalms).

Specifically one of these blessings is Yahweh's crowning of the king (v 3*b* [4*b* HB]), perhaps referring to a liturgical drama reenacting the king's coronation. This claim of Yahweh's disposition to initiate profound blessing for the king may provide the logical and theological base for the preceding lines, that is, "*For* you welcomed . . ." (LXX, ESV, KJV, NASB, et al.) or may simply be an emphatic conclusion to the first few lines (e.g., NABRE, NIV, NJPS, REB; compare v 6 [7 HB]).

■ **4-6 [5-7 HB]** Yahweh answered the king's prayer for life—abundant and long life. Neither here nor in v 6 [7 HB] should we think in terms of eternal life as theological abstraction involving afterlife or immortality. The NIV signals this by translating **length of days, for ever and ever**. It is life sufficient to experience the promises and blessings of Yahweh. And not simply for the sake of the king! The king was the pivotal person through whom much of Yahweh's blessing of the nation would flow.

Victories Yahweh granted established the renown of the king; this itself presented a deterrent from attack (v 6 [7 HB]). Perhaps Craigie (with Dahood 1966, 133) is right to say **Yahweh causes the king to see his face** rather than **made him** [the king] **glad** (1983, 188-89). In either case, as with the king's appearing (v 9 [10 HB]), so here with Yahweh's **presence** (v 6 [7 HB], **your face** (*pānêkā*) is an expression of the power of the king's and Yahweh's appearance.

■ **7 [8 HB]** The only line in the poem describing in third person what the king does names his chief and perhaps only absolutely necessary task—he **trusts** in Yahweh. Habitually, regularly, dependably (note the participle) he trusts the person of Yahweh and, implicitly, also the **unfailing love** [*ḥesed*] **of the Most High**. This provides the anchor for his reign and explicitly undergirds the first half of the psalm. This present faith makes possible the foregoing history and the promised future.

■ **8-12 [9-13 HB]** Turning to the king himself the poet promises full-scale victory by Yahweh's might. Standard but still meaningful conquests are envisioned, perhaps by the voice of a temple prophet who will speak for God. The king will hunt down all his enemies (v 8 [9 HB]). He will make them like fuel for the furnace (v 9 [10 HB]). He will cut off their progeny (v 10 [11 HB]). They will prove unable to carry out their evil schemes (v 11 [12 HB]). He will make his enemies turn their backs, as he takes aim with his bow (v 12 [13 HB]).

■ **13 [14 HB]** The psalmist by inclusion takes the reader back to v 1 [2 HB] and the celebration of Yahweh's strength/might. Here the prayer is that the display of Yahweh's might on behalf of his chosen king will leave him exalted above all rivals. And the promise is that Yahweh's people will praise him precisely at this point of his unrivaled might. It is one of two basic claims of the psalm. Yahweh has the strength to protect and prosper Israel's king. Not only is Yahweh able, but he is also willing to intervene on behalf of the king and his people. His proven disposition is to intervene with lavish good for his people by way of their king (vv 3, 6 [4, 7 HB]).

FROM THE TEXT

Psalm 21 underscores the preeminent place and privilege enjoyed by Israel's king in prayer. He could ask with strong hope for an answer. But, like all others in his realm, what he hoped to receive he had to request. "None of his gifts and endowments were inherent in his person," Mays reminds us. They were gifts of God. The king modeled "the indispensable place of prayer in human relationship with God" (1994b, 103-4). A marvel of the Psalter and its royal songs is that promises once uniquely made to the king are now the property of all the people of God.

Thanksgiving for Delivery from Desertion (22:1-31 [2-32 HB])

BEHIND THE TEXT

Psalm 22 presents probably the most memorable thanksgiving song in the entire Psalter. This is true in part because of Jesus of Nazareth's quotation of its opening lines from the cross (e.g., Mark 15:34), the so-called cry of dereliction. But its extensive, dramatic account of the psalmist's plight also contributes to this assessment. Lack of an explicit description of the psalmist's rescue, which nevertheless seems clearly assumed, adds to its interest.

See the Introduction, C.1.b, C.1.a, and C.3.c, for an explanation of the elements in the SS.

IN THE TEXT

The plight from which the psalmist had been rescued he narrates in the first twenty-one verses. The psalmist draws an extended contrast (vv 1-18 [2-19 HB]) between his present plight, forsaken and surrounded, and other testimonies and faith stories. The interchanging pattern, or chiastic structure, by which he presents this contrast, keeps his ironic distance from deliverance before the reader. (See below.)

■ **1-2 [2-3 HB]** (A) *'Ēlî 'ēlî lāmāh 'azabtānî*. **My God, my God** the psalmist cries out. **My God** locates this saint clearly within the community of believers, but it also launches the prayer less personally than use of Yahweh's covenant name might have. Verses 1-21 [2-22 HB] have five references to God, only one to Yahweh. The poet is forsaken in that God has not rescued him. Whether or not God is ontologically present in his crisis lack of rescue means God might as well be far off. His prayer groanings sound like a lion in distress. Day in and day out God's silence is deafening.

■ **3-5 [4-6 HB]** (B) Affirmations of faith and stories of his ancestors' trust stand in stark contrast to the psalmist's plight. They provide a solid ground on which to stand. From ancient faith he knows Yahweh as **the Holy One**. The praise God inhabits, perhaps is **enthroned** on, recounts the ancestors' salvation by grace (e.g., Exod 15). They cried out and God delivered them, so the stories go. That is the way it is supposed to be! They were not disappointed (Ps 22:5 [6 HB]), unlike the psalmist.

■ **6-8 [7-9 HB]** (A') But the poet's story is far removed from Israel's ancient tales of faith—the two stand in stark contrast. God's failure to deliver the psalmist in response to his cries has left him open to such severe derision that he sees himself unworthy of God's response. In his own eyes he's but a worm (v 6 [7 HB])! To make things worse, his adversaries know precisely where to lean on him. His claims to faith and his own reliance on Yahweh are called into question by his situation, and they know it. They use his very words against him (v 8 [9 HB]).

■ **9-11 [10-12 HB]** (B'A') In addition to stories about the ancestors, the psalmist has his own habit of faith. ***But even you!*** he exclaims, putting God at odds with his plight (v 9 [10 HB]). From infancy Yahweh has been his God. And this Yahweh remains. But where now is the helper customarily thought to be Yahweh (v 11 [12 HB]; compare 10:14; 30:10; 54:4; 72:12; 107:13; 118:7). *Ēlî 'attâ*, **You are my God**, and *'al tîrqaḥ*, **Don't be distant!** tie back to v 1 [2 HB]: *'ēlî 'ēlî . . . rāqôḥ*, **My God, my God . . . why so far from helping?** His lifelong faith constitutes simultaneously the anchor for his soul and the center of his present problem.

■ **12-18 [13-19 HB]** (A'') Although these lines are filled with obvious similes and metaphors, they appear to place the psalmist in a crisis of major proportions. His adversaries are wild bulls, snarling lions, a pack of dogs (vv 11, 12, 14 [12, 13, 15 HB]). They have done him physical harm and taken booty from him (vv 16, 18 [17, 19 HB]). He is physically and mentally traumatized, pushed to the very end of his personal and spiritual resources (vv 13, 14 [15, 16 HB]).

We are ill informed as to the specific historical circumstance we should think of, if indeed we are to move in that direction at all. Clearly the one who prays this prayer stands in desperate straits.

■ **19-21 [20-22 HB]** Here the first half of the psalm describing the psalmist's plight, forsaken and surrounded, comes to a stirring climax. More than able should he choose to act, Yahweh stands over against the crisis just described—**But you, LORD** (v 19 [20 HB]; compare vv 3 and 9 [4 and 10 HB]). The horrific situation leads inexorably to pleas for help. The cries for rescue gather up strands of the preceding lines in the vocabulary chosen. **Do not be far off** (v 19 [20 HB]; see vv 1 and 11 [2 and 12 HB]), **Rescue my life from dogs** (v 20 [21 HB]; see v 16 [17 HB]), **Save me from the lion's mouth** (v 21a [22a HB]; see v 13 [14 HB]), from the horns of the wild **bulls** (v 21b [22b HB]; see v 12 [13 HB]). The psalmist trusts Yahweh as more than a match for the troubles he faces.

Verse 21 [22 HB] should end with an imperative, reading *ănîtānî* in the B colon as a precative perfect, **Save me!** to stand parallel to the imperative **Deliver me!** in v 21a (with NIV, NRSV, probably LXX et al.; contra ESV, NASB).

■ **22 [23 HB]** Having cried for deliverance the psalmist promises to spread Yahweh's fame **to my people** (or perhaps he asks permission, **Let me recount . . .**). This whole drama has played out in the temple, so it is the gathered congregation who will hear testimony of God's mighty works when they appear, as surely they will.

■ **23 [24 HB]** Then promises turn to exhortation. The psalmist invites a wide circle to join him in praising—**You who fear the LORD, and all the descendants of Jacob and Israel**. These latter titles suggest we have an old song, perhaps already David's, when all the tribes are in view, not simply those of the Judean or Israelite kingdoms.

■ **24 [25 HB]** In the course of giving the reason why he will praise Yahweh, why those who revere Yahweh should join the praise, the poet provides the key to construing the psalm as a whole. Why? Because **he has not despised or scorned the suffering of the afflicted one; he has not hidden his face from him but has listened to his cry for help.** The psalmist is at pains to counter each one of the complaints voiced earlier. The terrible crisis, though told at length, has already passed. The cries uttered in all their pain have been heard. The one abandoned has been saved. What follows flows out of that past victory.

■ **25-26 [26-27 HB]** The psalmist confesses that when he speaks in the **great assembly** in the temple, Yahweh will be the source of his praise. During the crisis, though we were not informed in the first half of the psalm, the afflicted one made vows. He made promises that he would keep, should Yahweh hear his cry and deliver him (v 25 [26 HB]).

Psalm 116 provides an instructive sample of just such a votive service (i.e., a service for the paying of vows). It is a service for the offering of a thank offering or a votive offering (or some combination of these). It involves fervent praise, a liturgical libation, and fellowship with friends and family. Leviticus 7:11-21 provides the priestly instruction. Some of the sacrifice is burned to **the LORD**, some given to the priest, and some eaten by the worshippers (and probably their guests). Thus in our psalm **the poor will eat and be satisfied**, guests of the one making sacrifice (compare deVaux 1965, 417-18). **Those who sought him**, that is, sought some particular response or answer from him (*dāraš*) (as in vv 21-25), will join his praise, because their cry has been heard. The mysterious **May your hearts live forever** may be a greeting or benediction from just such a service.

■ **27-28 [28-29 HB]** The poet's horizon now moves to the ends of the earth. The promise made to the fathers (v 4 [5 HB]) that **all the families** of the earth would experience blessing through their faith is at least partially to be realized here (compare Gen 12:3). The fact that the poet grounds this hope in the universal **dominion** of Yahweh **over the nations** may set the bar for understanding the metaphors of vv 12-21 [13-22 HB]. Perhaps this is a royal psalm, like the several psalms preceding it, and the bulls, lions, and dogs are national leaders.

■ **29 [30 HB]** The topic shifts from the territorial reach of Yahweh's praise to the demographic range of those who join in submission to Yahweh, that is, the sorts of persons involved. Short answer? Everyone! Specifically the wealthy on the one hand, and **all who go down to the dust** on the other (all mortals?). In contrast to v 29*a* [30*a* HB] we might expect **those who cannot keep themselves alive** (v 29*c* [30*b* HB]) to mean the poor, those who do not have enough to sustain themselves. It could, however, simply exegete the preceding line.

■ **30 [31 HB]** Finally the poet turns to the chronological breadth of those serving Yahweh. Not only his contemporaries but generations on into the future will hear and join in telling the story of this deliverance.

■ **31 [32 HB]** At the city gates and in worship like that earlier referenced (vv 25-26 [26-27 HB]) **they will proclaim** [*Yahweh's*] **righteousness.** In so doing they recount not simply a feature of his character, that is, his uprightness and his sense of justice. They extol his uprightness as seen in his rescue of the needy, his accomplishment of justice and/or vindication for the psalmist (Reimer 1997, 762).

Logically (*for*) and experimentally all of this rests on the last two words of the MT, *kî 'āśâ*, *for* **he has done it.** Normally we expect a direct object with this verb, **he has done it** (NIV and most English versions). Here it appears absolutely, that is, without the object: *For he has acted*—period (see NJPS, REB)! Less likely these words could provide the content of the proclamation, "[They will] proclaim . . . saying that he has done it" (NRSV). Righteousness is here an act. Yahweh alone, in his sovereign governance of the nations, will make it happen.

FROM THE TEXT

Only Ps 110 rivals Ps 22 for its impact upon the NT. And none rival it for its influence on the shaping of the passion narrative. In Mark, for example, as much as Zech 13:7; Exod 24:8; Isa 53:6, 7, 9; Amos 8:9; Ps 69:21; and 109:25 together, Ps 22 provides a lens through which to interpret words and deeds of Jesus' death and resurrection (and perhaps exaltation).

The evangelists take their clue from Jesus himself who expressed his unspeakable anguish in the words of Ps 22:1: "My God, my God, why have you forsaken me?" (Mark 15:34). Right off, Ps 22 clarifies the meaning of abandonment/forsakenness. Signs abound that the God and Father of Jesus is present and active at the cross (the darkness, the torn veil). He is present, but he is choosing not to deliver his righteous Son. That is the agony of it.

But according to first-century piety, it is possible that Jesus referenced the entire psalm by citing its opening words. Following the righteous sufferer of Ps 22, Messiah Jesus thus voiced his abysmal loneliness and simultaneously confessed confidence in ultimate vindication. The fear that such an interpretation of the cry of abandonment could romanticize and thus trivialize the agony of Jesus' suffering is legitimate (Marcus 2009, 1063-64). But it may not take adequate account of the reports we have of the deaths of Jewish and Christian martyrs at the hands of the Romans. If the martyrs could find dying grace to bless and pray for their executioners, surely the Son of God might muster strength and faith to affirm the resurrection he had repeatedly linked directly to his crucifixion (Mark 8:31-33; 9:30-32; 10:32-34).

We can be more confident of the impact of Ps 22 on Mark's write-up of the passion than of Jesus' state of mind on the cross. Clearly Mark had the whole psalm before him, and he read Jesus' abandonment in context with the righteous sufferer's vindication. Interestingly, the subsequent proclamation of the psalmist's deliverance to all the nations in Ps 22:27-31 would appear to argue against the shorter ending of Mark. Although it is pretty obvious that we do not have the longer ending Mark himself penned, Mark's repeated reference to this psalm for the passion itself argues for a narrative that followed Ps 22 through to the end.

Not only so, but innocent persons suffering in spite of, perhaps even because of their righteousness, still find comfort in this psalm that emphasizes "the rest of the story."

Praise Yahweh the Royal Shepherd (23:1-6)

BEHIND THE TEXT

One of the most fruitful metaphors for kingship in the ancient world was the king as shepherd. This picture of kingship is at least as early as the Old Babylonian King Hammurabi. On the prologue to his famous Law Code he declared that Marduk had ordained him to lead, feed, and protect Marduk's people. As their shepherd, King Hammurabi carried the people on his bosom and found peaceful pastures for them (Meek 1955, 164-65, 177-78). God through the prophets addressed Israel's kings and also lesser leaders as shepherds (Ezek 34:1-10) and in the process described himself as Israel's shepherd (Ezek 34:11-24). In all of these places the shepherd in mind was the royal shepherd. The shepherd is none other than King Yahweh.

This insight, that Israel's shepherd is *King* Yahweh, makes best sense of Ps 23 and unifies its two main metaphors, Yahweh the shepherd and Yahweh the host—around its central claim, Yahweh is King.

The placement of Ps 23 beside Ps 22 may give a clue to its original setting, though certainty eludes us. It would have provided a stirring testimony to Yahweh's rescue and provision at home in the worship called for by the rescued supplicant in 22:23.

IN THE TEXT

■ **1** Foundational claims meet us immediately. First, Yahweh God of Israel is the writer's personal God. Second, because Yahweh is his own, personal God he will **lack nothing**. Yahweh has promised to bless the nation that obeys him. While this is a blessed truth, it is not the point here. Instead, he claims with Yahweh as his own God, he himself will **lack nothing**.

■ **2-3** This "lack nothing" state he particularizes (vv 2-3). He eats well in a peaceful environment. He enjoys tranquillity and a sense of being guided by Yahweh. By the grace of God he finds himself refreshed and energized. He experiences justice and vindication. And all of this full provision life he has at God's own initiative, simply because of who Yahweh is. Some such summary would probably get at the psalmist's core claims. But his testimony gains warmth, flexibility, and liveliness by being cast in the form of a metaphor. Picturing Yahweh as the royal Shepherd opens easily into themes of provision, protection, commitment, intimacy, and more, and it does so in a form that invites endless reflection, turning the pictures in one's mind. Lying in lush grass and grazing beside clear, calm streams picture marvelous provision. Patrick Miller helpfully recalls that the very act of lying down is often a picture of peace and tranquillity (Isa 11:6-7; 14:30; Jer 33:12; Ezek 34:14-15) and often carries with it the added assurance that "none shall make them afraid" (Job 11:19; Isa 17:2; Zeph 3:13; compare Mic 4:4) (1986, 114-15).

Being guided in **paths** profoundly **right** for the flock, being restored at the end of the day, and being able to count on all of this just because of who the shepherd is rather than what the flock has done—a picture of incredible blessing. Brevity and metaphor lead to ambiguity at points, as in the familiar "in paths of righteousness" (ESV, KJV, NASB). It can be taken to mean either *leading the psalmist to walk in the way of justice and righteousness* (compare Prov 2:9; 4:11) or *in safe and correct paths where no harm will befall* (compare Pss 5:8; 16:11). But the ambiguity, rather than presenting a problem may instead "belong to the richness of the psalm" (Miller 1986, 115). It all pictures either a marvelous hope or, more likely, a truly abundant life (depending on the tense).

■ **4** This abundance is not true because no challenges to it exist, but because of the presence of the shepherd even in or especially in frightening places. **With me** taps directly into a tradition of saving promise stretching all the way from the patriarchs, the Exodus and conquest, through to the incarnation itself and the last words of Jesus to his disciples (Gen 26:3; Exod 3:12; 33:14; Deut 31:8; Josh 1:5; Isa 43:2; Matt 1:23; 28:20). The KJV's "Yea, though I walk through the valley of the shadow of death" conjures a truly foreboding experience even though the LXX on which it depends probably stands erroneously on a folk etymology. The word in question more likely names an **impenetrable gloom**, a pitch darkness darker than dark (*HALOT*, 1029, and bibliography there).

The shepherd's presence is an active presence, guiding and defending. As attested in ancient glyptic art, the shepherd had two instruments, a **rod** (*šēbeṭ*) and a **staff**, that is, **shepherd's crook** (*mišʿenet*). With the shepherd's crook he reaches out to draw back a straying sheep. The *šēbeṭ* plays on the fact that the word designates not only a shepherd's club but also the king's mace (Keel 1997, 229-30). Yahweh as King is close to the surface through all of this. Yahweh is more than a passive bystander; he is prepared to enter the fray on behalf of the sheep.

■ **5-6** Verse 5 anticipates the setting revealed in v 6, the *bêt Yahweh*, the **House of Yahweh**. The temple at Jerusalem is called the *bêt Yahweh* because it is King Yahweh's earthly palace/house. In v 5, changing the metaphor from shepherd to host, the psalmist already finds himself in the king's palace. The king has brought him there and made him guest of honor at his special table. The table set for God's people is one of several reminiscences of the wilderness experience in this psalm (compare Ps 78:19) (D. N. Freedman, cited by Miller 1986, 116, n. 3).

Meanwhile, the psalmist's adversaries are also present. Noting this is critical to discerning the scene. The king has brought the enemies to the banquet as well, but not to honor them. Instead, while the king fetes the psalmist, vindicating his cause, the psalmist's adversaries, now counted among the adversaries of the king himself, watch the proceedings from the side and contemplate their fate. One thinks here of scenes something like those in Esth 7—8.

This is not a matter of vindictiveness on the part of the psalmist, against E. Vogt (1953, 155 ff.), as noted by Weiser (1962, 230-31). It is the king himself who has initiated this banquet. He has already anointed the psalmist's head (note the perfect tense). During the feast attendants make sure the psalmist's cup is filled to overflowing.

Finally instead of being pursued by his enemies, usually the subject of the verb **follow** (*rdp*), Yahweh's attendants, expansive good and *faithful love* [*ḥesed*], **pursue** him. And he either gets to dwell in Yahweh's house forever or gets to return there repeatedly in pilgrimages. Following the LXX and reading the Hebrew as *wěšibtî* gives **dwell**; the MT *wěšabtî* gives **return**. Either end spells joy for the psalmist. The poem ends with an inclusion tying the last three words of the psalm to the first word, **Yahweh**.

FROM THE TEXT

King Yahweh as Shepherd is a theme of particular interest to NT readers. That Yahweh would decisively shepherd his people was central to his announced intentions to redeem them from exile. And he would do so through a Davidic son who would himself be the good shepherd par excellence (Ezek 34:23-31). Against this backdrop Jesus of Nazareth said he himself was the Good Shepherd (John 10:11). The early church saw Jesus' resurrection as authentication of that claim (Acts 2:36). Later Peter picked up the oversight and caregiving side of the metaphor by telling his readers they had "returned to the Shepherd and Overseer of [their] souls" (1 Pet 2:25). Later he touched the Royal Shepherd motif by anticipating the eschatological appearance of Jesus the Chief Shepherd (1 Pet 5:4). This hope is reminiscent of the "great Shepherd of the sheep," vindicated by having been "brought back from the dead" (Heb 13:20).

As in ancient Israel, modern readers have every right to appropriate this psalm personally, individually. By the Spirit each member of the flock has confidence in the Good Shepherd as one's own God and Guide. The fact that this song is often read or sung at Christian funerals does not trivialize it. It rests on the Good Shepherd's conquest of the last enemy, death. The time of death may present its most potent context. Looking back on a lifetime of provision and blessing prompts confidence in God's continuing care.

Praise Yahweh the Glorious King (24:1-10)

BEHIND THE TEXT

Although no scholarly consensus exists on exactly what festival(s) procession might lie behind this psalm, some surely did. Its three sections suggest as much. Verses 1-2 laud Yahweh's universal ownership of the universe by virtue of his having created it. Verses 3-6 present an entrance liturgy (a Torah liturgy) for determining the worthiness of pilgrims for entry to the temple courts. Verses 7-10 appear to accompany the entry of the glorious King Yahweh into either the city or the temple precincts.

If it includes a liturgy for entry to the temple, "Of David" would have to do not with authorship but with association with the Davidic collection, perhaps songs for the Davidic king. On the SS, see the Introduction, C.1.a and C.4.a.

IN THE TEXT

■ **1-2** A claim regarding Yahweh's ownership of the whole world lays the groundwork for the poem. This the psalmist attributes to the fact that Yahweh made it. **Everything in it [*in the world*]** translates ***its fullness***. The term deals with everything on the earth—people, plants, animals, everything! The parallel term, **the world**, deals with the planet itself.

Verse 2 presents Yahweh's creative work in terms of securing the earth on the chaotic primordial seas (*yammîm*). He presses old Canaanite ideas into the service of lauding Yahweh's creation and mainly his kingship. Founding it on the seas probably pictures subjugation of the Canaanite god Yamm to Yahweh, here parallel to ***the rivers*** as at Ugarit. (More on this below.)

■ **3** Now the lines of the poem seem especially well suited to serve as a liturgy for screening entrance to the temple, Yahweh's **holy place**. **Ascend** assumes a walk up to the sanctuary, either from the valley outside the walls or up the temple hill itself. The requirement for entry is character, inner and outer holiness, with particular attention to integrity and regard for Yahweh's name involved in that. See Othmar Keel (1997, 120-27) on the whole business of safeguarding temples and their sacred space from profanation.

■ **4-5** **Who does not trust in an idol** presents a puzzle. **Idol** translates the MT *šāwĕ'*, **worthless** or **destructive**. The MT carries an article, ***the worthless thing***, which could refer to a particular idol or deity such as Asherah or Baal (compare Andersen and Freedman 1989, 318, on Amos 2:17-19 and "the girl" as Asherah). Even though translating the MT *nepeš* as **soul** perhaps works, it seems misleading. Hebrew *nepeš* rarely names something one has; it usually labels something one is. Humans *are* a *nepeš*, a living, breathing creature with wants, needs, passions, as well as thoughts and judgments (compare Gen 1:20 and 2:7). **Does not engage himself** (considered from the vantage point of desires and wants) **with the Worthless One**. Most versions take this meaning. All these assume a correction from "my" *nepeš* to "his" *nepeš*, following the LXX, which is probably best. Less likely, staying with the MT, it could give "By my life" as an oath to avoid (NJPS).

■ **6** Some interpreters seem eager to emphasize that this integrity and purity of heart required for entry into the holy place cannot be taken as an absolute purity. One suspects this strikes them as presumptuous and Pelagian—we know no one is really pure in heart!? Craigie rightly turns to the psalm itself to describe these potential worshippers: they **seek** Yahweh's **face**; they look to God for guidance (consult God) (v 6). But he continues, "They are prepared [to enter] in the sense that the desire to worship God has become an integral part of their lives, providing direction and focus. Though they lacked absolute righteousness, they desired it; in part, they would receive it as a consequence of worship" (1983, 213). It seems preferable to this interpreter to take for granted that the biblical writers were aware of the fact that only God is absolutely pure. We can hear the text actually claiming these persons will be pure in heart, a claim we can celebrate and expound rather than set aside.

Who seek your face, God of Jacob. The MT omits **God of**, an error corrected by the LXX and some contemporary versions (ESV, NABRE, NLT, REB). Even though the MT is the more difficult reading and therefore to be preferred, attempts to make sense of it have not yet really succeeded (e.g., KJV, NKJV, NASB, NJPS). The LXX's solution is preferable.

■ **7-10** These antiphonal lines call the gates to give entry to Yahweh and celebrate the person of Yahweh as the glorious King. Once again lines whose meaning seem obvious because of the context prove less clear upon closer examination.

Lift up your heads, you gates; be lifted up, you ancient doors. What would it mean for gates to **lift up** their **heads**? Gates do not have heads. And ancient gates did not include the portcullis design as they did later, and consequently did not **lift up**. Instead they opened swinging outward, pivoting on side posts. And what are the **heads** of gates?

Frank Moore Cross calls attention to Ugaritic Text 2.1.19-37 with a possible bearing on our psalm. The Ugaritic line identical in syntax to our line and very similar in vocabulary reads: "Lift up, O Gods, your heads!" Psalm 24:7 and 9 have **Lift up, O Gates, your heads!** Both texts have <verb imperative + vocative noun + object noun> syntax (Cross 1973, 98-105).

Ugarit

Ugarit was a Canaanite city on the Mediterranean coast north of Israel that thrived in the mid and late second millennium B.C. Ugarit shared a wide range of cultural and religious ties with Israel as well as a language similar to Hebrew.

In the Ugaritic text the council of the high god El is convened in the mountain of El. Emissaries from Baal's arch foe, Prince Sea [Yamm], approach. At their appearance the gods are overcome with fear and drop their heads to their knees. But the young king Baal shouts encouragement: "Lift up, O Gods, your heads!" Baal will handle the foe. The scene was likely repeated at the beginning and the end of a drama sending Baal out to battle against Prince Yamm.

There is no need to think of literary dependence. Instead, it is quite possible that we have texts that tap into a common stream of myth and literary topoi. Cross suggests we have language related to holy war and scenes from a ritual conquest in which Yahweh now returns from battle with the forces of chaos.

We should think perhaps of a personification of the gates, whose heads (in the minds of the procession) droop in feigned fear at the outcome. A liturgist or a guard or the gathered crowd at the gates shout the ancient word to take heart, because Israel's glorious King returns victorious from the battle! (see Cross 1973, 99-105). With gates opening wide, the promise is given: **The Glorious King will enter!**

The liturgist or the priestly guard or the crowd call the approaching entourage to identify the claimant to the throne: **Who is this Glorious King?** The response identifies King Yahweh with ancient titles elaborating his identity as the warrior king who fights for his people: **Yahweh, Strong and Mighty One, Yahweh, Battle Hero**, and **Yahweh of [Israel's or the Heavenly] Hosts**. Then finally for the fourth time for emphasis—**This is the Glorious King**.

Students of this psalm have generally assumed that a procession featuring the ark of the covenant was involved. Not infrequently in ANE literature one hears of priests carrying the idol of the national deity in parades of the sort envisioned in Ps 24. But Israel had no idol of Yahweh. Their theology and their founding documents ruled it out (compare Exod 20:4-6; Isa 44:6-20). Yahweh was thought to dwell on the ark of the covenant and was closely identified with it (Num 10:35-36; 14:44). Although Israel could not compel Yahweh to travel with the ark or fight on Israel's behalf against his will (1 Sam 4—5), still the ark served as the portable throne of Yahweh (Josh 3—4; compare Ps 132). A processional of the sort apparently assumed by Ps 24 would surely have involved the ark.

FROM THE TEXT

The three movements of this brief psalm bring vast areas of life together. We are told where we are and whose we are. We are in a world whose very order is a victory of the will of God. Life ordered by the Creator's will and participating in his victory is the only life worthy of the world he has given us. Finally we are told the glorious King now comes to his people. With his characteristic aptness Mays comments, "He comes as the victor who has prevailed against the chaos of unbeing and so is able to prevail against the chaos of evil. . . . Our existence depends on his creation; our blessing and righteousness depend on his coming" (1994b, 124).

Prayer for Rescue and Instruction (25:1-22)

BEHIND THE TEXT

Psalm 25 is an acrostic poem, the first letter in most lines beginning succeeding letters of the Hebrew alphabet, from *aleph* to *tau*. It is a slightly disrupted acrostic, with the *waw* (*w*) and *qoph* (*q*) lines absent but two *resh* (*r*) lines in the MT, the (*q*) line gone also in the LXX. No suggested textual repairs have gained wide support.

Just what the poet was trying to accomplish, if anything, with the acrostic design we do not know. A recent interpreter has suggested that the acrostic, running from the first to the last letters of the alphabet, suggests an "A to Z," comprehensive treatment of the topic at hand, thus giving it a "distinctive power and dynamic" (Goldingay 2006, 366). The suggestion fails for lack of evidence and for lack of a particular "power and dynamic" in the poem at hand.

One possible result of the acrostic design is that the psalm does not appear to have an overall logic or design. The logic may have been dictated by the acrostic demands. One can detect three units that move back and forth between lines making petitions in second person to Yahweh based on the character of Yahweh and of the psalmist himself (vv 1-7 and 15-22) and affirmations about Yahweh in third person (vv 8-14). Although two or three lines are upon occasion knit together by vocabulary or sense/syntax, the units suggested above do not clearly develop any singular topics. Against this assessment, some, prompted by several possible vocabulary pairs, have gone so far as to propose a chiastic structure for the psalm (Moller and Ruppert cited by Craigie 1983, 217-18). Most have judged the attempt a failure.

Though somewhat fragmented, the poem scores numerous strong points that easily stand on their own for instruction in faithful covenant life.

IN THE TEXT

■ **1** ['] The psalmist declares his allegiance at the outset. A double vocative (**Yahweh** and **my God**) emphasizes his focus on Yahweh the object of his trust. Lifting up the "soul" (MT and most modern versions) speaks of focusing the psalmist's whole, embodied person on Yahweh in worship or prayer. This important confession is too important to be lost for stylistic reasons (NIV, against most versions).

■ **2** [*b*] Yahweh is the object of the psalmist's **trust**, his hope of not being **put to shame** for want of help from his God, of finding himself the brunt of jokes from his **enemies**. This [*b*] line happens to be full of [*b*'s], calling attention to each word of the poem.

■ **3** [*g*] The psalmist undergirds his request in v 2 with the affirmation that **no one** who, like the psalmist, **hopes** in Yahweh will be **put to shame**. Similar sounds *gam//rēqām* at the beginning and the end "sew up" the line. See similarly in vv 9 and 15.

■ **4** [*d*] The MT *dĕrākêkā*, **your ways**, opens the [*d*] line, which itself has three *d*'s. The line reflects wisdom teachers' interest in **your ways, Lord** and in Yahweh finally as the one who must and does instruct his people in his ways. Parallel with **paths** in v 4*b*, these words speak of relationship with Yahweh as a journey best taken on a prescribed course.

■ **5** [*h*] This [*h*] line continues the interests of v 4. **Guide me in your truth** (**Make me tread**) is a single verb, *hadrîkēnî*, formed on the same root as *dĕrākêkā* in v 4*a*. Yahweh's way is not intuitive, not native to the untaught or ill-taught person. Yahweh will have to teach that one. And that instruction is tantamount to or at least an aspect of Yahweh's salvation upon which the untaught depends (v 5*b*).

■ **6** [*z*] In preparation for the petitions of v 7, the psalmist calls to mind the compassion (*rahămêkā*, an abstract plural) and loving-kindness (*hesed*). More important he asks Yahweh to respond according to these character traits for which he has been known for generations (Exod 15:13; 20:6; 34:6-7).

■ **7** [*h*] The request for Yahweh not to keep **the sins** of his **youth** in mind but instead to have Yahweh's own compassion in memory was the large matter v 6 prepared for. Very odd syntax at the close of this line forcefully underscores Yahweh's opinion as the decisive matter in this issue. Reasoning like the poet in 23:3c, "for his name's sake," Yahweh's forgiveness would occur in part for the sake of his own storied goodness (compare 25:11).

■ **8** [*t*] On a different topic, the fact that Yahweh takes it upon himself to instruct sinners is because of his own goodness and uprightness. That he does not simply dispatch with sinners, but bothers himself with their instruction is a mark of these gracious ways.

■ **9** [*y*] Not only sinners but also **the humble** (*those bowed low*) receive Yahweh's guidance. He enables them to walk in **his way** (note the singular, here summarizing the ways/paths of v 2 as a single orientation to life). **He guides them in what is right**, in the instruction on the basis of which right decisions can be made (Yahweh's *mišpaṭ*). Again a series of claims about the character of Yahweh (vv 10 ff.) provide the basis for this claim.

■ **10** [*k*] **All the ways of the Lord are loving and faithful**, and this proves most obviously so for persons who pay close attention to Yahweh's covenant. It is true generally, as we saw before, and also more specifically in the multiple, particular facets of the Lord's paths (pl.).

■ 11 [*l*] Because the **iniquity** for which the psalmist wants forgiveness is so massive, he must ground the petition in an equally weighty claim—the reputation of Yahweh himself. With the NIV I am reading *sālaḥtā* as a precative perfect, **forgive**.

■ 12 [*m*] To **fear** or ***reverence*** Yahweh is the very foundation of wisdom (Prov 1:7) and the essence of godliness in general in the OT. This descriptor gathers up trust and obedience and awe in a single, dense term. His reverent obedience finds footing since Yahweh instructs his people **in the ways they should choose**.

■ 13 [*n*] This verse may give the result of the instruction in v 12. Because of the instruction given those who fear Yahweh, they lodge in the ***extensive provisions*** of Yahweh (prosperity) and his posterity will experience the covenant promise of inheriting **the land**.

■ 14 [*s*] Continuing lines regarding those who fear Yahweh, we are told they have access to Yahweh's confidential counsel, perhaps even moving toward Yahweh's friendship with these whom he trusts (RSV, Keil and Delitzsch 1989, 345, and Craigie 1983, 216-17). Compare Gen 18:17 as an example of this confidential converse. But to what end? It could simply be for their instruction, for teaching the **covenant**, making it **known to them** (ESV, KJV, NIV, Kraus 1988, 318, 322) or making them "know [it]" in this sense of instruction (NASB). The clause could also preserve the more technical use of "knowing covenant" in the sense of making and keeping covenant, as promised in Jer 31:31-34.

Having noted several features of the psalm that tie it to the wisdom community in Israel, we must also emphasize the psalmist's interest in covenant life (explicitly in vv 10 and 14 and implicitly in vocabulary often linked with the covenant more than with wisdom pieces). A tendency to assume wisdom teachers and covenant theologians in Israel inhabited different worlds with few paths running between them does not square with the concerns we find in this psalm.

■ 15 [ˊ] Habitually the psalmist looks to Yahweh, because Yahweh will be his way out when he finds himself taken in a **snare**—a ***net*** entangling his feet. The *net* was apparently not all that unusual a weapon, not only for war but also for local predators. Nets could be thrown, for example, for trapping birds or a fleeing fugitive (Hos 7:12) or hidden by the path to entangle the feet (Pss 9:15; 57:6). A favorite metaphor of Ezekiel's warned of Yahweh's own net (Ezek 12:13; 17:20; 19:8). Apparently the psalmist's life includes adversaries who want to trap him. This plight, which reveals the psalmist's tenuous situation, figures in the next verses to the end of the psalm.

■ **16** [*p*] Lonely and afflicted the psalmist asks for Yahweh in grace to turn to him. The request assumes a sense of being out of Yahweh's protective sight or attention.

■ **17** [*ṣ*] The psalmist expresses his inner struggles in terms of being pressed in. So the request for Yahweh to **give me space**, that is, to make room for him to think and act reasonably makes sense (so the MT and LXX). Compare the NRSV's "relieve the troubles." Read as imperative or precative perfect. There is no need to emend the text to *rbb* or to read *rḥb* against its usually positive meaning, for example, **troubles of my heart**.

■ **18** [*r*] Similar to v 16's call for Yahweh to turn his attention to him, the psalmist here wants Yahweh to **look on** [his] **affliction**. He is afflicted and troubled, which may give rise to v 18*b*. The fact that he is troubled may prompt the conclusion that he has sinned, hence the call for forgiveness. To this point in the psalm no specific sins have been mentioned that could be in mind here.

■ **19** [*r*] A second *resh* [*r*] line repeats the opening verb of v 18, a repetition lost in some English versions. He urges Yahweh to take saving note of his enemies. They are violent persons who hate the psalmist.

■ **20** [*š*] **Guard my life** (my *nepeš*), or simply **Guard me**, the whole, embodied me. Why should Yahweh thus keep the psalmist? Because he has taken refuge in Yahweh, as urged at the outset of the psalms (2:12). Without Yahweh's guard the psalmist will be publically shamed. Either his God has been unable or unwilling to help him, or the psalmist's disreputable character has made Yahweh disinterested in helping him.

■ **21** [*t*] Aspects of the psalmist's godly character, his **integrity** and **uprightness**, provide protection for him. This is so because he sets his hopes on Yahweh. It is Yahweh, not his own uprightness, that spells deliverance for him.

■ **22** [-] Either the psalmist himself or an editor working this psalm into a collection now adds the request for Yahweh to **deliver Israel**. His horizon shifts from his singular interests of the acrostic to the needs of his people as a whole. Most likely the tenuous situation of the postexilic period is the setting of this prayer, but several occasions would work as a backdrop for it.

FROM THE TEXT

Goldingay titles Psalm 25 "The Bases of Prayer from A to Z" and at the conclusion of his treatment of the psalm lists implications for the life of prayer (2006, 366-78). The focus on prayer is well taken, full of insight as one would expect from Professor Goldingay. The focus on prayer, however, comes mainly from the fact that the psalm is itself a prayer. The petitions lodged and the affirmations made actually deal with covenant life as a whole.

The whole psalm arises in the heart of a poet reaching out to Yahweh with outstretched hands (vv 1, 2). This gesture of dependence and trust frames not only prayer but all of life. This prayer locates the psalmist among those who fear Yahweh (vv 12, 14), who seek instruction in the way of the Lord and his covenant (vv 4, 5, 9). Humility prevents claims of moral perfection and allows recourse to forgiving grace (vv 7, 11, 18).

The psalmist's affirmations most often provide the basis on which the various petitions rest. They outline a robust trust of Yahweh. In spite of threats inside and out to his well-being, the psalmist registers a foundational trust and confidence in Yahweh that shapes his response to all aspects of life (vv 2, 5, 15). Yahweh himself is good (vv 7-10). Everything follows from that.

Prayer for Vindication of a Blameless One (26:1-12)

BEHIND THE TEXT

The temple, among other things, was a place for resolution of legal cases. At first glance one might be tempted to read Ps 26 in such a context. The psalmist has come to the Lord's throne under false accusation. He wants Yahweh himself to clear his name. But, as Broyles persuasively shows (1999, 136-40), further examination associates this psalm more with the liturgies of entrance to the tent or the temple (as in Pss 15 and 24) than with cries for vindication.

IN THE TEXT

■ **1-3** The psalmist asks Yahweh to render a judgment concerning him (v 1). Reasons for the request follow immediately. First, the psalmist claims to conduct his life with complete integrity. He does what according to ancient tradition God Almighty first requested of Abraham: **Live before me in complete integrity** (Gen 17:1). Second, he trusts **Yahweh**, emphasized by word order, and is willing to rest his case with Yahweh. And third, he is confident he will not be shaken by Yahweh's test.

Three other requests specify what Yahweh's assessment will involve (Ps 26:2). Using two terms from the world of smelting and refining of metals the psalmist asks Yahweh to **assay** him (*běḥānēnî*) and to **refine** him (*ṣěrôpâ*). As here these terms are often associated with the intense examination of the human "kidneys and heart" (compare Jer 11:20; 12:3; 17:10; Ps 7:10, and see Zech 13:9 for the concrete experience upon which this metaphor rests).

The heart and the kidneys were both thought to be sites of human thought and emotion, human motives, and decision making. To examine the heart and kidneys was to examine the human interior life, one's thoughts, commitments, dispositions.

Psalm 26:3 gives further reason for the psalmist's request of this character test before Yahweh—his ongoing attention to Yahweh's **unfailing love** and his practice of Yahweh's faithfulness as revealed in his covenant. This line includes in parallel two terms frequently used together to summarize the Mosaic covenant: Yahweh's **unfailing love** (*ḥesed*) and **faithfulness** or dependability (*'ĕmet*). (Compare Mic 7:20.) He knows he is on safe ground and that his life is above reproach. This is not arrogance. He looks to Yahweh's grace and salvation. It is a candid assessment of his own with regard to fitness for entering the courts of the Lord to worship. See Othmar Keel (1997, 120-27) on the whole business of safeguarding temples and their sacred space from profanation.

Scripture readers know the term ***walk*** (lived) as a common place reference to the doings of life as a journey. To ***walk*** is to carry on life. Occasionally the OT writer uses a form of this word that emphasizes a back and forth, in and out, walking all about sort of journey, emphasizing the business and complexity of life (compare, e.g., Gen 3:8; 13:17; Job 1:7; Ps 105:13). That form stands behind ***walk*** in Ps 26:3.

■ **4-5** Five lines now particularize the character claims made in the opening verses. The psalmist has claimed integrity above reproach. He now gives representative details of that life. First the psalmist speaks negatively (vv 4-5), distancing himself from certain crowds. The psalmist does not seek the company of those who devote themselves to spiritually and practically worthless matters (compare 12:3), nor of persons whose lives are covert, their real selves hidden (26:4; compare 1:1).

Two groups of persons the psalmist rejects in strong terms. He abhors **evildoers** and does not keep company with **the wicked** (v 5). He separates himself completely from these persons, perhaps from the persons he has falsely been accused of accepting or of being like.

We note that neither here nor elsewhere are the specific sins of the **wicked** much catalogued, nor are they pursued specifically as attacks on the psalmist from which he seeks deliverance. He sees acceptance by Yahweh for entrance, not deliverance.

■ **6-8** Now speaking positively the psalmist claims heartfelt, enthusiastic participation in the sanctuary. He has ceremonially washed his hands, probably at the entrance to the shrine, symbolizing and declaring his **innocence** (v 6). (See Othmar Keel [1997, 120-27] on the whole business of safeguarding temples and their sacred space from profanation.) He has been among those who circle Yahweh's **altar**, caught up in offerings to God. He has done this in order to hear up close the service of the Todah—the offerings of thanksgiving, and to participate in the testimonies to Yahweh's mighty deliverances celebrated at the Todah (v 7). This is just as the writer of Ps 22 said it should be (22:22-31).

These acts of worship and devotion are simply expressions of his love for Yahweh's dwelling. This is the place where Yahweh's glory camps (26:8). The psalmist is not a person scraping together bits of evidence barely to clear his name. He is a worshipper in love with life lived for Yahweh and worships at Yahweh's house. Being accredited for entry to this blessed worship is what the psalmist seeks.

■ **9-10** Based on the preceding claims and disclosures the psalmist now asks God in v 9 to make a discriminating judgment ("Vindicate me" [v 1]). He asks God not to gather him up summarily with **sinners** or with violent persons. He wants decisions regarding his life and well-being not to include him in their exclusion from worship. Verse 10 again particularizes briefly these sinners of v 9. They are schemers and people who use their financial advantage to disrupt justice (bribers). This is the sort of people the psalmist does not want to be bundled with.

■ **11** On the other hand, in contrast with these wicked persons, and returning to the vocabulary of the opening lines, the psalmist reminds God that he lives blamelessly, with untainted integrity. As such one final time he asks for Yahweh to **deliver** or ***redeem*** him and **be *gracious*** to him. ***Redeem*** conjures the picture of a person hopelessly in debt to someone or completely locked in some obligation that never can be met, only to discover that someone has paid the insurmountable bill or met the undoable obligation, and you, the one redeemed, now go free! That is what the psalmist needs to get out of the predicament assumed by the opening verses.

■ **12** The psalmist supports his case by the claim that he, unlike his accusers, stands **on level ground**. It must be a metaphor for inhabiting a place where justice is done. Finally, presumably when he has been delivered, he promises to praise Yahweh in the assemblies gathered for worship.

FROM THE TEXT

At first blush the great concern with safeguarding the temple and the worship precincts from profanation seems distant to NT readers. Perhaps this is due to the marked decrease in and then disappearance of the role of the temple itself in Christian worship. Worship was typically in houses, as in those of Chloe and Stephanas at Corinth (1 Cor 1:11, 16) and Gaius in Rome (Rom 16:23) where the church gathered.

But further reflection reminds us that Paul considered certain attitudes and certain kinds of behavior totally inappropriate for Christian worship, even in a house church. The Corinthians' unworthy approach to the Lord's table was sufficiently outside the bounds of the meaning and spirit of the Lord's Supper that (1) it brought not simply censure but also lethal condemnation down upon them (1 Cor 11:30) and (2) actually disqualified the gathering as a legitimate Lord's Supper (1 Cor 11:20; compare also 5:1-8). (For a related but slightly different episode see Acts 5:1-11.)

Regarding the psalmist's confidence in his own innocence, NT believers had similar clarity about their character. They knew themselves to be sinners saved by grace and deserving of judgment (1 Tim 1:12-17). But in appropriate contexts they could also speak of their own spiritual maturity and the differences between them and others who they knew as enemies of the cross (Phil 3:12-20).

While I know of no church liturgy guarding the entries against profane intruders, there was an obvious concern for morally acceptable worship. Trivialization of the worship of the living Christ was an inexcusable affront to the risen Lord himself (1 Cor 11:27). The apostle calls worshippers at Corinth to examine themselves to avoid eating and drinking judgment upon themselves.

Yahweh, My Light and Life (27:1-14)

BEHIND THE TEXT

In genre and structure Ps 27 is similar to Ps 26. The first half of the piece contains the psalmist's affirmations of vibrant trust of God in the face of adversity (vv 1-6), culminating in his intense desire to stay in the temple (vv 4-6). The second half lodges petitions for Yahweh's guidance and protection and instruction (vv 7-13), with a concluding exhortation to hope in Yahweh (v 14).

Like Ps 26 this piece shows intense interest in the temple, in being in the temple and in gazing on Yahweh (v 4), being protected in Yahweh's pavilion (v 5), of joining in the singing there (v 6). This could hint at a pilgrimage as the setting for the song. The troubles faced in the psalm would then be the troubles encountered in the pilgrimage journey to Jerusalem. Warfare vocabulary (vv 3, 4) and talk of enemies (vv 2, 6) could suggest a royal concern, perhaps a king's return to the temple from battle. The number of stock phrases in the poem cautions against overly precise reading of these items. The psalm could have a number of settings.

If it is Davidic in terms of authorship, it has a narrow window of composition—when the tabernacle was in Jerusalem under David. If it is more generally "Davidic," anytime during the First Temple period would suffice.

IN THE TEXT

1. Confident Trek to Temple (27:1-6)

■ **1-3** Rhetorical questions in the two opening lines assume the answer "You should fear no one!" The reason: because Yahweh illumines all of his life, Yahweh rescues his people, and Yahweh functions like a fortified stronghold that secures life.

The succeeding lines of vv 2 and 3 raise specific, possible causes of terror, including even war. None disquiet the psalmist. **To devour me** should be taken metaphorically, as in 22:13. These enemies **will stumble and fall**, victims of Yahweh's providential intervention. Hence the result that his **heart**, the seat of thought subject to disturbance, **will not fear**. Verse 3*b* uncovers the secret. **Even then** is literally *in this*, that is, in these circumstances. Broyles wants the phrase to refer not to the war but to the following experiences in the sanctuary (1999, 142). As edifying as this would be, it sets aside a straightforward reading for questionable syntax. In all of this upheaval the psalmist remains or will remain anchored by his trust in Yahweh.

Broyles is also at pains to caution the reader that these stock lines do not describe the psalmist's experience of trust and tranquillity. Rather they present faith toward which the psalmist aspires or should "resolve to adopt" (1999, 143). Perhaps so. The military imagery could point in that direction, unless the poem is associated with the king and is more than metaphor. In either case, even stock phrases succeed because they provide words for the worshippers' experience. This "shalom" life need not be beyond the actual experience of God's people.

■ **4** Verse 4 presents a remarkably focused claim, the one thing he has requested and continues to seek: that he **may dwell in the house of the** LORD **all the days of** his **life**. We should probably not think of a servant of the Lord for whom the temple is his permanent address, but the pilgrim who takes the presence of the Lord home with him. Having been to the temple to attend to the things of Yahweh, he now lives in the light of that vision (with *lĕbaqqēr b-* perhaps a technical expression; *HALOT*, 151). At one time the term may have referred to inspecting sacrifices or witnessing the offering to look for an omen. Now in the OT it instead had to do with looking for or expecting a word from Yahweh (Kraus 1988, 334, comparing *sph* in Ps 5:3 and Hab 2:1).

■ **5-6** Continuing the metaphor the temple now becomes the covert hiding place where Yahweh will keep a guard over him. The clause is emphatic by redundancy: **hide in a hiding place**, a metaphor for protection. But Yahweh's **sacred tent** or **portable tent** was not in itself secure. It was secure because of Yahweh's presence, because the tent belonged to Yahweh. The **rock** upon which Yahweh **sets [*him*] high** could be any high rock where Yahweh could lift the psalmist above the fray and out of harm's way, very much as in v 6. Or, in view of the temple/sanctuary complex, it could well refer to the rock on which the temple was built.

Yahweh having answered the psalmist's one request (v 4), he will offer sacrifices and sing praises to Yahweh. Music and loud, jubilant shouts will accompany these sacrifices (compare 33:3; 150:5). These will no doubt be thank offerings where deliverance is proclaimed or votive offerings where vows made in distress are paid to the accompaniment of glad song and recounting of the deliverance (compare Ps 22:21-31 and Ps 16).

2. Pleas to Be Heard (27:7-12)

■ **7** The psalmist turns from affirmations of confidence to petitions for deliverance. He does so not necessarily because he lacks the faith he just confessed but because he knows that affirming the victory of Yahweh does not automatically make it happen. He will ask Yahweh to make good on the confidence his word has inspired.

■ **8-9** The general idea is clear here. The psalmist either wants to or will seek Yahweh's presence (his **face**). But no really satisfactory rendition has yet been offered. With language from v 5 he prays for the God who hid him there not to **hide** from him here (v 9). What would this mean? Cultically, it could mean no clear word from Yahweh at the sanctuary. It could mean circumstances raising the question of Yahweh's presence or pleasure with him.

He prays, as a **servant** of Yahweh, not to be turned aside, that is, not to have his request brushed aside. Like a servant standing before the king or governor (compare Neh 2:1-5), the servant is dependent totally on the king's good graces. In the end he has no leverage of his own. Perhaps the psalmist leverages Yahweh with a reminder of Yahweh's gracious history with his servant: **you have been my helper** (taking the perfect, *hāyîtā*, as a narrative form; most English versions, Kraus 1988, 331). Or ***Be my help!*** taking the verb as a precative perfect (LXX) is possible.

■ **10** Verse 4 presents one of the most singular statements in Scripture; v 10 presents one of the most poignant. It contemplates the unthinkable, that one's **father and mother** might **forsake** one, the forsakenness emphasized by vocabulary repetition with v 9*d*.

■ **11** The guidance and leadership sought here could imply the need for directions on pilgrimage, since some clues to a pilgrimage context appear in the psalm. Or they could as likely refer to guidance needed for everyday living. The fact that enemies figure in the reason for the request could have to do with enemies encountered along the way on pilgrimage or could argue for connection with the king again.

■ 12 The psalmist's adversaries included **false witnesses** who "breathe out cruelty" or "violence." This makes tolerable sense and follows a textual correction as old as the LXX, deriving the MT *yph* from *pûh*, **to breathe** (so the KJV, NASB, and still ESV, NRSV). This is one of those many places, however, where discovery of the Ugaritic corpus from the second millennium B.C. has sharpened and corrected our understanding of the Hebrew language. It turns out the MT *yph* should be derived from a root, *yph*, meaning "witnesses." This gives the phrase ***even violent witnesses***, clearly parallel to the preceding line, where **false witnesses** rise up **against** the psalmist. Like many such lexical corrections from the Ugaritic data, this enhancement of our grasp of the Hebrew text is not earthshaking. But the cumulative effect of these "small" corrections and clarifications has had a profound impact on our grasp of the language of the OT.

3. Concluding Affirmation and Exhortation (27:13-14)

■ 13 The psalm now concludes with a robust affirmation and exhortations to fellow worshippers, encouraging them from the psalmist's own experience. The first four letters of the MT in v 13, *lwl'*, have dots above and below each of them. The Masoretes have thus marked them as one of the fifteen so-called Puncta Extraordinaria (i.e., sites of extraordinary pointing) (Tov 1992, 55-56). Unfortunately we do not know what the Masoretes intended by the marks. Erasure? Emphasis? Some versions ancient and modern have ignored them (LXX, ESV, NIV, RSV); others have translated, usually as a conditional or contrasting conjunction (Tg., Vg., NABRE, NJPS).

In any case, the affirmation voices confidence that Yahweh will hear his cry. He will live to experience Yahweh's covenant **goodness** among the **living**. He will not be destroyed either by the wicked in their animosity or by Yahweh in judgment. He expects vindication and protection.

■ 14 A tricolon with identical opening and closing members concludes the psalm. **Wait for the LORD**, the tricolon repeats, with the encouragement to **be strong and take heart** in the center colon. Hebrew *qwh* means not only ***to wait*** but ***to hope***. The encouragement is not to wait passively, twiddling one's thumbs, but to wait expectantly, convinced of the affirmations made at the outset of the psalm and cognizant of adversity that will attend a significant faith journey.

FROM THE TEXT

This psalm speaks with two complementary voices. First we hear the voice of the confident pilgrim, fearless and steady in trust of God (vv 1-6).

Then comes the voice of the same saint, calling for Yahweh who embodies salvation (v 1) to bring that salvation about in the face of adversity and attack (v 9). We note carefully, however, that the psalmist nowhere in his "second voice" speaks of being afraid or cut off from God, of feeling betrayed by hesitation in voicing such disorientation. While the petitions in this psalm *may* imply such desperation, it is not necessarily the case. We may have the opportunity here to hear the trusting, confident one praying for help he actually needs. The two are not necessarily incompatible.

Prayer for Yahweh to Shepherd His People (28:1-9)

BEHIND THE TEXT

An invocation with opening plea (vv 1-2), petitions (vv 3-5), thanksgiving (vv 6-8), and intercession (v 9) mark this as a typical prayer song. Hints remain of the poem's use in liturgy (lifting of the hands, attention to the "Most Holy Place" [v 2]). Concern for the Lord's anointed may indicate royal participation (see *lĕdāwîd*; compare Introduction, C.1.a).

IN THE TEXT

1. Invocation and Opening Plea (28:1-2)

■ 1 Using an ancient name for Yahweh, the **Rock** (compare the ancient poems, Deut 32:4, 13, 15, 18, 31, 37; 1 Sam 2:2; 2 Sam 22:32), the psalmist calls for God not to greet his prayer with a deafening silence. That, he fears, will invite comparison to **those who go down to the pit** (Ps 28:1), that is, **with those who die**. All human beings are among those to **go down to the pit**, that is, are mortal. To **go down to the pit** in old age, full of years is not a problem. But to die prematurely or disgracefully, this is a problem (compare Ezek 32:25, 29). To be classed with those going **down to the pit** because of illness or threat of enemies is to have one's mortality painfully underscored. In our passage, without deliverance the psalmist's life will be in jeopardy. Not to be heard is not to be delivered.

■ 2 He now asks positively for his **cry for mercy** to be heard. Regarding the psalmist's cries we should think more of screams, of pleadings than of simple cries. And the cries are pleas **for mercy**, the "expressions of a mind beset with terror which do not have established formulations" (*HALOT*, 1719).

Although it is not necessarily the case, the fact that these prayers are accompanied by lifted hands (Ps 28:2c) probably does locate them in the temple, part of a fervent liturgical act. The lifted hands direct the psalmist's eyes to the **Most Holy Place**, the most sacred space on earth. In this portioned space, the *dĕbîr*, the psalmist saw the earthly counterpart to the heavenly realm itself, the throne room of Yahweh, housing the ark, the footstool of Yahweh (Beale 2004, 34-36).

2. Petitions (28:3-5)

■ **3-4** The psalmist's core prayer strikes two notes. First he asks not to be dragged **away with the wicked** upon whose deeds he will elaborate (v 3). Second he calls for strict judgment of these evildoers (v 4). **The wicked** names a way of life, as the participle makes explicit in *those who as a habit of life do evil*. And this habitual evil is a matter not only of acts but also of **hearts** poisoned by **malice**, and that directed toward the neighbor, fracturing community.

Four times in the space of two bicola the psalmist calls for retribution according to the deeds of the wicked, further underscored by the repeated **repay them . . . repay them** (v 4).

■ **5** Now the psalmist taps the root of the evil he wants judged: **they have no regard for the deeds of the LORD and what his hands have done**. The **deeds** of Yahweh would include his creation of the cosmos (compare 19:1), his rescue of Israel from Egypt and granting them a covenant (compare Exod 19:1-7), and giving them the land (compare Josh 24:1-14). Disdain of any of these planks of Israel's faith and story would undercut covenant faithfulness and breed contempt for the Lord.

3. Thanksgiving (28:6-8)

■ **6** Emphasizing that Yahweh's gracious deliverance has matched the psalmist's "cry for mercy" (v 2) he now shouts out what he before had prayed. **Yahweh has heard** [*šāmaʿ*] **my cries for mercy** (v 6), matching **O my Rock, hear** [*šĕmaʿ*] **my cries for mercy** (v 2)! Such a match between human prayer and divine response can only lead to celebration: **Praise be to the LORD** (v 6). Literally **Blessed be the LORD.** Blessing for humans is a prayer prayed for the one to be blessed, usually in the hearing of the blessed one.

Example: "May God give you heaven's dew" (Gen 27:28), prayed by Isaac for Jacob in his hearing. Related to the divine, however, *blessed* functions as an exclamation of **praise**. The logic of blessing seems inappropriate voiced by humans of/to God.

■ **7** Beyond Yahweh's response to the psalmist's cries for mercy Yahweh's own person calls forth praise. The psalmist has experienced the Lord as his **strength and . . . shield**. Between the psalmist and harm Yahweh has stood as sure defense. Yahweh has proven trustworthy, the embodiment of help. The poet responds in exultation, praise, and song. Both his trust and his exultation are functions of his **heart**. One does not want to overinterpret these expressions, which are roughly equivalent to using the personal pronoun (**my heart** for "I").

Nevertheless, **heart** does name the person from the perspective of the human capacity to think, reason, evaluate, feel, decide, commit, and the like. Perhaps it is not too much to say the psalmist's thoughtful, critical response to Yahweh's help is to trust and to leap for joy. And he does so not with any song but rather **my song**, composed or specially selected by the poet.

■ **8** The community's experience of Yahweh mirrors that of the psalmist: Yahweh is **the strength of his people**, just as he was of the psalmist (following the LXX rather than the MT). This is particularly seen in Yahweh's preservation of his own anointed, the king of Judah. Yahweh relates meaningfully to individual Israelites through the liturgy and beyond it. But he relates to his people uniquely through the king whose task it is to understand Torah (compare 89:16-29). As noted above, this reference to the king may indicate a liturgical background to this poem.

4. Concluding Intercession (28:9)

■ **9** The concluding intercession focuses on Yahweh's role as Shepherd of his people. Viewing Yahweh's people as his inheritance uses an ancient metaphor to picture the permanent, special relationship between Yahweh and his land and his people. Here, no doubt, the people are in mind, referenced in the pronouns and the focus of the blessing (Wright 1997, 77-81).

Be their shepherd. Picturing leaders, especially kings, as shepherds was an ancient move already by the psalmist's time. This warm picture opened easily to tender, attractive elaboration. Shepherd Yahweh leads his people by gentle streams to lush pasture (23:1-3). Here Yahweh picks up his people and carries them in his arms to safety and shelter. Yahweh provides for his people what they could never manage for themselves.

FROM THE TEXT

The psalmist's knowledge of Yahweh as his strength and defense supports his confident approach to Yahweh in days of distress. Prayer for himself and his people rises easily from the lips of the pilgrim who has seen Yahweh carry his people.

Praise to the Enthroned One (29:1-11)

BEHIND THE TEXT

This song of praise features a theophany—a self-disclosing appearance of Yahweh, here in a thunderstorm. The unusual similarity of this poem's theology, literary form, and poetic artistry to Canaanite thought and language known especially through the Ugaritic corpus has made it of particular interest to students of the Psalter. So striking are the comparisons that some have seen in Ps 29 a Yahwist editing of a Canaanite poem, replacing the name of Baal with that of Yahweh (compare Craigie 1983, 244-46, for a history of scholarship on these issues).

While there is no direct evidence of such a vorlage (a specific document standing behind the one with which we deal), the proposal has merit. As Kraus, a bit overconfident, put it, "From the very beginning we will have to consider the probability that a Canaanite Baal hymn with its description of a theophany was handed down without radical revision on the part of the OT tradents in Israel. The archaic, pre-Israelite themes and conceptions are recognized without difficulty" (1988, 346). But given the chronological distance between the Ugaritic known to us from several centuries before Israel and the fact that this body of poetry comprised the immediate literary backdrop for biblical poetry, we should not be surprised if the poets make use of "images, phrases, and even mythological elements from the antecedent tradition with which they were acquainted" without thinking in terms of a simple translation or transposition (Alter 2007, 98).

This Davidic psalm could actually have been from David's pen. Points of comparison with the ancient song of Moses (Exod 15:2-18) suggest an early date for its composition. See Introduction, C.1.a, for more on the "for David" SS.

IN THE TEXT

1. Acclaiming Yahweh's Glory (29:1-2)

■ **1-2 Ascribe to the LORD, you heavenly beings.** The opening line situates the reader and the action in the Jerusalem temple, exhorting the **heavenly beings** in the corresponding heavenly temple to ascribe **glory** to Yahweh. A similar reference surfaces in Job 1:6 ff., Pss 82 and 103:20-22. In a Canaanite song these **heavenly beings**, the *běnê ʾēlîm*, **the sons of gods**, would be lesser gods attending to Yahweh. Here we would expect them to have been "demythologized," understood not as lesser deities but as heavenly messengers at attention to do Yahweh's will. The exhortation to **ascribe . . . glory and strength to Yahweh** finds response in the acclamation in 29:9.

These heavenly attendants are to acclaim Yahweh's **glory and strength**. Taken concretely **glory** has to do with weight, heaviness. Abstractly it has to do with social and cultural "weightiness," that is, with honor, being of high repute, distinction, splendor. Colloquial English has a similar semantic play when it describes a person as "a heavyweight." To **ascribe . . . glory** is to attribute proper, fitting honor. To **ascribe . . . strength** is to attribute fitting, reputation-building strength to Yahweh.

The last line of v 2 caused confusion early on. In the MT the **heavenly beings** are called to **worship the LORD in the splendor of his holiness.** The word **splendor** (MT *ḥdrt*) poses the problem. The LXX, trying to solve the problem, has *"in his holy court,"* reading *ḥṣrt.* Based on a Ugaritic word, *ḥdrt* standing parallel to *ḥlm* ("vision" or "dream") in KTU 1.14.iii.50-52, some scholars have suggested a meaning of "appearance" or "apparition" for the MT here. Thus Kraus translates "at his holy appearance" (1988, 344; see Cross 1973, 152-53, n. 28). This seems quite possible, though not everyone is persuaded (see Craigie 1983, 242-43, n. 2a).

2. Celebrating the Voice of Yahweh (29:3-9)

■ **3** The name of Yahweh, the Tetragrammaton (*YHWH*, i.e., Yahweh) dominates this song. It appears four times in the opening pair of bicola, as again in the closing pair of bicola that match these (vv 1-2 and 10-11). In between the **voice of Yahweh** appears seven times, called the "Seven Thunders" by earlier interpreters.

Now begins the theophany, the revelation of Yahweh through the storm, with the first of seven thunders. The poem captures the awesome power of the storm, focusing particularly on its terrorizing blasts of thunder, the loud voice of Yahweh. In **the waters** and **the mighty waters** the psalmist sees the primordial waters subdued in creation and continually kept at bay by the command of God, especially in fierce storms (compare Prov 8:23-29). Thus the voice of Yahweh **over the floods** signals victory for Yahweh. Eventually this involves his kingship.

The God of glory thunders. Frank Cross may be correct that here and in v 9 the word **glory** is a technical term. In these places it may designate not simply the honor and gravitas of Yahweh but "the refulgent and radiant aureole which surrounds the deity in his manifestations or theophanies" (1973, 153 n. 30). This gives due weight to the MT's article to be translated "God of *the* [theophanic] Glory."

■ **4-5** The impact of Yahweh's thunderous voice on nature reveals his great power. Here Yahweh's voice is linked with accompanying lightning and thunder probably indistinguishable to the ancients. When Yahweh speaks he splits the mighty **cedars of Lebanon.** These gigantic conifers had been famous throughout the Fertile Crescent and the Mediterranean world since time immemorial. They were referenced already in the royal annals of Sargon the Great and in the Epic of Gilgamesh from the third millennium B.C. These trees apparently evoked something of the awe moderns feel at the sight of a redwood or sequoia. The lightning strikes split these giants from bottom to top, scattering bark in every direction.

In **cedars of Lebanon** Lebanon names a region, the Lebanon mountain range north of Israel. In **Lebanon // Sirion** Lebanon specifically names Mount Hermon, the dominating peak of the Lebanon range. Deuteronomy 3:9 explains that the Sidonians call Mount Hermon "Sirion." Scholars have called attention to the fact that the geographic references in Ps 29 are all to spots outside of and north of the land of Israel and have seen this as one piece of evidence for the Canaanite origins of the poem.

■ **6-9** Under the light display of the storm, the swaying trees and the mountains themselves seem to skip and dance. Flashes of light catch the landscape at different poses, creating a jerking, whirling scene. Only a little imagination is required to see dancing calves (v 6), ***whirling deer*** (instead of **twists the oaks**) (v 9) in this display of Yahweh's power. The hinds have been moved to writhe in birth of their little ones. See similarly Ps 114:4, 6. ANE iconography showing Baal holding lightning arrows in both hands reminds us how close to Canaanite thought the concerns of these verses stand (Pritchard 1958, n. 136). Here the poet enters theological territory held by Baal and captures it for Yahweh, true God of the thunderstorm and more.

Strips the forests bare. This colon has resisted confident interpretation. The NIV follows the LXX in assuming Hebrew "forests," normally pointed as a masculine plural can also be pointed as a feminine plural. Kraus follows G. R. Driver (1931, 255) in translating "makes the kids squirm with [birthing] pain" (1988, 345). This works but has kids reproducing though young.

Another tie to the north surfaces in the shaking of the Wilderness of Kadesh (v 8). We should probably take this to mean not the Kadesh in the southern desert and the period of the wandering, but instead in the desert associated with the Kadesh north of Damascus and east of the Lebanon Mountains.

And in his temple all cry, "Glory!" (v 9). This makes reasonable sense and supplies the congregational affirmation sought in v 2a. But the MT behind the **all** is awkward and should probably be deleted as a dittography. Cross's suggestion that the Hebrew *'mr*—usually translated "speak, say," or "cry" (as in NIV)—should be taken with its archaic sense of "see" or "appear" has merit. He then reads the line: *In his temple (his) Glory appears!* (1973, 154-55, n. 39), with the possessive suffix in the first word carrying through to the last as well.

3. Yahweh's Strength for His People (29:10-11)

■ **10** Having elaborated upon the thunder and lightning of the storm, the psalmist returns to Yahweh and the mighty, primordial waters. Yahweh's victory over those waters he now connects to the theme of Yahweh's rule over chaos and the cosmos: **the LORD sits enthroned over the flood.** His enthronement as **King forever** bursts the bounds of the cyclical kingship of Canaanite lore.

■ 11 The **strength** (*'ōz*) ascribed to Yahweh in v 1 he now grants to his people, mentioned twice in the final bicolon. The inclusion signals the poem's conclusion. Mention of Yahweh's **people** brings to the surface the first distinctively Israelite meter in the song. Yahweh has a shared history with Israel, reaching all the way back before Sinai. So far as we know, Baal has no such "family" or "people."

FROM THE TEXT

This text is by no means the only point from which to raise the subject of "plundering the Canaanites." But with its remarkable similarities to Canaanite language and thought it is a good one. It reminds us that the people of God always live with the challenges of redeeming the cultures in which they find themselves. Without adoption of the language of our surroundings there is no prospect of communication with and redemption of those surroundings. Without critical assessment, however, the word of the kingdom will be compromised.

All of Ps 29 is surely at home in Israel, but not necessarily distinctive of Yahweh, God of Israel. If Ps 29 were the only poem in the Psalter, we probably could not say whether or not the poet really knew the God of Israel. The final two bicola stake out theological territory critical to authentic faith in Yahweh but leave large gaps for us to fill. Happily, we read Ps 29, like all other individual psalms, within the canonical context of the Psalter and then the rest of the Bible. From that perspective this revelation of Yahweh's voice in the thunderstorm makes its own contribution to the faith.

Thanksgiving for Wailing Turned to Dancing (30:1-12 [2-13 HB])

BEHIND THE TEXT

Psalm 30 offers a classic *Tôdâ*, an individual song of thanksgiving. In its testimonies to answered prayer it implies, as do prayers for deliverance, brief narratives of the plight from which rescue was sought (vv 1-3 [2-4 HB], 11-12 [12-13 HB]). It assumes the worshipper speaks in the company of fellow worshippers, persons whom the poet invites to join in praise to Yahweh (v 4 [5 HB]).

The SS places this song in the Davidic collection and associates it with the dedication of the temple, *habbayit*. This poses a puzzle, in that so far as we know David neither built nor dedicated a temple. The SS could refer to the dedication of David's palace (2 Sam 5:11-12). But we know of no such palace dedication. Even if we did, one wonders what place such an occasion might have in temple worship. And the definite noun *habbayit* usually designates the house of Yahweh.

Most likely we should think of a song composed for individual praise later pressed into service at the dedication of Yahweh's temple because of its forceful beauty. Whether it was first associated with the dedication of Solomon's temple (1 Kgs 8:63 in view of 1 Kgs 8:17-24), with the second temple after the exile (Ezra 6:16-17), or with the rededication following the desecration by Antiochus Epiphanes (compare 1 Macc 4:52-59), and used thereafter in celebration of that dedication we do not know (compare Goldingay 2006, 425). It was the last one that gave rise to Hanukkah, the celebration at which it is now used.

For more detail on the SS, see the Introduction, C.1.a, C.4.a, and C.6.

IN THE TEXT

1. Praise for Rescue from the Grave (30:1-3 [2-4 HB])

■ **1-2 [2-3 HB]** The first line of the psalm follows the reasoning that governs the song as a whole. The psalmist promises praise—**I will exalt you, Lord**, and then lays out the reason—**for you lifted me**. Here worship flows from life experience.

The psalmist's plight involves **enemies** eager to make sport of his adversity. It also involves poor health, judging from his gratitude for healing (v 2 [3 HB]). Sadly the two misfortunes go together in the psalmist's situation where it was assumed that illness, especially lingering or chronic illness, signaled God's displeasure (e.g., Ps 41). Judging from the strong verb used to describe the psalmist's call for help, he was sick indeed (30:2 [3 HB]). But the language of the pit and Sheol remain general enough that others can join the song, bringing their own specific ills to the light.

■ **3 [4 HB]** What the psalmist implies in v 1 [2 HB] he now plainly states. He saw himself on the brink of disaster, already in the clutches of the grave. He numbered himself among those actually **going down to the pit**. Elsewhere psalmists pictured themselves as caught in cords or ropes pulling them down into the grave, threatening death (compare 18:5 [6 HB]. From this grave plight Yahweh rescued him (compare 16:10; 49:15 [16 HB]; 86:13).

2. Call for Saints to Praise (30:4-5 [5-6 HB])

■ **4 [5 HB]** Now the psalmist invites the congregants to join in singing to Yahweh, probably with accompaniment (Seybold 1990, 86). These **faithful people** (*ḥăsîdîm*), already pictured in Ps 1, are those who are faithful to *ḥesed*, that is, they *keep covenant*. The call to praise Yahweh's **holy name** employs an expression that calls to mind the larger memory of God. Not simply his name but his renowned saving exploits prompt praise. Even though the LXX and Vulgate preserve this nuance, most contemporary English versions have settled for **name**, perhaps for want of a crisp translation option.

■ **5 [6 HB]** Now the reason for the invitation in v 4 [5 HB]. The enduring cause for song in spite of momentary experience of Yahweh's anger drives the praise. This line contrasts short-term displeasure, from which he has just emerged (vv 2-3 [3-4 HB]), with a **lifetime** in Yahweh's **favor**, and a **night** of **weeping** with the prospect of jubilation in the **morning**.

3. Testimony of Deliverance (30:6-7 [7-8 HB])

■ **6 [7 HB]** The psalmist elaborates the boast that led to the recent chastisement by Yahweh. Claiming he would **never be shaken**, he had actually taken up the mantra of the wicked (10:6). This overconfidence proved no more pleasing to the Lord in the mouth of the righteous than in that of the wicked (Keil and Delitzsch 1989, 377).

■ **7 [8 HB]** He sees clearly that he stands securely in **Yahweh's favor**, not his own strength. The specific expression, however, remains a challenge. Most likely one should supply a direct object pronoun for the verb: ***You make [me] stand [on] my strong mount*** (i.e., David's Mount Zion; compare RSV), not a genera comparison, like a mountain (e.g., NABRE, NJPS, NRSV). When Yahweh hides his **face**, he finds himself discomfited. His sense of ease, he had forgotten, was due to Yahweh's grace.

4. Plea for Mercy (30:8-10 [9-11 HB])

■ **8 [9 HB]** Having elaborated the plight from which he celebrates deliverance, the psalmist turns to detail his cry for help. He emphasizes the direction of his cry—to Yahweh, and names it as a plea **for mercy**.

■ **9 [10 HB]** His approach is to leverage his plea for mercy. He reminds Yahweh that the dead (i.e., those in the **pit** and those returned to **dust** or laid in the **dust**) will not praise him or **proclaim** his **faithfulness**. **Faithfulness**, usually translated *truth*, refers to covenant-keeping (compare Mic 7:20).

■ **10 [11 HB]** The cry itself is a call for Yahweh to **hear** him. **Hear**, of course, signals answering the psalmist's plea. This calls not for a sound check to discern whether Yahweh can make out the cry of his saint. To **hear** is to save. He calls out for mercy (as just spoken in v 8 [9 HB]) and for Yahweh to be his **help** (or helper). Repeatedly in the Psalter this word **help**/ʿōzēr is associated with indispensable aid without which the one in need is lost or undone. We should think here not of minor assistance but of help roughly equivalent to salvation, help necessary for survival.

5. Praise for Wailing Turned to Dance (30:11-12 [12-13 HB])

■ **11 [12 HB]** According to the psalmist Yahweh achieved a huge, saving reversal in his life. Using a celebratory metaphor, Yahweh took him from mourning over the dead to **dancing** with the living. Using a liturgical metaphor, Yahweh took him from wearing **sackcloth** signaling sadness and mourning to **joy** and gladness.

■ **12 [13 HB]** The poem closes with another telling of the psalmist's rescue from the pit, with the verse providing the purpose and a commitment. The purpose reads: **That my heart may sing.** The MT has *kābôd* (liver) doing the singing, with **heart** a reasonable English translation. Both the **heart** and the liver, along with some other internal organs, were thought to be the seat of human emotions. Thus Paul's (to us) odd expression in Phil 2:1: "bowels and mercies" (KJV). The RSV's "soul" and NJPS "my whole being" run along the lines of the NIV (Ps 30:12). The KJV, LXX, and ASV rendering, "My glory may sing," is formally possible but makes poor sense. A promise to **praise** Yahweh his God **forever** concludes this beautiful song.

Nine times the name of Yahweh has been on the psalmist's lips in this brief song, speaking the name of his Deliverer. Indeed, "to utter the name of the rescuer . . . is to give praise and thanks" (Brueggemann 1984, 126).

FROM THE TEXT

According to Walter Brueggemann the Psalter contains psalms that enable the people of God to sing their way through times of orientation, disorientation, and then new orientation. In the course of rendering praise this song has told the "story of going into trouble and coming out of trouble" (ibid.). The thanks for which the poet calls in Ps 30:4 [5 HB], and which he promises as his perpetual stance toward Yahweh in the final word of the psalm (v 12 [13 HB]), is more than gratitude. Giving thanks here (Hebrew *hdh*), says Brueggemann, is confession, acknowledgment of the one who has given the new life, a relying on and commitment to that One. Thus this piece lets us narrate the "whole career of the relation to Yahweh from *well-being* (prosperity) to *Pit*, to *new life*" (ibid., 127).

A Prayer for Refuge in Yahweh's Love (31:1-24 [2-25 HB])

BEHIND THE TEXT

This psalm presents a lengthy and repetitive prayer song for an individual. Affirmations of faith (v 1 [2 HB], 5-7 [6-8 HB], 14 [15 HB], 19-20

[20-21 HB]) set a positive tone for much of the song, but in the end are in the service of petitions for deliverance (vv 8-9 [9-10 HB], 15-18 [16-19 HB]) and exhortations to fellow supplicants (vv 23-24 [24-25 HB]). Smaller units show coherence, but no sustained logic governs the psalm as a whole. This has led some to see this song as a composite, forged from the uniting of two or more smaller pieces (vv 1-8 [2-9 HB] and 9-24 [10-25 HB]). This is possible, but not necessarily so (see Kraus 1988, 360-61; Gerstenberger 1988, 136-37).

Psalms showing similar repetition reside in the neighborhood, for example, Pss 30 and 42—43. Goldingay aptly refers to this telling of the story twice as "the rhetoric of prayer," where it is "natural to go through the story more than once" (2006, 437).

See the Introduction, C.1.a, C.1.b, and C.4.a, for technical terms in the SS.

IN THE TEXT

I. A Cry for Rescue (31:1-4 [2-5 HB])

■ **1-2 [2-3 HB]** The psalmist's opening claim provides the foundation for all that follows: he has taken **refuge** in Yahweh (v 1*a*). The preverbal preposition—**in you, LORD, I have taken refuge**—emphasizes his identification of Yahweh, among all possible choices, as his refuge.

The need for refuge implies threat of some sort, difficulty exceeding the psalmist's capacity to manage alone. The pleas are urgent (**come quickly** [v 2 (3 HB)]). **Deliver, rescue, save** all convey the idea of a serious, perhaps lethal plight in which the psalmist finds himself.

Metaphors throughout the psalm will fill the word **refuge** with content. Either in testimony or petition Yahweh appears as a **rock** and **strong fortress** (v 2 [3 HB]), as a ***secure crag in a cliff***, a ***stronghold*** (v 3 [4 HB]), all pictures of rescue by offering a place of protection. He apparently accesses Yahweh as refuge by trusting him right in the stresses of life (v 5 [6 HB]). He also brings his need for refuge to the temple. There, as with this psalm, he rehearses both his need and his anticipated rescue for his countrymen to hear.

The lead plea, particularized in the following verses, is that the psalmist **never be put to shame** (v 1 [2 HB]), presumably by Yahweh's failure to heed his cry for deliverance (see v 17 [18 HB] again below). For Yahweh to **deliver [him] in your righteousness** would have Yahweh working justice on his behalf by setting things right by a standard established by Yahweh himself.

■ **3-4 [4-5 HB]** These verses logically support the psalmist's pleas in a pair of tricola bracketed by *kî* clauses (***for*** . . .). His cries find foundation in Yahweh's unique role as his **rock**, [his] **fortress**, [his] **refuge**. They stand further on Yahweh's vested interest in protecting his own reputation.

Further, the petitions for Yahweh to **lead and guide** him indicate that Yahweh will not simply extract him from his circumstances. Yahweh will also enable him to make choices consistent with his cries for deliverance. In these petitions we learn that the psalmist suffers not as a victim of natural disaster (earthquake, windstorm). He is the target of enemy plots to **trap** him (v 4 [5 HB]). In the repetitive movement of the poem, this citation of the foundations of faith surfaces again in v 13 [14 HB].

2. Yahweh's Faithfulness Rehearsed (31:5-8 [6-9 HB])

■ **5 [6 HB]** Addressing Yahweh directly, the psalmist turns from his pleas for deliverance to testimonies of his own response to his adversaries. The committing of his **spirit** into Yahweh's **hands** constitutes the core of this response. Spirit here translates the Hebrew *rûaḥ*, roughly equivalent to **oneself** (Van Pelt, Kaiser, Block 1997, 1073-74). **Commit** has the sense of depositing for safekeeping (*HALOT*, 957-58). This basic entrusting of his entire person to Yahweh informs everything else. A similar confession of profound trust surfaces again in v 13 [14 HB].

■ **6-8 [7-9 HB]** This positive attachment to Yahweh has as its correlate the rejection of all rivals. The MT *hablē šawě'* can be taken generally as ***empty folly***, which the psalmist detests (e.g., ASV, NJPS). But more likely, in this context of contrast with devotion to Yahweh himself, we should think of these empty follies as **worthless idols**, and those who devote themselves to them as the object of the psalmist's disdain. In contrast to these worthless gods, Yahweh has proven worthy of trust.

It is Yahweh's saving intervention in his life that fuels such strong devotion. Yahweh has redeemed him, released him from debts he could not meet. This key verb regarding Yahweh's rescue of the poet could be taken as a precative perfect, ***redeem me, Lord***. More likely the psalmist continues testimony to Yahweh's deliverance (LXX, most English versions). Yahweh shows himself to be **God of Truth** in these exploits (v 5*b* [6*b* HB]). "Truth" here one suspects has to do with covenant faithfulness. Not the simple opposite of falsehood is in mind, but the God who acts in accordance with the covenants he swore with his people (compare Mic 7:20) (Ps 31:7-8 [8-9 HB]). Thus the poet is eager to rejoice specifically in Yahweh's *ḥesed*, his **love**, his ***loving kindness*** often associated with his covenant faithfulness. This God has seen the psalmist's affliction and adversities and acted on his behalf. Space provides the salvation metaphor here. Negatively Yahweh has not left him boxed in to his enemy's reach; positively Yahweh has stationed him in an open place with room to maneuver.

3. Call for Mercy in the Face of Enemies
(31:9-13 [10-14 HB])

■ **9-10 [10-11 HB]** An implicit causal move now takes the psalmist from testimony to petition. Encouraged by the recollection of Yahweh's past deliverance he returns to his present need for rescue. A single plea for mercy prompts an extended rehearsal of his distress (v 9 [10 HB]). One bicolon (v 9a) triggers line upon line in a litany of suffering. His vexation has taxed his whole person—his **eyes**, his inner self, his **body**, his **bones**. He is consumed with grief. **Years** have been wasted in agony (v 10 [11 HB]). This chronic, long-term problem has sapped all of his strength.

■ **11-13 [12-14 HB]** His adversaries construe his long suffering as a sign of Yahweh's displeasure. They celebrate the reproach this brings him, even among his **neighbors**. He strikes fear even to his **friends**. When they meet him out and about they turn away from him. He might as well be dead, so far as they are concerned. He has actually overheard some plot his demise (echoing 2:2).

4. Contrasting Trust of the Psalmist
(31:14-18 [15-19 HB])

■ **14-15 [15-16 HB]** Over against this frightful adversity the psalmist emphatically states his trust in Yahweh. Note the subject pronoun brought to the head of the sentence for emphasis: *As for me*. He openly confesses Yahweh as his **God** (v 14 [15 HB]). In language reminiscent of v 5 [6 HB], he affirms, **My times are in your hands** (v 15 [16 HB]). With that assurance he calls for rescue. Yet again, he acknowledges Yahweh's *faithful grace* as the source of his confidence (v 16 [17 HB]).

■ **16 [17 HB]** Let your face shine on your servant is an obvious idiom for conveying affirmation, here the approval of a subordinate by a superior. In the Psalter the shining of God's face repeatedly stands with blessing, restoration, and salvation (compare 67:1 [2 HB]; 80:3 [4 HB], 7 [8 HB], 19 [20 HB]). Among Israel's neighbors Egypt celebrated the beneficent shining of the Sun god, Re's, face most extensively (Keel 1997, 208-12).

■ **17-18 [18-19 HB]** **Shame**, public shame, presents a persisting issue in this prayer song and others like it. Should Yahweh fail to deliver the psalmist, both the poet and his God, Yahweh, would be open to humiliation. The psalmist would suffer community **shame** either way. Either his God, Yahweh, has refused to deliver him (which would imply sin on the psalmist's part) or his God is unable to deliver him (which would imply an inadequate God). The psalmist calls for the **wicked**, not himself, to be covered with **shame**. This would amount to a heaping upon the **wicked** the contempt in which they have held the righteous.

5. Yahweh's Goodness Extolled (31:19-24 [20-25 HB])

■ **19 [20 HB]** Against this public shame, Yahweh is known as the one who stores up good for those who **fear** him. To "fear Yahweh" describes persons who live consistently trusting and obeying him. Yahweh's goodness should not be seen as an abstraction, a character trait deduced from certain teachings. Instead, this good is the public deliverance Yahweh works for those who take refuge in him, accomplished in plain sight of the world.

Fearing Yahweh

Fearing (*yārē'*) the Lord can name simple terror or fright of God, a response encouraged by several psalms (23:4; 33:8; 46:2). Persons understandably tremble in the presence of the God who made heaven and earth and who speaks in the thunderstorm and the earthquake. To fear God can also name an attitude of devotion to God (86:11; 96:4). The fear of God as devotion to God assumes an appropriate reverence for him but puts to the fore a profound trust and consistent obedience to Yahweh's Torah (40:3; 119:63).

■ **20 [21 HB]** These people who take refuge in Yahweh he hides in a covert place beneath his wings (reading *kănāpêkā* from the MT *pānêkā*, with *BBHS*; compare Ps 91:4). He shields them from **human machinations** (the MT has *hl*, of uncertain meaning). With v 20a and b roughly parallel to v 20c and d, the latter bicolon reads *You conceal them in your covert from the contentions of those who hate [them]*.

■ **21 [22 HB]** The psalmist extols Yahweh with a blessing. For humans a blessing is usually a prayer petitioning good for a person in their hearing (i.e., "May Yahweh preserve . . ."). When directed to God, for whom the logic of the blessing for humans does not apply, the blessing is another form of praise.

This praise extols Yahweh's display of his *ḥesed*, his **faithful mercy**, now appearing for the third time in this psalm (compare vv 7 [8 HB] and 16 [17 HB]). Both the petitions and the praises of this song have been grounded in Yahweh's proven grace. Here Yahweh has marvelously exhibited his *ḥesed* by proving himself to be a "veritable bastion" in time of siege (with NJPS, taking the initial *b-* as *bêt* of essence, that is, **as a veritable bastion**). **In a city under siege** (compare LXX, RSV, et al.) also makes sense.

■ **22 [23 HB] In my alarm I said**, the psalmist recalls a complaint he made, crying desperately for mercy as though his plight was hopeless. But he recalls that cry now to register his report to the contrary. Yahweh heard his cry! He lived to render praise!

■ **23 [24 HB]** He invests the rest of the song in inviting fellow worshippers to **Love the LORD**, an exhortation appearing only three other times in the Psalter (116:1; 122:6; 145:20). It sounds like an expression of Deuteronomic piety, with its focus on loving Yahweh. Psalm 31:23b and c [24b and c HB] explains why the saints should love Yahweh. On the one hand he **preserves** the faithful; on the other he fully **pays back** the "investment" of the proud.

■ **24 [25 HB]** A final exhortation urges strength of **heart** for those **who hope in Yahweh**. He addresses those who even now are awaiting the deliverance for which they will one day give praise.

FROM THE TEXT

The content and structure of this sort of prayer song remains instructive for the church of Jesus. Life inevitably finds us in situations whose resolution lies beyond our resources. Without the intervention of the God of Israel we will be lost.

Giving voice to these situations—clear, soul searching voice—is itself part of God's answer. And we are not alone in these cries. While fellow worshippers joining in our prayers take heart for their own journey, they also lift us up.

Further, we are reminded that prayer is about much more than simply changing the ones praying. Prayer may accomplish that transformation of the petitioner, but this prayer song at least is about much more. It actually aims to receive deliverance from God, to be answered in terms of rescue one could not have cobbled together on one's own.

A Witness: The Blessings of Forgiveness (32:1-11)

BEHIND THE TEXT

This brief prayer song is known for the overtly instructional lines with which it begins and ends (vv 1-2, 8-11). These include surprising instruction from Yahweh himself (vv 8-9). The SS designates this psalm as a *maśkîl*, the first one in the Psalter. If we are correct in associating this designation with the verb *lĕhaśkîl*, having to do with instruction and bringing insight, the designation would fit the content of the song. Of course the lack of this tag on any one of several other instructional psalms gives one pause. The plight from which this song celebrates deliverance is also striking. It recalls the affliction and misery reaped from failure to confess the psalmist's sin.

For more on the SS, see Introduction, C.4.c and C.1.a.

IN THE TEXT

I. The Blessing of a Clear Conscience (32:1-5)

■ **1-2** Paired exclamations with *'ašrê* throw open the doors of the song, **Oh the happiness of the one who . . .** (compare Ps 1:1). This unusual emphatic device only appears elsewhere at 84:5-6; 119:1-2; and 144:15 (compare 128:1-2). In addition to the paired *'ašrê* beatitudes the highly cryptic nature of the first line jars the reader's sensibilities: ***[Oh the] happinesses of [the one who] forgiven [his] rebellion, covered [his] sin.***

Whose transgressions are forgiven starts by naming sin as rebellion, one of the stronger terms in the OT's repertoire of terminology for sin. The second line picks up the more general term, ***sin***. **Forgiven** translates an idiom that trades on the notion that forgiveness involves carrying another's moral culpability. Goldingay translates, "The good fortune of the one whose rebellion is carried" (2006, 451).

Several perspectives from which to view human sin appear in these opening lines. From the perspective of naming and analyzing the infraction involved, the vocabulary just noted is important. The perspective of the one resolving the moral question surfaces in the *carrying* of the culpability for the sin and cultic covering of it. There is the issue of moral reckoning, by which the Lord does not count the crime done to the doer's account (v 2). The internal calculation concerns the integrity of the transaction and ascertains the state of the prayer's spirit being without guile.

■ **3-4 When I kept silent**. The origin of this song appears in this earlier day, before forgiveness and covering and reckoning. Silence means there was no confession of sin, no song of forgiveness. Silence means the interior festering of unacknowledged betrayal. This silence exacted a heavy toll on the psalmist, registered in his body (**bones wasted away**), in a sense of being weighed down by Yahweh's heavy, palpable presence (Yahweh's **hand**). The second half of v 4 is difficult, but the MT makes sense as rendered: **My strength was sapped as in the heat of summer** (similarly RSV).

■ **5** Now to the miracle itself. Positively the psalmist **acknowledged** his **sin**; negatively he stopped covering it. He recalls the very words of his commitment to **confess** his rebellion against Yahweh. Dramatically he speaks directly to Yahweh, even though the psalm is not primarily a prayer.

2. Exhortation to Prayer and Praise (32:6-11)

■ **6** The compelling turnaround triggered by the psalmist's confession and God's gracious forgiveness now prompt instruction and exhortation for those who will hear. Based on Yahweh's forgiving record, the poet urges every devout worshipper to pray ***in the time of distress, in the flood of many waters*** (v 6c-d), taking the repeated *l-* phrases as clues to parallel lines. The MT for v 6c seems disrupted. The translation assumes minimal emendation, close to the RSV, rejecting more extensive alteration of the text by the NJPS as unnecessary ("discovering [his sin], that the rushing mighty waters not overtake him").

■ **7** Meanwhile, the psalmist himself addresses Yahweh directly: Yahweh himself is his **hiding place**, protecting him from trouble (dropping the "joyous shouts of deliverance" [NJPS] by dittography).

■ **8** Surprisingly now a voice speaks for Yahweh in the liturgy. First Yahweh speaks assurance, promising to guide the psalmist. He will give insight for success, instruction one might have in Torah. Yahweh promises counsel based on careful examination of the psalmist. Then he gives instruction in the form of a warning.

■ **9** The psalmist should not think and act like **the horse or the mule**, creatures who require restraint—**halter** and **bridle**—to do what even their Creator wants of them. They lack sufficient insight. Or, putting it positively, he should on his own choose the way of the Lord, should stay with Yahweh without coercion.

■ **10-11** This maskil closes with distinctive instructions characteristic of wisdom teachings. First comes a foundational claim regarding the nature of life itself (compare Ps 1). The ***wicked person*** can expect life filled with pain. The person who lives trusting Yahweh (note the ptc.) is surrounded by Yahweh's ḥesed, his merciful, unfailing love. Finally, the truth of that claim and the deliverance elaborated in this psalm evoke a call for the righteous to celebrate lavishly: **rejoice . . . be glad . . . sing *out***!

FROM THE TEXT

James Luther Mays' sensitive treatment of this song discerns three realities emphasized by it (1994b, 145-48): The blessedness of the forgiven sinner, the crucial importance of the confession of sin, and the necessity of integrity in repentance. The psalmist knew by experience the multifaceted suffering brought about by attempts to ignore or cover one's sin. Authentic confession of his sin had been the gateway to profound joy, exuberant celebration.

This psalm reminds us that sin often leads to suffering of various sorts. We are rightly reminded by the book of Job, by other psalms, and by the teaching of our Lord that not all suffering has sin as its cause. Hence, we are ill advised to make hasty diagnoses blaming another's suffering on sin. Nevertheless, much suffering is the result of sin, directly and indirectly. This psalm acknowledges that reality and celebrates the blessing released by the confession of sin.

Praise for the Creator's Counsel (33:1-22)

BEHIND THE TEXT

One of the loveliest of the ten or eleven songs of praise and thanksgiving included in the "prayers of David" (Pss 3—72) meets us in Ps 33. From start to finish it has the marks of a liturgical piece, urging fellow worshippers to join in the praise (vv 1-3) and giving testimony to Israel's experience of Yahweh's provision (vv 18-21). Yahweh's righteous character and creation by his word provide the major reasons for the praise.

Psalm 33 is an "alphabetizing" song, not that it is a typical Hebrew "acrostic" but that it has twenty-two lines, one for each of the twenty-two letters in the alphabet. Some suggest this intends to present the psalm as "complete and comprehensive in covering its subject as the alphabet is in listing the letters" (Mays 1994b, 148-49). This completeness may be indicated in the extensive music vocabulary pressed into service in vv 1-2 (see below) and in expansive realms treated as the sources of praise to Yahweh in vv 6-19 (ibid.).

Psalm 33 is one of only six psalms lacking an SS in the first two books of the Psalter (Pss 1, 2, 10, 33, 43, 71). Why it should lack an SS is unclear.

IN THE TEXT

1. Call for a New Song (33:1-3)

■ **1-3** Yahweh's singular character and his marvelous works of creation and salvation move the psalmist so powerfully that he launches this song with a veritable thesaurus of Israelite music. Calling his fellow worshippers, the righteous, to praise he exhorts: **Sing joyfully** (*rannēn*, of ***boisterous praise***), **praise the** LORD (*hôdah*, often of ***confessional praise***), **make music** (*zammēr*, usually music with accompaniment), **sing** (*šîr*, ***make melody***), **play skillfully** (*hêṭîbû naggēn*, ***strumming a stringed instrument***). He calls for the **lyre** with the attached resonance box, ***the ten-stringed harp***, along with other stringed instruments to accompany this praise. (For an informative introduction to music in Israel check Klaus Seybold's *Introduction* [1990, 85-99].)

As the RSV and some other versions rightly have it, Yahweh names both the *topic* of praise, "Be glad *in* Yahweh" (*b*-Yahweh, with the LXX in v 1), and the recipient *of* the praise, **Sing to Yahweh** (*l*-Yahweh, v 2). The praise takes the form of elaborating the amazing works and person of Yahweh and against that backdrop addresses Yahweh himself with adulation (v 22).

All of this is fitting **for the upright**, eminently appropriate for them (v 1). What better endeavor could occupy these saints than this robust **praise**? It calls for a **new song** (v 3); but "new" in what sense? Perhaps the **new song** celebrates new awareness of Yahweh on the part of the poet or some new work of Yahweh (Goldingay 2006, 465; Craigie 1983, 272). Some suggest an eschatological newness in the song that sings about a new world Yahweh is even now creating (Brueggemann 1984, 33; Kraus 1988, 375). Or the song could be new in the sense of being newly composed (Weiser 1962, 290).

Since the adjective **new** modifies the song itself and not some phenomenon outside of the song, perhaps with Weiser we should think of a "newly composed" piece. This song could either now be freshly composed or could be an old song known since its composition long ago as a **new song**. **New song** could even be the name of a type of song, something along the lines of our "country songs" or "folk songs."

What we discern from these opening lines is that music is fitting for the people of God if those singing and playing the music are actually upright, and if the subject engaging the songs is the good news of God himself.

2. Creator Yahweh's Powerful Word (33:4-7)

■ **4-5** Predictable but still important in these praise songs, the poet explains why the saints should shout praise to Yahweh. The reasons given do double duty. They provide logical and experiential foundation for the call to praise. Furthermore they themselves extol Yahweh. The character and force of Yahweh's word and the esteem in which his person is held occupy the poet's attention.

First, Yahweh's **word** is **(*up*)right**, like Yahweh himself and like his people (v 1*b*). Not only is his **word** of proven character but his deeds exhibit faithfulness (v 4*b*). Yahweh's **word** and his works reflect his character as one who continually **loves righteousness and justice** (note the ptc., v 5*a*). That **the earth is full of** Yahweh's **unfailing love** most likely has to do with the creation's capacity to reveal its Maker as himself filled with *ḥesed* (compare Pss 19; 104). Perhaps Yahweh's obvious love for the earth's people, evident at every hand in his world, is the claim.

■ **6-7** Not only the character of Yahweh's word but its creative power and genius appear in his capacity to create the world simply by his **word**. Here the poet quite clearly thinks along the lines of Gen 1. **The heavens** and all their **host** Yahweh spoke into existence. The claim is doubly potent. First, by his **word** alone Yahweh created all that is. This stands in stark contrast to some ANE accounts of creation involving sexual materials or the corpses of other gods. Second, he made the **heavens**, the realm of the gods who were also creatures of Yahweh's making. The spheres others worshipped as gods who could not speak, Yahweh himself spoke into existence.

This concept of divine creation by **word** proves not to be utterly unique in the ancient world. But the perception of Yahweh's true lordship and the unique nature of his redeeming relationship to the world he has created set Israel's claims apart from the nations (Kraus 1988, 377; see 376-80).

Yahweh's **word** is joined with his *ruaḥ* as the agents of creation (v 6). As in Isa 11:4 and 34:16 Yahweh's mouth gives the command; his *ruaḥ* carries it out.

Continuing the series of participles by which he elaborates the works of Yahweh, the psalmist has God gathering (*konnēs*) **the waters of the sea** together into **jars** (*kannô'd* with the LXX and Tg., parallel to **storehouses**, instead of the MT *kannēd*, ***into heaps***). The MT probably has Exod 15:8 in mind, as in Ps 78:13.

3. Creator Governs the World He Created (33:8-12)

■ **8-9** One bicolon states the results of Yahweh's creative work. Earth's people **fear** him, an occurrence where **fear** carries not only awe but some terror as well. **All the earth** here designates the people of the earth, as sense demands and the parallel dictates (***those who inhabit the world*** [v 8*b*]). Then reversing the logic the peoples' fear of Yahweh is substantiated by reference again to the astounding fact of Yahweh's creation by word. ***He spoke and it came into being. He commanded and the creature stood at attention*** (v 9). The brevity and directness of the formula puts it in italics. In the process of creation itself, the only connection between the Creator and his vast creation is his word.

■ **10-11** Continuing the reasons for the world's fear of Yahweh, two bicola focus on Yahweh's sovereign governance. **The nations** take counsel, but Yahweh can frustrate it, if he chooses. The peoples invest energy in complex and considered plans (compare 2:1-3), but Yahweh has the last say. One is reminded again of God's interventions at the Tower of Babel (Gen 11:1-9).

■ **12** Consequently the **nation** with which Yahweh sides, whose plans he inspires and blesses, is blessed indeed. But **the nation whose God is the Lord** is a matter of covenant commitment, not a vague preference for one god or perhaps another. Already in the introduction to the Sinai covenant and in stark contrast to their plight in Egypt Yahweh promised, "I will take you as my people, and I will be your God" (Exod 6:7; compare 19:4-6). If Yahweh is this nation's God, it is a matter of sworn covenant relationship. Throughout the history of God's people, these words—"I [Yahweh] will be your God, and you will be my people"—repeatedly define the issues at hand (compare, e.g., Hos 1:6-10; Joel 2:27).

The complementary truth, implied above, is that Israel is Yahweh's people, here **the people he chose for his inheritance**. Yahweh appropriates the image of chosen property to picture his ownership of Israel. An old poem, Deut 32:1-12, explains how Israel in ancient days became Yahweh's own people. He created Israel and also chose her from all the peoples of the earth.

4. Yahweh Alone Saves His People (33:13-19)

■ **13-15** Although Yahweh's special and ancient relationship with his people Israel is to be celebrated, the poet emphasizes all the nations of the earth live in his purview. He surveys them like a king overlooking his realm (v 14).

And they are known individually by him. Who they are and what they do are known to him like the pot is known to the potter (v 15).

■ **16-17** As the one particularly invested in and acquainted with Israel, Yahweh is the secret of her strength. The assets upon which persons are inclined to depend must defer to Yahweh as the source of Israel's might. Not the king's valor, nor the warrior's strength, nor the warhorse's deployment in the end save God's people (compare Hos 14:3). All of these are false hopes, in spite of their lure.

■ **18-19** The result of Yahweh's full awareness of the nations—including his people, celebrated in vv 13-15—now comes to the fore. He keeps his eye on them in order to rescue them from **death** itself (v 19) and to preserve them **alive** in such catastrophes as **famine**. His people hope in his gracious and faithful character (his *ḥesed*). It is his mercy that makes his awareness of his people a cause for praise and not for terror.

5. Yahweh Is Our Hope (33:20-22)

■ **20-22** The song concludes now in confession. The worshippers **wait** for Yahweh, **wait** in the sense of trusting for and anticipating decisive help from him (v 20). This waiting is virtually the same as the **trust** affirmed in v 21*b*. Parallel to that **trust** is the psalmist's gladness (v 21*a*).

The poem's final bicolon and only petition flows directly from the preceding affirmations (v 22). That Yahweh's grace would be upon the worshippers, just as they have claimed it throughout the song of praise, that is the poet's prayer.

FROM THE TEXT

In the NT as much as in the OT, praise from the people of God is eminently fitting. Sometimes it is encouraged (e.g., Eph 5:19); sometimes praise from the redeemed simply cannot be restrained (Rev 5:9-10).

In the NT as in Ps 33 God's just and gracious character and his astounding creation by word alone prompt marvel and praise. All things were made by the Word, says John (1:1-2), a mystery only apprehended by faith (Heb 11:3).

Instruction in Yahweh's Goodness (34:1-22 [2-23 HB])

BEHIND THE TEXT

The abecedary (alphabetic) form of this psalm and the instructive tone in the latter half of the song lead us to call this a wisdom psalm. It shares features of the praise and thanksgiving songs as well. Its abecedary approach also means that the poem does not exhibit a long or sustained argument. Instead it moves through shorter units of praise and instruction. The poet achieves something of a sense of unity by using seven different words three or more times. Almost without exception its bicola show a beautiful 3 + 3 scansion one after another.

Along with Ps 25 this abecedary lacks a *waw* (*w*) line but adds a line at the end outside the alphabetizing structure. Interestingly its *pe* and *'ayin* lines (vv 16 and 17 [17 and 18 HB]) are reversed. Students have long observed that the subject of v 18 [19 HB], the righteous, appears to be out of place, back in v 16 [17 HB]. Conversely, v 17 [18 HB] fits better as a sequel to v 15 [16 HB] than it does to v 16 [17 HB]. This leads readers such as Hans Bardtke to propose reversing the order of these lines in the MT (*BBHS*, ad loc.) to read vv 15, 17, 16, 18 [16, 18, 17, 19 HB]. In light of the recent discovery of ancient (twelfth-century) abecedary texts carrying the "reversed" lines, we should in texts like Ps 34 probably see an older, alternate alphabet rather than a confused text. In our text it appears the text was composed with the older abecedary in mind.

Scribes have "corrected" the text toward the more recent alphabet, straining the sense a bit in the process (First 2012, 54-55). Chapters 2 and 3 of the book of Lamentations also exhibit this *pe*, *'ayin* order, which means it was known as late as the early exile.

The psalm's SS relates this poem to the occasion when David feigned madness to escape the clutches of Abimelek, the Philistine king. We know of the incident from 1 Sam 21:10-15, though it is likely that our poet relies on some other source. The 1 Samuel passage has the king's name as Achish, king of Gath, whereas our SS calls him Abimelek. Following Delitzsch and others, Craigie quite reasonably suggests Abimelek was the title of Philistine kings, as Pharaoh was of Egyptian rulers (1983, 278; Keil and Delitzsch 1989, 407-8). Achish would have been the king's personal name.

Although the poem does not relate directly and specifically to the historical setting evinced by the SS, it is relevant at several points. And, even if it might not appear clearly related, the tradents who gave us the Psalter have directed us to read with this episode in mind.

The SS and v 9 of Ps 34 share a word that sounds very similar: *ṭa'mô*, "his [David's] discernment" in the SS and *ṭa'mû*, "taste," a verb in v 9. But one doubts this alone would account for attaching the SS to this particular psalm.

IN THE TEXT

1. Invitation to Praise Yahweh (34:1-3 [2-4 HB])

■ **1 [2 HB]** Before all other agendas the poet declares his intent to bless the Lord. It is a declaration made with eagerness (note the emphatic verb). He will express this blessing in every single circumstance and will do so without interruption.

■ **2 [3 HB]** *My soul* [*nepeš*] **will boast** in the LORD, says the psalmist. The expression is roughly interchangeable with the simple pronoun, *I will boast . . .* , but names the psalmist as a flesh-and-blood person. It also provides a full word for the subject in v 2*a* [3*a* HB], yielding a nicely balanced 3 + 3 bicolon.

While boasting over one's own person or accomplishments would not be a virtue, boasting in Yahweh as the focus of the boast shifts from the psalmist to Yahweh from whom come all good gifts. Not only is such redirected boasting virtuous, but also it brings joy to the lowly who hear these boasts. The fact that another has cause to boast of Yahweh's deliverance gives glad anticipation that relief may be close at hand for them as well.

Verse 2*b* [3*b* HB] is one of a number of lines in this psalm in which the poet plays with sound to lovely effect. The purpose and scope of this commentary does not allow frequent comment on the numerous lines that catch one's eye. But here is one: *The lowly will hear* [*yišmĕʿû . . .*] *and be glad* (*yiśmāḥû*). Lovely!

■ **3 [4 HB]** The psalmist's invitation for others to join his song of praise would seem to indicate that at least part of this psalm had its roots in temple liturgy. He seeks a community of praise, moving from **me** to **us**. Although no tight logic controls these opening lines, perhaps one can discern a particularizing movement from the general declaration in v 2 to the aspects of that declared praise in vv 3-4. These include the hortatory verbs in v 3.

2. Foundations of Praise (34:4-10 [5-11 HB])

a. The Psalmist's Own Deliverance (34:4-6 [5-7 HB])

■ **4 [5 HB]** Now the poet shifts from praise to testimony about memorable deliverance. The testimony supports the call to praise. It recalls an incident or incidents when he sought Yahweh and found in him a saving answer. "Seeking" (*drš*) Yahweh has the sense of making supplication for an answer or a word or a deliverance, not looking for something or someone lost. The fact that Yahweh's response involved deliverance from **all** the psalmist's **fears** indicates multiple situations difficult or dangerous enough to generate trepidation and anxiety. From all these distresses Yahweh has delivered him.

■ **5 [6 HB]** If we follow the MT in this *ḥet* line, we lack a subject for the claim that *They look(ed) to him and are radiant; their faces are never ashamed.* One can supply that missing subject, as for example, the NJPS's "Men look to Him" or the NIV's **Those who look to him are radiant.** The most direct solution, I think, is to follow the LXX in reading the opening verb as an exhortation and in making necessary, related emendations (so RSV). The exhortation sits well in this series of lines that move back and forth between exhortation (vv 5, 7, 9 [6, 8, 10 HB]) and declaration (vv 4, 6, 10 [5, 7, 11 HB]).

The metaphor itself of looking to Yahweh is especially interesting in that Yahweh cannot be seen. He has no image and no visage literally to be seen. "Seeing" Yahweh then involves a turning of one's attention so fully to God that one actually apprehends his being, his presence.

■ **6 [7 HB]** Another testimony, somewhat parallel to that in v 4 [5 HB], speaks of Yahweh's deliverance in response to prayer. Framed in the third person and speaking of himself a bit formally, the psalmist describes himself as an *ānî*, **a poor, afflicted one** (pl., *ăniwîm*, compare v 3). He is among an identifiable cultic and social group. "At the mercy of powerful enemies and forces at work in society" these powerless ones lay out their desperate situations, turn to God, appeal to God, trust in his intervention and rejoice at his intervention (Gerstenberger 2001b, 246).

He continues his testimony: Yahweh had delivered him. The fact that Yahweh **saved him out of all his troubles** shows something of his plight (**from all his** *troublers* in the parallel line in v 4 [5 HB]). He has been under assault enough for his fears to become a trap and a drag on him.

b. The Goodness of Yahweh (34:7-8 [8-9 HB])

■ **7 [8 HB]** With a military image the psalmist claims **the angel of the LORD encamps around those who fear him**. The acrostic flow draws the verb, *ḥônêh*/**camps**, emphatically to the head of the *ḥet* line. This messenger of Yahweh is present, near in the sense of intervening to save. That is one of the benefits of those who **fear** Yahweh. Such a ***messenger*/angel** of Yahweh comes from the heavenly court and does the bidding of Yahweh (compare 103:19-22).

■ **8 [9 HB]** Once again the psalmist exhorts his fellow congregants (compare v 3 [4 HB]), this time to **taste and see that the LORD is good**. "Tasting" Yahweh, it appears by v 8*b* [9*b* HB], will involve taking **refuge** in Yahweh. **Taste** here would mean to experiment with trusting Yahweh and discovering that trust is rewarded. The one who tastes is profoundly **blessed** by taking **refuge in *Yahweh***. This taking **refuge** vocabulary brackets the last half of this poem, here in v 8 [9 HB] describing the one who "tastes" Yahweh and there in v 22 [23 HB] giving the stance of the servants Yahweh redeems. If we go with the NIV here—"The LORD will rescue his servants"—we do well to note that redemption is the particular sort of "rescue" the poet had in mind (with most modern versions). Beyond that the opening poems of the Psalter pronounce supremely happy (i.e., "blessed") those "who take refuge" in God's anointed one (2:12).

c. No Lack for Godfearers (34:9-10 [10-11 HB])

■ **9-10 [10-11 HB]** Another foundational concept, *fearing Yahweh*, opens v 9 [10 HB]. Several words carrying this idea have already surfaced in this psalm (compare vv 4 and 7 [5 and 8 HB]). **Fear** occurs now twice in v 9 [10 HB] and will surface again in v 11 [12 HB]. Early in Israel's history and then increasingly so, "fearing Yahweh" became one of the most frequently used expressions to describe persons who trusted Yahweh and kept his covenant joyfully and faithfully. (See Deut 6:2, 24; 10:12; 31:12, 13; Josh 24:14; 1 Sam 12:24; Pss 19:9; 111:10; Prov 1:7; 2:5; 19:23; Mal 4:2.) In this psalm **those who fear Yahweh** are protected by Yahweh's guard, a source of great blessing. They are numbered among **his holy people.** Living with plenty, they are known as teachers. These who take refuge in Yahweh really **lack nothing**.

3. Instruction in the Fear of Yahweh (34:11-22 [12-23 HB])

a. Living for Love of Life (34:11-14 [12-15 HB])

■ **11-14 [12-15 HB]** These lifestyle concepts—such as fearing the Lord and taking refuge in the Lord—are sufficiently defined that they can be taught. In a section reminiscent of wisdom instruction, the psalmist offers to teach his "sons" **the fear of *Yahweh*** (e.g., Prov 2:1; 3:1). "Sons" is probably a designation for the student in ancient teaching/learning situations, although it could address the psalmist's children as well.

The **fear of *Yahweh*** has several important and practical repercussions. It engenders longevity and a love of life (v 12 [13 HB]). It supports honest and grace-giving speech (v 13 [14 HB]), by developing character compatible with such use of the tongue. It builds character so that persons regularly choose good and reject evil (v 14 [15 HB]). These persons assume responsibility for their own actions, guided by Torah.

b. Yahweh and the Brokenhearted (34:15-21 [16-22 HB])

■ **15-21 [16-22 HB]** The psalmist turns now from concepts of fearing Yahweh and being good to the involvement of Yahweh in such living. Yahweh's involvement in life supports growth in grace longed for in this poem. This involves Yahweh's awareness of the circumstances and doings of both the righteous and the wicked (vv 15-16 [16-17 HB]). He is neither confused nor in the dark regarding human being and doing. He actively hears their cry (v 15 [16 HB]). He has particular interest in persons who make evil choices (v 16 [17 HB]). This spells disaster for those who do evil. On the other hand, he has a special interest in those whose hearts are broken, whose spirits are crushed (vv 16-18 [17-19 HB]). The Lord's interest translates into saving action for these needy ones. He rescues (vv 4 [5 HB], 17 [18 HB], 19 [20 HB]), redeems (v 22 [23 HB]), saves (v 6 [7 HB]), answers (v 4 [5 HB]), hears (v 6 [7 HB]), takes over (v 7 [8 HB]).

A note on poetry (v 19 [20 HB]: the *rēš* line exhibits alliteration (the series of "r's") and assonance (similar interior sound, the series of "a" sounds). Many/*rabbôt* [*are the*] troubles/*ra'ôt* [of the] righteous/*ṣaddîq*.

c. Codicil: Yahweh Redeems His Servants (34:22 [23 HB])

■ **22 [23 HB]** A concluding line is added, filling out the twenty-two lines of this alphabetic poem in lieu of the lost *waw* line. It makes two substantial claims. Positively Yahweh redeems his servants' lives. Negatively, those who take **refuge in him will** not **be condemned**. The positive claim pictures Yahweh's servants captured and held for ransom, their lives to be forfeited unless the ransom price is met. Yahweh's habit (note the ptc.) is to redeem the lives of his servants.

Alternatively, those who take refuge in him are pictured as indicted, evidence mounting of their guilt. But his servants have cried out to Yahweh, pleading for his mercy and deliverance from the court. He persuades the court of their innocence—exposing the false witnesses enlisted by their enemies—and assumes the cost of any real guilt they have.

FROM THE TEXT

Two ways NT writers use OT texts are illustrated in Ps 34. First, Peter quotes Ps 34:12-16 [13-17 HB] to present the specifics of Christian life in which, following Christ, believers speak blessing in response to reviling (1 Pet 3:10-12). In this case disciples of Jesus and OT followers of Torah are called to the same behavior and promised blessing for it.

Second, Ps 34:20 [21 HB] and John 19:36 have different contexts. But the wording of Ps 34:20 describing the righteous man as one who will keep all his bones, not a one of them being broken, supplies just the words John needs to describe the situation of Jesus, the quintessential righteous sufferer. Both of these uses of the OT Jesus would probably have called "fulfillment."

This song's strong contribution to Christian faith is its call to a life of praise and its model for buttressing that life. Psalm 34 calls for a life of nonstop praise, bringing to mind Paul's exhortation to give thanks always for everything (Eph 5:20; compare Col 3:17). It commits the psalmist to a life dominated by and marinated in praise. This call and commitment, then, are informed by personal testimony to deliverance by Yahweh. They are buttressed by personal experience of the goodness of God and encouraged by strong teaching regarding the goodness of life lived taking refuge in Yahweh.

Prayer for Vindication and Rescue (35:1-28)

BEHIND THE TEXT

Psalm 35 offers a standard example of the prayer of an individual for rescue from persecution and distress. Even so it is clear that the psalmist speaks for a group of persons who share his distress (vv 27, 28) and reports his adversity as the work of a host of wicked (vv 24-26). The repetitive movement of this psalm makes discernment of a clear outline difficult. Repeatedly the poet registers a complaint or voices a request to the Lord, with the complaint or the request then followed by a series of descriptions of either the psalmist or his adversaries, either commending his innocence or exposing their guilt. There is emphasis in the repetition, but not much discernible movement.

IN THE TEXT

1. Fight My Battles for Me (35:1-10)

■ **1-3** The psalmist pictures his spiritual and moral battles (v 1) with the language of armed warfare. He starts with prayers for Yahweh to **contend** for him, that is, to press his legal contention, and moves quickly to talk of a **shield** (v 2) and the wielding of **spear and javelin** (v 3; or perhaps a battle-ax, *HALOT*, 743). These prayers tap deep into the ancient tradition of Yahweh as a warrior. They also use vocabulary illuminated by art and artifacts known from Israel's world (Keel 1997, 218-25). In addition, the psalmist prays for an awareness spoken to him by Yahweh himself that Yahweh is the psalmist's salvation.

We have enough information in these opening lines to say our poet is under legal attack. An accusation has been leveled; his reputation and standing in the community are at stake.

■ **4-6** He prays now for Yahweh to turn the schemes of the wicked ironically back on their heads. Although both the conflict and the instruments of battle include metaphor, it appears that the struggle itself is not only real but mortal conflict as well. There are **those who seek** [the psalmist's] **life** and who **plot** [his] **ruin** (v 4).

Stressing his own innocence ("without cause" twice in v 7), the psalmist prays that the destiny promised the wicked would appear in the life of his adversaries. His prayer is that they would **be like chaff** driven by **the wind** (v 5), indeed driven by the force of Yahweh's **angel** himself (v 6).

■ **7-10** These verses exhibit a strange, compact repetitive style that underscores the innocence of the psalmist, the guilt of his adversaries, and the consequences for which the psalmist prays. Twice in v 7 we are told the adversaries acted **without cause**. The behaviors of these persons would be evil even if caused. But the psalmist feels especially assaulted because of his innocence. He prays for retribution particularly well suited to the infractions committed by his enemies—thus, having **dug a pit**, that the wicked will fall in it; having laid the snare, that the perverse will be caught in it (compare vv 7, 8).

When this happens **all [his] bones will say, "Who is like you, O Yahweh?"** (v 10). This unusual expression, **all one's bones**, is a palpable way of referring to one's whole self. The NIV translates it well, **My whole being will exclaim.** The force of this introduction matches the breadth of the exclamation: "Who is like you?" Of course the answer anticipated by this rhetorical question is the resounding "*No one* is like you, O Yahweh! You are incomparable" (compare Pss 71:19; 89:8 [9 HB]; and Mic 7:18).

And the point of Yahweh's incomparability celebrated here is his penchant for siding with the disadvantaged, the materially and culturally poor. Yahweh puts his strength at the service of those who are overpowered by their enemies. This describes Yahweh's habit, not exception to his rule.

2. Requite the Guilt of the Psalmist's Enemies (35:11-21)

■ **11** Some of the enemies the psalmist faces are **witnesses** known for their violence. These are hostile **witnesses** that raise questions beyond the competence of the psalmist. These **witnesses** aim to intimidate more than they want to effect justice. These lines take us all the way back to v 1, where the legal terminology began in the call for Yahweh to "contend," which had its setting in a legal proceeding.

One of the weapons of the adversaries is surprise, bringing before the court matters that are unknown to the psalmist. Most English versions, following the LXX, are probably right in understanding the surprise to be the range of questions being asked, rather than the identity of the witnesses.

■ **12** Several lines now stress the impiety of his enemies and the contrasting innocence of the psalmist. And not simply his innocence but his demonstrated, pious character. Generally, he claims, the protagonists have repaid him **evil for good**, leaving him feeling **bereaved**.

■ **13-14** The psalmist, on the other hand, has responded to news of his enemies' illnesses and adversities with rites of grief and concern appropriate to the community. He dressed in **sackcloth**, engaged in **fasting** and prayer as though it were his own **friend** or **brother** or even his **mother** that was ill. This exemplary behavior, in stark contrast to his adversaries, at one and the same time underscores his innocence and emphasizes the guilt of his enemies.

These lines may give clues to the sort of adversity the poet faces. Simple disagreement or slander is not the problem. Rather, the psalmist's enemies were once his friends, persons to whom he gave significant aid and support. Now a breach has occurred; those who accepted his aid now accuse and abuse him.

◾ **15-16** Once again the poet emphasizes the culpability of his foes by describing their despicable behavior. They not only seek to do him harm but also delight in his suffering. Unfortunately the MT of v 16a nearly defies confident translation. Compare the NIV, **Like the ungodly they maliciously mocked**, and the ESV, "Like profane mockers at a feast." When such striking differences surface in the versions, one can be sure the MT carries unsolved riddles. Even so, it is clear these tormenters are intent in making the psalmist's life miserable.

◾ **17-18** The psalmist's **How long**? question is, of course, not an inquiry looking for a timed response. It rather expresses disappointment and urgency. He needs and wants deliverance now! Sooner, not later! These are **lions** with which he deals and devastating events from which he needs rescue. When that rescue comes he will publish it to the whole congregation.

◾ **19-21** Their speech is totally inappropriate. The psalmist's enemies are gleeful when they deceive (v 19a). They make unprovoked, hateful gestures (winks, mouth gestures) (vv 19b-21). Their talk is disruptive and filled with deceit (vv 20-21). They can be counted on to disrupt the peace of the community. Just what the gestures are to which the poet returns we do not know. Of this we can be sure—they were signs of disdain, rejection, mockery, and personal attack understood by all.

3. Contend for the Innocent Psalmist (35:22-28)

◾ **22-26** A series of requests asks Yahweh to leave the sidelines and enter the fray immediately. In view of what you have seen, O God, speak up (v 22)! Wake up (v 23) and judge my case (v 24a)! Stop their revelry over my plight (vv 24b-25). Bring **shame** to those who celebrate my troubles (v 26).

◾ **27-28** On the other hand engender boisterous praise in those who applaud **my vindication**. Inspire these colleagues continually to say, **The Lord be exalted, who delights in the well-being of his servant** (v 27). He promises to ponder Yahweh's justice and engage **all day** in his praise (v 28). These lines climax a theme of praise that has run throughout this song. Even in trouble the psalmist is eager to praise (vv 9, 10, 18, 27-28).

FROM THE TEXT

The genius of these prayers for deliverance from accusation and persecution is that the business of reconciliation is brought right into the temple. They provide liturgical means for facing community breaches, language with which to say what one is thinking about friends who have betrayed you or enemies who still harass.

Christians might benefit from keeping these prayers in mind when they are thinking of exercising the Matt 18:15-20 option.

Prayer for Yahweh's Keeping Love (36:1-12 [2-13 HB])

BEHIND THE TEXT

Considerable disagreement exists regarding the genre of this poem. Nine of twelve lines provide instruction regarding the deeds and character of the wicked (vv 1-4 [2-5 HB]) and then of Yahweh (vv 5-9 [6-10 HB]). The latter unit moves into prayer language (i.e., second person address of Yahweh). Then the poem ends with petitions and claims typical of the individual prayer for help (vv 10-12 [11-13 HB]). Because of this ending, we follow Gerstenberger in designating this a prayer of the individual (he has "complaint") (1988, 156). Because of the two opening sections one can understand seeing the poem as instruction of some kind, though wisdom language is not prominent. The poem is brief, but the MT bristles with difficulties.

The SS carries a distinctive designation of David as the **servant of Yahweh** [v 1 HB], only here and in the SS of Ps 18. Especially in the form "my servant," Yahweh positions himself as King or Lord with the prerogative of appointing particular persons to special service for him. One thinks especially of Abraham (Gen 26:24), Moses (Num 12:7-8), Joshua (Josh 24:29); even outside God's people, he commissions Cyrus (Isa 44:28) and Nebuchadnezzar (Jer 25:9) as his special agents. Recall that at the end of Ps 35 David identified himself as Yahweh's servant.

IN THE TEXT

1. Life without Fear of Yahweh (36:1-4 [2-5 HB])

■ **1 [2 HB]** The opening lines present syntactic difficulties as yet unsolved. The MT's *nĕ'um* appears almost without exception as the prescript or postscript of an oracle. Kidner honors that pattern in translating "An oracle of Transgression is deep in his [the wicked one's] heart" (1973, 145-46). The ESV's "Transgression speaks to the wicked deep in his heart" (compare, similarly, the RSV and NASB) follows the LXX in personifying "transgression." If we go this direction, Weiser's insight is worth mentioning. "It is obvious that the psalmist wishes to say by using that phrase: the voice of sin which man hears speaking in his heart has for the wicked the same authority and power as the voice of God has for the prophets" (1962, 307). But neither of these makes real clear sense, nor do most other attempts (see Kraus 1988, 396-99, for a summary of options).

I have a message from God in my heart concerning the sinfulness of the wicked makes progress by allowing the MT's *nĕ'um* outside its normal syntax as a simple noun. *Peša'* names the sinner's preoccupation as spiritual rebellion, insurrection against the God of Israel. That the wicked one lives with no fear (*paḥad*) of God is a strong claim because of the vocabulary choice. *Paḥad* has a heavy dose of fright in it and is not generally the word choice when the author/speaker wants to talk about the "fear of Yahweh"; normally *yir'âh* would be the choice. While *yir'âh* can carry the idea of fright, it generally has a softer nuance. But this sinner is not afraid of God.

■ **2-4 [3-5 HB]** This is because sinners handle things to their own advantage, flattering selves. As a result they find nothing in themselves to hate. But their speech betrays their character, full of deception and idolatry (v 3 [4 HB]); these habits will bring their prosperity to an end.

A tricolon brings the first paragraph to conclusion. The thoroughgoing evil of these persons proves evident, **even as they ponder wickedness on their beds**. Against the habits of the truly happy one in Ps 1:1, these wicked ones deliberately take their stand along the road with the "not good" population. They do not find the wherewithal to reject evil. On the contrary their self-induced captivity to sin has them shackled.

2. Yahweh's Salvation for Humans and Beasts (36:5-9 [6-10 HB])

■ **5-6 [6-7 HB]** The poet now turns his attention to extolling the basic features of Yahweh's character that form the basis for all he has claimed and will say. Yahweh's *ḥesed*/**his loving kindness**, his *'ĕmûnâ*/**faithfulness, truthfulness**, his *ṣĕdāqâ*/**righteousness**, and his *mišpāṭ*/**justice** are the cornerstones of grasping Yahweh's person. His **loving kindness** and **faithfulness**, though known here in the blessings of Yahweh, reach to the highest heavens. That is, they reach to the realm of the gods (v 5 [6 HB]). Citing opposites, the psalmist claims Yahweh's **righteousness** could be compared to **the highest mountains** (lit. *the mountains of God*), and his **justice** to the fathomless, **great deep**. In v 6c [7c HB] Yahweh's **loving kindness** extends to both humans and **animals**, that is, to the full range of creation.

■ **7-8 [8-9 HB]** The realization that all life is dependent upon Yahweh's *ḥesed* evokes confession regarding the great worth of that *ḥesed*. Human beings find shelter in the **shadow of** Yahweh's **wings**, a reference to the cherubim and the ark. They feast from the abundance of Yahweh's palace (i.e., the temple). And from a luxuriant wadi, perhaps flowing out of the temple, as in Ezekiel's vision

(Ezek 47:1-12), Yahweh gives them to drink. Or the psalmist may simply have in mind here Yahweh's lavish provision for all his world.

■ **9 [10 HB]** The reason humans and beasts all flourish in Yahweh's luxuriant provisions, says the psalmist, is that Yahweh himself is the source of **life**. And Yahweh's own **light** shows the way to light for living. The meditation on the wicked with which the psalm opens implies also that these persons are a threat to the righteous. We recall that all this talk of provisions is metaphor for the characteristics of Yahweh, especially his *hesed* that sustains his people.

3. Extend Your Love, Yahweh (36:10-12 [11-13 HB])

■ **10 [11 HB]** Now the petitions flowing from reflection on Yahweh's character. **Continue your love to those who know you, your righteousness to the upright in heart.** It could be a temporal extension, as the NIV has it. It could be a demographic extension, that is, *Extend your love, let your love reach* to all **who know you**, all you people.

■ **11-12 [12-13 HB]** The arrogant **foot** and **hand** of the **wicked** represent the threat the **wicked** pondered earlier. Supremely arrogant, committed to evil, fearless before God—in the face of this evil the psalmist knows his need for Yahweh's protection (i.e., his *hesed*). A concluding description of the defeat of the wicked has the force of affirming the victory of Yahweh in response to the preceding prayer.

FROM THE TEXT

Paul quotes v 1 [2 HB] as the climax of his catena exposing the sinfulness of all human beings: "There is no fear of God before their eyes" (Rom 3:18). Psalm 1 contrasts the wicked with the righteous, Ps 36 the wicked with the love of God. The glory of the gospel expounded in the book of Romans as a whole is that the psalmist's prayer for victory over human sin and arrogance has been answered. "The Spirit" of God in Christ Jesus "has set [us] free from the [way] of sin and death" (Rom 8:1; see vv 1-4), both bridging the chasm between us sinners and our Creator and enabling us to live his will.

A Teaching: Trust Yahweh; Don't Fret (37:1-40)

BEHIND THE TEXT

Along with psalms 9/10, 25, 34, 111, 112, 119, and 145, Ps 37 is an acrostic poem. With some exceptions the first letter of every two lines carries the abecedary pattern. There are three lines, not two, under the *het* (vv 14-15). And there is no *'ayin* line (compare v 28c).

The acrostic design has complicated development of a detailed, extended outline in this poem, as in the other acrostics seen to this point in the Psalter. But three concerns receive repeated emphasis in this psalm: (1) avoiding anger at evildoers, especially the powerful, rich evildoers; (2) the doings of the righteous and the wicked; and (3) the contrasting futures of these persons.

The acrostic form and the focused study of "the two ways" suggest a didactic purpose for this piece and probably a source in the wisdom community. Perhaps the most obvious feature of the psalm is the string of fifteen hortatory expressions within the first eight verses. These exhortations, such as **Do not fret because of . . . evil** (v 1), remind one of the book of Proverbs. They also suggest a teaching community, such as the wisdom instructors, as the source of this piece. Just how such compositions might have figured in the community's worship remains unclear. The poem itself provides no clues to liturgical use. The exhortations are all singulars, addressed to a solitary reader.

For the brief SS, see the Introduction, C.1.a, on *lĕdāwîd*.

IN THE TEXT

I. Guidance for Responding to Sinners (37:1-11)

Attempts at an outline beyond the verses tied together by the string of exhortations mentioned above prove difficult. Several topics cycle through the poem without a clear plan. Although these verses are concerned with more than "sinners," they present the largest single agenda.

■ **1** ['] The first three words of the poem express its most prominent concern: **Do not fret because of . . . evil**. **Fret** picks up the reflexive aspect of the verb (*tithar* > *ḥārāh*). But **fret** seems too tame to render adequately a word usually invested in actual anger, not just inner turmoil. **Nor be envious of evildoers**. The issue is just plain jealousy over what these people often have, largely due to their lack of scruples. This attitude mixes well with the fretful anger of v 1a and is to be avoided.

■ **2** This bicolon supports the opening exhortation by providing a reason anger and jealousy directed at the wicked is such folly. Why? Because they and their accomplishments are so ephemeral.

■ **3** [*b*] The exhortation to **Trust in the LORD and do good** provides a brilliant companion to the opening directives against angry and jealous fuming over evildoers. As a matter of fact, **trust in *Yahweh*** is actually the issue at stake in the anger and envy proscribed in v 1. Can Yahweh provide adequately for his people or can he not? Do we need more than he has provided to be satisfied?

Doing good takes control of one's own life. The psalmist cannot control the attitudes and actions of the wicked, but they can control their own doings. ***Doing good*** asserts by behavior that God's people **do good** because they choose to live faithful to the covenant come what may.

Dwell in the land and enjoy safe pasture. Another interest of this poem surfaces here: the inheritance of the land (compare also vv 9, 11, 22, 27, 29, 34). One wonders whether there may be signs here of competing approaches to inheriting the land. One approach involves peaceful pasturing; the other, by contrast, would involve taking over a neighbor's land violently (Kraus 1988, 405-6). Some English versions take the last half-line as referring to enjoying safe pasture, which is possible (NEB, REB). The ASV's "feed on his faithfulness" is difficult to decipher. The NJPS's "abide in the land and remain loyal" stays with the issue of Israel's relationship with the land. Retaining that emphasis I might translate, ***Dwell in the land and shepherd (your flocks) with integrity.***

■ **4** The insight that **delight** in Yahweh is the clearest path to getting what you really want presses the concerns of v 1 even further. Here the realization of one's deep desires is a by-product of delighting most in Yahweh himself (compare 73:25-28). The opening word of the line is a strong word, urging ***sheer, exquisite delight*** in the Lord.

■ **5** [g] We can paraphrase this admonition, ***Roll the burdens of your journey off onto Yahweh. Depend on him; he can handle it all.*** Commit your way—way in the sense of life's journey and all the burdens and challenges that come with it. **Trust in him** states plainly the crux of the metaphor in v 5a. Rolling life's burdens off onto the Lord is an act of profound trust. We should confidently do this because, says the psalmist, Yahweh will respond appropriately. Literally, ***and he will act***: *wĕhû' ya'ăśeh*. The final verb, *ya'ăśeh*, nine times out of ten expects a direct object, something the subject does or makes. Here used "absolutely" (standing alone) it invites some such assurance as ***he will handle it all.***

■ **6** Verse 6 appears to state the effect/result of the trust in v 5. The psalmist will have demonstrated his integrity, or to be more precise, Yahweh will have brought his indirection out into the light of midday for all to see. The promise of vindication implies the need of it. At the moment, apparently, the psalmist may be the brunt of accusation and legal duress. It is possible that those of which he is tempted to be jealous and angry at in vv 1-2 may be persons trampling the psalmist's character and bringing it into question.

■ **7** [d] The best response to these attacks is to place oneself quietly before Yahweh and wait there patiently. The exhortation not to be angry when the wicked succeed in their plans is repeated in succeeding lines. To say the psalmist is concerned about this issue is an understatement for sure. At least in these opening lines, the opposite of trusting Yahweh, of living with a sense of inner quiet, with sheer joy and pleasure is this corrosive anger, this toxic jealousy at the successes of the wicked.

■ **8 [*h*]-9 Refrain from anger** pictures a person releasing his hold on **anger**, letting it go. No need to hold on to this destructive set of mind. It can only lead to evil.

The predictable bad results of this disquiet counsel against it. But that is not all. In addition, the wicked who generate such destructive frustration **will be destroyed**. How we are not told, but they will actually be **destroyed**. On the other hand, those who make Yahweh their **hope**, these shall **inherit the land**. Those who schemed and connived to get land not legitimately theirs will lose what they have. Those who trust Yahweh will actually get their inheritance.

■ **10 [*w*]-11** The [*w*] lines extend the reasons why we as readers should heed the teacher's admonitions and let go of our anger. Why? Because the destruction of the **wicked** is not only assured but also close at hand. Soon. A search of the wicked one's former haunts will be in vain; there will be no sign of the **wicked**. The repetition of several words may form a loose inclusio to mark the end of this opening, hortatory unit (compare **land** [vv 3, 11]; "delight"/**enjoy** ['*ng*] [vv 4, 11]; and "those who are evil" [vv 1, 9]).

2. Doings and Destiny of the Wicked (37:12-27)

■ **12 [*z*]-13** Earlier lines have warned against the preoccupation of the godly with the doings of the **wicked** (compare vv 1, 7, 8). Now it becomes clear that the **wicked** also obsess about the **righteous**, scheming to do them harm and publically intimidating them. Yahweh finds this behavior laughable, because he knows the end of the story, the fate of the **wicked**.

■ **14 [*ḥ*]-15** Talk of swords and bows is stock material but should not be ignored. These were no doubt life-and-death quarrels over fundamental matters of faith in Yahweh. But they also work metaphorically, allowing appropriation by readers faced only with serious battles with words.

But Yahweh has made a world where those who would slay with the **sword** often find themselves pierced by it, and the drawn **bow** splintering in the hands of the one who drew it. This is the nature of the world, says the teacher. It is not that Yahweh takes the **sword** and wields it. This is just how the **wicked** find the world.

■ **16 [*ṭ*] Better the little that the righteous have than the wealth of many wicked.** That's what the proverb says, according to the NIV and several other English versions (e.g., NABRE, REB). It contrasts financial resources (**wealth**). Those renderings are probably better, however, that leave the nature of the resources unspecified, translating "abundance of many wicked" (e.g., ESV, NRSV, RSV; compare NJPS). The Hebrew word involved can rightly be taken either way. But the teaching is more likely about the whole life experience of the **righteous** and the **wicked**, not simply about their financial dealings.

■ **17** And that is how v 17 probably understands it, because the reason given for this state of affairs is a general claim about how resources come to be adequate or not. The strength of the **wicked** (their physical, spiritual, moral, financial resources) **will** eventually **be broken**. On their own they will not have unending, unfailing resources. On the other hand, the **righteous** have ongoing strength not because of a relatively larger "supply" of resources, but rather because of the support of Yahweh. And Yahweh's resources never fail.

■ **18** [*y*] Translations that state the matter of Yahweh's knowing with the grammatical passive are acceptable. But the active voice, **The blameless spend their days under the Lord's care**, more adequately preserves Yahweh's providential engagement in this knowing (also LXX and RSV).

The proverb is not mainly about Yahweh's awareness of data—he has full information about the days of **the blameless**. No, this returns the reader to 1:6, where the knowing of Yahweh spells the difference between flourishing and perishing. That's why NJPS renders this "The Lord is concerned for the needs of the blameless," and the REB, "The Lord watches over the upright."

And it is with **the blameless** that the proverb deals, not simply the upright or the righteous. That is the particular semantic niche this noun fills. And it is a programmatic niche reaching in its verbal form all the way back to El Shaddai's covenant with and command to Abraham (Gen 17:1-2). The psalmist has not turned Pelagian, and the theological issue has not suddenly become how **the blameless** earn their salvation. It is about the fact that God calls his people to live with full loyalty and faithfulness to him and that a group of people called **the blameless** did just that.

■ **19** More likely we should stick with the MT and say the proverb claims the upright will never be shamed by their God. In difficult times he will provide for them (compare Joel 2:16-17). They will have **plenty** during **famine**.

■ **20** [*k*] These lines take the reader back to Ps 1 with the claim that the **wicked** simply **perish**. The enemies of Yahweh fade away like precious pasture. The general sense is clear, but the lines can be scanned several ways that make tolerable sense, none of which is strongly convincing. I am inclined to read two bicola with 3 + 2 rhythm: *For the wicked perish, even the enemies of Yahweh; like prize pasture they fade away, fading away in smoke.*

■ **21-22** [*l*] The issues here are generosity and integrity. The **wicked** take loans, secured by their promise to repay. But they do not honor their promise. The **righteous**, on the other hand, even though they know these facts of life, still exercise grace and give as there is need. Those who are blessed of Yahweh **will inherit the land** as part of that blessing. They need not resort to stingy dealings to get that inheritance (compare v 17). Those under Yahweh's curse will not inherit the land, their stinginess notwithstanding.

■ **23** [*m*]-**24** Again the poet places in tandem (*a*) the path a person chooses, (*b*) Yahweh's evaluative response to those chosen steps, and (*c*) Yahweh's consequent providential engagement in that chosen way, affecting the durability of the chosen way. Verse 24 describes one way this plays out. The person who **stumbles** will not lie dashed to pieces, because Yahweh gives support **with his hand**.

■ **25** [*n*] The teacher makes a bold claim. Once **young**, now **old**, the teacher has **never seen the righteous forsaken or their children begging bread**. This tricolon reveals the genre of our poem. It is instructional wisdom, not disputational. Readers would have known, of course, that the teacher's claim is hotly contested. One thinks only of Job 21 and 24 where the patriarch reports a very different take on life, denying any dependability in God's providential provision for the needy. But debate over these issues is for another day and another composition. This acrostic inculcates thoroughgoing trust in God's goodness, not out of ignorance but from didactic purpose.

■ **26** The claim in Ps 37:25 is supported in part by the character of those who have received from Yahweh's hand. These people are **generous** persons, providing loans for those in need. **Their children** are conduits of the Lord's **blessing**.

■ **27** [*s*] Talk of the consequences of locating oneself among those who trust in Yahweh and delight in his ways (vv 3, 4) leads inevitably to the exhortation to **Turn from evil and do good**. This turning would be both a definable event and a way of life. Persons who **turn from evil and do good** would be those who *trust in Yahweh* (v 3), *who delight in Yahweh* (v 4), *who roll their way over onto the Lord* (v 5), *who quiet themselves before Yahweh* (v 7), and *who let go of anger and wrath* (v 8) for starters. Added to these descriptors, which are mainly attitudinal, these persons also act out their trust of Yahweh by *doing good*.

Most English versions translate v 27*b* as the result of v 27*a*, like the RSV: "Depart from evil . . . , so shall you abide for ever." Better, perhaps, to follow the MT and LXX and treat **dwell**/*šekōn* as imperative, as does Goldingay (2006, 516). The causal reading makes sense, of course, but stumbles on the *w-* conjunction in *wškn*. The exhortation then asks the reader to "be what you are," in OT terms. You who turn from evil are the legitimate inheritors of the land. Now live in that inheritance.

3. Observations on the Life of the Wicked (37:28-40)

■ **28** ['] Yahweh's love of justice and his unfailing commitment to his saints (his *ḥăsîdîm*) provide the basis for the exhortations in the "s" line (v 27). Yahweh's character underwrites his people's obedience and hope of endurance on the land.

These saints will be preserved forever. Their durability receives emphasis by the disruption of the acrostic precisely at the point of claiming the "to/forever" aspect of the saints' preservation (with *lĕ ʿôlām* in the [ʾ] line). In contrast, the wicked will **be cut off**, the passive implying Yahweh's hand in their demise.

■ **29** The bicolon recycles material from earlier maxims dealing with the inheritance of the land by the righteous (vv 3, 11, 18, 22). These instructions would be very much at home in the restoration period when disputes arose over land rights.

■ **30** [*p*] Another theme valued by wisdom teachers was speech, that is, the use of the tongue. We are referred again to Ps 1 and its claim that the righteous meditate on Yahweh's Torah. Here wisdom is the topic of meditation. This meditation is a type of "self-talk" that paves the way for judicious speech. First thought; then speech is the wise one's way.

■ **31** The connection between wisdom and Torah is clear in these interlocking claims about meditation. It is by meditation on wisdom materials that Yahweh's Torah finds its way into the heart. These virtues that internalize Yahweh's Torah make for stable steps.

■ **32** [*ṣ*]**-33** The **wicked** spy out the **righteous**, intending to do them harm, to kill them if possible. But Yahweh does not allow it; nor does he do them ill when their case comes up in court.

■ **34** [*q*] Waiting and hoping are linked here by faith and trust. Waiting does not settle for simply passing time. It is watching the wicked lose their land, while those setting their hope in God are inheriting theirs.

■ **35** [*r*]**-36** The poet returns to Yahweh's providential care probed earlier (vv 9, 10, 13, 16). He cites the strong contrast between the sprawling, luxuriant ***wicked one***, obvious to all who pass by his land, on the one hand, and his surprising gap, the startling absence of any signs of the wicked one's presence on the other. Even if you probe for signs of the wicked's stuff, you will come up empty-handed.

■ **37** [*š*]**-38** This pair of bicola treats the contrasting futures of **the blameless**, **the upright**, and the peaceful on the one hand and ***the transgressors*** and **wicked** on the other. The contrast is simple and blunt. The **righteous** have a future; the **wicked** do not. They will be destroyed, their **future** cut short. The so-called divine passives again hint that the tragedy to befall all the **wicked** is the work of God. This contrast is a matter of simple observation: **Consider . . . .** , says the poet (compare on v 25 above).

■ **39** [*t*] The *tau* line is disrupted by the preposing of the conjunction *w-* to the *tau* word, *wtšwʿt*. Not the sort of interruption caused by a scribal accident, this looks deliberate. We should probably translate, **And now, finally [we must acknowledge], the salvation of the righteous is from Yahweh . . .**

■ **40** Two matters that were suggested in v 37 the teacher now makes explicit. First, Yahweh (and Yahweh alone) rescues the righteous from the **wicked**. (The pronouns refer back to the righteous in v 39.) Second, it is because these persons **take refuge** in Yahweh that he saves them. This "taking of refuge" assumes the confession of need of Yahweh's salvation, and it implies trust and confidence in Yahweh as a worthy source of help. All of this he emphasizes by concluding the poem with a 3 + 3 + 2 tricolon.

FROM THE TEXT

The most direct use of Ps 37 in the NT is Jesus' use of v 11 in the beatitude, "Blessed are the meek, for they will inherit the earth" (Matt 5:5). Psalm 37 is a parade example of traditional wisdom teachings, a brilliant presentation of "the two ways" to which we were introduced already in Ps 1. Although the poem touches topics elsewhere argued among Wisdom thinkers, Ps 37 is mainly a strong personal witness. It presents testimony of actual human experience from which we are to learn, and from which we are to take comfort and instruction.

Kraus presses the point that Ps 37 is not primarily about retribution but about God and the nature of his participation in our lives (1988, 408). This may be true, but the contrasting consequences of living as a righteous person or as a wicked one are clearly delineated. Still, Kraus is correct that appeal to a theology or principle of retribution does not appear. We are called not to a principle but to Yahweh, to find refuge in him, to trust him, take sheer delight in him.

Prayer for Rescue from the Consequences of Sin (38:1-22 [2-23 HB])

BEHIND THE TEXT

Psalm 38 is a prayer for gracious correction rather than angry contention. It begins almost verbatim like Ps 6:1. The SS designates this work as a *mizmor* and as a "Davidic" psalm (on which, see the Introduction, C.1.a, C.4.a, and C.5.a). The designation *lĕhazkîr* should have to do with making remembrance or memorial and quite likely with making an offering. First Chronicles 16:4 implies as much when it brings together the offering of thank offerings, Hallel readings, and *lĕhazkîr*.

IN THE TEXT

1. Prayer for Relief from Yahweh's Angry Rebuke (38:1 [2 HB])

■ **1 [2 HB]** Only three of this psalm's twenty-two lines are devoted to prayer in the sense of petition, this bicolon and those in vv 21-22 [22-23 HB]. The rest of the psalm, vv 2-20 [3-21 HB], is prayer in the sense of converse with God but is devoted to elaborating before Yahweh the psalmist's plight. There we see the psalmist is plagued with painful and putrefying physical maladies, with crushing guilt, with harassment from adversaries.

Already in the opening petitions we learn the theological frame of reference from which the prayer makes sense. The psalmist understands his adversities as **rebuke** and **discipline** at the hand of Yahweh. The prayer is not that the psalmist experiences no **rebuke** from Yahweh but that Yahweh not **discipline** the psalmist in **anger** and **wrath**. Presumably Yahweh would **discipline** him in mercy, though this prayer does not actually state that request. Here and in Ps 6 the prayer is for deliverance from the plight.

2. The Physical, Spiritual, Personal Burden of the Psalmist (38:2-10 [3-11 HB])

■ **2 [3 HB]** The physical sufferings the psalmist endures are, in his judgment, manifestations of the anger of Yahweh. Yahweh's **arrows** (compare 91:5) have hit their target in him. Yahweh's **hand** is pressing **down** on the psalmist.

■ **3-5 [4-6 HB]** The psalmist's widespread illness, as he sees it, is due on the one hand to the anger of Yahweh and to the psalmist's sin on the other. A particularly long bicolon emphasizes this. His guilt *has gone over his head*, well put by the NIV as **overwhelmed me** (v 4 [5 HB]). His **guilt** constitutes a burden too heavy to bear. The MT can be translated either "iniquities" (ESV, NJPS, RSV) or *the guilt incurred by the iniquities*. The latter is perhaps better in the sense of pressing down like a burden. He further describes his behavior as foolishness, not so much a lack of intelligence as a deficit in moral sense (v 5 [6 HB]), but nevertheless **sinful folly**.

■ **6-8 [7-9 HB]** Physical and emotional aspects of the psalmist's misery intertwine and crush him. He has **searing pain** (v 7 [8 HB]), feels totally brought down. He goes around like one in **mourning** (v 6 [7 HB]), groaning in **anguish** (v 8 [9 HB]).

■ **9-10 [10-11 HB]** None of this is **hidden** from God. The Lord knows all of his sufferings, indeed, he is responsible for them. The Lord knows what the psalmist longs for, including what he has just divulged in prayer. Direct address of the Lord (*'ădōnāy*) here may signal a transition from prayer detailing his condition to attention to others' response to his plight. "LORD" appears only in vv 1, 15 and 21 [2, 16, 22 HB]; Lord appears in vv 9 and 15 [10 and 16 HB].

3. Family and Associates' Response to the Psalmist's Condition (38:11-20 [12-21 HB])

■ **11-20 [12-21 HB]** His family and neighbors react to his pitiful state by withdrawing, with both halves of the bicolon ending in forms of the verb "stand"/*'md* (v 11 [12 HB]). Others who would like to snare him keep right on slandering him and plotting deceptions (v 12 [13 HB]).

Because of the connection drawn between sickness and sin, the penitent will find accusers among his close **friends**. They ponder how it is that their friend or family member remains ill so long. They wonder why Yahweh reproves them, what sin the penitent has actually been hiding.

He responds to these accusations as though he were **deaf** and **mute** (v 13 [14 HB]), unwilling, as though he were actually unable to speak in response to those accusing him. Instead he places his hope solely in the LORD (v 15 [16 HB]).

The series of four bicola from v 15 to v 18 all begin with **for**/*kî* and support his silent response.

4. Plea for Yahweh's Salvation (38:21-22 [22-23 HB])

■ **21-22 [22-23 HB]** Two bicola with four petitions conclude the penitent's prayer. He prays not to be deserted. For God to be near means for him to act on the psalmist's behalf. Not only does he ask for Yahweh to act on his behalf, but also he claims his LORD is his salvation, his help in person. In the course of these prayers, he names Yahweh, the covenant God of Israel (v 21*a* [22*a* HB]), he calls Yahweh **my God** (v 21*b* [22*b* HB]), and affirms Yahweh as **my Lord**, *'ădōnāy* (v 22 [23 HB]).

FROM THE TEXT

The OT's "majority report" joins this penitential prayer in seeing a close tie between sin and sickness. Struggle with chronic illness signaled guilt for sin that needed to be confessed. Even though that close tie is questioned at some points in the OT and repudiated in the NT (John 9), it is still wise to begin prayer for healing with confession of sin. To say there is not a direct tie between the two is not to say there is no connection. This song would be an encouragement to such prayer.

Prayer of the Transient Sinner (39:1-13 [2-14 HB])

BEHIND THE TEXT

Broadly speaking, Ps 39 is the prayer of an individual (a *tĕpîllâ*). Specifically it reads like the thoughts of a writer in the wisdom tradition, a literary, private song, with no signs of association with the worship apparatus.

This is a strange little prayer that depends on the reader's seeing between the lines to make sense of it. Apparently the psalmist is or has just been very ill, perhaps in danger of dying (vv 9, 10, 11, 13 [10, 11, 12, 14 HB]). Apparently also some evil acquaintances are threatening him (v 1 [2 HB]). It carries a pessimistic outlook and an intense awareness of the brevity and ephemeral nature of human life. These are the sorts of prayer thoughts Qohelet could have prayed, had he a bit more faith (Craigie 1983, 308).

For more information on the SS, check C.1.a, C.1.b, C.1.h, and C.4.a in the Introduction.

IN THE TEXT

1. The Poet's Troubled Silence (39:1-3 [2-4 HB])

■ **1-3 [2-4 HB]** The psalmist opens his prayer by unveiling his inner turmoil. For fear of sinning with his words, he resolves not to speak but instead to **muzzle** himself while the **wicked** are present (vv 1-2 [2-3 HB]). Then he decides to remain quiet even when conversation could have been on noble topics. Information in the context leads us to think the **wicked** he mentioned were persons of means, who had accumulated goods, heaped up with fanfare, in spite of the fact that no one knew where their treasure would wind up when they died (vv 4-6 [5-7 HB]).

But these resolves only increased his disquiet. The questions raised by these matters pained him. His **heart** burned within him (vv 2-3 [3-4 HB]). The poet describes this inner burning with the expression used in Torah to designate the passion with which the angry blood avenger pursued the one under warrant and fleeing for his life (compare Deut 19:6).

Because of the intensity of the poet's inner struggles and because of the possibility of his distress actually leading him into sin (Ps 39:2 [3 HB]), one suspects the issue at stake is the suffering of the righteous and the apparent prospering of the wicked. This sort of reflection easily moves from investigation to indictment, to reservations about the justice of Yahweh.

2. The Ephemeral Nature of Human Life (39:4-6 [5-7 HB])

■ **4-6 [5-7 HB]** Instead of pursuing the question of God's justice, the psalmist turns to questions regarding his own existence. His petitions center on one, perhaps two critical points. He asks Yahweh to let him see the **end** of his own existence. The Hebrew term in the MT and the LXX Greek vocabulary selection usually mean **end** in the sense of terminus, edge, boundary, or the like, not end in the sense of goal or purpose. It is possible that the psalmist does ask about the purpose of his life (so Craigie 1983, 309). But it is more likely he asks in both v 4*a* and 4*b* [5 HB] about the extent of his **days**, and implicitly then about the significance of his life.

He acknowledges how brief the **number of** his **days**. Their **span** would be measured with a **handbreadth**, four fingers wide, the smallest measure of width in the OT (v 5 [6 HB]; Jer 52:21); like nothing before God himself! Three cola, each beginning with the emphatic particle (*'Ak/surely!*), elaborate on this brevity of life and the corresponding pessimism about significance of human life. *'Ak/surely* everyone, even standing full height is a mere **breath**. *'Ak/surely* everyone goes about like a passing shadow. *'Ak/surely* in vain they pile up goods with great fanfare, not even **knowing** who will finally garner them.

Thus, beginning with the brevity and transient nature of his own life he soon moves to the same judgment regarding all human existence. These thoughts, which at first he had resisted, can only lead now to cynicism or hope, to accusation of God or to profound trust in God.

3. Prayer from the Poet's Hope (39:7-11 [8-12 HB])

■ **7-11 [8-12 HB]** Now the poet speaks to Yahweh as **Lord** and affirms Yahweh as his **hope** (v 7 [8 HB]), his way to resolution of these life puzzles. What follows is based on this hope foundation. With confession of sin implicit in his request, he now petitions his Lord to rescue him from the repercussions of his **transgressions** (v 8 [9 HB]). He asks not to be made the laughingstock of **fools** who wind up with more perception than he exhibited. He again commits himself to silence, this time because he knows God has been the chief actor in the events lying behind his inner turmoil and his insight (v 9 [10 HB]).

Although he has not specifically described them, clearly the psalmist is experiencing some events in his life as a **scourge** from God. He asks God to turn those blows aside from his life (v 10 [11 HB]). He will be consumed by them if God does not desist. He acknowledges that it is in this reproof for iniquity that the Lord disciplines persons. But in the process he consumes their treasures like a **moth** is snuffed out (v 11 [12 HB]).

This part of his prayer closes with another *Ak*/**surely** exclamation. Again it is the ephemeral, vapor-like life of every human being that strikes him now. Beginning with *Ak*/**surely** and ending with *selâh* this line (v 11c [12c HB]) repeats v 5cd [6cd HB] nearly verbatim, dramatically underscoring the insignificance of all human life. When the *selâh* appears to have significance as it does in these verses we will retain it, contrary to the NIV.

4. Prayer for Sojourner to Be Heard (39:12-13 [13-14 HB])

■ **12-13 [13-14 HB]** His summary petitions ask God's attention to his prayer, his **cry** and his **tears** (v 12 [13 HB]). If Yahweh is to hear his prayer, he will need to act promptly, lest the psalmist be **no more**—a bleak outlook indeed (v 13 [14 HB]). But he asks God to **look away from** him, that is, stop attending to him with discipline, and let him be cheered (compare Job 7:16-21 for a similar but much darker request by Job).

Even his identity as a sojourner and his family's resident alien background emphasize from yet another vantage point his transience. But the sojourner identity also carries memory of Yahweh's special regard for sojourners and aliens, as disadvantaged persons needing particular grace (Lev 19:34; Deut 10:18).

FROM THE TEXT

The psalmist's clearest identification of himself is as a sojourner (*gēr*) in a line of resident aliens (*tôšāb*). In the psalm it acknowledges both the particular need of the sojourner and Yahweh's special regard for them. What the psalmist applies to himself King David applied to the nation of Israel as a body (1 Chr 29:14-19). He works from the fact that the sojourner and alien are in fact guests of the host country, and thus Israel as guests of Yahweh in his land are recipients of his grace and largess (Lev 25:23).

New Testament writers use this language to acknowledge that Messiah's people also live conscious of their impermanent status in their native lands (1 Pet 2:11). They live by their identity as God's own people (1 Pet 2:10), with their futures as sojourners and aliens entirely transformed by the resurrection of Jesus Christ.

Prayer: Deliver from the Pit—Again! (40:1-17 [2-18 HB])

BEHIND THE TEXT

This song begins with an extended testimony of a past deliverance, the resultant new song in the psalmist's heart, and reflections on what Yahweh really desires in worship. Although these features occupy a bit more than the first half of the psalm (ten of eighteen verses), in the end this is a prayer song of an individual crying out for rescue from evils that threaten to overwhelm him (vv 11-17 [12-18 HB]).

The two halves of the psalm (vv 1-10 [2-11 HB] and 11-17 [12-18 HB]) are sufficiently different and complete that some have insisted they are two separate poems simply joined, and that without warning, to make the present work. Thus Kraus treats this poem as Ps 40A and Ps 40B (which he divides as 40:1-11 and 40:12-17) (1988, 421-23). The appearance of vv 13-17 [14-18 HB] as Ps 70 in Book II of the Psalter could support such a notion. It could just as well indicate that vv 13-17 [14-18 HB] of Ps 40 have been dislodged from Ps 70 and circulated as a separate piece. Either could be the case, or the psalm may have been composed whole cloth as a unit (e.g., Craigie 1983, 313). For one thing, several psalms exhibit a lengthy song of praise as a prelude to complaint or petition (compare Pss 9—10, 27, 89).

For SS details see the Introduction, C.1.a, C.1.b, and C.4.a.

IN THE TEXT

1. Out of the Pit to a New Song (40:1-4 [2-5 HB])

■ **1 [2 HB]** As do prayers for rescue, Ps 40 begins with the story of the psalmist's unforgettable rescue by Yahweh. The story begins emphatically (cognate infinitive construction in the MT), stressing the psalmist's waiting upon, hoping in the Lord. One wonders how to translate "emphatic hoping" or waiting. Several versions (e.g., KJV, NLT, RSV, and others) translate "waited patiently," while the NEB has "I have waited, waited for the LORD." In either case the poet's sense of dependence upon Yahweh is clear. When the Lord did respond, the psalmist pictures God leaning down to listen to him.

■ **2 [3 HB]** The salvation itself he sees as rescue from a terrible **pit**. Here one must envision a wretched, loathsome dungeon, where the prisoner sinks down to his ankles or knees in mud and mire from the urine and excrement of scores of prisoners. No drain; no fresh water. A floor difficult even to stand on. Comparing the plight of Jeremiah at the hands of Zedekiah can inform our imagination (Jer 37:11—38:13). The metaphor chosen indicates the seriousness of the psalmist's adversity.

Like Ebed-Melek's fearless rescue of Jeremiah from the pit—requiring three men with ropes and cloths around Jeremiah and under his arms to pull him out before he dies of starvation (Jer 38:11-13)—God pulled the psalmist out onto dry ground! Out of mire onto solid rock!

■ **3-4 [4-5 HB]** This dramatic rescue ignited **a new song** in the psalmist. Clearly this will have been **a hymn of praise**. And the testimony carries sufficient inspiration that those who hear it would be moved with awe and holy **fear** and would **trust** this God. Such persons who actually make Yahweh their trust are supremely glad (see comments on Ps 1:1 for notes on **blessed/**ʾašrê [40:4 (5 HB)]). Negatively their trust of Yahweh will be matched by their humble integrity, eschewing insolence and lies.

2. What Yahweh Wants from the Rescued (40:5-10 [6-11 HB])

■ **5-6 [6-7 HB]** Turning from testimony to prayer, the psalmist reflects on the greatness of his God as seen through his astounding works. These **wonders** are not simply mind-boggling displays but are almost always works of deliverance in the OT. These works unveil the thoughts and plans of God for his people. They and the God who did them are incomparable! The psalmist feels compelled to proclaim these divine **wonders** but realizes they are **too many to declare**.

The next several verses challenge interpreters with their strongly worded, apparent rejection of animal sacrifice, puzzling talk about a book and of the psalmist's participation in the congregation's worship.

Still in prayer the psalmist claims Yahweh does not desire the offering of the popular fellowship offering (*zebaḥ*), the cereal offering (*minḥâh*), the whole burnt offering (*ʿôlâh*), or the sin offering (*ḥaṭṭaʾt*), all mainstays of Israelite worship. And in the middle of the tricolon, v 6*b* [7*b* HB], he includes something about his ears—God has ***dug out my ears*** (MT), **my ears you have opened**, "given [him] an open ear" (RSV), "receptive ears" (REB). Most likely the idea is that Yahweh has prepared him to hear this bold revelation about God's attitude toward **sacrifice**.

40:3-7

■ **7 [8 HB]** The psalmist now speaks (or spoke), perhaps as part of a liturgy for entry into the temple (compare Pss 15 and 24). **Then I said** (or *I say*, describing a pattern of worship rather than a single event), **"Here I am, I have come—it is written about me in the scroll."**

Precisely what is in mind here is not known, but it appears to be a book, the consulting of which was a part of temple entry process (so Broyles 1999, 350-51). One thinks here of a "book of life" that recorded the names of the righteous (Exod 32:32-33) or more likely a "scroll of remembrance" recording the names and deeds of those who fear Yahweh and hear his word (Mal 3:16-18). Or perhaps, as Kraus conjectures, these words come from the liturgy of a festival of thanksgiving (1988, 426). **The scroll** then could contain the new song inspired by Yahweh, something like the opening testimony (Ps 40:1-3 [2-4 HB]).

The worshippers would normally bring their sacrifices at this time. Instead the psalmist declares his desire to do Yahweh's will and his praise for Yahweh's deliverance as his sacrifice. Kraus cites Ps 118:19 and also similar inscriptions from Asia Minor (1988, 426-27). "Eighth- and seventh-century prophets rejected the sacrifices of Israel because they were offered by a disobedient people whom sacrifices could not make acceptable" (Mays 1994b, 170, citing Isa 1:11; Jer 7:22; Amos 5:22).

■ **8-10 [9-11 HB]** I desire to do your will, my God; your law is within my heart. In this context the psalmist declares his desire to do Yahweh's **will** (compare Ps 19:14 [15 HB]). He has internalized Yahweh's Torah. He has proclaimed Yahweh's *righteousness*, in the sense of Yahweh's victory or righteous **saving acts**, not simply Yahweh's righteous character (compare Isa 40:9; 41:27; 52:7).

Several prophetic voices from the exile promise Yahweh will one day make for himself a people who will actually have Yahweh's Torah in their hearts (so Jer 31:31-34; Ezek 36:25-28). Some psalmists experienced this promised blessing. "It was in these circles of prophets and temple singers," says Mays, "that sacrifice was relativized in favor of the proclamation of the Lord's saving righteousness (Pss. 40:6; 50:7-15; 69:30-33; cf. Isa. 66:1-4)" (1994b, 170). See also Othmar Keel for evidence of similar claims among Israel's neighbors (1997, 325-28).

We can see the importance of this proclamation as part of the psalmist's worship of thanksgiving by catching the repeated notice given the topic. In five successive cola he claims he has given testimony to Yahweh's saving acts and the faithful, loving character of the Lord from which these acts of deliverance come (vv 9-10 [10-11 HB]). What he stated positively, *I have told . . .* , he now states negatively. He has *not* kept word of Yahweh's **righteousness** hidden away in his **heart** (v 10 [11 HB]). Then still another time, closing this unit with an emphatic tricolon, he claims he has spoken of Yahweh's **faithfulness**, his salvation, and, conversely, he has not hidden word of Yahweh's lovingkindness. These testimonies/proclamations have been in the **great assembly**, matters of public record, if you will.

3. O Lord, Save and Preserve Me (40:11-17 [12-18 HB])

■ **11 [12 HB]** The concluding tricolon of v 10 [11 HB], the dependent bicolon of v 12 [13 HB], and the need for a line to be substantiated by v 12 [13 HB] lead us to draw a break at v 11 [12 HB]. Now the poem reaches the point toward which it has been heading all along. Once again the psalmist needs deliverance at Yahweh's hand. *Do not, O Yahweh, withhold your compassion from me. Let your mercy and your truth perpetually guard me.*

■ **12-16 [13-17 HB]** The psalmist is surrounded by countless troubles, which he attributes to the fact that his **sins have overtaken** him. This is not formally a song for the confession of sin(s) such as we encounter, for example, in Ps 51. And neither do the acknowledgment of his sins nor petitions for forgiveness and deliverance from his sin occupy significant space. Nevertheless, the psalmist's theological context, including Sinai covenant thought, standard wisdom instruction, and the default theological construct of the world of ancient Israel will intuitively interpret his ongoing adversities as divine discipline for sins (Thompson 1993, 250-51), from which he needs deliverance. He does not specify divine action specifically aimed at rescuing him from his iniquities—no prayers for forgiveness or for cleansing. These are included in the rescue, in the display of Yahweh's mercy and grace for which he prays (vv 10-11 [11-12 HB]).

He is no longer able to **see** (v 12 [13 HB]). His troubles are more than **the hairs** on his **head**! His **heart fails** him; he is thoroughly distraught and paralyzed with his **troubles**. Just what he has in mind here one cannot know. He literally cannot see? He figuratively **cannot see** a way out of his plight? It makes little difference. What he needs is Yahweh to hasten to his rescue (v 13 [14 HB]) and that as a mark of his good pleasure. Among the psalmist's troubles are persons who would do him harm if they could (v 14 [15 HB]), who also mock the psalmist publically (v 15 [16 HB]).

The poet would like these who want to sweep him away to be shamed and humiliated. This could happen if their shameful ways are made public. Their shame could also involve theological humiliation, having to face the fact that Yahweh has delivered the one they mocked and that God is on the side of those they despise. One would not be surprised to learn that the psalmist's adversaries are "the wicked" who seek not just his ruination but the ruination of all the godly and the disadvantaged.

In contrast to this shame and embarrassment the psalmist prays for the joy and gladness of all those who seek Yahweh, who actually **rejoice** in Yahweh himself. The psalm has uncovered persons of contrasting quests—those who **want to take** the psalmist's **life** (v 14 [15 HB]) and those who **seek** Yahweh himself. The former occupy themselves shouting mockery at the psalmist and those like him. The latter are those who continually say "[*Yahweh*] **is great!**" (v 16 [17 HB]). They **say** as in exclamations during worship and in their ruminations "day and night" (1:2).

■ **17 [18 HB]** The song closes with two strong identifications by the psalmist. First in v 17*a* [18*a* HB] he states who he is. The psalmist is a **poor** and afflicted one. In the Psalter these are typically the disadvantaged, the mistreated. These are the poorest of the poor, suffering at the hands of the wicked or simply caught in the wheels of life. That Yahweh would take thought of him is his prayer.

Then in v 17*b* [18*b* HB] he states who Yahweh is: Yahweh is his **help** and his **deliverer**. It is not simply that Yahweh does help and deliver him, but that Yahweh himself is that **help**. Now the prayer is that Yahweh, who is his God, **not delay** in his help.

FROM THE TEXT

The insight regarding God's preference of obedient people rather than traditional sacrifice speaks in three registers. First the classical prophets, without setting aside Levitical sacrifice, knew that, forced to a choice between the two, Yahweh would choose his Torah on their heart rather than lavish sacrifice from polluted hands (e.g., Isa 1:11; Amos 5:22). Second, exilic voices, listening to these earlier prophets, actually set aside the sacrifice of animals in favor of piety fulfilling Jeremiah's and Ezekiel's hopes.

Finally the writer of Hebrews has seen that this prophetic hope has been realized through the life, death, and resurrection of Jesus Christ (Heb 10:5-7). By the power of this one who offered himself up once for all, we as did he walk with God's law in our hearts to the glory of God (Heb 10:8-18).

Prayer of the One Betrayed (41:1-13 [2-14 HB])

BEHIND THE TEXT

This simple prayer of the individual for healing could be at home either in a cultic setting or in private meditation. The lack of particular, specific clues to its setting and the abundance of stock expressions make it appropriate for either.

For specifics of the SS see Introduction, C.1.a, C.1.b, and C.4.c.

IN THE TEXT

1. Yahweh's Record of Healing (41:1-3 [2-4 HB])

■ **1 [2 HB]** The poem begins with an account of Yahweh's healing power and of his merciful response to those who, having shown regard for the poor, are now blessed by God. Book I of the Psalter ends as it began—with a beatific exclamation with *'ašrê*/**O how marvelously happy is the one who** . . . In 1:1, the one pronounced blessed is the person who does not walk in the sinner's ways. Here the one who has had **regard for the weak**, for the helpless is the happy one.

Poor (*dāl*) here speaks not only of life with scant provisions but of "little people," insignificant persons at the fringes of society (*HALOT*, 221-23). Persons who attend to these dispensable ones are the sort of persons Yahweh deigns to rescue. Just how high this regard for ***the poor*** ranks in Yahweh's estimation perhaps can be seen in that this is the only description of the psalmist's piety in the entire poem until we come to v 12*a* [13*a* HB]. It carries much freight.

■ **2 [3 HB]** Then the recounting of Yahweh's healing and saving works provide warrant for the psalmist's own petitions later in the song. The poet's praise for Yahweh moves back and forth between the telling of Yahweh's gracious deeds (third person) and appeals directly to Yahweh (second person). Positively Yahweh watches carefully over him, preserves his life, and sees to his blessed status in the land. Negatively Yahweh does not hand him over to his enemy's desires.

■ **3 [4 HB]** References to the psalmist's **sickbed** and Yahweh's healing presence imply at least part of the psalmist's trouble is sickness, probably chronic **illness**. Indeed, the following verse implies that at least some of his enemies expected or anticipated his death (v 5 [6 HB])!

Most versions translate the Yahweh clauses here as grateful descriptions of Yahweh's present or future actions (MT, NRSV, most English versions)— "the LORD delivers, . . . protects, . . . keeps, . . . sustains . . ." and so forth. A few others follow the LXX and take the colas as supplication (NJPS). Taking these lines as narrative rather than prayer fits the logic of the prayer song better than do the petitions.

2. Prayer for Mercy in the Face of Slanderous Foes (41:4-9 [5-10 HB])

■ **4-9 [5-10 HB] Have mercy on me**, the poet cries. Switching clearly now from report to petition, the poet prays for God's saving grace in the form of healing—*his* healing (v 4 [5 HB])! He supports his petition by the explanation that he has **sinned against** Yahweh. Clearly sin often leads to illnesses of various sorts, and such may be the case here. But just as likely the psalmist's repentance/confession is prompted as much by his theological assumptions as by his medical condition.

The theological assumptions derived from the Sinai covenant, from standard wisdom teaching, and from the prevalent folk theology of the psalmist's world connected sin and illness causally. This shaped Israel's thought so much that one could reason from sin to suffering as an expected result. The sick one will often have difficulty knowing just what cause explains his illness, especially when the reference to his sin has no specifics.

We notice the psalmist's confession in v 4 [5 HB] is brief and general: **I have sinned against you.** In that environment a confession of sin is always appropriate. The psalmist's misery comes in part from the slander of his enemies. The account here of their miserable attacks on the psalmist occupies the majority of the lines in this unit (vv 5-9 [6-10 HB]). They speak ill of him, eager for his demise (v 5 [6 HB]). They come to see him, feigning sympathy but actually gathering fodder for the gossip they will spread abroad (v 6 [7 HB]). His despisers gather together to plan ill for him (v 7 [8 HB]). They predict the worst for him; some lethal force has fastened on him, they claim; he will not rise again from the place where he now lies (v 8 [9 HB]). In other words, his adversaries celebrate the plight of this poor one, interpreting his illness in the worst possible terms, perhaps implying severe judgment for sin the poet should, in their opinion, confess, and gladly anticipating a bleak future for the psalmist.

The fact that these attacks upon him are the work of an erstwhile **close friend** only increases the pain of the psalmist's plight (v 9 [10 HB]). This is a trust betrayed. These friends had shared at the psalmist's table. Now they are alienated—perhaps over the cause of the psalmist's illness. This is the situation from which the psalmist cries out for the mercy of Yahweh (v 4 [5 HB]).

3. Mercy to Show Yahweh's Favor (41:10-13 [11-14 HB])

■ **10 [11 HB]** A second time (compare v 4 [5 HB]) the psalmist cries **have mercy on me**, launching the final movement of the psalm with its focus on the needed display of Yahweh's mercy. Without elaborating he explains the desire to repay his enemies when Yahweh has shown mercy by raising him up.

■ **11-12 [12-13 HB]** When Yahweh thus displays his mercy so that the poet's enemy does not **triumph** over him, he will know Yahweh holds him in favor. His reasoning is the reverse of that seen near top. There he is ill and therefore confesses his sin. Here his enemy has been vanquished and he concludes that the rescue was Yahweh's gracious response to the psalmist's own integrity. Pleased with the psalmist, Yahweh has rescued him in mercy. Yahweh has supported him and caused him to stand before him **forever**. Yahweh could make him stand before him for prosecution and as a prelude to judgment. But in this context being given direct access to Yahweh is an expression of grace. This signals vindication for the psalmist and the unending approval of Yahweh himself.

■ **13 [14 HB] Praise be to the Lord, the God of Israel, from everlasting to everlasting. Amen and Amen.** Numbered with the text, these lines make a fitting conclusion to Ps 41. The praise voiced for Yahweh also expresses humility and dependence upon Yahweh.

Having read the entire Psalter, however, we recognize these lines as the first of five blessings with which the books of the Psalter conclude. They appear here and then at 72:18-20; 89:52; 106:48; and finally at 150:6 (or perhaps the whole of 150). The blessings relate in different ways to their contexts, at the least providing scribal colophons to separate collections as they came under the umbrella of the forming Psalter. Psalm 89:52 provides an intriguing counterpoint to the strident objections in the closing lines of that psalm. Here the rubric could just as well have been penned with the psalm itself, though we suspect that not to have been the case. Even so, the fact that the Chronicler quotes Ps 106 *with the concluding blessing already in place* tells us these scribal rubrics were assimilated to their contexts early on and that they precede the Chronicler's work considerably (1 Chr 16:36).

FROM THE TEXT

This song exposes as well as any the plight of those dear souls who sought to understand their standing with God prior to the cross and resurrection of our Lord. When persons suffered chronic illness they stood in a double bind akin to the plight of Job. Their continuing illness gave their enemies ammunition for slander, because the illness implied sin that they apparently had not confessed. On the other hand, even close friends and family eventually were tempted to wonder why their friend or loved one continued in his illness if he was really as pious as he professed to be.

One can see this played out positively in v 11 [12 HB]. The psalmist's happy circumstances—his enemies have not triumphed over him—indicate that Yahweh is pleased with him. The life, death, and resurrection of Jesus of Nazareth occasioned a full reappraisal of this understanding. One will not in the NT find our circumstances cited as evidence from which to discern God's disposition toward us. Without fail we are cited instead to God's giving of his Son for us on the cross as the sole and indisputable indication that God loves us (e.g., Rom 8:31-39; 1 John 4:9-10) (Thompson 1993).

BOOK II: PSALMS 42—72

Prayer for Vindication of the Downcast (42:1—43:5 [42:2—43:5 HB])

BEHIND THE TEXT

The verbatim appearance of a two-line refrain twice in Ps 42 (vv 5-6 [6-7 HB], 11 [12 HB]) and once in Ps 43 (v 5) suggests the original unity of a poem now divided in the MT. The lack of SS on Ps 43 also suggests earlier union with the preceding psalm. Further the LXX divides the psalm and then cements that division by adding a Davidic SS to Ps 43. Other repetition of full bicola (42:9 [10 HB] and 43:2; compare 43:3 [4 HB] and 42:10 [11 HB]) also suggest this earlier unity as do thematic ties between the two songs.

Although no specific cultic setting is indicated by the psalm itself, the refrain certainly invites use in a worship setting with multiple voices. At the same time the poem positions the worshipper yet a distance from the temple and longing for it (42:6-7 [7-8 HB]).

We also note that Pss 42 and 43 are the first two psalms in the so-called Elohistic Psalter. It is apparent that the psalms now residing in Books II and III of the Psalter have been edited favoring the name Elohim over the name Yahweh. Whereas in Book I references to Yahweh outnumber those to Elohim 233 to 45, in Books II and III the reverse is true. References to Elohim outnumber those to Yahweh 186 to 69. That this boundary between Book I and Books II and III coincides with attribution to the Korahites and then the Asaphites is intriguing. Unfortunately, we lack sufficient information to draw secure inferences from these realities.

For the sons of Korah see the Introduction, C.1.d. This Korahite collection extends from Pss 42—49, assuming 43 originally to have been joined with Ps 42. Thus the attribution to the Korahites preceded the division of 42 into 42 and 43.

IN THE TEXT

1. Thirst in the Face of Mockers (42:1-5 [2-6 HB])

■ **1-2 [2-3 HB]** As the deer pants for streams of water, so my soul pants for you, my God. This psalm opens with one of the most, if not the most potent images in all of Scripture. It introduces the topic that will occupy the writer first—the psalmist's insatiable yearning for God himself and for the worship of him in the temple. With *BBHS*, by simple haplography we should probably read *'ayyelet* (*'ayyālâ*)/**doe**, or **deer** instead of *'ayyil*/**ram** in the MT.

The precise nuance of the word picture is debatable however. The verb involved occurs only here and in Joel 1:20 in the OT, complicating its interpretation. There, in a set of recurring calls for some sort of vocal response to a draught—weep, lament, wail, call, cry to the Lord, among others—we find the statements, "even the wild animals pant [*'rwg*] for you; the streams of water have dried up." If our passage carries the same idea, then we should expect more than yearning or panting here.

Assuming the psalmist's intense longing, we should expect some cry or moan or groan as an expression of that longing. The KJV's classic rendering, "As the hart panteth after the water," is so much with us, however, that we will be inclined to leave it as is here with a qualifying note like this. The NIV reads, **As the deer pants for streams of water**. But Jastrow is on the right track when he actually defines the word as "to groan (of the deer)" (1950, 1113).

The streams longed for both in Psalms and Joel are the *ăpîqê mayim*, the **water courses**. These are the seasonal streams on the edge of the arable land that dry up after the rainy season. The animals slake their thirst from them and protest their absence when they run dry.

The psalmist yearns not just for some general sense of divine presence (v 2 [3 HB]). No, he longs **for the living God**, for a particular God understood a specific way. This designation names the creator God, for to give and to sustain life is the Creator's unique prerogative (Gen 2:7). It is this characteristic, among others, that sets Yahweh, God of Israel, so clearly apart from the gods of the nations (e.g., Hab 2:18-20).

This desire of the psalmist to "drink" from Yahweh leads naturally into a longing to worship God. When can he go to the temple? The sooner the better the question implies. He wants to **meet with God**; to "behold the face of God" (LXX; RSV); or to "appear before God" (MT; NJPS). The NJPS "appear before God" follows the MT but changes the focus from the psalmist's yearning for Yahweh to the psalmist's being seen by Yahweh. In any case seeing God, literally *seeing the face of God*, follows well the desires and yearnings of vv 1-2 [2-3 HB].

The eyes, the mouth, and facial expressions are all instruments of communication. Relationships are born and maintained through them. To want to see God's face is to desire to open up to God and to maintain authentic, candid relationships with that God.

■ **3 [4 HB]** The agendas of the prayer have moved slowly and deliberately. First, and perhaps central to them all, the psalmist unveiled his hunger and thirst for Yahweh. Then he placed that yearning in the context of the community and his desire to see the face of Yahweh. Finally we get indications of the agenda that will, in the end, occupy the most space—his need for Yahweh's help against his adversaries.

The first we hear of his adversaries is his confession of **tears** flowing night and day. A nonstop assault on his faith comes through the twice-repeated question, **Where is your God?** (vv 3, 10 [4, 11 HB]). Once again we encounter the psalmist's adversaries as persons challenging both the faithfulness of Yahweh and the character of the psalmist.

■ **4 [5 HB]** In response to this assault the psalmist pours himself out to Yahweh and rehearses memories of bygone days when he joined in the celebration and thanksgiving of the festive crowd, leading the mighty throng to God's house, caught up in the energy of the joyful multitude.

The general meaning seems clear; but the best reading of the MT in v 4c [5c HB] is uncertain. The consonantal text in the two critical words is *bsk 'ddm*. While most English versions have something about leading a multitude to the house of God, it is not clear which of several parsings of either word could best support these moves.

■ **5 [6 HB]** **Why, my soul, are you downcast? Why so disturbed within me? Put your hope in God, for I will yet praise him, my Savior and my God.** The first of three appearances of this remarkable refrain establish the base line from which all the other emotional and spiritual movement in the psalm can proceed. The refrain is what we moderns would call self-talk, aimed it appears at encouraging himself. But the psalmist's choice to externalize his own **soul** in this self-talk—**Why, my soul . . . downcast?**—and address himself as a second party in the conversation, underscores and reinforces each part of the refrain—the questions, the admonitions, and the affirmations.

The questions challenge the necessity of the distress with which the psalmist approached the refrain. Other responses are possible. The admonition, **Put your hope in God**, directs the psalmist and the reader away from the soul's disquiet and threatening environment to the only resource that could match the psalmist's needs.

The poet hears the admonition to hope in God and responds with a promise yet again to **praise** God, to look beyond the present distress to a future marked by gratitude. This confidence actually provides the basis for the psalmist's encouragement to hope: *Hope . . .* <u>*because*</u> *I will yet again give praise.* The affirmation identifies the God of Israel as the psalmist's salvation and his own God. The statements function both as commitments to be faithful to this God and as identifications of the God to which the psalmist intends to look (compare Zeph 1:4-7; Joel 2:32).

2. Hope in the Face of Adversity (42:6-11 [7-12 HB])

■ **6 [7 HB]** As in the first strophe (v 4 [5 HB]), the psalmist's discouragement triggers his memory of God's role in meeting that distress. In this case he calls to mind the demonstration of God's graciousness revealed in nature. He thinks of the **land of the Jordan** associated with Mount Hermon, that is, the regions of the sources of the Jordan River on the south slopes of Hermon. He mentions a **Mount Mizar** whose location is not yet known, but, one suspects should be sought in the hills above Galilee, associated with the sources that fill the Sea of Galilee and eventually feed the Jordan.

■ **7 [8 HB]** The region is full of waterfalls, especially in the months of snow melt on Hermon. In the roar of these waterfalls, **deep calls to deep**. Just what this expression means remains a puzzle, but it seems hopeful. "One flood calls to the other" is *HALOT*'s rendering (1691). God's **breakers** and **waves** roll over the psalmist, nearly drowning him. But the eventual result is positive. He takes it all as a display of God's *ḥesed*, his loving-kindness.

■ **8-10 [9-11 HB]** These watery displays of God's grace prompt God's song in the **night** and prayer to the living God as well. The psalmist is drawn to God. He thinks not simply of the living God, but **the God of *his* life**, that is, the God who gives him life (v 8 [9 HB]). He calls to God as ***his* Rock** (v 9 [10 HB]), a firm place of unshakable relief.

In spite of the remarkably positive responses to the memory of God's revelation in the hills and waterfalls of the north country, the psalmist retains a certain disquiet regarding his relationship with this God. He has still a sense that God has **forgotten** him and wonders why (v 9 [10 HB]).

His circumstances prompt this question. First there seems to be no escape from his mocking adversaries. Second, unless he is simply speaking metaphorically in the strange expression, "with murder in my bones" (Alter 2007, 151), he has actually suffered physical attack or is under threat of death. As though that were not enough, his adversaries mock him, probably because of his circumstances. As in v 3 [4 HB], the mockers question **Where is your God?**

■ **11 [12 HB]** Once again the refrain brings the psalmist and worshippers and readers like us back to solid ground. The refrain asks the reason for our continuing discouragement. We take this as a set of rhetorical questions that challenge the legitimacy of his downcast face as the best response to his adversity. The questions do not actually expect a carefully reasoned response explaining or defending the psalmist's downheartedness.

The refrain provides space for the psalmist's own inner conversation to urge hope in God for a second time and to commit himself again to praise. Finally the psalmist identifies the God of Israel as his salvation. All of these moves anchor the psalmist and bring him back from the recitation of his plight to the memory of his faith foundation. The refrain creates a safe space within which the psalmist can wander theologically.

3. Worship and the Way of Hope (43:1-5)

■ **1-2** If talk about the enemies has continuity in Pss 42 and 73, then we have another peek into the psalmist's plight. His prayer is for God to judge his case. His predicament is at least partially a legal one. He has been dragged into court where he fears partiality at the bench and lack of integrity in the plaintiff's accusations and witness (v 1).

Emphatically over against this plight (*kî 'attâ*), suddenly the psalmist cries for help. He identifies this God as his **stronghold** of life. But he also feels betrayed by God and asks again for reasons for God's "adultery," that is, his perceived unfaithfulness to the psalmist (v 2).

■ **3** What exactly had taken place we do not know because the poet speaks in generalities and metaphors. But, as before, the psalmist's longings include the desire to find himself once again in the temple, at the altar of God, buoyed by the joy of God himself (vv 3-4). He personifies God's truth as messengers whom God can send to guide the psalmist to the mount of God, the **holy mountain** and divine dwelling. Then he will enter all the way into the courtyard to God's altar.

■ **4** When the psalmist goes into the temple he enters a sphere of great joy and blessing. The God of the temple is the source of the psalmist's **joy**, his **delight**. By God's light and truth he will be transported beyond his sense of betrayal to fellowship with God—who is himself gladness—to God who is specifically *his* God.

■ **5** For a third time, we recite the questions that make room for restoration and then the exhortation to move through downheartedness to praise, the urging to hope in God rather than rehearse discouragement. We see the promise to praise and the identification of this God as *the psalmist's* God, this time reading the refrain as a close to the entire psalm, reading Pss 42 and 43 as a single song.

FROM THE TEXT

Psalms 42 and 43 call to mind Walter Brueggemann's famous division of the Psalter into psalms of orientation, disorientation, and finally of reorientation (1984). In part because its refrain ranges back and forth through these textual states of mind, the poem leads us back and forth between them.

As do many complaint or lament psalms, this poem is filled with questions. Thirteen queries sprinkled the length and breadth of the song move back and forth through the mental dispositions. They express the psalmist's profound thirst for God and hunger for worship: "When can I go and meet with God?" (42:2 [3 HB]). They give voice to the psalmist's adversaries: "Where is your God?" (v 3 [4 HB]) and his present disorientation. "Why have you forgotten me?" voices the present disorientation but implies the time integration and tranquillity, now largely a memory, which preceded this present crisis (v 9 [10 HB]). "Why . . . are you downcast?" even anticipates the time of reorientation, when the singer will again praise God (43:5).

For reasons to be explored elsewhere, Christians regularly experience these sorts of circumstances different from God's ancient people. This change is triggered mainly by the fact that since the passion of Jesus, adversity is not routinely interpreted as evidence of alienation from God. Consequently disciples of Jesus frequently find God in the midst of suffering and disorientation. And at times Pss 42 and 43 provide a road map that helps Christian believers move more rapidly into God's reorientation.

Prayer to the Sleeping God (44:1-26 [2-27 HB])

BEHIND THE TEXT

Psalm 44 is a communal prayer for rescue that also incorporates numerous individual references (compare vv 4, 6, 15, 23 [5, 7, 16, 24 HB]), freely moving back and forth between the two. The first in the series of communal complaints in the Psalter, it stands unique among these complaints for its protestation of innocence in response to suffering attributed to God (vv 9-22 [10-23 HB]). It reads in the canon like a national reflection of Job, like Lam 3 and the Suffering Servant in Isaiah.

Psalm 44 situates itself after or anticipating a devastating military defeat, but it resists specific dating. Settings from Jehoshaphat (2 Chr 20:4-13 in Weiser 1962, 354) to the period of the Maccabees (Kraus 1988, 445-46, citing Calvin and the Antiochian fathers) have been suggested as context for this psalm. Sennacherib's invasion in 701 B.C. during the reign of Hezekiah or Pharaoh Neco's slaying of Josiah in 609 B.C. would provide excellent settings for this psalm (Broyles 1999, 201). But its general reference allows appropriation in many situations marked by suffering.

For the sons of Korah see the Introduction, C.1.d. For the *maskil* see C.4.c.

IN THE TEXT

1. Report of God's Conquest (44:1-3 [2-4 HB])

■ **1-2 [2-3 HB]** The opening lines of this psalm lay the groundwork for the cry for help that will appear in vv 23-26 [24-27 HB]. The psalmist reports what the community has heard regarding God's great works. Their **ancestors** (v 1 [2 HB]) have taken it upon themselves to rehearse the wonders God performed among them, especially when he gave them the promised land. The psalmist recalls that in those days God had dispossessed the **nations** (v 2 [3 HB]), setting his own people free in the new land. (Thus most versions.) The LXX, however, is open to the interpretation that both verbs in v 2*b* [3*b* HB] have to do with the defeat of the nations (so REB). I am inclined to side with the majority here, taking the string of third person suffixes as referring to God's people: that is, God disposed the nations, thus making room for his people.

■ **3 [4 HB]** The wonder in the report was that by their telling the ancestors themselves had virtually nothing to do with the conquest and possession of the land. Neither their weaponry (**their sword**) nor their strength (**their arm**) enabled them to possess the land. The resources were all God's—his **right** hand, his strong **arm**, the glorious radiance of his presence (**the light of** his **face**); these achieved victory in the conquest. They were all expressions of God's favor toward them.

2. Trust in God as King (44:4-8 [5-9 HB])

■ **4-8 [5-9 HB]** In these marvels the psalmist experiences God as his **king**, the one whose commands achieve salvation for his people (reading v 4*b* [5*b* HB] with the LXX and *BBHS*). It is not that God's people did not engage militarily with the nations God dispossessed. No. God's people gored their adversaries and put them down. The psalmist carried his **bow** and his **sword** (v 6 [7 HB]).

The issue instead is a matter of trust. The psalmist trusts God, not his **bow**; God, not his **sword**. God's people experienced the victorious outcome as the work of God's **name**, that is, God's person. The result is that they live in **praise**, expressing thanksgiving all the time (v 8 [9 HB]).

In this first half of the song we encounter ancient tradition being picked up by the psalmist. Twice in these lines the psalmist refers to God's **name** as equivalent to referring to God's self. But, as we are seeing, this psalm has been edited so that the name of Israel's God, the name Yahweh, does not appear in it. Nevertheless, its composition assumes a time when **your name** would have been glossed with the name "Yahweh."

In addition, the notion that God himself dispossessed the peoples of the land, not the Israelites' bows and swords, is an old, old way of understanding the conquest. Joshua 23:3—24:13 already understands Israel's entry into the land in these terms. This faith is critical to the story the fathers had told their children (v 1 [2 HB]). But here it forms a setup for the following lines. That happy story happened long ago. Now the psalmist has a different story. This turnabout presents an excellent place for a liturgical pause (so the *selâh*, against the NIV).

3. God's Humiliating Acts (44:9-16 [10-17 HB])

■ **9 [10 HB]** A strong reversal marks the beginning of the current story (reading *'ak*/**but now** with the LXX, for MT *'ap*/**anger**). Here virtually all of the wonders of the former days have been traded for episodes of shame and defeat. Just as God was credited with the victories of old, now he is charged with the present defeats.

■ **10-12 [11-13 HB]** Turning now to military metaphors, the psalmist claims God has abandoned Israel's troops, leaving them defenseless. God has turned them back before their enemies, has failed to go to battle with his people. He has left his people like **sheep** destined to become "food," that is, they will be or have been slaughtered and devoured. Their adversaries have **plundered** them. The claim that God has **scattered** them **among the nations** (v 11 [12 HB]) could be a clue to its date of composition. Exilic or postexilic situations appear to be in mind.

The accusations and claims laid out before God here are interconnected. The psalmist has already praised God as his King (v 4 [5 HB]). It is in God's role as King that he is leader of the "hosts," that is, the armies of Israel, which he is here accused of deserting. We recall the temple entry liturgy: *Who is this glorious king* [i.e., this king of glory]? *Yahweh of hosts, he is the glorious king* (24:10). Psalm 59:5 [6 HB] brings these concepts together: *You, Yahweh God of hosts, are God of Israel.* Note also 84:3 [4 HB], *Yahweh of hosts,* my King and my God. Psalm 46:11 [12 HB] makes claims opposite from our passage: *Yahweh of hosts* is with us, the God of Jacob is our *refuge*.

■ **13-16 [14-17 HB]** A major concern of this unit, first mentioned in v 9 [10 HB] and then elaborated by repetition in vv 13-15 [14-16 HB] is God's shaming of his people. Not giving them aid militarily, he shamed them with defeat. It was as though he **sold** them on the open market, and **for a pittance** at that (v 12 [13 HB]). He made them **a reproach to** their **neighbors**, a mockery and **derision** to everyone around. He treated them so badly, says the psalmist, their shameful state became proverbial among the nations (vv 13-14 [14-15 HB]). Passersby *made obscene gestures* at them (i.e., **shake their heads**). The situation is so embarrassing that his whole day is colored by it (vv 15-16 [16-17 HB]), by the sound of blasphemers.

In Israel's theological context and also in the thought world of the ANE, Israel's military defeat and other catastrophic events that had befallen her have only one or two possible explanations. It is possible that Israel has broken covenant with her God Yahweh. In keeping with the provisions of that covenant, Yahweh has brought destruction upon them. She is shamed in that case because of her unseemly behavior; Yahweh is shamed because of the unbecoming character of his people.

Or it is possible that Israel has been defeated in battle because her God Yahweh is too weak to defend her or unwilling to do so. In these cases Israel is shamed because of the unworthy behavior or character of her God. Or Yahweh is shamed because of his weakness or his poor judgment. See Jer 23:40; 24:9; 44:12; Ezek 5:14-15; 16:52, 57; 22:4-5; and Joel 2:17 for examples of Jerusalem or Israel being shamed.

4. Protest of Innocence (44:17-22 [18-23 HB])

■ **17-22 [18-23 HB]** Here the psalmist takes a most surprising turn. He speaks for the group and denies that they have done anything worthy of the suffering exacted from them by Yahweh or the reproach he has put upon them. It is not unusual to find persons claiming innocence in the face of judgment past or coming. For example, some of Ezekiel's audience objected to his preaching to his contemporaries in Jerusalem and in exile. They insisted that their parents, not they, were to blame for the judgment Yahweh had sent (18:2).

Here the worshippers claim they **had not forgotten** God nor broken his **covenant** (v 17 [18 HB]). Their ***hearts have not pulled back*** from him nor have their steps veered from his ways (v 18 [19 HB]). In neither their attitudes nor their conduct had they betrayed Yahweh. Nevertheless, in spite of their innocence God has brought the covenant's curses upon them. ***He had crushed them in the haunt of jackals and covered them over with darkness*** (v 19 [20 HB]).

Emphasizing the sense of betrayal, the psalmist acknowledges that God's actions would be justified had his people been unfaithful to him, especially had they sought other gods (v 20 [21 HB]). Not only so, but they could not have avoided God's judgment, for their God knows the **secrets of the heart** (v 21 [22 HB]). He would not have been fooled or left ignorant of their betrayal. To make matters worse, it is because of their loyalty to the God of Israel that they are being slain. Their fate is trivialized and set, like **sheep** marked for **slaughter** (v 22 [23 HB]).

5. Cry for Sleeping God to Awake (44:23-26 [24-27 HB])

■ **23-24 [24-25 HB]** On both sides of v 23 [24 HB] the poet presses surprising material into service to express his desperation. The lines in vv 17-22 [18-23 HB] we would generally have expected from the mouths of persons trying to sidestep the consequences of their own sin. They protest their innocence in the face of the God's indictment through the prophets.

We know these malcontents from passages such as Ezek 18, where Yahweh specifically addresses the claim that it is not the sins of Ezekiel's audience that have brought destruction upon them. No. As their favorite proverb says, "The parents eat sour grapes, and the children's teeth are set on edge" (Ezek 18:2; so also Jer 31:29-30). That is, they suffer because of the sins of their parents and grandparents. They claim to have nothing of which to repent. Ezekiel and Jeremiah indict the wrong people, they claim.

The historic statement of faith from Sinai seemed to support this claim. Did Yahweh not identify himself as the gracious God who nevertheless "punishes the children and their children for the sin of the parents to the third and fourth generation" (Exod 34:7). And preaching from the time of Ezekiel and just before him claimed that Manasseh's sins were so great that even if Judah repented and followed Josiah's reform, God would still send judgment upon them (2 Kgs 21:10-18; 23:24-28).

But finding these lines in their present context in the Psalter, we are led to expect them to speak in a faithful voice. We are inclined to believe their protest that ***they have not forgotten God, have not been untrue to the covenant*** (Ps 44:17 [18 HB] ff.), etc. In all likelihood they are "collateral damage" from the complete destruction of Jerusalem or from some other catastrophic loss. If we date this poem to the days following Josiah's death, these will have been the people who followed him in sincerely observing Passover and renewing covenant with Yahweh (2 Kgs 23:21-25). The Babylonians gave special treatment to very few persons. The rest, these righteous ones as well as the wicked, were marched in large caravans to settlements in Babylon. At the same time, judging from the "why" questions in Ps 44:23-24 [24-25 HB], they may not understand the larger catastrophe in which they had been caught up.

But the voice of innocent protest is not the only surprise in these lines. Vocabulary awkwardly addressed to the God of Israel confronts us. The psalmist urges God to ***wake up*** and asks ***why Adonai sleeps.*** This language, rarely applied to Yahweh and then metaphorically (only Ps 78:65), we associate first with Elijah's taunting of the prophets of Baal (1 Kgs 18:27). There Elijah probably means to be taken literally as an insult to Baal. "Maybe he [Baal] is sleeping and must be awakened." Assurance that the God who keeps Israel "will neither slumber nor sleep" (Ps 121:4) makes sleep a category of being that does not apply to the God of Israel and underscores our surprise at the psalmist's words.

44:25-26

A significant military reversal is the cause of the questions and pleas of these lines. God has rejected (*zānaḥ*) them, that is, he has not gone into battle with Israel's troops (44:9 [10 HB]) and has ***hidden his presence*** from them (v 24 [25 HB]). (Note the similar vocabulary clustered around the strong notion of Yahweh's rejection of his people: 60:1, 10 [3, 12 HB]; 88:14 [15 HB].)

■ **25 [26 HB]** **We are brought down to the dust** is to be preferred to "Our soul is bowed down" (RSV). ***Soul*** here refers not to some aspect of persons that they possess, but rather what we are—living, breathing persons with creaturely desires, aspects of flesh-and-blood existence. The perceived absence of God presses the psalmist into postures of absolute dereliction and dissolution or to abject penitence.

■ **26 [27 HB]** A bicolon with two final cries concludes this poem. Celebration of God's famous deeds, the psalmist's commitment to that God, recall of God's inexplicable forsaking of his people in their time of need, and protest of the people's innocence all reach their goal in the psalmist's pleas for help.

Arise as our help! evokes the picture of God's riding into battle on the ark of the covenant, his throne (contra v 9 [10 HB]; compare 1 Sam 4). He stands to survey the battle and lead his people to victory. ***Redeem us*** uses the language of the Exodus in which **redeem** is tantamount to "deliver" (Deut 7:8; 9:26), the deliverance only God can accomplish with his mighty hand. Here, however, the plea rests not on that divine strength but on God's faithful compassion. This *ḥesed* brings to mind the covenant whose theology raises the community's questions but also provides the only place to stand from which to ask those questions.

FROM THE TEXT

How to take the protestations of innocence and the accusations of God is the crux of Ps 44. Taking these as the "beginnings of Pharisaic righteousness" (R. Kittle) or "Pharisaic self-righteousness" (H. Gunkel), cited by Kraus (1988, 448-49) is probably anachronistic. These people are not necessarily self-righteous; they are righteous. Contrary to some in their community, they actually have kept covenant. On the other hand, their God is ultimately responsible for their plight. God has brought suffering to them either directly (in response to sin in the community) or indirectly as the Lord of all history. In either case, from the community's perspective justice has not been served.

Theological resources at their disposal will not take them farther in resolving their problem. They lack a clear view of afterlife, which could provide a path to resolution. The insight that righteous suffering can be redemptive is yet to take hold for the community. Still this psalm serves the community well by stating three realities clearly without forcing a premature "answer." First, God is their King. He is the one who has rescued them to this point. They will never cease to praise him (vv 4-8 [5-9 HB]). Second, this God has now cast them aside, without reasonable cause and without prospect of gain (vv 9-12 [10-13 HB]). Third, the God of the covenant is both their most vexing problem and their most promising hope of deliverance (v 26 [27 HB]).

Verses for the King's Wedding (45:1-17 [2-18 HB])

BEHIND THE TEXT

Psalm 45 is a love song—to be precise, a love song for/about the king. Information normally placed in the SS has in this psalm found its way into the body of the song. The composer himself labeled it a "composition for/about the king" (*ma'ăśê lĕmelek*) (v 1 [2 HB]). The SS tells us it is a song of/about love (*šîr yĕdîdôt*). Whether *yĕdîdôt*/love names a specific kind of song/*šîr* or simply describes the content of this one is not clear.

Psalm 45 is unique among royal songs in its apparent attribution of divinity to a Judean or Israelite king (v 6 [7 HB]). Celebrating the king's wedding, on the surface at least, it also presents a surprisingly "secular" psalm, raising the question as to how it came to be in the Psalter. The text of the psalm has also suffered in transmission, another testimony to the difficulties encountered in this song.

IN THE TEXT

1. The King Extolled (45:1-8 [2-9 HB])

■ **1 [2 HB]** The composer speaks for himself in the first person here at the beginning and then again at the conclusion (v 17 [18 HB]). At the outset in a rare move the composer opens a window on the compositional process itself for this song. His heart is stirred, his artistic aspirations aim at a *good* (*tôb*) piece, assuming the reader will know the criteria by which the "goodness" of a song are to be measured. He plans to recite this work and already has in mind the psalm genre he wants to produce—the *ma'ăśê lĕmelek*, a royal song. This will be the work of a gifted and experienced scribe, precisely what the writer by implication claims to be. He will compose orally, his **tongue** doing the work of the scribe's stylus.

■ **2 [3 HB]** Addressing the king directly in the body of the song, our composer takes up first the striking attributes of the king. The royal groom has no peers in appearance, among humans with whom he locates the king. He is handsome without rival, and graciously endowed, speaks articulately and elegantly. As a result (*'al kēn*) **God has blessed** him **forever** (*lĕ'ôlām*). (The two Hebrew expressions transliterated appear again as an inclusion in v 17 [18 HB].)

■ **3-4 [4-5 HB]** The psalmist urges the king as warrior to **gird** on his **sword**. We should not think here of the king preparing for battle but instead of the groom donning his dress uniform. He, like his bride in the lines below (vv 10-17 [11-18 HB]), is preparing for his wedding, not for battle. Even so, the various roles of the king will be on parade here. So the song calls the king to ride out to victory, as he would do in his role as defender of **truth** and meekness and right. Only after defeating the forces of evil and chaos in battle can he take his throne as king.

> ***May your right hand teach you/show you awesome exploits!*** Almost all versions since the LXX translate in some such fashion. But what the clause means remains unclear. How does one's right hand lead one or teach one or show one? By holding and pointing the sword? As a symbol for the king's strength and prowess?

■ **5 [6 HB]** Further attention to the king's dress uniform beyond the sword finds his archery equipment passing muster. His **arrows** are **sharp**, aimed at the **hearts** of his **enemies**. From their barrage, people fall beneath his **feet**.

■ **6a [7a HB]** This verse contains the major crux of Ps 45, its claim regarding the throne of the king whose marriage the poet celebrates.

*a. **Your throne, O God, stands forever and ever!*** (compare LXX, ESV, KJV, and NABRE). This traditional rendering employs the most straightforward syntax but also presents the problem most clearly. It appears to address the human king as divine—***Your throne, O God*** . . . (emphasis added). This rendering contradicts the OT's consistent rejection of attempts to deify any human, including the kings of Israel and Judah. Thus in Ps 2 we saw Yahweh's anointed one declared to be Yahweh's son, but apparently by adoption (2:7). And Nathan's programmatic oracle to David in 2 Sam 7 promises David that his offspring will be Yahweh's son and Yahweh his offspring's father (v 14), and that his dynasty and his offspring's rule will stand forever (vv 13, 16), but with no indication that this son and offspring would be divine. These passages use language elsewhere reserved for the gods, but in contexts obviously referring to human beings. See, for example, Isaiah's promise of the "Mighty God, Everlasting Father" (Isa 9:6).

*b. **Your divine/your great throne endures forever!*** (compare NJPS, RSV). Some propose the special use of the word "Elohim," where it appears simply to mean "great," not "god." But the syntax of the expressions put forward in *HALOT* (53) is different from our passage.

c. "Your throne is like God's throne, eternal" (NEB). This translation, though technically possible, is very unusual, pushing the syntactical parsing needed to its limit.

d. Some attribute the problem to the editing of the Elohistic Psalter. An original "Your throne, oh Yahweh, is forever" was edited to read "Your throne, O Elohim, is forever," thus creating the problem (Broyles 1999, 207). The fact that the string of second person references on both sides of this colon seem clearly to refer to the king himself militates against this solution.

e. Broyles also suggests that an aural reading of the poem in the festival may have made clear the reference to Yahweh in v 6a [7a HB] (ibid.). The same objections that challenge "d" call this into question.

f. "The eternal and everlasting God has enthroned you." Dahood repoints the MT and parses "your throne" as a verbal clause, "God enthrones," rather than the usual verbless clause (1966, 272-73) (compare REB). This works reasonably well, the main objection being stylistic.

I am inclined to stay with the traditional rendering, understood as "divine hyperbole" or to repoint with Dahood. Most important here are the clear statements in the immediate context that make it very clear that the king is not God and that he and the congregation know that. On these contextual limits see vv 7bc [8bc HB] and 17 [18 HB].

■ **6b-8 [7b-9 HB]** The king's rule is not only enduring but also of admirable character. His **scepter** (v 6b [7b HB], a symbol of his royal authority and rule, is upright. He loves **righteousness** and hates **wickedness** (v 7a [8a HB]), and his **scepter** in the service of Yahweh is the final adjudicator of legal cases (remember Solomon in 1 Kgs 3:16-28). **Love** and **hate** speak of his stance toward covenant values. Consequently Elohim, his God, has anointed him.

The celebration of the king's wedding involves a festive anointing (thus the **oil of joy** [v 7c (8c HB)]). Secondarily it reenacted or at least called to mind the anointing by which God put him on the throne. The clear place of anointing in the string of official acts leading to kingship in Israel can be seen in the OT passages that associate kingship with either the verb ***anoint***/*māšaḥ* or the adjective **anointed**/*mīšĕḥâ*. Through them a messianic hope developed as Israel's eschatological hope was more and more associated with the appearance of a new, Davidic king (e.g., Jer 23:5-6; Ezek 34:23). The fact of this anointing is also used here to underscore his superiority to others who might vie for the throne.

Verse 8 [9 HB] brings the reader back to the marriage festival. The on-site result of the anointing with **oil of joy** is a palace and temple filled with the fragrance of **myrrh** and **aloes** and **cassia**, the fragrances of royalty.

45:6b-9

Contrary to *BBHS*, because of the gender of the audience in v 8b [9b HB] we should probably read v 8b [9b HB] as parallel with v 8a [9a HB] rather than as joined with v 9 [10 HB].

As the king approaches the palace he is delighted by **music** wafting from it. The music comes from palace rooms decorated with ivory inlays that amplify the sounds. We have hints of the luxurious and luxuriant decorations quite likely in mind here. **Ivory** inlays on walls, on furniture, on toiletry articles, and much more were prized booty for invaders, especially Assyrian invaders. Megiddo, Samaria, including Ahab's palace, have been confirmed as sources of ivory (Pritchard 1962, 773-75). From the OT itself, we know of Solomon's ivory throne (1 Kgs 10:18), of Ahab's ivory palace, that is, decorated with ivory (1 Kgs 22:39), and of the prophet Amos' references to ivory as a sign of northern Israel's decadence (Amos 3:15; 6:4). Here this art and finery befit the king.

2. The Bride and Her Entourage (45:9-15 [10-16 HB])

■ **9 [10 HB]** Attention shifts now from the king groom to the royal bride. Among her "ladies of honor" (RSV) stand **daughters of kings** with whom the king or his father has political alliances. She stands at his **right**, a place of submission but also of influence (compare Neh 2:6). Her wedding garment is embroidered with fine **gold**.

■ **10-15 [11-16 HB]** How to make best sense of theses verses is a puzzle. The MT has been disrupted at several points. This prevents us from reconstructing well the situation envisioned by the poet.

The bride now is introduced to the realities of her situation implied in the preceding verse's reference to royal daughters who join the wedding party. She herself will have been the **daughter** of one of these kings! The poet urges her even now to **forget** her **people** and her family back home (v 10 [11 HB]). This is part of being a "daughter of Tyre" (v 12 [13 HB]). On the one hand, the king is captivated by her **beauty**. On the other hand, he will be her **lord** and she will bow in deference to him (v 11 [12 HB]).

As a daughter of the king the wealthiest of the nations will at times come to seek her favor. She will be dressed in beautiful gowns, woven with **gold** (v 13 [14 HB]). On other occasions she will be brought to the king, arrayed in the loveliest of **embroidered** gowns, her entourage of virgins following in her train (v 14 [15 HB]). They will be brought in celebration to the royal palace. This life in the king's newest bride is an exhilarating mix of romance, opulence, power, influence, and risk. This song introduces her to all of these realities.

3. The King's Enduring Renown (45:16-17 [17-18 HB])

■ **16-17 [17-18 HB]** Back now to the king, the days will soon come when he will be preoccupied more with the placement of his **sons** in responsible positions than with paying deference to his predecessors (v 16 [17 HB]).

And back also to the voice of the psalmist who also spoke the opening lines of this song (v 1 [2 HB]). The narrator's disclosure of himself is a distinctive of this psalm. Speaking once more with royal hyperbole he purposes to make the king's renown to reach unending **generations** (v 17 [18 HB]). How he does not say. Probably through the very writing of this psalm.

FROM THE TEXT

Questions of the life of this unique poem after its incorporation into the psalms are bound up with the question regarding its entry into the Psalter. What role would this celebration of the king, indeed of his wedding, have played in the psalms for their first readers? To be blunt: why is Ps 45 in the Psalter?

As v 2 [3 HB] tells us, it may simply have been a poem for the king or commissioned by the king, in this case for his wedding. It may have been a celebration of kingship itself as it was in Israel and thus, indirectly a celebration of God who gave kings to his people (compare Deut 17:14-20). Its voice would then be something like Ps 78.

The Targum already takes it messianically, translating v 2 [3 HB] "Your beauty, Oh king, Messiah . . ." One suspects that this allegorical interpretation brought it into the Psalter. This messianic reading the writer of Hebrews exploits in Heb 1:8-9. Psalm 45 expresses for him both the divine kingship of Jesus and also his unique revelation of God from whom he is in some sense distinct. As James Luther Mays puts it, this reading of the psalm safeguards "against attributing the divine right of rule to any other save Christ, in whose hands it is utterly safe" (1994b, 182).

Praise for the City of God (46:1-11 [2-12 HB])

BEHIND THE TEXT

This song extols Yahweh as the people's enduring refuge. In the process it pays sufficient attention to Jerusalem as to merit designation as a Song of Zion. Among its distinctives is a refrain that appears twice in the song (vv 7 and 11 [8 and 12 HB]). See the Introduction, C.1.d, C.3.d, and C.4.b on the details of the SS.

IN THE TEXT

1. Help in Trouble (46:1-3 [2-4 HB])

■ **1 [2 HB]** Verse 1 [2 HB] stakes the claim that the rest of the psalm will elaborate. The claim is a causal reality. God is the community's refuge; the result ("therefore . . ." [v 2 (3 HB)]) is calm in the face of global collapse.

God is our refuge and strength. Refuge implies protection from an exterior threat. **Strength** implies need for inner fortification. Claiming God as their fortress, the community implicitly rejects those pseudo-protections that promise much but deliver little.

This confident faith has emerged through trial and experience where Israel has to be their most enduring and substantial refuge. The specifying parallel here exegetes the **refuge and strength** of colon A with **help in trouble** of colon B. Literally it reads: *a help in troubles he has been found to be much*. The concluding **much** is an adverb that modifies the entire preceding statement regarding God's proving to be help. Most English versions register this word with **ever-present** or "very present" (RSV), "very near" (NJPS), or the like. We might paraphrase a bit awkwardly: *God really has proven to be indispensable help in grievous trouble.*

■ **2-3 [3-4 HB]** This confidence and proven reality has a predictable result: the people are unafraid, even in the most threatening circumstances. ***The earth***

giving way and ***mountains tumbling into the sea*** surely depicts catastrophic situations. The psalmist may picture a real earthquake here. Repeatedly in the ancient world the hills were shaken with the convulsing of an earthquake. (See Amos 1:1.) Or a tsunami with foaming, rolling waves has brought catastrophe rushing in upon them (Amos 5:8). Or the poet may have in mind social chaos and political upheaval that troubled Israel and Judah repeatedly, before and after the exile.

We should remember that in the ancient world God's people would not have thought of "natural" disasters. An earthquake signaled turmoil in the underworld. The Sea itself was a terrifying god, always threatening to break out of its bounds. In either case their experience of proven refuge with God provides foundation for confidence and freedom from fear in the middle of these soul-shaking events.

2. Yahweh, Present Refuge (46:4-7 [5-8 HB])

■ **4-5 [5-6 HB]** Without notice the subject switches to the **city of God** and its beauty. The city has an artesian spring—just one (Gihon)—that waters the citadel on the flank of the northern mount. The Temple Mount is a uniquely sacred space, where God **Most High** himself **dwells**, from which his rule is broadcast. This fact, the reality of the presence of God in his city, accounts for its stability. He is her help.

■ **6 [7 HB]** The earthquake metaphor of vv 2 and 3 gives way to political realities. Political turmoil and national upheaval threaten. God thunders and the **earth melts**. By context the melting earth apparently is a picture of calm, of fluidity brought about by the command of God.

■ **7 [8 HB]** *Yahweh of Hosts* is with us; *our refuge is* the God of Jacob. The chiastic refrain taps two streams of tradition to form a potent affirmation. ***Yahweh of Hosts*** names Yahweh as leader at once of the heavenly army and of the armies of Israel. The traditional language is strong enough that even in this "Elohistic" psalm Yahweh's name is preserved. **God of Jacob** reaches back behind the monarchies to the identity of the nation as the sons of Jacob. This God is Israel's refuge; his presence constitutes protection and refuge for all who seek him.

3. Yahweh, Breaker of Bows (46:8-11 [9-12 HB])

■ **8-9 [9-10 HB]** *Come, gaze upon Yahweh's works* (v 8*a* [9*a* HB]), comes the invitation. The works now are elaborated in the following lines. In short, Yahweh brings peace to a war-torn, troubled earth. First come the **desolations** (v 8*b* [9*b* HB]) left in the wake of his battles. Then comes an earth-wide armistice, brokered by the God of Jacob, the Lord of Hosts, in view of his mighty exploits on the battlefield. Finally Yahweh disarms all combatants, breaking bows, snapping arrows and burning chariots. Armaments large and small are destroyed.

These lines are reminiscent of Assyrian royal annals where Shalmaneser or Sargon rehearse their conquest of town after town, nation after nation, capturing the army and destroying their weapons.

■ **10 [11 HB]** The second exhortation (compare v 8) calls for quiet in view of the uproar of war, even conflict that brings peace. In this the only place where we hear the voice of God in the song, he asks for sufficient quiet that we can know that the one who has done these things is God. These mighty works will elevate Yahweh above all gods among the nations and to the ends of the earth.

■ **11 [12 HB]** The psalm ends with a verbatim repetition of the refrain, v 7 [8 HB]. The recurrence elevates the reality of Yahweh, **God of Jacob** as refuge as the dominant theme of the poem. Among the several emphases that could have been selected, it is this mighty work we are to think of first.

FROM THE TEXT

Psalm 46 is rich in the language of chaos and desperation. The language of earthquakes and floods is appropriated to picture social and cultural upheaval. In these extremities of life, only God can provide shelter and deliverance by his saving presence.

According to Luke, Jesus used this language to describe the circumstances of the coming of the Son of Man (Luke 21:25).

A Song for the Great King Yahweh (47:1-9 [2-10 HB])

BEHIND THE TEXT

Psalm 47 is a classic song of praise, extolling God as King of all the earth. Sparse information limits our ability to pinpoint a historical and cultural setting for which the psalm may have been written. The exile and the postexilic centuries provided decade after decade in which confidence in Yahweh as King of the world were surely challenged and encouragement to trust the King of kings would have had a hearing. Memory of Yahweh's past deliverance would have been welcome. For information on the technical terms of its SS, see the Introduction, C.1.b, C.1.d, and C.4.a.

IN THE TEXT

■ **1-2 [2-3 HB]** A call for all people to join in boisterous praise of God opens the poem. Hand clapping, loud shouts fill the air. And there is good reason for these responses to God. This is **Yahweh Elyon**, the **Most High** God. He strikes awe into the hearts of worshippers and is acknowledged as **great King** of the world. The title commandeers language used to address the great monarchs of the biblical period, designating Yahweh—not Pharaoh or Ramesses—as the world's great King. In Israel Yahweh sits invisibly enthroned over the cherubim on the ark of the covenant.

■ **3-5 [4-6 HB]** The song recalls times when Yahweh **subdued** (v 3 [4 HB]) enemies under their authority, indeed whole **peoples** under their rule. Before that came Yahweh's choice of the land as his own **inheritance** (v 4 [5 HB]; Deut 4:38; 32:8-13). The land can also be referred to as *Yahweh's* inheritance, but it need not be so here (compare LXX; Deut 32:9). **The pride of Jacob** refers to the land as the gift of Yahweh of which Jacob (the collective people) are justly proud. This is the land Yahweh particularly loved and chose for himself (Deut 4:34). Yahweh's "love" of Israel should be read as an entry into covenant with her, but the term should not be stripped of all its warmth and affection.

Finally in this movement Yahweh has risen at the trumpet's signal, at the blast of the shofar. This pictures Yahweh seated on the throne on the ark, rising as he advances into battle on his palladium (Ps 47:5 [6 HB]).

■ **6-7 [7-8 HB]** Three bicola call for jubilant celebration of God as King. Four out of six words in the MT of v 6 [7 HB] are the exhortation **Sing!** (*zammērû!*). **Sing to God! Sing! Sing to our King! Sing!** Why sing? Because **God is King of all the earth** (v 7 [8 HB]). But God is specifically and particularly Israel's King, to whom song is directed. We are invited to sing a particular song—a *maśkîl*. Unfortunately we do not know much about this sort of song beyond its name. See the Introduction, C.4.c, for more information on this song type as sometimes found in SSs. Something about it must have made it particularly fitting for extolling God as King.

■ **8-9 [9-10 HB]** As King, God rules **over the nations** (v 8 [9 HB]), having taken his seat upon his sacred **throne**. As a **holy throne** it belongs first to Yahweh and then to his king. The princes from the people are gathered, **the people of the God of Abraham** (v 9 [10 HB]). This expression, **the God of Abraham**, appears only seventeen times in the entire OT, first in Gen 26:24 in the patriarchal narratives. It conjures up the God of ancient times, whose promise of the land sustains Israel (compare Ps 47:5 [6 HB] above). It looks as though **the people of the God of Abraham** may reach here beyond Israel, if v 8*b* [9*b* HB] stands parallel to v 8*a* [9*a* HB], and if **the shields of the earth** (v 9*c* [10*c* HB]) is parallel to v 9*a* [10*a* HB]. **The shields** of the earth refers to the **kings** or rulers of the earth, as in 89:18 [19 HB] where "shield" stands parallel to "king." No wonder he is highly exalted (47:9*d* [10*d* HB]): Yahweh Most High, the great King, Israel's King, God of Abraham, and God of the kings of the earth!

FROM THE TEXT

A song that celebrates the sovereignty of Yahweh over all the nations of the earth and their kings must have presented a challenge to those saints who edited and gave us the Psalter. Some circumstances lent themselves better than others to the confession of the faith that *Israel's God was Great King of all the earth, who ruled all the nations* (vv 2 and 8 [3 and 9 HB]). At the height of David's reign, or Hezekiah's, or Josiah's it seemed to make sense. At other times, such as when Josiah died at the hands of Pharaoh Neco, one could not have avoided the irony of the claim. On the other hand, sometimes it is precisely when the irony is sharpest that the claim of the Lord's rule carries greatest weight.

Perhaps this is why Augustine expounds as he does. Taking vv 6-8 [7-9 HB] about the enthronement of the Lord, Augustine asks, "So the heavens are his holy throne? Yes, but do you want to be his throne too? Do not think of such a thing beyond you; if you prepare a place for him in your heart, he comes and is pleased to set his throne there" (Boulding 2000, 331).

Praise for the City of the Great King (48:1-14 [2-15 HB])

BEHIND THE TEXT

Psalm 48 is the second of the so-called Songs of Zion we encounter in the Psalter. Psalm 46 was the first. Psalm 48 is distinctive for its extended attention to the topography of Zion and its environs and to its fortifications.

IN THE TEXT

■ **1-2 [2-3 HB]** The opening lines of the poem (parallel tricola) present agendas that occupy the song as a whole. First, the character of Yahweh, Israel's God, is **great**, eminently deserving of *the great praise he receives*. Second, receiving major attention, Yahweh occupies his own city, Zion, situated on his storied mountain (v 2 [3 HB]). The psalmist reels off a string of verbless clauses, or simple descriptors, giving an emphatic staccato effect to these lines. *Yahweh (is) great / and eminently (to be) praised / in the city of our God / (on) his holy mount. / Lovely in elevation / (it is the) joy of the whole earth. / Mt. Zion in the far reaches of the North / (in the) city of the Great King.*

Zion first referred to the rocky escarpment on the ridge separating the Kidron and the Tyropoean Valleys. It had long been inhabited by the Jebusites before David conquered it and made it the capital of his kingdom (2 Sam 5:7; 1 Chr 11:5). The ridge, roughly 1,250 by 400 feet and shaped like a large footprint, became the city of David or Zion. There David built his palace. He acquired the threshing floor of Araunah (2 Sam 24:18) further up the hill and built an altar there. Later his son, Solomon, constructed his large temple at the summit of the ridge of Zion. Eventually Zion came to refer to the whole city of Jerusalem (Ps 126:1).

Description of Zion was influenced by Canaanite lore that located the mountain of the gods in the far north high on Mount Zaphon (meaning "north"). There the high god, 'El, had his palace, and from there he ruled the earth. Baal's dwelling was also associated at times with Mount Zaphon and established in battle with Yamm (Lord Sea). Zaphon was also in Canaanite mythology located near primordial rivers.

Talk of Zion situated on a high mount in the far north took inspiration from the Canaanite traditions just noted. **Mount Zion** was not a particularly high mountain, was not located in the far north (that was Mount Hermon), and was not associated with lavish waters. Never mind. The borrowed vocabulary enhanced thought of Zion and her location as Yahweh's dwelling.

This was the city of **the Great King**, "King of the World" (v 2 [3 HB]), a title that enhanced the significance of both the city and the king. "The Great King" was the title the empire builders of the first and second millennia B.C. gave to themselves. Thus, the language of Shalmaneser III's chief officer, the Rabshakeh in 2 Kgs 18:28. Appropriating this language for Yahweh both elevated Yahweh and put limits on human pretenders to greatness.

■ **3 [4 HB]** The city's **citadels** would be the heavily defended, government buildings at the top of the ridge, the palace, and the temple especially. Together with the formidable wall and heavily defended gates, these buildings and fortifications make Zion herself a fortress. But in battles and sieges, Yahweh has shown himself to be Zion's **fortress**. His protection has been key to her survival.

■ **4-7 [5-8 HB]** Upon occasion kings have joined forces against Zion, marching by as in review. But at the sight of Zion, they have fled, overtaken with terror (v 6 [7 HB]). *Trembling has seized these leaders, fear like that of a woman in travail, like the east wind [that] destroys sea going vessels* (vv 7-8 [8-9 HB]). This translation reads the wind as the subject of the comparison, extending the doings of **trembling**. The verb can be conjugated as 2 ms., *You shattered the ships, like the east wind . . .* , as well as 3 fs., and *the east wind shattered the ships. . . .*

Tarshish in the MT can mean simply "sea faring ships" (so Cyrus Gordon, "The Wine-Dark Sea," *JNES* 37 [1978] 50-51, cited by Goldingay 2007, 89), or can designate a geographic location, probably Tartessus, a Phoenician colony in Spain. The net effect is virtually the same either way (vv 7-8 [8-9

HB]). The reading that extends **trembling** by the parallel **like that of a woman in labor // *like the east wind breaks . . .*** , with minimal emendation is to be preferred.

■ **8-9 [9-10 HB]** As did the kings in v 5 [6 HB] so now the poet's fellow worshippers find themselves moved by actually seeing the city about which they had to this point only heard (v 8 [9 HB]). This city belongs to their God like no other city.

The city of God and the celebrations and festivals tied to it prompt reflection on Yahweh's steadfast love, as do few other situations (v 9 [10 HB]). This is the sort of thinking that has worshippers comparing with each other situations and liturgy that recalled Yahweh's *ḥesed*, and reflected on it as they processed through the **temple**. The **temple** here is literally ***the palace**/hêkāl* of Yahweh the great King (v 2 [3 HB]), the place of his throne, center of his dominion.

■ **10-11 [11-12 HB]** Yahweh's steadfast love/*ḥesed* is part of his reputation spread **to the ends of the earth** (v 10 [11 HB]). His character and reputation are known far and wide. His fame is based also on his victories, translating **Your right hand is filled with *victory*** (not **righteousness**). Consequently, because of Yahweh's character and also his victories, **Mount Zion** has great cause to be glad (v 11 [12 HB]). Joining in the song are (LXX, NJPS, RSV) the ***daughters of Zion***, meaning either the **villages** or "towns" (NJPS) around Zion or the people who live under her protection.

■ **12-14 [13-15 HB]** The worshippers are called to join in a procession around the city. As they go they are to imprint on their minds **her towers, . . . her ramparts, . . . her citadels** (vv 12-13 [13-14 HB]), the architecture of a great fortress. They are to **count her towers** so that they can *recount* the city's grandeur and God's identity to another **generation**. The message? **This God is our God for ever and ever** (v 14 [15 HB]). That is, the God who founded and protected this, his city, is Yahweh. (We would expect the name Yahweh in these lines in the MSS standing behind the Elohistic psalm.)

The closing confidence of the song is that ***God will guide them even to the end***, retaining the MT, *'al mût*, literally, "unto death." This statement about God's actions (i.e., he will lead them) is stronger than a claim about his identity (i.e., **he will be our guide**) and is a better translation. It is remotely possible that the final two Hebrew words in the MT should be joined to the SS of the following Ps 49 (see the Introduction, C.3.d, for *'al mût*). The resulting word order, however, does not favor this move.

FROM THE TEXT

The appropriation of Canaanite language of Mount Zaphon and the headwaters of the primordial rivers actually underscores the relatively less imposing realities of Mount Zion and her city. The psalm establishes again that God chose Israel, here Jerusalem, not because of her greatness but because of his loving purposes.

A Poem for Dealing with Death (49:1-20 [2-21 HB])

BEHIND THE TEXT

Like Pss 1 and 37, Ps 49 is a piece of wisdom instruction, not a prayer. The writer speaks directly to the reader or worshipper, not to God. The word "God" occurs twice in this teaching (vv 7, 15 [8, 16 HB]). Vocabulary at home in wisdom literature catches our attention immediately: "words of wisdom" (literally *wisdoms*) (v 3 [4 HB]), "understanding" (v 3 [4 HB]), "proverb" (v 4 [5 HB]), "riddle" (v 4 [5 HB]), "wise [men], . . . foolish, . . . senseless [ones]" (v 10 [11 HB]). Whether this psalm trades in wisdom discerned from observation or insight from another world and revealed by God is difficult to say. Its confrontation of death itself and of the problems created when persons of inadequate understanding venture to deal with death show sensitivity that could well have come from the psalmist's own experience.

IN THE TEXT

1. An Appeal for Worldwide Attention (49:1-4 [2-5 HB])

■ **1-4 [2-5 HB]** The teacher makes a universal appeal for attention to his wisdom: **all you peoples,** specified as **all who live in this world** (v 1 [2 HB]). Verse 2 [3 HB] further particularizes this audience as **both low and high, rich and poor alike. Low and high** translates *gam běnê 'ādām gam běnê 'îš*, **both offspring of a human being and offspring of an individual.** The line clearly plays on a nuanced difference between **the human** and **an individual.** Most English versions take the expression as indicating persons of low then high standing, as does Weiser in the Old Testament Library. The REB takes it just the reverse, **the human** indicating a person of high standing; so also Brueggemann (1984, 107). The NJPS deftly cuts the knot with "Men of all estates, rich and poor alike." Some such play is no doubt at work, with the order of v 2*b*, **rich and poor alike** perhaps giving the nod to the REB.

In any case the agenda has been set for the early portion of the psalm. It claims that neither wealth nor status should effect the seriousness with which his teaching should be received nor the breadth of the audience that should attend to it. The psalmist offers no basis for his universal claim, either theological or practical. We will have to look elsewhere to find such bases (e.g., Prov 1:7).

He proceeds immediately to locate his teaching among that of the sages (Ps 49:3 [4 HB]). What he will say (**words of wisdom**), what he will meditate upon ("matters of discernment"), what he will listen to ("maxims"), and what he will elevate by adding accompaniment on the lyre ("riddles")—all of this will be couched in literary genres at home among wisdom teachers and scholars. The fact that he will "open" (i.e., investigate, solve) riddles with accompaniment of the lyre (v 4 [5 HB]) indicates crossover between worship leaders and scribal (i.e., wisdom) personnel.

2. No One Can Bargain Successfully with Death (49:5-12 [6-13 HB])

■ **5-6 [6-7 HB]** Verse 5 [6 HB] moves toward the central concerns of this teaching. The sage faces troubled times, trouble primarily monetary. The psalmist has enemies aimed at subverting him, whose character itself is a threat to him (so LXX, NIV, and RSV). All this is enough to raise fear, but he finds no reason in these troubles to fear.

His assailants live an alien way of life. They are known as persons who **trust** primarily in their own **wealth** and strength—and they want the community to know of their arrogance (v 6 [7 HB]). They will boast in their accumulated wealth. The Psalter has already identified the focus of human trust as the defining feature of life (compare 27:3; 28:7). Our teacher implicitly claims, in contrast to these enemies, to have made Yahweh his trust.

■ **7-9 [8-10 HB]** In order to live such arrogance, the wealthy, alas, must ignore the fact that **no one can redeem** themselves. The word "God" appears only twice in this psalm (vv 7, 15 [8, 16 HB]), both occurrences used to make a claim about God's redemption of a person. Our sage underscores his claim with a redundant infinitive in the MT. The cost of the **ransom** for their lives is too steep to pay God off. What they raise will never suffice to allow them to **live on forever** (v 9 [10 HB]) and not see the pit, that is, not die.

■ **10-12 [11-13 HB]** Verse 10 [11 HB] either provides support for the preceding claim that no one can avoid death by paying ransom (taking the initial *kî* as the conjunction "for") or emphasizes the fact that everyone can see that **the wise** and **the foolish** alike **perish**. The NIV and most English versions follow the LXX, reading it this way. The RSV and Kraus take it as emphatic, "yea" or the like. Either makes sense, though the fact that v 10 [11 HB] introduces a new aspect of the instruction favors the emphatic construal (also marked by the longer tricolon). Oddly, the NRSV and NLT omit this word. To this point the sage has emphasized the impossibility of avoiding death by paying a ransom for oneself. Now we are told that neither **the wise** nor **the foolish** has an advantage in avoiding death. **The wise** and **the foolish ... perish** alike, just like the brutes they are, leaving their **wealth** to those who survive them.

These all wind up with the grave as their perpetual home, their dwelling **forever** (v 11 [12 HB]). Neither wisdom nor folly seems to have any effect on that reality. Even those important enough to have had parcels of land named for themselves suffer this lot (v 11 [12 HB]). Now the refrain, underscoring the sobering claims: **People, despite their wealth, do not endure; they are like the beasts that perish.**

The refrain, appearing again in v 20 [21 HB] carries a puzzling variant in its main verb. Here **do not endure** translates the MT *bal-yālîn* and stands parallel to the claim that beasts do not endure. As in Ps 73, beasts are mentioned for their subhuman thinking as well as their demise (compare 73:22). In 49:20 [21 HB] the refrain says a "people who have wealth but lack understanding are like the beasts that perish." Here instead of *bal-yālîn*, **do not endure**, the MT has *lō'-yābîn*, **lack understanding**. Most English versions and contemporary interpreters follow the MT here, for example, Weiser, Goldingay, and Craigie. The LXX and the Peshitta read *lō'-yābîn*, "lack understanding," both times followed by Kraus (1988, 479) and Broyles (1999, 222), whereas the RSV, NRSV, and REB read *bal-yālîn* in both refrains. Whether the refrain should read the same in both instances or should read differently, and, if read the same, which verb should be read is impossible to tell with certainty. Against the majority opinion I am inclined to follow the RSV, reasoning that lack of longevity is more apt to have been the point of the refrain, rather than lack of understanding.

3. Neither Wealth nor Wisdom nor Poverty nor Folly Alter Death (49:13-20 [14-21 HB])

■ **13-15 [14-16 HB]** Verses 14-15 [15-16 HB] present one textual problem after another, so that one frequently can only make educated guesses as to what the writer had in mind. Perhaps Weiser is to be commended for simply putting dots on the line (i.e., ". . . . . . .") for the latter part of v 14 and declaring the restoration of the corrupt text "hopeless" (1962, 384-85; compare also Kraus 1988, 479).

The psalmist sees this is the destiny of the dullard; even those whose words have a following (v 13 [14 HB]). **Like sheep** set for Sheol, **Death** itself will feed on them, *while the upright also go down to the grave* (reading the MT *yrdw* as from *yrd*, *go down*, and *lqbr* instead of *lbqr*, *by metathesis*; compare *BBHS*). **Death**, with capital "D," is the fearful deity of Canaanite mythology. Even if personified here, it would carry potent overtones.

Textually and theologically we are on more secure ground here. The second of only two occurrences of the word **God** in the poem (compare v 7

[8 HB]) is used here to affirm God's capacity to rescue the psalmist from the grip of death that has shadowed this entire psalm. No one can redeem either another or themselves (recall vv 5-9 [6-10 HB])—but God can. He can snatch one from the clutches of the grave.

From the realm of the dead, literally *from Sheol*. *Sheol* is simply the place of the dead. While Sheol was not considered a place of punishment (like the later hell), neither was it generally considered a desirable place. Being **ransomed from the power of Sheol** would have meant to be rescued from a premature death, saved from the grave that in a person's illness or life-threatening situation already has its grip on one.

He [God] will surely take me to himself. Old Testament evidence does not reveal a well-developed doctrine of afterlife. Glimmers of a confidence that Yahweh would (perhaps even in Sheol) take or receive dying righteous persons to himself in such a way as to comfort and/or vindicate them may appear. In our case, parallel to the claim that God would redeem him from Sheol, the psalmist affirms God **will surely take me to** *God's self.* Take me here translates a Hebrew verb, *lāqaḥ*, used elsewhere to describe the departures of Enoch (Gen 5:24) and Elisha (2 Kgs 2:3). Again in Ps 73:24 it is used in a way similar to our passage. It appears to carry the positive notion of God taking or receiving godly persons to himself, with salvific overtones.

■ **16-20 [17-21 HB]** Again the teacher warns against fear. In v 5 [6 HB] his concern had been fear of wicked deceivers and their fraudulent ways. Here the concern is the intimidation generated by the wealthy as others defer to them and their influence. But once again death is the universal equalizer. No matter how wealthy and influential, these persons will die and **will take nothing with them** (v 17 [18 HB]), not even their impressive reputation. Indeed, they counted themselves **blessed** because of what people are inclined to say about the wealthy (v 18 [19 HB]). But this does not change their destiny. Instead they **will join** the generations of their ancestors, **who will never again see the light** of day again (v 19 [20 HB]).

Then once more the refrain provides the concluding bicolon and drills home its sober point: *A man, though wealthy, will not abide; he is like the beasts which perish* (v 20 [21 HB] = v 12 [13 HB]). (→ on v 12 [13 HB].)

FROM THE TEXT

The sage who wrote Ps 49 was for the moment clearly and completely dominated by a single verity. Everyone dies, wise and foolish, rich and poor—everyone. No one has the resources it would take to avoid that end. The ploys humans use to mask this reality—reputation, fame, exhibition of power and influence—will in the end prove pointless. Everyone dies on equal footing.

While death is certain, the sage has found that trust in God can deliver from the fear and intimidation experienced by persons who foolishly trust their own strength in their face-off with death.

Indeed, only God can be trusted to redeem a person's life and offer a positive entrance to Sheol. Although the teacher mentions this hope (v 15 [16 HB]), he apparently purposes not to elaborate a hope in the face of death but instead to emphasize the universal certainty of death and the resources the godly have for living en route to the grave. As Broyles so aptly puts the matter, the key is "the realization that life is determined not by what you possess but by what or who possesses you" (1999, 222).

We are aware that the Christian reader can scarcely resist the urge to move on to a full-blown conquest of death in the power of Jesus the Messiah who has conquered death and the grave. But we will for the moment resist that move in order to hear the psalmist's sober teaching.

Instruction on Feeding God (50:1-23)

BEHIND THE TEXT

According to the Chronicler, Asaph and his family were worship leaders in the Jerusalem temple (1 Chr 15:1-17; 25:1-2). Some led music and others functioned as prophets who spoke God's word during worship and accompanied by various instruments and singing. One can easily imagine how such persons might become engaged in composing pieces aimed at enriching, even correcting and elevating worship in the great temple in Jerusalem. (Note the reference to Zion in v 2.) Psalms 81 and 95 are usually cited as pieces having a similar prophetic tone.

We lack sufficient information to describe precisely the setting for which this psalm was composed. Even so it seems clear from vv 5 and 16 that it involved in some way a declaration from God and/or recitation of covenant. (See Kraus [1988, 488-91] for a summary of scholarly inquiry into precisely what sort of occasion this may have involved.)

IN THE TEXT

The psalm divides clearly into three parts. An introductory unit (vv 1-6) calls all the earth to hearken to God. He is appearing as Judge (vv 4, 6) and as Judge is about to speak to his people. The two other parts of the psalm carry God's declared word, as Kidner puts it, to "the unthinkingly religious" (vv 7-15) and to "the hardened and hypocritical" (vv 16-23) (1973, 185).

1. The Judge Speaks from Zion (50:1-6)

■ **1** The Mighty One, God, the LORD, that is, *'El 'Elohim Yahweh*, addresses his people (v 1). **The Mighty One** translates the Hebrew word *'ēl*, which simply means **God**. The word is known to OT students since the discovery of the Ugaritic corpus as the name of the high God of the Canaanite pantheon. The name appears often in the OT in conjunction with other terms, such as *'ēl 'elyôn*, God Most High. 'El and 'Elohim, however, are practically synonyms, when *'ēl* is not functioning as a divine name, it makes the set of divine names almost impossible to translate well (as the NABRE translators note). The NIV rendering, supported by most English versions, as **the Mighty One, God, the LORD**, has little to commend it, since *'ēl* means neither "mighty" nor "Mighty One." The REB and NJPS read "God, the LORD God," while the NABRE has "God . . . , the LORD," little improvement.

In addition to these divine names the psalm also has *'elyôn*, **Most High**, as a stand-alone divine name in v 14. Like *'ēl*, *'elyôn* is at home in the Canaanite religious world, but in our context may well be the ancient name of Jerusalem's God, now fully identified with Yahweh (Craigie 1983, 364). The presence of both of these archaic divine names in the psalm has led some to suggest an early date for it.

Having opened with ponderous divine names, the psalmist announces the speaking of Yahweh, calling for global attention. Perhaps we should think not just of "East to West" but actually of worshippers scanning the eastern skyline for the first light of day as a sign of the arrival of Yahweh.

■ **2-4** This word goes out **from Zion**, that is, from the temple in Jerusalem, famous for its beauty and situation. The psalmist speaks from within the community of Yahweh, claiming that **our God** comes. And with him will come his word, for he will not be silent.

A fire devours before him, and around him *the raging storm* (v 3*b,c*). This is theophany language, language of the powerful self-disclosure of Yahweh. Calling heaven and earth to account, God arrives with the purpose of judging (v 4), with his identity as Judge emphasized again in v 6 (compare Exod 19:16-19; Deut 33:2; Judg 5:4 ff.; Ps 94:1-2; Isa 30:27). According to what follows Yahweh's role as **judge** here involves a critical review of worship at the Jerusalem temple as well as instruction to rectify deficiencies uncovered.

■ **5-6** Yahweh calls for the gathering of his saints for critical review. These are persons known for their devotion, for their faithful practice of the **covenant**. Here v 5*b* particularizes these devout ones as persons who regularly make **covenant** with Yahweh **by sacrifice**. Craigie stresses that the participle that names these persons as covenanters, *kōrĕtê bĕrîtî*, must be construed as the so-called immediate future (1983, 365). This would be translated "those who are about to, are going to make covenant" and would clearly locate these persons in a covenant renewal/making ceremony. These persons could also be identified as persons who regularly, as a habit, make and keep covenant with Yahweh.

The **heavens proclaim his righteousness** (v 6), the psalmist claims. **The heavens** refers to God and heavenly agents surrounding him. As in other theophanies, the heavens have been called as witnesses to the proceedings. Interpreters generally take **his righteousness** as an attestation to the righteousness of God himself. This would be significant because he will function as divine Judge (see Craigie 1983, 363-67). The ***selah***, which is not included here, signals a pause or some other break at an appropriate place this time, marking out the introductory verses.

2. God's Rebuke of Theological Confusion and Inexcusable Ignorance (50:7-15)

■ **7** A direct appeal to **my** [i.e., ***God's***] **people** opens the second unit of the Psalms, moving from the universal appeal of the opening verses to those souls who became God's people by covenant at Sinai. In spite of some commendation offered to his people, the overall tone is accusatory. His speech to his people will include ***bearing witness against them***, this witness is based in his role as ***their*** God (compare v 4*b*).

■ **8-12** The logic is a bit confusing. On the one hand, God claims he is not rebuking them for the sacrifice of which they provide a constant and more than ample supply (v 8). On the other hand, he says he will accept no more **bulls** or **goats** from them. The literal ***from your houses*** may signal the corporate approach to worship and sacrifice, which the psalmist assumes (v 9). Most interesting, God bases his rejection of further offerings from their households on the fact that, were he to be hungry—which he is not!—he would not look to his people for food. After all, he knows where plenty of food is to be found among the animals and birds of the wild, which all belong to him (vv 10-11; compare Ps 104).

■ **13** Having taken some worshippers' viewpoint for the sake of argument regarding his need for food, God now simply denies his need for food altogether. Using rhetorical questions he rejects (better, ***mocks***) the idea that he eats and drinks at all (v 13).

One is a bit surprised to find persons otherwise positively addressed chided because of their ignorance regarding the God of Israel's need for food or the lack thereof. There was in Levitical law a description of the peace offering, one of Israel's burnt offerings, as "food" for Yahweh (Lev 3:11, 16). This language remained in Leviticus as fossilized language long after the archaic theology behind it had been rejected.

Sharing a Meal with Yahweh

Among Israel's Mesopotamian neighbors, the "care and feeding of the gods," as Oppenheim put it, was a huge industry consuming considerable resources and directly linked to the bureaucracies of the royal palace and main, national temple (1964, 183-97). In Israel sharing a meal with Yahweh, whether literally or metaphorically, was part of family celebration at the temple, not a royal, federal priestly event.

Psalm 50 shows that at some time in Israel's history this expression came to be understood as a metaphor. Understanding this "food" of Yahweh as literal, physical sustenance for Yahweh was a crass misunderstanding of the person of Yahweh himself. In our passage God wants his people to be done with any confusion about this matter as a precondition of participating in covenant life (vv 5, 13-15). Yahweh's instruction in a sentence? Don't even think about it!

■ **14-15** The last two bicola link sincere sacrifice with deliverance from Yahweh, understanding v 15 as causal exhortations. ***Offer a sincere thank offering to God, and faithfully pay your vows to the Most High. Then call on me with this sincerity and expect that I will rescue you, and you will honor me.*** That is, it is possible these lines are simply about the need beyond correct theology to offer sacrifices from a sincere heart and obedient life, a need made obvious in the larger contexts both preceding and following these exhortations.

It is also possible that these lines press through to the insight that the sacrifices themselves were at heart metaphorical. Although there was a peace offering sacrifice called a *Todâ*/***thank offering*** and used for expressing thanks to Yahweh, our psalmist may suggest that the attitude of being truly thankful is itself a thank offering (Lev 7:11-15). Similarly, while there was a Peace offering to be offered when one paid the vows made along with an earlier prayer for healing or deliverance, the psalmist suggests that the paying of the vows themselves could be understood as the votive offering (Lev 7:16-18).

3. God's Disdain for Compromised Covenanters (50:16-23)

■ **16-17** The second section of the psalm was addressed to God's people (v 7), theologically confused but nevertheless faithful covenanters (vv 7-15). The concluding section addresses **the wicked** (v. 16), hypocrites who want to participate in temple worship but have no interest or only perverse interest in authentic covenant life.

God's concern here is similar to that heard in the Prophets, for example, Isa 1:12-17 or Amos 5:21-24. God condemns those who think there is benefit in joining in worship while one rejects covenant life, disobeying and disdaining that covenant. With a rhetorical question God specifically condemns those who actually have the gall to recite the **covenant** at appropriate points in the liturgy (v 16). Verse 17 completes the ironic accusation that these frauds actually **hate . . . instruction**. They toss it like so much trash over their shoulder and into the gutter. This scheming hypocrisy reminds one of the conniver in Deut 29:16-21 who foolishly thinks to gain the benefits of the covenant while secretly rejecting it in his heart.

The fact that the psalmist assumes recitation of parts or all of the covenant in the course of worship, even by sinners, surely argues for some sort of worship focused on or deliberately using covenant. This is true even though we are at a loss to fully describe and locate this festival.

■ **18-20** Three bicola then expand on this basic accusation. These people, claims God, take every opportunity they find to join thieves and **adulterers** in their obvious rejection of the covenant. That's where they find their lot (v 18). Their speech spews wickedness; they **harness** their **tongue to deceit**, says God, employing an animal metaphor (v 19). Even against close family, against their **brother** and perhaps their half-brother, they speak shamefully (reading *BBHS* rather than the MT) (v 20).

■ **21-22** Verse 21 uncovers a colossal miscalculation of these sinners. Without question they did the sins of which God had accused them, while God remained **silent**. But they misunderstood that silence on God's part, imagining he was like they—impotent, forgetful, ineffective, and confused. His terrifying announcement sweeps aside this confusion: **But I now arraign you and set my accusations before you.**

God invites these sinners who forget him to consider the fact that he is going to **tear** them **to pieces** like a marauding lion tears his prey, with not a chance of escape or **rescue** (v 22).

■ **23** The closing bicolon of this psalm devoted to the purification of worship draws a connection between the offering of sacrifices—by this time we may surely assume these to be legitimate sacrifices—and God's commitment to save his people. Such sacrifices, offered with integrity, actually prepare the way for God to show these worshippers his salvation. There is a causal link between the worshippers' authentic sacrifice and their experience of the work of God celebrated in the liturgy.

FROM THE TEXT

Intertextual reverberations between our Ps 50 and vv 16-19 of Ps 51 show already a long line of working "from the text" before we ever took it up. The writer of Ps 51 assumes the sort of authentic, spiritually significant offering of sacrifices demanded by Ps 50. This trajectory on God's true desire regarding worship climaxes in offering our very lives as sacrifices to God, as in Col 3:17 or Rom 12:1-2.

Indeed, Augustine claimed that Christ Jesus himself was the salvation God promised to show those who honor him with the sacrifice of praise. Everyone who offers such a sacrifice of praise is good, he says, "because whoever offers it is also living a good life, praising me not only with the tongue, but with tongue and life in harmony" (Rotelle 2000, 408).

Prayer for Confession and Recreation (51:1-19 [3-21 HB])

BEHIND THE TEXT

Psalm 51 presents us with perhaps the most moving prayer song/*tĕpillâ* in the entire Psalter. The Anglican liturgist J. M. Neale titled it "The Psalm of All Psalms" (Waltke and Houston 2010, 446). Psalm 51 dominated the Roman Breviary for thirteen centuries, being read seven times daily during those years. Because of the first person reference of the psalm we might be inclined to think first here of an individual psalm. James Luther Mays has pointed out, however, that the language of the prayer is sufficiently reminiscent of Jeremiah, Ezekiel, and Isaiah as perhaps to suggest composition or editing in the early decades after the exile and with the community in mind (1994b, 199).

The psalm's SS locates this poem in the life of David, specifically at the point when the prophet Nathan confronted him regarding his affair with Bathsheba (2 Sam 12:1-14). Both Pss 51 and 52 emphasize the specifically situational location of the two pieces—"When the prophet Nathan came to him," and "When Doeg the Edomite had gone to Saul." Scholars disagree on who attached the SSs to the poems, but clearly the editors who gave us the Psalter wanted us to read these psalms as written for or from these specific contexts.

This works wonderfully for Ps 51, prompting fruitful reflection, even though other contexts are also easily addressed by the prayer. The SS for Ps 52 may not seem as fitting nor as fruitful immediately as a prompt for meditation. But it also repays reflection. Some have taken the SS as indicting a prayer for relief from illness occasioned by some sin (so Wurthwein according to Hossfeld and Zenger 2005, 14-15). I think they are on target when they read it instead as a penitential psalm, whose final form has been determined by the needs of the postexilic community.

For more information on this psalm type, see the Introduction, E.1. And for more on the historical notation in the SS, see the Introduction, C.6.

IN THE TEXT

1. Pleas for Mercy in Pardon (51:1-4 [3-6 HB])

■ **1 [3 HB]** Have mercy on me, O God, according to your unfailing love. The rest of the psalm is, for all practical purposes, an exposition of this opening petition. In the process the psalmist provides a veritable thesaurus of terms related to God's dealings with his covenant people and especially with repentant sinners. We will discover just what it will mean for Yahweh to **have mercy** on the psalmist, thus displaying his **unfailing love**.

Without the SS the psalm itself informs us the penitent one in this psalm is guilty of murder, as indicated in the "guilt of bloodshed" of v 14 [16 HB]. If we read as instructed in the SS with King David's story in mind, to this murder we will add the sins of adultery and lying, if not more. No sin offering is available to cover these sins. They are capital offenses, done with the "high hand" (Num 15:22-36). The psalmist should only expect death. The regimen of sacrifices covers only unintentional sins and sins not done with deliberate rebellion (Averbeck 2003, 719; Hartley 1992, 55-57). The whole psalm is based, then, on mercy apart from sacrifice. The penitent here has no recourse but to throw himself on the **mercy** of God.

This he does from the very first word of the psalm, *ḥānnēnî*/**have mercy on me**, tapping into language familiar from God's self-disclosure at Mount Sinai. There Yahweh revealed himself as "compassionate and gracious God, slow to anger, abounding in love and faithfulness, maintaining love to thousands, and forgiving wickedness, rebellion and sin" (Exod 34:6-7).

Here he asks for God's mercy measured not by God's justice, nor by God's righteousness, but measured by his *loving kindness*, his famous *ḥesed*. This term is often thought to be "covenant love" because of its frequent use in covenant environments. Kindness and faithfulness join hands in this word.

The second petition, *mĕḥēh*/**blot out my transgressions** (v 1b [3b HB]), trades on the image of one wiping out a bowl (2 Kgs 21:13) or blotting out a record (Jer 18:23) to picture the removal of the record of a sin or the stain of the sin itself. Yahweh is known to Isaiah as the one who blots out transgressions, which in that case will involve erasure of even the memory of Israel's sin (Isa 43:25).

As in the first colon, so in the second, the psalmist prays for God's action measured by the scope of his mercy. The term emphasizes the tenderness in God's mercy. **Transgressions** (*pĕšāʿîm*) translates a term that sees sin as the disregard of a law, a criminal act.

■ **2 [4 HB]** The petitions in v 2 [4 HB] both conceive sin as a contaminant and therefore ask for cleansing. "Wash me" (*kabbēs*) is used commonly of the washing of garments (Lev 13:59), thus rendering them liturgically or cultically "clean." So as in Ps 51:7 [9 HB] *kibbē* is parallel here with the verb *ṭahēr*/*to cleanse or make clean*, constitutionally clean.

Because of the psalmist's **iniquity** and because of his **sin** he is unfit for relationship with Yahweh. To be made clean is to be restored for life with God. Both of these terms can appear in the plural, designating multiple acts of sin and crookedness (e.g., sins and iniquities [v 9 (11 HB)]). But here in the singular the petitions reach beyond specific actions to the psalmist's sinful and iniquitous condition. His behaviors flow out of this inner reality. His relationship with God will be restored.

■ **3-4ab [5-6ab HB]** The psalmist is keenly aware of his transgressions and sins. He is aware of specific breaches of the will of God and of his sinful condition as well. This awareness encumbers him like a burden carried on his back.

Verse 3 [5 HB] could simply be emphatic confessions that clear the ground for God to pronounce judgment (v 4 [6 HB]). But interpreters ancient and modern have taken these confessions as the first of a series of lines that substantiate the opening petitions in vv 1-2 [3-4 HB], while at the same time providing the basis for v 4*b* [6*b* HB].

Verse 4 [6 HB] stresses the fact that it is against God and him alone that the psalmist has **sinned**. It would be a serious misunderstanding of the poet to take the psalmist's claims here as a denial of his accountability to the human beings also involved in his sins, indeed, as victims! The editors of the Psalter no doubt had this possible misconstrual in mind when they related Ps 51 to King David. The SS makes sure we do not forget Bathsheba, Uriah, Solomon, the armies of Israel, and others. Some of them even lost their lives as a result of David's sin (Weiser 1962, 403).

But in confession of this sin the reality of David's indebtedness first to Yahweh, Creator and Judge of all the earth, takes theological priority. Without this realization no foundation exists for concern about others also entailed in David's sin. The poet repeats his admission that the deeds done—deeds already called transgressions, sins, and iniquities—were **evil** in God's estimation. The psalmist makes no attempt to minimize the nature and impact of his sin. He calls them **evil**, not mistakes or missteps or slipups or any other trivializing labels.

■ **4cd [6cd HB]** He reaches the purpose for which his full confession has been given, the vindication of God and his word through his servant. God's indictments through the prophet Nathan were correct, and the sentences he will impose are warranted. Though the justness of God's sentences and the rightness of his judgments (compare NJPS) are not the major concerns of this poem, they are important and legitimate matters to broach.

2. Yahweh's Desire for Inner Truth (51:5-9 [7-11 HB])

■ **5-6 [7-8 HB]** Two cola introduced by the Hebrew *hēn*/**behold** and placed side by side make assertions that illuminate the surrounding materials by stating cryptically the human predicament and promise. Verse 5 [7 HB] asserts the sinful history of humans and their surroundings. In an iniquitous world the psalmist was conceived. He has never lived in a culture tilted away from sin and toward obedience to God. Even prior to his birth, in this sinful world his mother conceived him. These lines continue the confessional form of the preceding verses and should not be taken as teaching original sin, certainly not the sinfulness of the acts of conception and birth.

Verse 6 [8 HB] asserts God's preference to the contrary for inner **faithfulness** or truth and godly **wisdom**. While the psalmist has lived in a sinful world since birth, God's desire has been for truth, even in the secret places (though the meaning here is unclear). Pursuing his preference for truth, God has influenced the psalmist prenatally toward **wisdom**. (Compare Ps 139:13 ff. on God's interest in the unborn fetus.) Standing side by side with 51:5 [7 HB], it both complicates significantly the plight of the sinner there while at the same time talking of divine grace.

All of these comments on vv 5 and 6 [7 and 8 HB] must be taken with caution, since the lines are very difficult to translate, let alone understand. Interpretations that link sinfulness with human conception itself fly in the face of the whole OT. (Some of the more extensive notes on these lines to be seen in current commentaries can be found in volume 20, page 6 of Marvin Tate's Word Biblical Commentary.)

■ **7 [9 HB]** The central place of these two *hēn*/**behold** bicola in vv 5-6 [7-8 HB] is underscored by the chiastic arrangement of the verbs that surround them, an arrangement preserved in some versions (e.g., NIV) and not in others (e.g., RSV). The verbs go as follows: "blot out my transgressions" (v 1 [3 HB]), "wash away . . . my iniquities" (v 2a [4a HB]), "cleanse me from . . . sin" (v 2b [4b HB]) before these verses and **cleanse me with hyssop** (v 7a [9a HB]), **wash me** (v 7b [9b HB]), and "blot out all my iniquity" (v 9 [11 HB]).

Cleanse me as in **cleanse me with hyssop** translates a verb that stands outside the vocabulary actually having to do with cleansing or cleaning or making pure. As it happens, in Hebrew the verb translated "commit a sin" is the same verb rendered **to purify from sin**. This is sometimes registered by translating the verb to "de-sin" a person. Thus we have **I have sinned**/*ḥāṭā'tî* (v

3 [5 HB]) but also ***purge me***/"de-sin" me/*tĕḥaṭṭĕ'ēnî* (v 7 [9 HB]), both built on the *ḥṭ'* root, with no economic way of conveying these distinctions in English.

Hyssop was a leafy vine (compare 1 Kgs 4:33 [5:13 HB]) used to sprinkle the blood of sacrifices on persons or objects for which atonement or cleansing was being made. Thus the prayer for God to ***de-sin me with hyssop*** assumes a sacrifice whose cleansing power the psalmist wants applied to him. As a result he would be clean. The prayer assumes the contaminating power of sin. The impurity itself was an image for disruption in the psalmist's relationship with God. The need for "washing" was the need for restoration of relationship with God.

■ **8 [10 HB]** To this point in the prayer the psalmist has focused mostly on more "objective" aspects of his predicament—the fact that he had sinned, had broken relationship with God, that he stood under the judgment of God with no basis for his petitions beyond the sheer mercy of God. But these issues only address part of his plight.

Once a man of song and celebration, he now feels so miserable, it is as though God has crushed his **bones**. He begs for God once again to kindle **joy and gladness** within him. Not only had his sin wreaked havoc with his relationship with God, but it also had disrupted his relationship with himself, silencing his song. This matter of the relationship between his behavior and his emotional or personal state will figure increasingly in his prayer.

■ **9 [11 HB]** A request for God to **hide [his] face** from the psalmist's sins is tantamount to asking him not to attend to those sins, to put them out of his mind, so to speak. The parallel **blot out all my iniquity** gets at the same thing, that is, to have them erased from memory. ***Iniquities*** (pl.) follows the MT and the LXX, parallel to plural **sins** and has in mind getting each specific infraction and all of them out of the picture.

3. Sinners Restored; Praise Renewed (51:10-17 [12-19 HB])

■ **10 [12 HB]** With the petition that God would **create in [him]** a ***clean*** **heart** the psalmist breaks new ground. He moves from dealing with behavioral symptoms to confronting motivational and personal causes. The **heart** for Hebrew worshippers named the location of thought, reflection, commitment, and decision making, as well as feeling. Other worshippers could forgive the psalmist, could encourage or instruct him. Only God could create a ***clean*** **heart**. That ***clean*** heart would be the source of ***clean*** behaviors.

Renew a steadfast spirit within me. This moral and spiritual renovation (compare Joash's renovation of the temple, 2 Chr 24:4) will provide the inner fortitude to ground consistent, dependable obedience to God.

■ 11 [13 HB] Two negative pleas expose possible responses the psalmist might have faced—being cast away from the Lord's **presence** and having God's active presence (i.e., his Spirit) withdrawn from him. The poet's sins could have warranted either or both of these bleak prospects. Positively the prayers imply a desire for God to welcome him in his divine presence and for God to be creatively and powerfully at work in the life of the psalmist. Granting the Spirit's presence would be granting the presence of God himself.

■ 12 [14 HB] The petition that God might *restore the joy generated by the salvation he brings* recalls a time of joy that is now only a memory. He longs for both the song and the salvation that would inspire it. This joy sets the tone for spontaneous obedience that sustains both the psalmist himself and the community of penitents. The word translated **willing** in **grant me a willing spirit** (emphasis added) is associated with a family of words that regularly speak of willing, voluntary action, of free will and not being coerced. He wishes God to sustain him with such abandon. Note vv 14 and 15 [16 and 17 HB] for similar petitions.

■ 13 [15 HB] Now come results the psalmist foresees should God grant his several petitions for mercy. From his own unfortunate experience as a transgressor, he anticipates, perhaps promises, to instruct **transgressors** in God's **ways**. The long form of the verb carries some emphasis, perhaps indicating some eagerness in his desire to teach. The result he foresees may well be the purpose (as in NJPS), that his students, erstwhile **transgressors**, will turn to God.

■ 14 [16 HB] A tricolon emphasizes the only specific confession in the psalm—*blood guilt*—and pleads for God's saving intervention. He asks to be spared from the consequences of having slain someone, either accidentally or purposefully. If accidentally, then the family's avenger seeks his life along the lines of Num 35:9-29; if purposefully, then the community will seek his life unless God spares him in mercy. Interestingly the God to whom he addresses this most urgent request is characterized as the saving God, *the God who delivers me*. This will issue in loud, vigorous praise for the demonstration of God's right character in his rescue of this penitent.

■ 15 [17 HB] Following up the requests regarding restored song, inspired teaching, raucous **praise**, the psalmist now repeats the concern that God be involved in his **praise**, opening his **mouth**, as it were. Stopped by guilt, silenced by fear, it will take an act of God for **praise** again to be on his **lips**. This grateful proclamation of God's **praise**, as it turns out, will be the offering God desires.

■ 16-17 [18-19 HB] The insight that has guided the psalm to this point now surfaces as the explicit substantiation of the preceding lines. God does not **delight in sacrifice** or **burnt offerings**, claims the psalmist. Instead God prefers a disposition of **heart** that shows awareness of the gravity of what one has done in one's sin and gratitude toward God for his deliverance. Had God preferred **sacrifice** the psalmist would have offered it, and the psalm presumably would have contained evidence to this point of accompanying a **sacrifice**. But that was not God's preferred response to sin. The editors of the Psalter have already laid groundwork for this paragraph in the contiguous psalm's related treatment of authentic sacrifice (Ps 50:7-22).

The **sacrifice**/*zebaḥ* (Lev 3 and 7:11-21) was the communal offering used widely as the so-called fellowship or peace offering for giving thanks, for payment of vows, and simply to provide means for communal worship. With this offering relationships between God and the worshippers and between the worshippers themselves were nurtured.

The **burnt offering**/*'ôlâh* was a sacrifice of wide-ranging significance, distinctive in that the entire animal was consumed (except the skin). It often accompanied other offerings to add atoning significance to those sacrifices. To assert that the God of Israel did not desire these sacrifices strikes at the heart of animal sacrifice in Israel.

Instead, in another emphatic tricolon (v 17 [19 HB]), we learn that God desires **a broken and contrite heart** (literally *a crushed heart*) (compare 38:8 [9 HB]). These pictures contrast with the stubborn heart, the stony, adamant, arrogant heart that resists the prophetic word. The hard heart either avoids repentance or engages in superficial or insincere contrition.

4. New Walls and Pleasing Sacrifices in Zion (51:18-19 [20-21 HB])

■ **18 [20 HB]** If we had only Pss 50 and 51 through v 17 [19 HB] in our hands, we would be inclined to see them as a straightforward rejection of animal sacrifice. We would have located them in a day when sacrifice was metaphorical, when the need was not for perfect animals but for pure hearts. Or we would have taken them not as a rejection of all animal sacrifice but as a call for authentic worship. Here we would pay more attention to concerns and vocabulary shared between Pss 50 and 51 and the prophets Micah (6:6-8), Isaiah (1:12-20), Jeremiah (33:8), and especially Ezekiel (24:13; 36:25, 33; 37:23).

It is entirely possible that Ps 51 once ended at v 17 [19 HB] and functioned as a critique of animal sacrifice. But the petitions of vv 18 and 19 [20 and 21 HB] suggest another option now. They locate us in a time when God's pleasure would have included the rebuilding of Zion's walls, that is, a time when **Zion** either had no walls or had ineffective defenses. The mention of Yahweh's altar in v 19 [21 HB] could even imply a time without a temple and its altar.

This places us sometime between the fall of Jerusalem and the ministry of Nehemiah (Neh 1). In that setting, when God accomplishes his "good" for

Zion he will provide physical resources and for the refortification of the city. He would provide a splendid context for worship.

■ **19 [21 HB]** Then you will delight in the sacrifices of the righteous (emphasis added), implying that at the moment circumstances prohibited the offering of sacrifices truly pleasing to God. The person who penned these closing lines was convinced sacrifice that gave pleasure to God not only issued from a humble and contrite heart but also took place in a setting that itself suggested the worthiness of God for worship. A gloss clarifying the desired sacrifices as whole burnt offerings (the ʿôlâh, earlier called the kālîl), and placed at v 19*b* [21*b* HB], made a striking tricolon to draw his work to an emphatic conclusion.

FROM THE TEXT

The theological trajectory within which this psalm stands reaches its target in the death of Jesus once for the sins of the whole world. This involved abandonment of the offering of bulls and goats by the earliest Christians. The correlate of these realities was the transformation of animal sacrifice into a sacred metaphor. Our desired response to the gospel is the offering of our entire selves to God as a whole burnt offering (Rom 12:1) and all our doings as a thank offering (Col 3:17) to the Father. Our life of Christlike love becomes a sweet-smelling aroma, offered in imitation of God himself (Eph 5:1-2). The NT follows the OT's "minority report" in this matter.

A Psalm against Betrayers (52:1-9 [3-11 HB])

BEHIND THE TEXT

The form and type of song to which we should assign Ps 52 remains a puzzle to modern interpreters (Kraus 1988, 508-10). The first section (vv 1-5 [3-7 HB]) shares form and content with passages in the Prophets (e.g., Isa 22:15 ff.). The second section (Ps 52:6-9 [8-11 HB]) sounds something like the response to deliverance in a song of deliverance.

The SS brings 2 Sam 22:6-23 to bear on the reading of this song. It reveals the amount of damage that a malicious tongue can inflict by referring the reader to Doeg the Edomite and his betrayal of David. (On these historical notes see C.6 in the Introduction.)

IN THE TEXT

I. Indictment of Betrayers (52:1-5 [3-7 HB])

■ **1 [3 HB]** Why do you boast of evil, you mighty hero? is as much a rhetorically emphatic form of accusation as it is a question expecting an answer. The psalmist has in his sights the wicked who are powerful in the community because of their physical assets (v 7 [9 HB]) and also their willingness, indeed even their eagerness to speak falsehood against the godly (following the Syriac with most modern versions). "God's faithfulness never ceases" (NJPS) requires the least emendation of the text but seems to disrupt the thought flow.

■ **2 [4 HB]** "Like a sharpened razor that works treacherously" (NJPS). The differences between the versions are all within the realm of the possible. It seems to me that it is more likely the wicked rather than their tongues that **plot destruction**, and more likely that the participial clause "works treacherously" (NJPS) functions as a descriptor of the **razor**-like tongue than a direct address. In any case the indictment is against persons who are deliberately disruptive and whose **tongue** is their chief weapon.

■ **3-5 [5-7 HB]** The deceitful one's tongue does not function autonomously. It reveals the values, the theology of the person wielding this weapon. Speaking reveals moral and spiritual preferences. Given the opportunity the deceitful one chooses **evil rather than good**, lying over **speaking** righteously, preferring words of one who swallows up and the **deceitful tongue**. These deal with chosen associations.

Unfortunately for such persons, Yahweh, God of Israel also has preferences. And he also acts on the basis of those preferences. Consequently, the psalmist warns, Yahweh will ***permanently tear the betrayer down, will tear him and take him away from his tent, he will tear him up by the roots from the land of the living*** (v 5 [7 HB])!

2. The Different Destiny of the Righteous (52:6-9 [8-11 HB])

■ **6-7 [8-9 HB]** These acts of God against the ungodly are public matters, open to observation by the community. When the **righteous** see God's judgment unfolding it fosters awe-filled trust of God. Sight of this reversal also prompts laughter of disgust. Clearly this tragic soul did not make God his refuge. Instead he trusted in his **great wealth** and **grew strong by destroying others** (v 7 [9 HB])!

■ **8 [10 HB]** The psalmist is actually talking about the outcomes of alternative faiths. When life is at stake, in what or in whom does one trust, is the question. The betrayer trusts in his own, accumulated wealth (v 7 [9 HB]). The psalmist claims to stake his life on the faithful kindness and mercy of the God of Israel—now and **for ever** (v 8 [10 HB]). Consequently he sees himself like a lush **olive tree** that has taken root in the temple, whereas the deceiver has been pulled up by the roots (v 5 [7 HB]).

All of this prompts unending praise in the psalmist, the one who trusted Yahweh while his deceitful neighbor stockpiled goods. Why the praise? Because he knows God has acted to bring all of this about. His interesting expressions, simply **because God has acted**, emphasize the vastness of God's actions by omitting an expected direct object and various adverbs with which he might have qualified God's "doing" or God's "acting." (See similar syntax in Mal 3:17.)

■ **9 [11 HB]** Praise promised into an unlimited future implies hope to which the psalmist now turns. He **will hope in** [God's] **name**, that is, in Yahweh's person and character, which his **name** denotes. The reason? Because Yahweh is **good**. If we stay with the meaning "hope" or "wait" for the opening word of the poem's last line (so Hossfeld and Zenger 2005, 26; ESV, KJV, LXX), we will probably link **in the presence of your** *saints* with *I will praise you forever*, which opens the concluding affirmations. Several versions emend the MT to get a verb that means "proclaim" or "glorify" (so the NABRE, NJPS, NRSV, REB, and RSV). Tate reminds us that in a few contexts the verb normally translated "to hope" means instead "to cry/proclaim" or "to call," as in Pss 37:9; 40:2 (1990, 33-35). I am inclined to follow Tate here. It makes fine sense and solves the syntax problem with the very last phrase. The line still expresses enduring hope, but does so implicitly.

FROM THE TEXT

The several themes brought into conversation in Ps 52 are also found juxtaposed in the NT. Here the force of the boastful, deceptive tongue is emphasized, and the havoc it can wreak in a community (vv 1-2 [3-4 HB]). The insight that the tongue expresses the person's moral preferences and deeper spiritual commitments (vv 3-8 [5-10 HB]) is clearly pressed. God's active response to all of this in blessing or judgment is clear (vv 8-9 [10-11 HB]). These come together surprisingly in Paul's castigation of Gentile depravity in Rom 1:18-32. The basic human response to God in his creation prompts worship and loyalty. We either perceive God and are grateful to him or see mainly ourselves and spiral down in self-centered speech of ingratitude toward the Creator and dishonorable speech toward others, slandering, gossiping, and speaking in ways worthy of death, says the apostle.

The Godless Are Fools Still (53:1-6 [2-7 HB])

BEHIND THE TEXT

Psalm 53 presents a near duplicate of Ps 14, here edited for inclusion in the so-called Elohistic Psalter (Pss 42—83). All occurrences of the name Yahweh in Ps 14 are here rendered Elohim. Otherwise, beyond a minor variant in 14:4 and the replacement of v 6 the two texts are identical. (See Introduction, B, for additional treatment of the Elohistic Psalter.)

For technical terms of the SS, see the Introduction, C.3.a, C.1.a, and C.4.a.

IN THE TEXT

■ **1-2 [2-3 HB]** For the majority of our treatment of this poem, see Ps 14. In both poems the terrible situation is acknowledged straight off that the people of God include a host of fools who speak and act as though there were **no God** at all, who do not seek God, and who must anticipate the judgment of God (vv 1-5 [2-6 HB]). This is a prophetic word proclaimed in worship. Correction of this systemic corruption will only occur when God brings Israel's salvation from Zion itself (v 6 [7 HB]).

■ **3-4 [4-5 HB]** The variants in the first two words of v 3 [4 HB] are roughly synonymous. I see no way to judge between them, unless by the rule of the more difficult reading, which would favor our text over that in Ps 14.

■ **5 [6 HB]** The text of v 5 [6 HB] has suffered in transmission. Most English versions rely on the LXX but still show minimal agreement.

Prayer for Deliverance from Ruthless Attack (54:1-7 [3-9 HB])

BEHIND THE TEXT

Psalm 54 presents another of the several songs designated as Davidic *maśkîls*, located here in the middle of Book II of the Psalter. This psalm also carries a historical notation as do eight of the twelve psalms so annotated (51, 52, 54, 56, 57, 59, 60, and 63, along with 3, 18, 34, and 142). The historical note locates the psalm in the episode in David's life when the people of Ziph leaked the word to King Saul that David was hiding among them (1 Sam 23:19-24; 26:1). Ziph was also one of the places Jonathan secretly met David (1 Sam 23:14-16). Ziph is generally identified with Tell Ziph/Zif, a town on the eastern edge of the Judean desert, south by southeast of Hebron. For more detail on the terms in the SS, see the Introduction, C.1.b, C.2.a, and C.4.c.

IN THE TEXT

■ **1-2 [3-4 HB]** The psalmist identifies the form and genre of his own work in the course of crying out for deliverance. He asks God to hear his *tĕpillâh*, his **prayer** (v 2 [4 HB]). He cries out for God to **save** him, more specifically to

vindicate him (v 1 [3 HB]), and this probably by an honest court decision in his favor.

He calls on God to **save** him **by** God's **name** and by God's **might** (v 1 [3 HB]). God's own character and person are the means by which God's rescue of the psalmist will take place. **Name**, of course, in passages like this, refers to the whole person, especially one's character. As Kraus puts it, "the power of Yahweh present and active on earth and especially at the cultic center" (1988, 516). In this case God is assumed to be the Judge and to have sufficient strength as to back up any judgment he proclaims on the psalmist's behalf.

■ **3 [5 HB]** The reason for the urgent petitions now follows. Adversaries have risen against the psalmist—foreigners, strangers (or perhaps *cynics*), powerful foes who actually threaten the psalmist's life. These foes have no **regard for God**. We are not told explicitly, but these foes and the psalmist's petitions would seem to locate the psalmist among those in the community who lack power. They have few resources—other than God's covenant commitment to Israel—with which to resist the assaults on their person and property.

■ **4-5 [6-7 HB]** But over against these threats to his life the psalmist is profoundly aware of God, who continually rescues him and regularly provides indispensable help for him. He prays that the evil perpetrated by his adversaries will be brought back upon their head (compare Prov 1:15-19). He prays that God, his Lord (*ădōnāy*), will bring God's inimitable truth to bear on the psalmist's case.

■ **6-7 [8-9 HB]** Anticipating the rescue for which he prays, the poet foresees a celebration by gladly offering a sacrifice, perhaps paying a vow made during the trial. God has delivered him, in accordance with his petitions; a thank offering will be especially appropriate. Review Ps 116:12-19 as an example of what the psalmist may have in mind here.

Broyles notes this psalm's references to God by his "name" (Ps 54:1, 6 [3, 8 HB]) link it to the Deuteronomic "name theology" characteristic of Deuteronomic literature (compare Deut 12:5). This theology deals among other things with the tensions between God as the one who has chosen to dwell at his temple in Jerusalem, but also the one whom neither the temple nor the heavens can contain. It is perhaps best seen in Solomon's prayers at the dedication of the temple (1 Kgs 8:13, 30-45) (1999, 238).

FROM THE TEXT

No explicit references to Ps 54 appear in the NT, but its key themes are treated. In the process a major, inspired revision occurs. While believers in Jesus are assured of the eventual conquest of all evil and vindication of God and his people (Rev 20—21), Christians are in the meantime urged repeatedly to pray for the good of their adversaries (e.g., Matt 5:43-48). One of Augustine's chief concerns in his exposition of Ps 54 was that the people of God live with such clear devotion to the Master that they never be confused by others with the Ziphites (compare 1 Cor 1:12). "But love God for himself alone," he urges, "love him disinterestedly, for you cannot possibly think of anything he could give you better than himself" (Rotelle 2000, 51).

Prayer for Rescue from an Erstwhile Friend (55:1-23 [2-24 HB])

BEHIND THE TEXT

Psalm 55 carries an SS nearly identical to that of Ps 54, except for the fact that it includes no historical note. For the technical terms in the SS, see the Introduction, C.1.b, C.2.a, and C.4.c. As for its form the psalmist himself names it as a prayer. This form is expounded in the first few lines as a supplication, that is, a cry for mercy or simply a cry (v 1 [2 HB]). The prayer is almost completely comprised of the psalmist's personal calls, of descriptions of the psalmist's plight, and of his trust in Yahweh.

An uncommon feature of this prayer is that his enemy has been his close friend (vv 12-14 [13-15 HB], vv 20-21 [21-22 HB]). This broken trust gives the prayer a particularly poignant twist and provides the agenda that allows the psalm its particular contribution to the Psalter.

IN THE TEXT

1. Prayer for Help in Trouble (55:1-3 [2-4 HB])

■ **1 [2 HB]** Listen to my prayer, O God (emphasis added). As noted above, the psalmist names his **prayer** using the term scholars have come to use to identify the literary form of this poem and others like it. It is a **prayer** in which the psalmist cries out to God with petitions that address needs only the psalmist's God can meet. Early scholars of these forms call this type of psalm laments. This designation proved unsatisfactory mainly because they contained no actual laments in the usual sense of songs related to the dead.

The parallel term, *mittĕḥinnâh*, expounds the **prayer** as a plea for mercy. He desperately needs God to hear him. He especially wants God not to **ignore** him, a terrible prospect. This would have Yahweh not simply failing to hear him for some undisclosed reason (too busy? too far away? disinterested?) but deliberately choosing not to hear the psalmist.

■ **2-3 [3-4 HB]** The early lines of the song disclose the fact that the problems the psalmist confronts involve people, actually evil, noisy persons. He has enemies, adversaries; these persons seek to do him harm. They are not neutral acquaintances. No, these persons intend to injure the psalmist, and they mean to convey their hostility to him when they encounter him at the various points of public interaction. They threaten him and openly express their anger at him. They are **the wicked** (v 3 [4 HB]).

2. The Depth of the Psalmist's Distress (55:4-11 [5-12 HB])

■ **4-5 [5-6 HB]** In addition to these external issues for which he seeks God's mercy, the psalmist faces interior problems related to his response to his adversaries. His thoughts trouble him; he is "distraught" (v 2 [3 HB]). Fear and trembling have beset him. **Horror has overwhelmed** him (v 5 [6 HB]). His interior state has taken on a life of its own as part of the problem for which he cries for help.

■ **6-11 [7-12 HB]** To his petitions the psalmist adds his wishes that he **had the wings of a dove** (v 6 [7 HB]) to distance himself from his frightful situation. He would fly **far away**, lodging somewhere in the trackless wilderness (v 7 [8 HB]), away from the tempestuous life his enemies put him in (v 8 [9 HB]). Returning to life as he actually encounters it, he sets aside his wishes and the accompanying metaphors. Instead the city in real life confronted him with **violence** and contention (vv 9-11 [10-12 HB]). **Day and night** the violent circle the city, patrolling its **walls** to incite destruction and **malice** (v 10 [11 HB]).

3. Prayer against Friends Turned Enemies (55:12-21 [13-22 HB])

■ **12-14 [13-15 HB]** Now the psalmist names the issue that gives this prayer its distinctive contribution in the Psalter. "It is not an enemy who taunts me," he claims—then **I could endure it**; "not an adversary . . . —then I could hide from him. But it is you, . . . my companion, my . . . friend" (vv 12-13 RSV). But obviously his former companion is indeed now his **enemy**, his erstwhile **friend** is his adversary. Precisely this is what makes the situation so unbearable. **If an enemy were insulting me, I could endure it; . . . But it is you, . . . my close friend**. All the language used to describe his enemies has actually been aimed, and appropriately so, at a person formerly his friend.

Not simply a friend but a **close friend**. This one the psalmist could address straight on—"you." A person of comparable station, a compatriot, one to whom his ways are known; not just an acquaintance (v 13 [14 HB]). Among memories shared were treasured conversations—"temple talk"—prompted by worship of Yahweh and neighbors' desire to learn of the Lord from each other.

The strange manner in which the history of the psalmist's relationship with this particular enemy figures in the situation surfaces in the naming task.

The adversary is certainly a **foe**, an **enemy** (v 12 [13 HB]). But this foe, this enemy has also been his **companion**, his **close friend** (v 13 [14 HB]). Neither side of the description seems appropriate without the other now.

■ **15 [16 HB]** But for now the roles are set. The psalmist's prayer for the erstwhile friend is a prayer for the **death** of this enemy. It puts the friend back in the teeming throng, destined for an early and well-deserved departure to the grave.

■ **16-21 [17-22 HB]** Stressing now not his common ground with his colleague but instead his singular reliance upon Yahweh for deliverance, he returns to the pleas with which the psalm opened. He testifies to Yahweh's deliverance (v 18 [19 HB]), even though his friend **attacks**, violating **his covenant** word (v 20 [21 HB]). His friend attacks with words **smooth as butter**, yet **war** lurks **in his heart** (v 21 [22 HB]). Now he addresses Yahweh as the one who delivers (*ransoms*), the one **enthroned from of old** (v 19 [20 HB]).

4. Trust in Yahweh's Victory (55:22-23 [23-24 HB])

■ **22-23 [23-24 HB]** A teaching, encouraging voice exhorts the psalmist to **cast your [sg.] cares on** *Yahweh*, knowing he will provide for the needy (v 22 [23 HB]). Why so? Because he is convinced Yahweh will eventually bring his enemies to an undesirable end, to a premature end. **The pit of decay** (v 23 [24 HB]) would be the grave. Everyone dies, of course, but not everyone dies prematurely, living only half their potential. Avoiding this sort of end by the providence of God is good reason to look to God. His assertion that in contrast to these unfortunate souls he will **trust** Yahweh closes the psalm (v 23*c* [24*c* HB]). The concluding tricolon and the emphatically placed pronoun (**But as for me**, . . .) put an exclamation mark on the promise.

FROM THE TEXT

Peter quotes Ps 55:22 [23 HB] as he encourages Christian elders in central Asia Minor to "cast all [their] anxieties" on God as they "tend the flock of God" (RSV) according to Christ's example (1 Pet 5:7, 2).

Earlier in Peter's epistle without direct citation of Ps 55, the apostle does raise the issue of a Christian response to enemies who were at one time friends. Peter considers suffering unjustly an opportunity to find God's approval by responding to such suffering as did the Master (1 Pet 2:18-25). According to Peter, our Savior provides both an example that instructs us and also redemption that empowers us. These resources enable us to respond to betrayal by our erstwhile friends in ways not considered by the psalmist in Ps 55. For the psalmist the former friend is now an enemy to be treated as an enemy. For the Christian elders these "enemies" would represent a call to follow Jesus to the cross.

Prayer of Trust for Deliverance (56:1-13 [2-14 HB])

BEHIND THE TEXT

Psalm 56 illustrates well the folly of pressing the form of a psalm too forcefully. It puts hymned features together in rather inelegant ways, which the editors of the Psalter nevertheless apparently found edifying. The song begins with (vv 1-2 [2-3 HB]) and later returns to (vv 5-7 [6-8 HB]) the standard petitions and descriptions of plight common in the prayer songs. Interspersed among these petitions are affirmations of trust (vv 3-4 [4-5 HB]; 8-13 [9-14 HB]) more at home in wisdom pieces or praise songs than in the prayer of the devout.

As for the SS, this composition is entered into the Psalter as a Davidic *miktam* with two other features to its SS. First, it is situated in the story we know from 1 Sam 21 and David's brief capture by the Philistines. Second, it is apparently to be performed or sung to the tune of a piece popularly known as "The Dove on Distant Oaks." See the Introduction, C.1.a, C.1.b, C.3.b, C.4.d, and C.6.g.

IN THE TEXT

■ **1-2 [2-3 HB]** The first word in the body of the psalm gives us the only petition in the song related directly to the psalmist: *ḥānnēnî*, that is, **Be merciful to me, my God.** The following two and a half lines elaborate the plight prompting the cry for mercy (vv 1*b*-2 [2*b*-3 HB]).

Pursue is the key word (twice in two lines) in the psalmist's mind when he describes his situation, the reason for the call for mercy. It pictures wild animals panting after the chase. This is hard work for the ***mere men**/'ĕnôš*. These men press the attack, using a military metaphor. These foes are numerous, arrogant, and slanderous. Either figuratively or literally the psalmist is in a battle from which he cries for help.

■ **3-4 [4-5 HB]** Two states of mind stand at odds with each other in the psalmist's mind. On the one hand, his situation can produce fear, experienced as being **afraid**. Over against this fear he places his **trust** in God (v 3 [4 HB]). While the fear simply appears to rise from the situation, his trust in God appears to be a chosen set of mind contrary to being afraid. The result of trusting is not fearing.

In the center of these realities the psalmist asserts his praise of the **word** of God. Although we should probably not think here of extensive written texts of Scripture available to the psalmist, the word of God is clearly a sufficiently coherent reality to ground his conquest of fear in trusting God (v 4 [5 HB]). Prophetic preaching, priestly teaching, scribal publication, and perhaps other streams of divine word may be involved in the psalmist's concept of the word of God.

What **mere mortals** can **do** to the psalmist would be summarized in the trampling and attacking pictured in vv 1-2. **Mere mortals** here translates the Hebrew word for *flesh*, associated with human beings in their weakness and their constitutional difference from God. In light of the psalmist's trust and God whose word he praises, nothing mere mortals can do will plunge him into fear (v 4 [5 HB]; compare v 11 [12 HB]).

These statements of trust and praise in the midst of the psalmist's petitions are a distinctive feature of this psalm. Affirmations of trust and encouragement appear not only once but twice in a refrain-like restatement in vv 11-12 [12-13 HB].

■ **5-6 [6-7 HB]** The enemies spread disinformation, constantly twisting his words, taking them out of context to slander the psalmist. The psalmist confronts a group of persons plotting, conspiring. The picture is of predators lurking to attack, or of "special forces" set on taking his life.

■ **7-9 [8-10 HB]** "The text is meaningless," complains Kraus, of the MT in these lines (1988, 524). Actually the text of the whole psalm shows signs of rough treatment by tradents. Kraus's assessment may be premature but warns us of the textual difficulties that have yet to be solved here. Various "toe holds" show promise, but no version produces a crisp translation that honors the MT. The NIV is as good as any at this point. Tantalizing toe holds keep one looking. On the metaphor of God having a record book or various books, see Exod 32:32-34 and Mal 3:16, along with Rev 22:8-9.

■ **10-11 [11-12 HB]** The short of it is that when he calls upon Yahweh his enemies fall back and he emerges with the conviction that Yahweh is on his side. This he knows! This astounding claim of certainty is the theological foundation of the other statements of trust and confidence. These verses celebrate God's word. A refrain-like repetition of v 4 [5 HB] underscores his **trust** in Yahweh and the role of God's **word** in that trust. He speaks praise of God's word.

■ **12 [13 HB]** Convinced that no one will harm him while he is trusting, he promises God the **vows** he made during the thick of the battle he will pay. It is God's rescue of his life that prompts his concluding praise.

■ **13 [14 HB]** All of this reaches its purpose now, that he may conduct himself, in the **light of life**. He will live out his years before God, that is, related to and accountable to him. (See Gen 17:1-2 on living before God.)

FROM THE TEXT

That God is "for us" proves to be one of the foundational revelations of biblical faith. The psalmist comes to this conclusion apparently on the basis of his rescue by Yahweh in response to his prayers by the word of Yahweh, whom he praises lavishly. Exactly what word the psalmist depended on for this confidence we do not know.

The NT's critical contribution to the canonical dialogue on this matter appears, among other places, in Rom 8:31-39. The Christian's confidence that the God and Father of Jesus is "for us" is grounded in the fact that he sent his Son to reconcile us to himself (compare also 1 John 3:16; 4:9-12).

Prayer for Rescue from Ravenous Lions (57:1-11 [2-12 HB])

BEHIND THE TEXT

We have placed this delightful piece among the prayer songs concerned with deliverance from persecution, and rightly so. (See especially the psalmist's description of his enemies [vv 3, 4, 6 (4, 5, 7 HB)].) But his description of his general situation, his confidence in deliverance, and his anticipation of joyful praise when he is delivered give this song in several lines the atmosphere of a song of praise. It provides a model for buoyant petition.

For the SS see the Introduction, C.1.a, C.1.b, C.3.a, C.4.d, and C.6.h. This is another song in which the congregation is guided to sing the prayer according to a known tune, "Do Not Destroy," and to bring to mind the setting of David's choice not to harm King Saul when he had opportunity to do so in a cave in the Judean desert (so 1 Sam 24).

IN THE TEXT

■ **1a [2a HB]** **Have mercy on me, my God, have mercy on me.** By repetition and placement this prayer sets the tone for the entire psalm. Truth be told, it also provides the theological grounds for psalms like this. By the nature of the case the writers of these prayer songs find themselves in situations from which only God can extricate them and for which his mercy will in the end be the most critical feature of his motivation for favorable response. Thus v 1a.

Now v 1b provides the reason for his cry. In God is where he has chosen to take refuge. It is the basic, positive response to God that the Psalter has offered and has sought since the first pages (2:12). **For in you I take refuge.**

I, or lit., **my soul** appears here and again in vv 4 and 6 [5 and 7 HB]. In all of these the first person references, the "I" is given metrical and theological richness with the use of *my soul*. *My soul* is the I of substance, of desire, of thought and more. The writer affirms **In you *my soul*/*nepeš* takes refuge**. That is his habit, not his surprise move here.

■ **1b [2b HB]** **In the shadow of your wings**. The poet may call on a comforting picture from nature of the chick finding protection from the storm in the shade of its mother's wings. Just as likely in our case, it would be the wings of the cherubim filling the most holy place corner to corner under which Israel would find refuge (1 Kgs 6:27-28). And this ancient scene would itself find its roots in widespread artistic traditions depicting gods and other "heavenly" creatures with wings outspread to provide protection while claiming status (Keel and Uehlinger 1998, 248-77; Hossfeld and Zenger 2005, 70-74). **Take refuge**: the word occurs twice in two lines.

■ **2 [3 HB]** The psalmist calls upon God as *'elôhîm 'elyôn*/**God Most High**, with *'ēl gōmēr* in the parallel colon (3 B). *Gōmēr* is not used elsewhere as a divine name. The verb usually has to do with completing, finishing something, or providing. This latter sense probably fits here. We find a "shadow" and the "Most High" also in 91:1.

■ **3 [4 HB]** **He sends from heaven and saves me**. We should picture the Most High sending emissaries from the heavenly counsel—servants eager to do his bidding—in this case, saving the psalmist (compare 103:19-22). The servant rescues the psalmist, bringing reproach on the one who hounds him. Indeed, in this metaphor God sends his servants, **his love** [*ḥesed*] **and his faithfulness** (*ĕmet*), to do his bidding. These two words often appear together in contexts tied to Yahweh's covenant with Israel (Mic 7:20). Compare Ps 23:6, where God's *ḥesed* and *ṭôb*, "his mercy and goodness" in this case, follow him constantly.

■ **4 [5 HB]** Following his interchanging pattern he turns from his focus on God and his responses to devote two cola to his own plight. He complains that he dwells **among ravenous beasts**. He paints a military and hunting picture, speaking of **men whose teeth are spears and arrows**, their **tongues are sharp swords**. Both his person and his reputation are threatened.

■ **5-6 [6-7 HB]** Back to his petitions he envisions God demonstrating his lordship over **the heavens** and **all the earth** (v 5 [6 HB]) when he rescues the psalmist. His glory will be evident over all the earth. The futility of the enemy's ways will become evident when they fall in the **pit** they themselves had dug for the psalmist (v 6 [7 HB]). They demonstrate the ironic truth spoken at the outset of the Psalter and also of the book of Proverbs. Evil carries in itself the seeds of its own destruction. The sinner perishes in the pit he had carved out so carefully for the righteous (compare Ps 1:6; Prov 1:17-19).

■ **7-8 [8-9 HB]** In all of this the psalmist is centered on God, ***his heart is set on God*** (v 7 [8 HB]). Though he cries for help and assesses soberly the strength of his enemy, he is not overwhelmed. He looks forward to song in praise of his deliverer. With the dawn of day he will give song. **Awake, my soul!** (v 8 [9 HB]) translates well the MT (so also several other versions). The ESV, following the LXX, translates "Awake, my glory!" The MT *kĕbôdî* can be translated this way, but what does it mean? Better (with NIV, NABRE, RSV, and some other versions) to take *kābôd* as roughly equivalent to soul or heart or self.

■ **9-11 [10-12 HB]** Turning one last time to his praise of God, he anticipates giving praise among great throngs. This is because of the greatness of Yahweh's **love** (*ḥesed*) and **his faithfulness** (*ĕmet*), brought together now for the third time in this poem (v 10 [11 HB]). Asking for the praise of God's greatness **over all the earth** and unto the **heavens**, that is, from A to Z, is asking for God's person to be celebrated in all earth (v 11 [12 HB]). From one extremity to the other emphasizes the great range over which the psalmist wishes God's renown to be spread. This echoes Habakkuk's claim that "the earth will be filled with the knowledge of the glory of the LORD, as the waters cover the sea" (Hab 2:14).

FROM THE TEXT

This psalm that sees the glory of God evident over all the earth appropriately prays for his glory to be everywhere praised and manifest. When the distance between the believers' affirmations of faith and their own trials of faith are disturbing, a prayer like Ps 57 is called for. We may need the one who is exalted over all the earth to exalt himself. This is the faith Christians repeatedly exercise when they pray "Thy kingdom come, thy will be done" (Mays 1994b, 210).

Prayer for Deliverance from Uncharmed Snakes (58:1-11 [2-12 HB])

BEHIND THE TEXT

As with many psalms a confident conclusion about the date and setting of Ps 58 escapes us. A number of settings could be suggested by the social upheaval and rampant injustice evident in the psalm. If this turns out to be a piece in which Yahweh is moving to theological supremacy (compare, e.g., Ps 82), this could suggest an earlier date, but not necessarily so.

Discerning the genre of Ps 58 also proves challenging. The lines one might expect to find in its petitions sound instead like instructional material. Thus Gerstenberger designates it material for communal instruction (1988, 233). Tate and others have noted that the "instructional" material sounds not simply instructional but prophetic (1990, 84), perhaps to be linked with cultic prophets either at the Jerusalem temple or the various sanctuaries both north and south.

Perhaps this prayer is underscored by a chiastic reversal that hinges on v 7 [8 HB]. Following Doyle, Hossfeld argues for the following concentric structure: vv 1-2 [2-3 HB] (A), vv 3-5 [4-6 HB] (B), v 6 [7 HB] (C), vv 7-9 [8-10 HB] (B'), and vv 10-11 [11-12 HB] (C') (Hossfeld and Zenger 2005, 79-82).

On the SS, see the notes on Ps 57 (whose SS is the same as that of Ps 58, except for its historical note).

IN THE TEXT

1. Injustice Rules (58:1-2 [2-3 HB])

■ **1-2 [2-3 HB]** According to the MT a speaker addresses a mute person (*'ēlem*) asking (rhetorically?) whether or not he speaks justice and apparently implying that he does not. Perhaps the mute one is prohibited from speaking or refuses to speak. In either case, righteous proclamation does not occur and injustice prevails. Bardtke (*BBHS*, ad loc.) and others read the MT *'lm as 'ēlîm*, god (or gods) or mighty one(s). In this case the speaker is probably Yahweh. The "mighty ones" are the world leaders charged with proclaiming and maintaining justice and order. These have failed, resulting in a terrible breakdown of righteousness and order.

Or it is possible that we should take *'ēlîm* as the gods in Yahweh's heavenly court charged with maintaining righteousness. Yahweh here rebukes them for their failure, along the lines of Ps 82. Perhaps we have a remnant of an ancient account of Yahweh becoming the Most High, greatest of all gods (compare Deut 32:1-9).

2. Like Vipers from the Womb (58:3-5 [4-6 HB])

■ **3-5 [4-6 HB]** The result of the failed proclamation is that **the wicked go astray; even from the womb** (v 3 [4 HB]). They themselves speak falsehood, whereas they should have spoken righteousness. Their speech instead poisons the community like a serpent's **venom** (v 4 [5 HB]). They are like a serpent that closes its ears to the sound of the **charmer** so as not to be charmed (v 5 [6 HB]).

3. Break the Teeth, . . . God (58:6 [7 HB])

■ **6 [7 HB]** Verses 6-8 [7-9 HB] constitute the only petitions spoken to God in this prayer. Like the poet in Ps 22:12-21 [13-22 HB], the psalmist pictures national leaders as various vicious animals. This strident prayer is for God to **break the teeth** of the wicked, pull out **the fangs of those lions**.

4. Let the Wicked Be like a Slug (58:7-9 [8-10 HB])

■ **7-9 [8-10 HB]** Now the psalmist turns again to the state of the wicked with a series of disgusting, putrid metaphors. They wither, are like downtrodden grass, like snails dissolved into slime, a miscarriage that never saw the light. These picture the wicked when they have no word from God or when they will not receive it. The deplorable state of the wicked underscores the responsibility of the Mighty Ones and their call to speak righteousness among human beings.

5. The Righteous Will Be Glad (58:10-11 [11-12 HB])

■ **10-11 [11-12 HB]** The poet moves now from the plight of the wicked (vv 7-9 [8-10 HB]) to the joy of the righteous one who sees vengeance done and reward given to the righteous. The righteous **will wash his feet in the blood of the wicked**. Though clearly from another age, nevertheless the **righteous** is himself actively engaged in the vengeance for which he had prayed.

The last line of the psalm testifies to the validity of the claim standing behind the entire psalm, though only now spelled out. **Surely there is a God who judges the earth.** This is the proclamation asked for in v 1 [2 HB]. This is the assumption behind the intervention of Yahweh in v 6 [7 HB].

FROM THE TEXT

Breaking the sinners' teeth, washing the saints' feet in the blood of conquered sinners seem more strident than Christian ears want to hear in prayers for our enemies. But along with a number of other imprecatory psalms, they are quite well at home in the prayers of the Psalter (e.g., Pss 59, 69, 70, 79, and others). Among other issues, these prayers underscore the importance of a conscience sensitive to justice in the world and to the question of God's participation in it. In the end we will have to have the NT to give satisfactory account of the God who does justice in the earth.

Prayer for Deliverance from Snarling Dogs (59:1-17 [2-18 HB])

BEHIND THE TEXT

This is the third psalm in a row to be sung to the tune, "Do Not Destroy!" Apparently this melody enhanced the singing or reading of prayers for deliverance. The editors of the Psalter have also connected the song with a historical moment, the time when Saul placed David's home under surveillance in order to capture and kill him (1 Sam 19:11-17). The SS informs us this is another Davidic psalm, a *miktam*. Regrettably, although we can observe this genre data, we lack information to understand the significance of the notes.

IN THE TEXT

1. Prayer for Deliverance from Enemies (59:1-5 [2-6 HB])

■ **1 [2 HB]** The psalmist begins the poem's interchanging *pattern* with a call for his God to deliver him from his enemies. The line itself is beautiful and is closely parallel to v 2 [3 HB] in syntax, vocabulary, and rhetoric. Its chiastic syntax calls attention to the two verbs that rhyme and stand at the outer edges of the bicolon. Thus:

(Deliver me) (from my . . . ;)

//(*from my* . . .) (*rescue me*)

The expressions **enemies**, that is, persons with animosity, and **those who are attacking me** both capture the Hebrew words well.

■ **2 [3 HB]** Verse 2 [3 HB] has syntax and order nearly identical to that of v 1, underscoring the thought in both verses. **Evildoers** names persons known by what they habitually do—in this case evil! **Bloodthirsty men** names violent adversaries. These songs are written in such a way that they can be spiritualized and appropriated by persons whose adversaries are problems of life. This is legitimate. But petitions like this force one to recall the precarious nature of life in Bible times. The saints of old lived in truly violent situations, needing God's help to survive.

■ **3-4 [4-5 HB]** Explaining why he prays for rescue from violent adversaries, he pictures his enemies like predators. They hide along the road in ambush at sundown. These are strong men, and they attack without warning. Perhaps the psalmist could understand if he could recall or cite some transgression, some sin for which these attacks might be seen as chastisement or punishment. But that is not the case. Without cause these enemies rush to prepare themselves for attack. Thus, to his personal danger the psalmist must add spiritual confusion as the plight from which he seeks rescue.

■ **5 [6 HB]** The poet strengthens ground from which he prays by repeating affirmations foundational to his faith. He cites three points: (1) The God to whom he prays is Yahweh, the historic **God of Israel**, Israel's covenant partner since Sinai and the days of Moses. (2) This Yahweh is God of Hosts, here in a so-called absolute form (L ORD **God Almighty**) found elsewhere only in 80:4, 19; 84:8. That is, he commands the hosts of Israel whenever there is a standing army in Israel. And (3) This God, Yahweh, is God of Israel, making explicit what is implicit in the use of his covenant name, Yahweh.

The psalmist expands his plea to a national concern, that Yahweh would punish all the nations, showing no favor to these treacherous villains (compare NJPS).

2. Enemies like Prowling Dogs and Refrain (59:6-10 [7-11 HB])

■ **6-8 [7-9 HB]** Each evening these malcontents return to the walls of the city. They **prowl** around it, **snarling** like a pack of **dogs** (v 6 [7 HB]; compare also v 14 [15 HB]). Look how they foam at the mouth. With their lips they slice others as with sharp **swords** (v 7 [8 HB]). They think no one will hear! But the psalmist knows Yahweh laughs at these frauds. He mocks **all those nations** (v 8 [9 HB]).

■ **9 [10 HB]** But Yahweh, the psalmist's strength, will be his song as well (reading *'šyrh* with *BBHS*) and his place of refuge.

■ **10 [11 HB]** His *loving God* will go before him and cause him to look upon, that is, **gloat over** his enemies. They will get the point, God's greatness and their own distance from God.

3. Repay Them for Their Sinful Words and Refrain (59:11-15 [12-16 HB])

■ **11 [12 HB]** Interestingly, the psalmist prays that Yahweh **not** slay these enemies of God and his people, lest his people forget these events—their sins and God's decisive response to them. Instead he prays for God to bring these enemies **down** with an unforgettable demonstration of his might. All of this he addresses to the Lord (*'ădônay*), Israel's **shield**. **Shield** here can be roughly the same as "king" (as in 89:18), standing in apposition to the divine appellation. The term's use to refer to weapons of protection (Keel 1997, 222-23) is of course the use that stands behind its application to royalty.

■ **12-13 [13-14 HB]** Clearly the protagonists against whom the psalmist prays have spoken in ways rejected by the poet. His prayer is that they will become entangled in their own words. Their words showed **pride**, falsehood, and the misuse of cursing (v 12 [13 HB]).

His utterances were apparently in anger; now the psalmist prays they will be consumed by that anger (v 13 [14 HB]). As a result these abusers of speech will ***know that God reigns in Jacob to the ends of the earth***. Apparently it would be God's decisive response to this prayer, bringing down the arrogant, the boastful, and evildoers condemned before that would solidify this insight.

■ **14-15 [15-16 HB]** The psalmist repeats as something of a refrain the lines we encountered in v 6 [7 HB]. These **snarling ... dogs** return each night to the city, prowling around its walls, looking for food and a place to lodge overnight.

This is an image of opportunistic ruffians, terrorizing the city and never being satisfied.

4. The Psalmist's Song in Distress (59:16-17 [17-18 HB])

■ **16-17 [17-18 HB]** The song closes with the psalmist's promise to sing lustily, morning by morning of God's loving-kindness. He makes this commitment because he himself has experienced God as his **strength**, his **refuge**, his **fortress** (v 16 [17 HB]), his ***loving God*** (v 17 [18 HB]). The poem ends using a stylistic feature distinct to this psalm, the three-time repetition of select vocabulary. Three times the writer uses *miśgāb*, ***bulwark*** (vv 9, 16, 17 [10, 17, 18 HB]); three times *ḥesed*, ***loving kindness*** (vv 10, 16, 17 [11, 17, 18 HB]).

FROM THE TEXT

No references to Ps 59 appear in the NT. The NT does pick up with surprising seriousness the theme of the use of the tongue by the friends and foes of God. Although this is not the only theme of Ps 59, it is a major concern of the writer. Negatively, Paul includes gossips and slanderers along with haters of God as among the persons whose conduct the apostle thinks worthy of death (Rom 1:29-32). Positively, he urges the people being renewed in their mind after the will of God among other things to bless those who persecute them, to bless and not to curse their enemies (Rom 12:1-2, 14).

These representative exhortations affirm the seriousness with which the psalmist takes his enemy's use of the tongue in Ps 59. At the same time, the apostle points to a response to persecution shaped by the mind of Christ rather than the need to avenge.

A Prayer for Help from Neighbors (60:1-12 [3-14 HB])

BEHIND THE TEXT

According to the SS, Ps 60 is a Davidic *miktam* to be used for instruction of God's people. The editors associate the psalm historically with David's subjugation of Aram Naharaim and Aram Zobah, Aramaean entities in the far north of the land, and with Joab's and David's exploits among the Edomites in the far south, in the Valley of Salt below the Dead Sea (compare 2 Sam 8—10).

With its historical note and several geographic references, Ps 60 is best read with an atlas in hand. The revised edition of Carl Rasmussen's *Zondervan Atlas of the Bible* is a reader-friendly and very helpful resource for such a reading. *Carta's Atlas of the Biblical World*, edited by Anson Rainey and R. Steven Notley, offers a comprehensive, scholarly treatment for the same purposes.

The midsection of the psalm is an oracle, speaking a word from God directly to the congregant. This divine word would most likely have been delivered by a Levitical preacher or a cultic prophet. We can think of a number of settings for which this word that declares God's sovereignty over the lands surrounding Judah would be appropriate. Thus the oracle is not as helpful as one might have thought in dating the psalm or its compositional history.

That the psalm was eventually commended "for teaching" cautions us again against reading hard line divisions between the various schools or groups of influence in ancient Israel. We have here materials from prophetic, Levitical, and historical sources sewn together as though their collocation is perfectly natural and edifying.

A nearly identical copy of vv 7-12 [9-14 HB] appears in 108:6-13 [7-14 HB]. It is of slight help text-critically. For the details of the SS see the Introduction, C.1.a, C.1.b, C.3.f, and C.6.j.

IN THE TEXT

The metrics and genres of Ps 60 divide the poem into three obvious parts. An opening set of five, 3 + 3 bicola (vv 1-5 [3-7 HB]) cry out for deliverance. A closing set of four, 3 + 3 bicola (vv 9-12 [11-14 HB]) again pray for help. As noted above, an intervening oracle, a collection of three tricola (vv 6-8 [8-10 HB]) whose length and beat underscore a prophetic word from God.

I. Heal Your Broken Land and People (60:1-5 [3-7 HB])

■ **1 [3 HB]** Verse 1 [3 HB] carries the basic logic of the whole psalm. Based on the defeat of Israel's armies and the shaking of the earth in an earthquake the psalmist concludes God is angry at his people. He has rejected them. Only God can deliver from the plight he has created. So on behalf of the people, the psalmist cries to God for restoration. In spite of the information we have, it is not possible to date the psalm confidently. Times of distress under David, trauma during Hezekiah's struggles with the Assyrians, the fall of Jerusalem and exile, and even later situations could offer times that would suit this psalm.

■ **2 [4 HB]** A tremendous earthquake has **shaken the land**. But this event is not a simple natural phenomenon. Indeed, for the psalmist and his contemporaries there really were no natural phenomena, simply occurring without meaning beyond themselves. Happenings in the natural order all have causes in the spiritual world. In this case, not only has Yahweh caused the earth to quake, but he has split it apart, opening fault lines like gaping wounds for all to see. Thus the psalmist prays, **mend its fractures**.

Kraus, Tate, and others take the earthquake as a metaphor. That is, the horrendous troubles of God's people are *like* an earthquake (1988, 4-5; Tate 1990, 105). The breach in mind, then, is in the integrity of the nation; the welfare of the nation, comparing language of a breach to Judg 21:15 and 2 Sam 5:20. This is possible. Just as likely, however, given the propensity of the region for frequent and sometime severe earthquakes, we should think of a genuine quaking of the earth (compare Amos 1:1; Zech 14:5).

■ **3 [5 HB] You have shown your people desperate times**, and **you have given . . . wine**. The NIV translates well the so-called causal forms of the Hebrew verbs involved (as also in the previous verse). These causal grammatical forms convey the theological causation basic to the psalmist's prayer. God's giving his people wine to drink that causes them to **stagger** pictures his influence over them. Jeremiah has a similar picture of God causing his people to be senseless.

■ **4 [6 HB]** Having laid out the plight into which God plunged his people, the psalmist now affirms God's deliverance. With a military metaphor he claims God has **raised a banner** for those who **fear** him. "The **fear** of God" retains a holy terror, an awe of God. But the **fear** of God further describes persons who from their awe of God regularly trust and obey him. The **banner** provides a godly focus around which they can rally themselves against the well-armed foe (**the bow**). It is also quite likely possible that the first colon should be translated as a request, ***Give those who fear you . . . a banner***, parsing the verb as a precative perfect (with, e.g., NJPS).

■ **5 [7 HB]** Finally for the opening section, the psalmist prays for God's **right hand**, that is, God's active, saving presence, to rescue him and his fellow worshippers. This he prays in order that those whom Yahweh loves may be delivered. God has not simply chosen his people but also loves them! This the psalmist knows. Even in judgment, God loves his people. The psalmist emphasizes this by placing the purpose clause for the petitions in v 6*b*, prior to v 6*a*. This placement (as in the MT, ESV, KJV, and RSV) I judge preferable to renderings that perhaps for stylistic reasons move the purpose clauses to v 6*b* (so, e.g., the NIV, LXX, NABRE, NJPS, and NRSV).

2. Gilead and the Lands Belong to Me, Says God (60:6-8 [8-10 HB])

■ **6 [8 HB]** Now **God has spoken from his sanctuary**, the psalmist says. He spoke of Shechem, the place where Jacob put away foreign gods from his family, and centuries later the briefly used capital of the northern kingdom (Gen 35:1-4; 1 Kgs 12:25). God exulted as he spoke of dividing up and apportioning out Shechem's territory for whomever he might choose. **Measure off the Val-**

ley of Sukkoth** completes the brief picture of God dividing the land as spoils of his victory over neighboring peoples.

■ **7 [9 HB]** The second tricolon makes a set of simple claims to God's ownership of lands in the Davidic kingdom. **Gilead** and **Manasseh** belong to him, he claims. These tribal areas on the east side of the Jordan, the first to be claimed in the original taking of the land, remain the domain of God (Num 32; Josh 1:12-18). **Ephraim**, the heartland of the northern tribes and the northern kingdom, God says is his **helmet**, his most important piece of defensive armor. **Judah**, the tribe associated with the rule of God in Israel from the beginning (Gen 49:10), also belongs to God and remains the instrument of God's rule in Israel and the world.

■ **8 [10 HB] Moab**, enemy of God since the earliest days of Israel's arrival in the land, now stood as part of the land to be subdued by David (2 Sam 8). Calling Moab his wash pan registered not only his ownership of this rebellious subject but his disdain of them as well.

Edom, as the place God throws his **sandal** when he comes in from battle, has by a sort of reverse "pride of place" the distinction of being the most despised subject of David. This animosity reached clear back to Edom's refusal to let Israel pass through its land as they left Egypt, and still remained in place in the late prophet Malachi's day (Num 20:14-21; Mal 1:2-4).

Over **Philistia** God would raise the victor's **shout**. Out of a web of tangled relationships these latecomers to the land of promise became allies and then subjects of the kings of Judah. Several of David's own entanglements with Philistines have been referenced in SSs already encountered in immediately preceding psalms. By the hand of God David brought Philistia under his rule. Over these Philistines too God raised his shout of triumph. God has proclaimed his ownership and dominion over territories particularly storied in their histories of resistance to the God of Israel.

This is not an exhaustive list of the lands that God has brought under his rule. One suspects these are chosen representing all the nations of the earth. Indeed, God rules over all the lands whom his people met on their way out of Egypt, over all the lands ruled by David and Solomon. And, truth be told, God's kingdom embraces all the lands of the earth that he himself has made.

3. Give Us Real Help, O God (60:9-12 [11-14 HB])

■ **9-10 [11-12 HB]** The psalmist now asks wistfully for someone to take him to **the fortified city**. We should probably think either of returning in victory to Jerusalem or in conquest into a fortress in Edom, perhaps Sela, Edom's capital. The petition assumes God might once again take command of his troops and lead them to victory. He questions God himself as to whether or not God has deserted his people. He claims God has ceased going to battle with his people. This means they have failed in battle (compare 1 Sam 4—6 on Yahweh's relationship with the ark in battle).

■ **11-12 [13-14 HB]** Against the backdrop of God's apparent abandonment of his people, the psalmist asks God for help for his people against their adversary. In contrast to God's help he confesses that **human help** will not be adequate for this situation. With God helping them they will prevail valiantly. Left to human ingenuity they are lost. **God** will actually defeat their enemy. He is their only hope.

FROM THE TEXT

The NT people of God do not share the psalmist's confidence that they can reason directly back from any particular nation's well-being to the disposition of God toward that nation (Rom 8:31-38). Nevertheless, they remain confident that God providentially works his will in history, both judging and saving persons according to their response to the Creator and to Jesus his Son (Rom 1:16—2:29; 8:28-30). They remain firmly convinced that God and only God can deliver persons from the plight in which those alienated from God find themselves (1 Tim 2:3-7).

In light of Jesus the apostles thoroughly denationalized the gospel. Thus, even in Rom 9—11 with all its attention to Israel there no mention of land or boundaries or temple or other features of political or national identity. Israel is the people of God, composed of Jews everywhere who keep covenant with their God. John the Revelator's declaration that the Roman Empire would perish at the hands of the Lord God Almighty and the Lamb (Rev 18—19) shows that God is by no means done with the affairs of nations. This is true even though the primary appeal of the gospel seems addressed to individuals (2 Cor 5:14-21).

A Prayer at the Paying of Vows (61:1-8 [2-9 HB])

BEHIND THE TEXT

Among the artifacts most frequently found scattered throughout the ruins of ancient temples are so-called votive cones or votive objects. These votive objects were used by worshippers to mark the fact that they had followed through on whatever they had promised *under oath* to do. A cone or peg often contained a brief record of the oath and the faithfulness of a worshipper, along with praise to the god before whom the oath was taken.

Psalm 61 is a poem to be used at just such an occasion. Psalm 116 and Jonah 2 are also from this part of Israel's worship. "Votive" has to do with demonstrating, assuring, or guaranteeing by means of an oath.

IN THE TEXT

1. Lead Me to a High Rock (61:1-3 [2-4 HB])

This prayer divides into three brief sections, each containing a petition, a comment on the psalmist's situation, and finally a reason for the plea.

■ **1 [2 HB]** The psalmist prays that God would **hear** him, indeed that God would give ear to his **prayer** (using the technical genre designation for this sort of prayer, the *těpillâh*).

■ **2 [3 HB]** He prays **from the ends of the earth.** The MT has singular. Clearly the psalmist locates the place from which he prays. His words, however, are open to several different readings. Taken geographically and literally the psalmist prays from a distant place, probably far from the temple, given the reference to God's "tent" in v 4 [5 HB]. One would think then the exile and of praying from Babylon or some other distant land. One could also take it as reference to David's expulsion from Jerusalem under pressure from Absalom.

Following the MT's singular, *from the end of the earth/or the land* it could locate the supplicant at the far boundary between the land of the living and the underworld of chaos and death, or simply afar from the temple. Taken metaphorically it could simply locate the psalmist at the end of himself and his resources.

Moving from his location to his condition the psalmist says he is **faint** in **heart**. The **heart** names the psalmist himself, with particular attention to his capacities to think, commit, evaluate, and live, intellectually and emotionally engaged. At this place of depleted personal resources, at the end of his psychological, spiritual, and physical resources he cries out to God. He is weary of making decisions that alter his world, tired of staying the course when others fall by the wayside.

The petition here is that God *led him to a rock higher than himself.* The MT, LXX, and a few modern versions read "a rock" (singular). Most English versions translate "to *the* rock." Translating as a definite singular **(the rock)** leads easily to identifying the rock as the Temple Mount or even as Yahweh himself (compare 62:2 [3 HB]). But the preferred reading is singular. It conjures the picture of being led to a rock in a wilderness wadi that is high enough to let one climb on it out of harm's way. This petition sounds the main note of this psalm—that God can rescue his people individually and corporately from difficulties beyond the reach of humans.

■ **3 [4 HB]** The psalmist's own experience provides the bases for his prayer. God has proven to be a place of **refuge, a strong tower**. The image is from the design of a fort or fortified city, with walls and towers providing protection against the enemy. Based on this experience with God, he turns to him again in prayer.

2. Let Me Dwell in Your Tent (61:4-5 [5-6 HB])

■ **4 [5 HB]** The second petition of the prayer is that God would let him **dwell in** his **tent forever**. This reflects a tradition in which matters of the old Mosaic tabernacle were transferred to the Jerusalem temple. **Forever** exercises the right of royal hyperbole. He speaks not of exact chronological age or of being that escapes the bounds of time, but with language that extols the king. This language indicates that Yahweh's kingship, though not explicitly articulated nevertheless stands in the background.

The parallel colon continues the motif of finding protection in Yahweh, this time in the covert provided by God's **wings**. One thinks immediately here of finding refuge under the **wings** of the cherubim in the temple. This is possible, but several observations raise reservation about this identification. First and most important, the protecting wings here are God's wings, not those of the cherubim. Second, when we encounter the cherubim they are not known for their protection but rather for their role as porters for a divine throne (compare Keel 1997, 190-92).

■ **5 [6 HB]** In the course of explaining why he wants to dwell forever in God's tabernacle the psalmist tells us more of the situation assumed by this psalm. He is paying his **vows**. This recalls some deliverance in the past when he promised that, should God rescue him, he would bring a gift of some sort to the temple. That deliverance is in the past; he comes now to pay his **vows** aware that God observes these transactions (compare Lev 7:16-18; Ps 116, especially vv 16-19). God guards the integrity of these vows and blesses persons accordingly. It is in these settings that God grants the inheritance of the land to those who trust him and obey him in reverent awe.

3. God Save the King (61:6-8 [7-9 HB])

■ **6 [7 HB]** The psalmist prays God will extend the days and years of the **king's life**, reading the MT *twsyp* as a jussive. This is in effect a prayer for the ongoing well-being of the kingdom, since the king represented the most tangible and most immediate link between God's rule in the heavens and the realization of his will now on earth (compare Ps 72).

■ **7 [8 HB]** **May he [the king] be enthroned in God's presence forever.** The prayer particularizes the request of v 7 [8 HB]. The request presents God as the great King before whom the vassal king (here the king of Israel) rules and stands accountable. Casting mercy and truth as servants who do the will God (compare 103:19-22), the psalmist asks God to **appoint** his emissaries **love and faithfulness to protect** the king. The welfare of the land and its people are tied to the well-being of the king.

■ **8 [9 HB]** Then I will ever sing in praise—**then** carries causal force here. As a result of the answer to his prayer, which he anticipates, he likewise eagerly (note the extended Hebrew verb form) extols the name of the Lord. Specifically he anticipates **praise** in the context of the payment of his **vows**. That is, he closes this prayer song fully expecting that in the future he will again find himself in desperate straits, which will evoke **vows**. He expresses confidence that he will again experience God's rescue. Again he will make good on his **vows** in the temple.

FROM THE TEXT

Psalm 61, even with its formulaic language, supports the turning of our hearts toward heaven when we find ourselves at the end of our resources. Through the paying of our vows and other reminders of deliverance past, God transforms present crises into occasions of insight regarding the fortress God has become. The NT has only two references to vows (Acts 18:18; 21:23).

A Song to God, My Only Hope (62:1-12 [2-13 HB])

BEHIND THE TEXT

Psalm 62 presents us with an artistically crafted piece. Six of its lines begin with the Hebrew particle *'ak*/"surely," registered in different emphases in different versions. It carries a nearly identical refrain in vv 1-2 [2-3 HB] and 5-6 [6-7 HB], and uses an "n // n+1" poetic device in v 11 [12 HB]. With all of this care for an attractive text we might have expected a transparent work. Alas, as Goldingay observes, "A number of elliptical expressions tax readers and drive them to work hard to stay with the poet (vv. 1a, 3b-4a, v. 7)" (2007, 245). No indications of date appear. For more information on the details of the SS, see the Introduction, C.1.a, C.1.b, C.1.h, and C.4.a.

IN THE TEXT

1. God Alone Gives Relief against Slanderers (62:1-4 [2-5 HB])

■ **1-2 [2-3 HB]** The poet rests the entirety of the following lines on the claim that God alone is his **salvation**, his **fortress**, his **quiet** [rest]. Both in v 1 [2 HB] and in v 5 [6 HB] he identifies quiet as a source of strength and renewal. Here he speaks to fellow worshippers about his God and then about their moral failures. Direct address of God will appear only in the closing line of the poem.

■ **3-4 [4-5 HB]** Immediately we encounter the lines that led Goldingay to say the poem contained "elliptical expressions" and that the reader was "taxed" just to keep up with the poet (2007, 245). He launches a set of indirect accusations in the form of probing questions begun with **How long . . . ?** This is clear enough. But what do these accused ones do that brings the wrath of the poet (and God) upon them?

The two key verbs involved in v 3 [4 HB] in the MT are *tĕhôtĕtû* and *tĕrāṣṣĕhû*. The former, if from *htt*, has to do with "overwhelming with reproof" (*HALOT*, 257); if from *hwt* then perhaps "shout, attack" (BDB, 223), with LXX translating *epitithēmi* "to put, place, attack." The latter, if from *rṣḥ*, has to do with "murder" (*HALOT*, 1283-84); so the LXX. *BBHS* suggests deleting the first verb and reading the second one as from *rwṣ*, having to do with "running."

Context indicates these lines should probably be asking (rhetorically) about adversity the psalmist endures. A review of ancient and modern attempts to translate the lines leaves one, unfortunately, with the impression that we have not yet discerned specifically what the poet is saying. And after all of this one comes away wondering if one has caught the intended sense precisely.

62:3-10

Here it seems the poet may be the brunt of a group focusing their animosity on him. All of them press upon him, forming a circle of murderous disregard. They press on him as on a bulging **wall**, a distended **fence** ready to break.

2. God Alone Proves Worthy of Trust (62:5-10 [6-11 HB])

■ **5-10 [6-11 HB]** As in the case of the first refrain, the psalmist discovers the secret of his protection not in a formula of divine presence but in recollection of actual deliverance. In those experiences of deliverance he has actually known God as his rock, his refuge, his salvation. In the refrain, the affirmation of God as the psalmist's salvation is replaced by the claim of God as his hope (vv 1//5 [2//6 HB]). Indeed, strength belongs to God. But to God also belongs Yahweh's loving-kindness.

He turns now to exhortation, commending the worship and **trust** of Yahweh to all the people (v 8 [9 HB]). To him they can **pour out** their inner selves, their **hearts**, to Yahweh. On the one hand, human beings prove incredibly ephemeral and prone to **extortion** (v 10 [11 HB]). When you put them on a scale, virtually nothing is weighed. So trusting in human violence is a bad mistake, and following it even when it seems worthwhile is not a place to **set** one's **heart**.

3. Strength and Love Belong to Yahweh (62:11-12 [12-13 HB])

■ **11-12 [12-13 HB]** The N + (N+1) device locks together these lines. They are anchored in the prophetic word of God that the palmist himself has heard.

The God known both for his strength and his loving-kindness is known also for his role as Judge of all the earth. He will repay human beings rightly according to their work (v 12*a* and *b* [13*a* and *b* HB]). This is not to be read as "works righteousness" but rather as grateful obedience as a *response* to God's deliverance.

FROM THE TEXT

Verses 11 and 12 [vv 12-13] bring together two claims essential to a correct and robust understanding of Yahweh, God of Israel. Either one of these without the other would not describe Yahweh adequately. On the one hand, not only is Yahweh powerful, but all power belongs to him. On the other hand, steadfast love belongs to him. He lives and acts steadfast love. This OT insight is affirmed also in the NT. The Creator of all things, Judge of all the earth, is generously loving and at the same time rigorously righteous. The temptation to dispense with one of these aspects of Yahweh's character must be resisted. Without Yahweh's full power and ability, he may prove unable to carry out some aspects of his will. He may be loving or just but prove impotent in the face of the forces of evil. On the other hand, without his steadfast love, his power may prove abrasive and more destructive than redemptive.

We see this problem when Christians try to pit the NT's loving God and Father of Jesus over against the OT's Judge of all the earth. This misunderstands the God of the OT and the God of the NT. The God of Israel and the God and Father of the Lord Jesus exhibit both power and love in a perfectly integrated divine person. Echoing Ps 62:12 Paul claims that "God 'will repay each person according to what they have done'" (Rom 2:6), this God from whose love nothing can separate us (8:31-39).

Song of the King's Hunger for God (63:1-11 [2-12 HB])

BEHIND THE TEXT

Psalm 63 provides evidence of the deeply personal piety and penetrating spirituality with which OT saints could approach the God of Israel. The psalm gives voice to the worshipper's hunger for God and praise for God's character.

Indeed, the confessions of confidence in God and expressions of yearning for God strike one as a form of praise. Even disclosure of a threat to the poet's life also comes in the form of testimony to the certainty of deliverance (vv 8, 9 [9, 10 HB]). Because of this, one may be inclined to see in this psalm an individual prayer of testimony and praise, not a straightforward prayer song. The final tricolon introduces the king, perhaps transforming the poem itself into a royal psalm (against Tate 1990, 125-26).

The SS designates this piece as a "Davidic *mizmôr*" (**psalm**) and situates it in David's sojourn in the Judean desert. Which of David's several flights into the wilderness the editors of this piece have in mind we cannot say (his flight from Saul in 1 Sam 23—24 or from Absalom in 2 Sam 15—16?). No evidence prevents us from assigning this poem to David, though several "wilderness" moments in preexilic Judah could have prompted the song. Its testimony to hunger and thirst in a ***dry and weary land lacking water*** is particularly apt to such a setting. But situating the psalmist as anticipating a pilgrimage through dry and barren land overburdens the metaphors in v 2 [3 HB] (against Broyles 1999, 260). For details of the SS, see the Introduction, C.1.a and C.4.a.

IN THE TEXT

1. Psalmist's Whole Self Hungers for God (63:1-4 [2-5 HB])

Scholarly consensus is scarce on the discernment of units within the psalm. I concur with those who divide the psalm into three units, vv 1-4 [2-5 HB], 5-8 [6-9 HB], and 9-11 [10-12 HB]. Each of the units begins with an occurrence of the Hebrew word *nepeš*/"soul" used with a slightly different nuance each time (with Ceresko [ZAW 92 (1980), 435], cited by Tate [1990, 125]). The units move from the psalmist's profound thirst for God, to his desires for God, to the end of those who threaten the psalmist's life.

■ **1 [2 HB]** Virtually every nuance of the psalmist's description of his relationship with God can be traced to the opening acknowledgment that God is his **God**. (In the Elohistic Psalter we should think "Yahweh" in these references.) **Soul** and ***body*** together as a merism in v 1 indicate the psalmist's whole person yearns for God. The physical location of the thirsty psalmist in a **dry and barren place without water** echoes his spiritual plight.

■ **2-3 [3-4 HB]** His thirst takes him to the **sanctuary** where he gazes on Yahweh's **strength** and **glory** (note the causal link, *kēn*, between these two ideas, between spiritual thirst and the longing to worship). One wonders precisely what this means, since there was no image of Yahweh to illuminate in the temple. Whatever he sees, it reminds him of Yahweh's loving-kindness, his *ḥesed*. This he claims is **better than life** itself and provides an additional reason for worship in the sanctuary.

■ **4 [5 HB]** Two promises flow from this in a soft, causal movement signaled again by the clause initial *kēn*. First and more likely, he will bless Yahweh either *while* he has *life*, that is, *in life*, or *with* his *life*, depending on how the preposition (*b-*) on the noun *life*/**live** is handled. Second, he **will lift up** his **hands** in Yahweh's name. Whether this is a gesture of praise or prayer or perhaps oath taking is not clear from the use of the expression.

2. Psalmist's Desires Are Satisfied in God (63:5-8 [6-9 HB])

■ **5-6 [6-7 HB]** As noted above, this second portion of the psalm uses the Hebrew *nepeš* with a different meaning than found in its use in v 1 [2 HB]. Here the psalmist effuses that his *desires* are satisfied. Literally, *as with marrow and fat his desires* [*nepeš*] *will be satisfied.* Marrow and fat would signal fine food, luxurious provisions (Tate 1990, 127-28).

Whenever he remembers Yahweh as he reclines on his bed, he meditates throughout the watches of the **night**. The NIV and some other versions omit the conjunction with which v 6 [7 HB] opens. The colon carries a rather unusual use of the conjunction *'im* and probably should be translated *When(ever) I remember*... (see *IBHS*, 643). He is reminiscent of the godly ones described in Ps 1:2 who meditate on Torah day and night.

■ **7 [8 HB]** The reason the psalmist's thoughts run as they do is that Yahweh has proven to be his **help**. We should think here not of minimal assistance but of divine intervention at a time of great need, **help** without which he may well have perished. He changes metaphors in v 7*b* [8*b* HB], picturing his **help** as the protection little birds find under the wings of their caregivers, that is, **in the shadow of** Yahweh's **wings**. Recourse here is understandably often made to the wings of the cherubim to explain this picture (Kraus 1989, 20; Tate 1990, 125, 127-28).

Keel rightly points out, however, that the reference is to Yahweh's wings, not the cherubims' wings, which are mentioned elsewhere (e.g., Ezek 1). Shelter under divine wings is a common theme in Egyptian glyptic art. While Israel's lack of representation of their God, Yahweh, complicates this matter some, the theme could easily be present without artistic representation (Keel 1997, 190).

■ **8 [9 HB]** *My soul clings* **to you** makes excellent sense here but does not give a hint as to how odd the MT sounds. *My soul clings after* [*'ḥrytk*] *you* translates the MT literally but accepts an unusual sense for the preposition (*ḥrytk*). Various translators try to convey this: "My soul clings fast to you" (Tate 1990, 123), "My whole person has stuck to you" (Goldingay 2007, 254).

We have evidence from Israel's neighbors of the gods expressing this sort of intimate embrace of the king. For example, Hossfeld and Zenger cite representations of the god Ptah in warm embrace of Pharaoh Sesostris I from ca. 1950 B.C. (2005, 127). Our passage radically democratizes this by claiming it is the God Yahweh who is in the embrace of the worshipper, not the reverse; and it is the unnamed petitioner and not the king who is received. Complementing this grip by the psalmist, God's saving presence (his **right hand**) has its own grip on him.

3. Psalmist's Life Is Spared by God (63:9-11 [10-12 HB])

■ **9 [10 HB]** The psalmist lets us see that his ardent pursuit of God has not been simple fair-weather devotion. On the contrary, it has taken place in the context of threats to his well-being. There are persons who seek his life (the last occurrence of *nepeš* in the psalm) with inflicting of trouble in mind. This is serious. The word for **kill/*trouble*** here is *šô'âh*. In modern Hebrew this noun has become the Shoah, the name for the holocaust. We cannot simply equate the ancient and the modern word, but the ancient word may well have carried some of the horrific sort of "trouble" the modern use underscores.

These adversaries are headed for lower parts of the earth, a reference something like Sheol. His enemies go there not particularly as a place of punishment, but not an attractive destination either. In this context their entry to the underworld is assumed to be the work of Yahweh's "right hand" (vv 7-8 [8-9 HB]). While going to the underworld/to Sheol was not punishment, how one entered the grave was a significant issue. Entering prematurely or disarticulated as the carnage of battle or desecrated or abused was a matter of shame (compare Pharaoh's unenviable plight in Ezek 31—32). Going to the grave with proper care, having lived a full life, clothed with honor—this is what one wanted.

■ **10 [11 HB]** We can assume enemies of the psalmist had none of these luxuries. Instead they are to be handed over to the edge of the **sword** (i.e., slain in battle) so that they become the fare of **jackals**. This assumes they have been slain and left out in the field to be abused by animals.

■ **11 [12 HB]** *So the king rejoices in God*, a mark of his devotion to Yahweh. He rejoices not in instruments of war (horses, chariots; compare Hos 14:1-3) or in great wealth or accomplishments. Instead he rejoices in Yahweh himself.

Consequently he delights himself in those who **swear by** God's name, that is, those who take and receive oaths in the name of Yahweh. This also is a mark of the king's devotion to Yahweh, since the god in whose name one would take an oath was the god in whose hands one placed one's destiny. The god named in the oath was the god who guaranteed the dependability of the person taking the oath and carried out the threat either implied or stated in the oath formulae.

Examples of Taking Oaths

Just what was involved in taking oaths can be seen, for example, in the closing paragraphs of a mid-second millennium B.C. treaty between Mursilis, a Hittite king, and Duppi-Tessub, his vassal king from Amurru. After a listing of Hittite and Amurru deities relevant to the taking of oaths in a treaty, these words follow:

> Should Duppi-Tessub not honor these words of the treaty and the oath, may these [previously listed] gods of the oath destroy Duppi-Tessub together with his person, his wife, his son, his grandson, his house, his land and together with everything that he owns. (*ANET*, 205)

An appropriate paragraph binding Mursilis also appears. This was all taken with much more seriousness than would be the case in contemporary Western culture. For the ancients, taking an oath was not just a mechanism for protecting against perjury but was actually a legitimate approach to securing loyalty and integrity. This was true because of the seriousness with which the ancients viewed the gods and their involvement in the securing of oaths.

Continuing with the king's integrity supported by the character of Yahweh, it is plainly declared that the **mouths** known to speak falsehood will not be allowed to speak or to conduct business with oaths (note the ptc. in Hebrew and the implied falsehood as a way of life). The implication is that, God being his helper, the king will rule a kingdom marked by truthfulness. This is true whether we imagine this being said of a ruling king or of any saint with which the king's blessings are now shared.

It is also quite possible that the reference here is to swearing by the king himself, not by God. As a matter of fact, many interpreters take it as a reference to the king. This understanding is based on the fact that in the OT persons are occasionally said to swear by the king (e.g., Gen 42:15; 1 Sam 17:55; 25:26; 2 Sam 11:11). But Goldingay rightly notes that, although reference to the king makes sense here, the phrase "swear by him" elsewhere in the OT invariably refers to Yahweh (2007, 262). One may also note that this makes excellent sense of the pronouns in v 11 [12 HB] and is adopted by the NIV, NJPS, NLT, and REB.

The final colon of the poem dramatically claims that either the king or Yahweh puts an end to the speech of all who live speaking lies. The verb pictures someone stuffing the liars' mouths with rags or some other obstacle to clear speech.

FROM THE TEXT

As noted several times now, Ps 63 exhibits unparalleled devotion to God and God's grace (*ḥesed*). It excels in expressing subjective aspects of life with Yahweh—he "thirsts" for God (v 1 [2 HB]). In the temple he fixes his gaze upon Yahweh's strength and "glory" (v 2 [3 HB]). Indeed, Yahweh's *ḥesed* is "better than life" itself to the psalmist (v 3 [4 HB]). Living for Yahweh, he claims, is like feasting on rich food (v 5 [6 HB]). All day and night he thinks about Yahweh (v 6 [7 HB]), he clings to Yahweh as in a strong embrace (v 8 [9 HB]).

All of this without a direct request for anything, an unusual omission for songs of praise, which often use their praise to leverage requests. And also all of this without reference to the Exodus, the taking of the land, or other objective aspects of God's revelation of himself to Israel. This highly subjective revelry of the psalmist in God himself von Rad calls an "almost mystical spiritualism," which makes Kraus nervous (von Rad referenced by Kraus 1989, 21). One suspects Kraus's high Lutheranism may be responsible for his fear that such "spiritualism" might undermine the objectivity of the bestowal of salvation and in the end prove "impracticable."

It is doubtless true that in the OT the subjective apprehension of God and God's grace is regularly grounded in the objectivity both of the bestowal of salvation and of the history of salvation. But in this psalm not a single reference to this objective grounding appears, though it is everywhere assumed.

Followers of Jesus are not foreigners to the "experience" of God. They know thirst for God and hunger for his grace of the sort expressed in Ps 63. The whole church is called, being indwelt by Christ, to know by experience the love of Christ, indeed to be "filled with all the fulness of God" (Eph 3:19 RSV; see vv 14-19). They know "God's love has been poured into our hearts through the Holy Spirit" (Rom 5:5 RSV). To the Corinthians Paul wrote, "So we do not lose heart. Though our outer nature is wasting away, our inner nature is being renewed every day" (2 Cor 4:16 RSV). See Ps 73:23-28.

Prayer for the Ambushed Innocent Ones (64:1-10 [2-11 HB])

BEHIND THE TEXT

Whether this is a prayer song buttressed by testimony to God's past deliverances or encouraged by anticipation of what God will do depends largely on how vv 7-9 [8-10 HB] are understood. The majority opinion treats them as futures or presents, even though the *wyqtl* and *qtl* verbs would normally be set in the past. Following Goldingay (2007, 265-66) and Hossfeld and Zenger

(2005, 129-31), I am inclined to treat them as narrative pasts. The song assumes the psalmist is under attack, with emphasis placed on rehearsing the circumstance threatening the psalmist. The petitions themselves are confined to vv 1-2 and 10 [2-3, 11 HB].

The brief poem is marked by paronomasia (repetition of words and sounds), which knits the sections of the poem together. Thus **hide me** (*tastîr*, v 2 [3 HB]), **ambush** (*mistār*, v 4 [5 HB]), **tongue** (*lešôn*, vv 3, 8 [4, 9 HB]), **suddenly** (*pit'ôm*, vv 4, 7 [5, 8 HB]), **arrows** (*ḥēṣ*, vv 3, 7 [4, 8 HB]), **words/plans** (*dābār*, vv 3, 5 [4, 6 HB]), **see** (*r'h*, vv 5, 8 [6, 9 HB]), **fear** (*yr'*, vv 4, 9 [5, 10 HB]), **shoot** (*yrh*, vv 4, 7 [5, 8 HB]), **doer/done** (*p'l*, vv 2, 9 [3, 10 HB]). Straddling the unit describing the wicked and the deeds of Yahweh, they give the impression that God's responses to the sins of the wicked suit them admirably.

According to the SS this is a Davidic mizmor. (See the Introduction, C.1.a, for more on the technical terms.) Whether from the pen of David or Davidic in some other sense, the song gives no clue to its specific setting. The general nature of the references makes one suspect it was written as a liturgy to encourage and support supplicants in their need.

IN THE TEXT

1. Petition for Cry to Be Heard (64:1-2 [2-3 HB])

■ **1 [2 HB]** The psalmist calls out for God to **hear** him, that is, to give a saving response to his prayer. He calls his prayer a "cry." By v 1*b* we know the petition involves an **enemy**, and that the psalmist's quality of life is in jeopardy, perhaps marred by threats. The cry is to be saved not from the enemy itself but from the psalmist's *fear of the enemy*. He prays not to be controlled by fear, which presupposes God will also tend to the enemy itself. He knows that to be captured by fear of an adversary is already to have conceded precious ground to that foe.

■ **2 [3 HB]** Hide me from *the secret plots*, he prays. Both the verb and the prepositional phrase trade in secrecy. This is only the start of a major preoccupation of the poet with secrecy and its various manifestations. The enemy is described as ones who do evil, described by a noun covering wide-ranging evil, including deceit (v 3; compare 36:4).

2. Picture of the Well-planned Ambush (64:3-6 [4-7 HB])

■ **3 [4 HB]** Having registered his petitions, the poet turns now to a description of the enemy. The picture of the foe is introduced by a relative clause, first with images of battle. These enemies **sharpen their tongues like swords.** *They aim toxic talk* like deadly arrows. Usually the expression has the bowman drawing the bow, rather than the arrow. Thus the versions are probably correct to extend the metaphor, making "their arrows" a comparative not the object of the verb. These weapons make sense in light of the preceding line and the plea to be delivered from fear. The foe slanders and misrepresents.

■ **4 [5 HB]** The battle metaphor continues as the enemy shoots **from ambush**. The **innocent** one (lit. *the blameless*) is the target for this slander. The innocent person is attacked behind his back, without opportunity to defend himself. Perhaps his case in court is undermined or his standing in the community is sabotaged.

■ **5-6 [6-7 HB]** The damage is quickly and fearlessly done, just as they boast— **Who will see *us*?** (with *BBHS*). These adversaries **encourage themselves with** or **they hold firmly to [their] evil plan, plotting to set traps.** They are confident they will not be detected. Emphasizing their arrogance and commitment to their wicked endeavor, the writer composes a line in which three of the five words are built on the stem *ḥpś*, **to search out**. Translating to convey the effect the line would read: **They planned out wicked [plans, saying] we have finished a planned out plan** (v 6*a* and *b* [7 HB]). They finish the plans overly impressed with their own intelligence, a manifestation, they opine, of human genius.

3. Payback by God (64:7-8 [8-9 HB])

■ **7 [8 HB]** But their confidence proved deceiving. God himself shot them with a divine arrow. Suddenly they found themselves nursing their own wounds. As noted above, by vocabulary repetition this line echoes descriptions of the well-planned ambush, hinting at the fitness of Yahweh's response (note **suddenly**/*piṭ`ôm* and ***arrow***/*ḥēs*, both in vv 3 and 7 [4 and 8 HB]). One is reminded of Prov 1:8-19 and the teacher's instruction precisely on this point of the lovers of ambush to get caught in their own traps.

64:4-10

■ **8 [9 HB]** God *caused them to stumble because of their tongue* (following *BBHS* and his minimal emendation). **Everyone who saw them were shaking their heads in dismay**. Again the suitability of the punishment to the crime with ***tongue***/*lāšôn*, ties v 8 [9 HB] to v 3 [4 HB].

4. Response of the Righteous (64:9-10 [10-11 HB])

■ **9 [10 HB]** Every person who experienced the divine retribution responded in fear. This response included some terror at the intervention of God, but it was more akin to the trust out of which consistent obedience could emerge. This is an issue that divides all persons. With regard to their fundamental response to God, their topic of conversation and the issue they ponder, these persons are oriented toward God.

■ **10 [11 HB]** Then there were those, **the upright in heart**, who, (1) seeing God's work and (2) penetrating its significance, celebrated. These were **the**

righteous and **the upright in heart**. The significance of the contrast between these persons and the scheming outlaws indicted in the earlier verses of the psalm can be readily detected. The difference is not that the one breaks Torah and the other observes it. The difference is more profound and basic. The critical issue is the fact that the righteous person actually delights in Yahweh, takes joy in Yahweh's person.

And these people are **upright in heart**. It is not just that they act in certain ways—these could be motivated by any one of a number of perspectives. Instead these persons who delight in Yahweh are actually attuned to him and his ways. He is the one in whom they place their trust.

FROM THE TEXT

This prayer asks for deliverance from wicked persons in the community that ambush the godly with their sharp tongues. First an individual and then the whole community call for deliverance. God heard their cry and showed himself to be the Divine Archer, willing and able to protect and deliver his people from these foes. One may be surprised at the sharpness of God's response. Then we recall that this issue of the human tongue surfaces all across the canon—in NT Epistles (Jas 3:5-6), where slanderers and gossips are said to be worthy of death (Rom 1:29-32). In the Prophets (Jer 9:8; Hos 7:16), in Wisdom literature (Prov 6:17; 26:28), and elsewhere God's concern arises regularly for human speech that glorifies him and edifies his people.

Praise for the Creator, Zion's Savior (65:1-13 [2-14 HB])

BEHIND THE TEXT

Although the themes of this song would have been eminently fitting for use at several of Israel's festivals, it is not possible to date the work confidently or specify its cultic connections more precisely. Generally, of course, it knows of worship on Zion, God's house, a place of prayer and praise, of paying of vows.

For more information on the SS and its technical terms, see the Introduction, C.1.a, C.1.b, C.4.a, and C.4.b.

IN THE TEXT

I. Praise Appropriate for God in Zion (65:1-4 [2-5 HB])

■ **1-2 [2-3 HB]** Two items receive particular note at the outset of this psalm: (1) the worthiness of the God of Israel to be praised; and (2) **Zion** as the locus of that praise. The three opening bicola in the MT (vv 1-2 [2-3 HB]) introduce this psalm's focus on the God of Israel with three nearly identical prepositional phrases ending in -*ḵā*/**you**. The MT reads the critical term in v 1a as either *dĕmîyyâ* or *dômîyyâ*, **praise is either waiting for God in Zion** or **eminently fitting of God.**

Zion named the ridge situated between the Tyropoean Valley on the west and the Kidron Valley on the east that leads up to the mount where the Muslim shrine, the Dome of the Rock, now sits. Later the name Zion came to cover all Jerusalem. Zion was a Canaanite fortress and worship site taken from the Jebusites by David, according to 2 Sam 5:7 (also 1 Kgs 8:1). In time the name came to refer to the mount above the old fortress. It became the Temple Mount when Solomon built his Yahweh temple there. It came to be known by such descriptors as the "Mount of Yahweh" (Pss 24:3; 132:13), "Yahweh's holy hill/mountain" (2:6; 3:4 [5 HB]; 15:1, etc.). The temple there became the preeminent locus of Yahweh's divine presence (Pss 5:7 [8 HB]; 15:1; 24:3; 28:2; 138:2 among other passages).

Yahweh was also hailed as the God to whom **vows** were paid. The significance of this prerogative was its implicit acknowledgment of the authority and integrity of this God by whose name one had made promises. He officiates at votive (vow payment) events as set forth in Lev 7:16.

Finally in Ps 65:2a [3a HB] God is uplifted as the one who hears the worshipper's prayer. The two are related, for payment of vows assumes some crisis in which vows were made in the course of praying for deliverance. The fact that God hears his peoples' prayers is attested by the fact that they come to him with payment for their vows in hand (see Ps 116:12-14). Answering or listening is an ongoing behavior of God (note the participle on **answer**/listen). (The NIV has **answer**. The reader might wonder where the word "listen" is in the text.)

■ **3 [4 HB]** The God of Zion is God of ***all flesh*** ("all people" [v 2 (3 HB)]), not simply a national deity. Peoples of the earth make their way to him because of their iniquities. For all flesh their iniquities prove more than they can manage. They confess to God that he forgives them. **On account of sins** actually names sins by virtue of human crookedness. The **transgressions** that prevail are named by a political term indicating rebellion, disrespect of boundaries.

Remarkably, all of these infractions God forgives or makes atonement for (frequently appearing in Leviticus; only three times in the Psalms [65:3 (4 HB); 78:38; 79:9]). Tate points out that, whereas this verb (*kappēr* [Piel imper.], "atone" or "forgive") in Pss 78 and 79 is generally associated with some human liturgical action related to the atonement, in the three references in the Psalter it is not so. Yahweh simply forgives! (1990, 141).

■ **4 [5 HB]** There is more to the praise of God in Zion than rendering praise and receiving forgiveness. Particularly blessed are those whom Yahweh chooses to be brought near so as **to live in** [God's] **courts**. The verbs **choose** (*bāḥar*) and **bring near** (*qāreb*) are at home in priestly materials related to Levitical matters. Perhaps Levites are in mind here for this blessing. But the participation of all flesh in worship in v 2 [3 HB] and the priestly quality of all Israel (as in Exod 19), and the pronouncement of blessedness as already introduced for all readers in Ps 1:1 inclines one to say all flesh has an invitation to dwell in Yahweh's (temple) **courts** (with Kraus [1989, 29] against von Rad [1962, 404, n. 49])!

The delight of *dwelling in Yahweh's courts* is now spelled out, with an inclusive, second person plural leading the way: *We shall be* [or are] *satisfied with the goodness* **of your house, of your holy temple.** Blessings spiritual and temporal await the worshipper in Yahweh's house. As Yahweh's people they share his altar and his table, feasting on meat from offerings (compare Lev 7:15-18).

2. God, Creator and Sustainer of His Works (65:5-8 [6-9 HB])

■ **5 [6 HB]** The NIV's translation of the verb *tā'ănēnû* (**answer**) here as present experience encourages the same treatment of the preceding verbs. The worshippers not only hope for these blessings, but they experience them now. Hence their celebration. ***Deliverance*** here is *ṣedeq* (**righteous deeds**), saving acts faithful to covenant and community. "God of our salvation" (MT) can support several different treatments of the genitive (**of**): *God from whom our salvation comes*; God who *himself is our salvation*; *our saving God*, *God who saves us*. Context indicates which of these is most appropriate. The claims are based in the psalmist's experience.

The second bicolon in v 5 [6 HB] stands in apposition to the first one. This means v 5*c* and *d* particularize and interpret v 5*a* and *b*. Thus one aspect of God's saving answer to prayer is his presence as **the hope of all the ends of the earth.** He is a God who has proven worthy of trust, of reliance. And not just for his people, but for those in distant reaches of land and sea.

■ **6-8 [7-9 HB]** Verse 6's bicolon and v 7's tricolon each begin with a relative clause built with a participle, a stylistic mark of songs of praise. They celebrate God as Creator of the **mountains**, with emphasis on the might of such a God. This involves battle for the God strongly girded like a warrior (Ps 93:1-2; Isa 51:9-11). Psalm 65:7c continues exulting God who brings order to the noisy **seas** and **their** crashing surfs, quiet to the tumult of earth's peoples. Those dwelling at the ends of the earth were struck with fear (**awe**) from Yahweh's "signs" (v 8 [9 HB]). These acts of creation carry a message sufficiently clear that the writer calls the aspects of creation itself *Yahweh's signs*/wonders.

Where morning dawns, where evening fades, you call forth songs of joy. This colon's issue/output of morning and evening stands in apposition to Yahweh's signs. This is more likely than the NIV's construal of morning and evening as places. Yahweh causes these celestial marvels to shout for **joy**. It is quite possible that the issue of dawn and dusk bring at least overtones of Canaanite twin deities, Dawn and Dusk, sired by the high god, El. These deities and abundant Egyptian art showing daily attention to the sun's birth at sunrise and consumption at sunset attest to the charged nature of these times and places. Yahweh subsumes these matters under his call for celebration.

The psalmist brings together language from different OT traditions to craft praise for God the Creator. Here God stills the primordial sea and its tumultuous waves, acts of creation that have continuing repercussions, bringing order and stability to creation. L. Köhler comments aptly here, says Kraus (1989, 30). This language is "neither outworn mythology, nor mere poetic figures of speech." They are facts in the consciousness of the Hebrew. The world of men is continually threatened and assailed by the destructive powers of chaos. If God were not there, chaos might become master of the earth, and disaster would be upon us. Thus, deep in his consciousness there slumbers a continual insecurity, or clear consciousness, whether it is an echo of the past or a foreboding of future fear, which will one day be real, this vague awareness of cosmic insecurity forms the basis of the Hebrew's feeling about the world.

The order forged in battle against chaos at the beginning cannot simply be taken for granted. That order is the mark of God's continuing sovereignty over forces of disorder.

3. God, Fructifier and Provider (65:9-13 [10-14 HB])

■ **9-10 [10-11 HB]** Yahweh's visitation often brings judgment with it, but not here. Signaling a change in topic, this visit brings with it saturating rain that profoundly enriches the land (v 9 [10 HB]). Some terms in this section are particularly troublesome, for example, the term translated **ridges** (v 10 [11 HB]). But the overall point is clear and potent, aimed at discrediting Baal as one to be trusted by Israel. Yahweh—not Baal—is the Rain Giver extraordinaire. He is the one who renders the land fertile and productive and in the process provides all good things for his people from the land he has given them.

The streams of God are *full* of water is probably to be thought of as a liturgical, not geographic, reality. Built on traditions tying primordial streams with the mount of God (e.g., Ps 46:4 [5 HB]), it symbolized the source of the lavish blessings showered upon the land in the form of rain.

The specifics of this blessing mentioned by the psalmist reveal the concerns of those who actually worked the soil and depended on Yahweh for rain.

He writes of **furrows**, of a soaking rain, of **ridges/*clods*** to be softened, and the real blessing when growth is sustained. He knows the disappointment of a season short of rain when the ground is not just dry but hard as rock. None of this simply happens as a fluke of good weather. Repeatedly in vv 9 and 10 [10-11 HB], we are told it is God who visits, waters, enriches, establishes, soaks, softens, and blesses.

■ **11 [12 HB]** Then, crowning (Ps 103:4) the year with goodness he makes his tracks to drip oil. ***Tracks/ma'gāl***—How do we picture wagon tracks or foot tracks dripping? Perhaps we should think of the land prospering, of ***trails*** or ***paths*** dripping with oil or fatness (compare Pss 17:5; 23:3; 140:5 [6 HB]).

■ **12 [13 HB]** The pastures of the **wilderness**, not the most luxuriant of land for running herds, will drip with fat. Meanwhile the **hills** are pictured girding themselves. The "weapon" with which they gird themselves is joy.

■ **13 [14 HB]** **Flocks** and fields experience the blessing of lavish rain as well. The hills clothe themselves with flocks; the **valleys** cover themselves with **grain**. These shout for joy; indeed they sing.

Understood correctly Yahweh was a fertility deity, indeed for Israel *the* fertility God. In this regard the benefits Israel sought from Yahweh were not significantly different from those sought from Baal at Ugarit. The major difference was the means by which the blessing was sought and clarity about the god(s) from whom the rain was sought (compare Hos 2:4-13). At Ugarit the rain was sought by means of sympathetic magic. In Israel, rain came as the result of trusting God and obeying his covenant (Lev 26:1-13; Deut 28:1-14).

FROM THE TEXT

The Ugaritic legend of King Keret, KRT C, celebrates Baal's role as giver of rain and the sweetness of Baal's rain to the fields and the earth. The document would have been roughly contemporary with Israel's period of the Judges.

After reading Ps 65's exuberant celebration of Yahweh and the rain he sends, the KRT C passage reminds us of the theological realities facing those who first read the Psalter. Every affirmation of Yahweh's role in providing for his people was also a denial that some other deity played that role. A reception of Yahweh's provision of rain was of necessity a rejection of Baal's "sweet rain." Rain was Baal's special territory in Canaanite culture; it could not have been discussed or sung or prayed about neutrally.

Jesus' remark was to another point, but it remains true that God sends his rain on the just and on the unjust alike (Matt 5:45). For the Christian this remains a claim with explanatory force, advances in meteorology notwithstanding.

Thanks for the One Who Answered Prayer (66:1-20)

BEHIND THE TEXT

Signs of composition for use in public worship abound in this song, for example, the repeated calls to participate by shouting (v 1), singing (v 2), speaking (v 3), blessing (v 8), and a narrative of worship acts (vv 13, 15). Although payment of vows is anticipated (v 13) this is more likely a general worship song that includes place for individual actions than a liturgy solely for the payment of vows. The placement of *selāh* at points that appear to coincide with literary units in the psalm itself (vv 4, 7, 15) is rare (hence NIV's omission). Here, however, contrary to the frequent practice of apparently random placement of this element, it would appear to have group performance in mind. And requests in the closing lines that make better sense on the lips of a worshipping community than they do spoken by individuals, even though the unit is controlled by a first person singular voice, tend toward a communal, cultic reading of this song.

For information on SS technical terms, see the Introduction, C.1.a, C.1.b, C.4.a, and C.4.b.

IN THE TEXT

1. Shout Praise from All the Earth (66:1-7)

■ **1-2** The psalm begins with a wide angle appeal to **all the earth**, exhorting boisterous **praise** to Yahweh. We are assuming that in the Elohistic Psalter we would have expected the name of Yahweh in these positions before the editing that excised the name and replaced it with the less specific Elohim. Worshippers from all the earth are exhorted to shout praise, sing Yahweh's glorious **name**, and **set glory** as is appropriate in a song of praise (*a tĕhillâ*). **Set glory his praise** is probably well rendered by **make his praise glorious**.

■ **3-4** A significant feature of worship with this song is the declarations worshippers are led to make. In this case (v 3) all the earth is exhorted to confess how **awesome** Yahweh's works are. To God's face they anticipate Yahweh's **enemies** will come cringing before him, because of his might. **All the earth** will worship and sing to Yahweh and his name, with **all the earth** repeated in vv 1 and 4, bracketing the opening unit, marked also with *selah* in the MT.

■ **5** Continuing the universal reach of the opening verses, the ***offspring of Adam*/mankind** (*bĕnê ʾādām*) are called to **Come and see** [*lĕkû ûrʾû*] what **God has done**. This exhortation will also be picked up again in v 16 with *lĕkû šimʿû*/"Come and hear" opening the last unit. It takes into account the awareness neighboring peoples had of the actions of their gods. The prophet Joel knew Israel's neighbor's mocked them and their God when it appeared Yahweh had either failed them or punished them. "Why should the [nations] say . . . , 'Where is their God?'" (2:17). Compare the king of Moab's similar theology in the Moabite Stone and his awareness of the doings of Israel's God (*ANET*, 320). Hence the psalmist's international reach.

■ **6** No larger deeds could come to mind than those associated with the rescue of Yahweh's people from Egypt and the establishing of his covenant people at Sinai. Mention of Yahweh's drying up of the sea brings the whole event to mind for the worshipper. The parallel, **they passed through the waters on foot**, actually has them going through the *river* (so RSV following the MT, LXX). The reference could be to Yahweh's bringing them through the Jordan River (Josh 3), of which it was said that at that event God began to "exalt [Joshua] in the eyes of all Israel" (Josh 3:7). Or it could refer to Yahweh's victory over Pharaoh and his forces at the sea—where they did break into song (Exod 15).

From the Canaanite documents from Ugarit we are accustomed to seeing "sea" and "river" in parallel, especially in settings where reference to primordial waters could be appropriate. On the other hand, reference to the Jordan would obviously fit the context. In either case we recall that to early Israel and probably also to the psalmist, the sea was actually Lord Sea, the god Yamm, and Judge River was also among the deities to be reckoned with. Though the full mythmaking had eventually been broken, these entities still carried more than "natural" impact.

■ **7** This is the God who **rules** the world in his might, God whose attentive gaze is on **the nations**. As the NJPS has it, "His eyes scan the nations." The clause is a participle clause that particularizes the preceding line. Let the rebels rise up against Yahweh, comes the warning. From the Psalter's introduction we know such rebellions are constant possibilities (2:1-3). This admonition, lodged with a ***selah*** in the third line of a lengthy tricolon, closes the first section of the poem. (Because the ***selah*** rarely has understandable significance NIV omits treatment.)

2. Praise Our God, All You People (66:8-12)

■ **8** Turning now from the nations of the earth to the **peoples** of the land, the liturgist calls God's people to ***bless***, that is, to **praise** God. There is a second reference here to the song type being used, a **praise**.

■ **9-10** Verse 9 is another participle clause, common in songs of praise, that elaborates on the preceding line. The one whom they blessed is the one whose care keeps them among the living. He does not let their foot stumble. But the adversities implicit in the praise just uttered are not just random sufferings.

On the contrary, Yahweh has tested them. He led them through suffering akin to the refining of **silver**.

■ **11-12** Changing the metaphor, the poet says Yahweh ensnared his people, as in a hunting net. He even made them wear trouble on their **loins** (v 11). **You let people ride over our heads** (v 12). In other words, they are overcome in battle, overrun by either the chariotry or infantry. **People** here translates *ěnôš*, often associated with humans in their weakness or frailty. Beyond frailty it appeared in Ps 9:19-20 as though *ěnôš* carried the notion of corruption, wickedness. They were put in desperate straits. That would work here. **We went through fire and water**, opposites covering all of life. But once again the poet concludes the unit with a long tricolon, the final colon bearing the good news. Through it all Yahweh brought them to a place of luxuriant provision.

3. Hear My Prayer, O God (66:13-20)

■ **13-15** The final movement of the psalm is signaled by the change to an individual subject. First the nations, then the peoples, and now the singular worshipper leads. Most likely instead of an actual individual, we should think here of the liturgist leading the first person lines so that individuals throughout the congregation can identify with the song (but compare Mays 1994b, 221). The address moves back to speak to God as **you** (v 13).

The worshipper has brought whole burnt offerings and come to the temple to pay his **vows**. These were vows he made during a time of distress. Clearly the worshipper was rescued from a significant plight. This is seen in the extent of the vows that are surmised by the number and variety of offerings now being offered: whole burnt offerings of fatlings, **rams, bulls,** and **he-goats**. Once again a tricolon and **selah** mark the end of a subunit.

■ **16** The last subunit opens with *lěkû šim'û*/**Come and hear**, an echo of v 5. Addressing **all you who fear God**, he asks for the opportunity to tell what God has done for him. Those who **fear God** are those who trust and obey, that is, who keep covenant faithfully. They want to tell what God has done for them.

■ **17** The psalmist's history is that he called for help; Yahweh heard him; now praise is on his lips: **his praise was on my tongue**. The line is difficult, as is evident from the versions. All three of its words are open to multiple parsing. **His praise**, as a subject noun, could also be taken as a verb, *and he was extolled with my tongue* (e.g., RSV, with the LXX). The MT literally has **under my tongue**, as does the LXX, but that presents an odd or at least minimally attested use of the preposition *taḥat*. But compare Ps 140:3: "They make their tongues as sharp as a serpent's; the poison of vipers is on [*taḥat*] their lips." This syntactic parallel inclines me to stay with the NIV. In any case, the general idea is clear.

The psalmist's history is this: he **cried out** for help, **his praise was on my tongue**, and in between the two, between the asking and the praising, one is to fill the theological gap with God's deliverance, that is, something like "God heard my cry!"

■ **18** But there is no magic formula in this experience. His judgment is that, had he harbored known **sin in** his **heart**, God would not have heard his cry. The covenant God's relationships with his people assume integrity and fidelity of thought and commitment. *BBHS* notes that the Syriac reads 2 ms., "If *you* had seen"; but no change to the MT is needed.

■ **19-20** The poet, however, emphatically rejects any hint of such duplicity by affirming that God did hear him, did incline to the sound of his **prayer**. The poem closes with a tricolon (3+2+2) pronouncing God blessed (v 20). Most versions have retained the traditional "Blessed be God" rendering. This is a praise formula, so the NIV translates **Praise be to God, who . . .** Two reasons support this emphatic praise. First, God did not turn aside his **prayer**. Second, neither did he turn aside (the verb brought forward by the parallelism) **his love** from the psalmist.

The richness of the word *ḥesed/chesed*, here rendered **love**, can be seen in the nuances elevated by the varying versions: "love," "steadfast love" (ESV, RSV); "faithful care" (NJPS); "mercy" (NABRE); "lovingkindness" (NASB). This *is* the attribute for which Yahweh is most widely known, ever since the beginning at Sinai (Exod 34:6-7).

FROM THE TEXT

When Israel called all the earth to join its exaltation of God on the basis of his mighty, awesome deeds, the congregation thought instinctively of celebrating God's rescue of them from bondage in Egypt. Even those who resist him must pay him respect. Not that individuals could not point to experience of deliverance in their own lives, as the concluding lines of the song show. But these events, almost larger than life, had sufficient power to gather up all peoples in praise to the God who did such things.

The NT people of God have a similar reflex in the call to the nations in the Song of Moses and the Lamb (Rev 15:3-4). This side of the eschaton, however, as did Israel, we look to sacramental portrayal of acts of God, larger than life, to prompt worship and gratitude to God.

A Prayer Song for All People (67:1-7 [2-8 HB])

BEHIND THE TEXT

Psalm 67 is a general prayer song. Its basic petitions (vv 1, 4, 7 [2, 5, 8 HB]) are buoyant, and its other prayer lines sound enough like exhortations to praise that the poem seems to straddle the prayer/praise boundary, celebrating God's person and mighty works. Few if any clues to its setting, date of composition, and such matters appear. The song is concerned that all nations come to know and be grateful to Yahweh. This would seem to indicate an exilic or postexilic audience, but we have no certainty here.

For technical terms from the SS, see the Introduction, C.1.b and C.2.a.

IN THE TEXT

■ **1 [2 HB]** The opening bicolon contains three general petitions for God's beneficent disposition toward his people (presumably Judah or Israel). The community (**us**) asks that God (1) might show them mercy, (2) might **bless** them, and (3) might make his countenance **shine** toward them (*IBHS*, 195). All three of these prayers appear inscribed on two silver amulets found in a wealthy family's grave in Hetef Hinnom in Jerusalem. They date from the late seventh or early sixth centuries B.C.

They are striking for the resemblance of the inscribed texts to the priestly blessings in Num 6:22-26. They constitute the earliest known textual witness to portions of the Hebrew OT. These texts found in situations of private devotion attest to their probable use also in public or Jerusalem temple liturgies.

One of the difficulties of this psalm is determining whether several verbs should be understood as plain statements or as jussives, that is, as petitions or wishes. For example, in v 1 [2 HB] the regular statement would read, **God is gracious** or **was or will be gracious**. The jussive, as these verbs are generally translated, would read: **May God be gracious to us.** This problem continues through the whole psalm.

Verse 1 [2 HB] may provide a toehold; however, since the verb translated **shine** differentiates the jussive from the non-jussive form. Here in v 1*b* [2*b* HB], the form is clearly jussive, as Tate (1990, 153) translates, "*May* he make his face to shine among us" (emphasis added). It is likely that the other verbs follow this line. This means we should probably understand the whole psalm as a prayer rather than as a thanksgiving song.

■ **2 [3 HB]** The stated purpose of praying for God's actions is that God's **ways** and his saving acts might be known **among all nations**, subordinating v

2a [3a HB] to the preceding lines, or so it may seem. English versions regularly translate this purpose in the passive voice, **that your ways may be known** on earth. This makes fine sense. But there is a problem masked by this rendering. Both the MT and the LXX show an active voice for this infinitive, **to know your way on the earth**, which seems awkward. The B colon context seems especially suited to follow a passive construal of v 2 [3 HB].

Tate, however, notes that the infinitive construct with a preposition, as in our text, can be used circumstantially (1990, 154 n. 3a; so also GKC, 1140). He thus translates: "Knowing your way(s) on the earth, . . . let the peoples praise you, O God." This subordinates the clause to the following verb, providing the circumstance in which the people praise God rather than the purpose of God's being gracious (v 1). And, taken this way we translate actively, *knowing* instead of "being known," with the MT and LXX. Either way, such a purpose of knowing God is compatible with the dreams of the later Isaiah and with the promise of "all the families of the earth" to Abraham (Gen 12:3).

■ **3 [4 HB]** The desired response of the nations to the knowledge of Yahweh's ways is gratitude, emphatically so. The emphasis comes by repetition and by the twice concluding *all of them!*

■ **4 [5 HB]** The people's response, it is prayed, would be more than cognitive. It is hoped that they would be **glad** at learning of Yahweh's ways, gladness expressed in boisterous, jubilant song. Some take the lines as indicatives, that is, "Nations will exult and shout for joy" (NJPS, following LXX). Continuation of the jussives seems more likely.

The reason the peoples will respond so jubilantly is that Yahweh judges them equitably, guides them in the land, and provides produce from the land.

■ **5 [6 HB]** This bicolon repeats verbatim the prayer found in v 3 [4 HB]. The two together bracket the centerpiece of the psalm, the prayer that the people will rejoice in Yahweh's judgment among the nations.

■ **6 [7 HB]** The syntax of this bicolon can be scanned several ways that would make sense. Verse 6a could state the cause/basis of v 6b: **Because the earth gives its produce, may God, our God bless us.** Verse 6 could provide the result of the praise mentioned in v 5 [6 HB]: **Then the land *will yield* its harvest.** Verse 6 can be a standalone petition for produce and God's blessing (NJPS). None of these has a strong claim to be preferred, except on grounds of compatibility with the way one has understood the preceding lines, as prayers or indicative statements.

This bicolon looks to God for the fruitfulness of the land. In the immediate book context, 65:9-13 [10-14 HB] expanded on Yahweh's indispensable gift of soaking rains to support the full fertility of the land. In our context, the produce of the land is also the blessing of **God, our God**.

■ **7 [8 HB]** Repeating most of v 6*b* [7*b* HB] in v 7*a* [8*a* HB] the psalmist prays that God might **bless** his people (**us**), with the result that **all the ends of the earth** *would* **fear him.** This repetition is one of the poem's most obvious stylistic features. In the process the poet lays emphasis on "God, our God" (v 6 [7 HB]), upon blessing as the work of Yahweh, on the ***nations—all of them*** (named by three different words)—being glad at Yahweh's ways.

FROM THE TEXT

In some ways this brief poem is an improvisation on Yahweh's blessing. Blessing is one of the general petitions given content by the contiguous lines. This song supports Westermann's idea that we should draw a distinction "between God's saving action in the sense of acts of attention or intervention and the continuous action of God's blessings" (Tate 1990, 159, referencing Westermann's *Elements of Old Testament Theology*, 102-4). He continues, "Blessing is not a series of events as much as 'the quiet, continuous, flowing, and unnoticed worship of God which cannot be captured in moments or dates'" (104).

Though **all the ends of the earth** constitutes the subject of the last sentence of the psalm, it provides the three final words of the poem. The psalm closes in the momentum of an ever widening arena in which God's saving acts, his upright judgment, are known by experience among all the peoples of the earth.

A Song for God on the Move (68:1-35 [2-36 HB])

BEHIND THE TEXT

Psalm 68 presents one of the most challenging Hebrew texts of the entire Psalter. An abundance of hapax legomena (words that occur only once in the OT and whose meaning therefore is often in question for lack of context), a plethora of odd or archaic expressions, puzzling syntax, and damaged texts lead to widely differing interpretations, none of them really secure. Trying to be positive about this challenge Derek Kidner calls Ps 68 a "rushing cataract of a psalm—one of the most boisterous and exhilarating in the Psalter" (1973, 238). Hossfeld calls work with this psalm "an exegetical experiment" (2005, 160). The upshot of this is that we proceed with caution and humility.

Major studies of Ps 68 fall roughly into two groups. One group concludes that the fragmented, disjointed appearance of the piece stems from its genre and not from ill-treatment. These scholars view Ps 68 as an anthology of sorts, a collection of independent poems or perhaps some type of list.

The most famous English representative of this view is W. F. Albright's article, "A Catalogue of Early Hebrew Lyric Poems" (1950). Citing Sumerian and Akkadian lists of literary works, Albright's catalog was composed of *incipits* or opening lines of poems. In such a catalog we would not generally expect to find a flow or logic to the work itself, though even a hymnal can show a compositional plan.

The other group contends that a design and overall meaning can be discerned, though no consensus on the genre and purpose of the song exists. Writing against Albright, Mowinckel found nine separate strophes and argued that the coherence of the psalm ought to be sought in the occasion for which it was written, not in an independent theme. The song, in this reading, would have been a liturgical piece or a collection of liturgical pieces (see Tate's summary of this research [1990, 172-73]). Broyles concurs. Citing four allusions to the cherubim-ark in the poem, he concludes we should see Ps 68 as "sung alongside a ritual procession with the ark and cherubim at its head" (1999, 281).

I find attractive Kidner's suggestion that the song may have been composed for David's transport of the ark from the home of Obed-Edom to the city of David (2 Sam 6:12) (1973, 238-39). Its apparent, archaic allusions to the Song of Deborah, its hymnic and narrative qualities and its attention to the ark could support such an origin, though certainty eludes us.

Following Mowinckel, Hossfeld finds nine strophes in the psalm. He further discerns matching "rings" that present the beginnings of a chiastic arrangement. His analysis runs as follows in verse divisions and the inner and outer rings, a, a', b, b':

    vv 1-3 Prelude on the victory of God and his people
      a vv 4-6 Call to praise the divine rider
        b vv 7-10 Victory over the One from Sinai
          c vv 11-14 The Almighty scatters kings
            d vv 15-18 Mount Bashan and God's sanctuary
            d' vv 19-23 God crushes enemies from Bashan
          c' vv 24-27 Procession of God and King
        b' vv 28-31 Victory over Egypt and Cush
      a' vv 32-35 Call to praise the divine rider

I have proposed rings c, c', d, and d'. If we have actually seen a valid feature of this psalm's structure, the identifying of the rings depends on matching vocabulary as well as matching themes. We see this already in Hossfeld's work with rings a and a' having the unusual "rider" name for God. Thus the lines containing "Bashan" may perhaps be a ring (d, d'), and so on. What we probably have are the remnants of a chiastic design that has suffered significantly in transmission. These observations must be offered very tentatively.

For treatment of the SS's technical terms, see the Introduction, C.1.a, C.1.b, C.4.a, and C.4.b.

IN THE TEXT

1. Yahweh Scatters His Enemies (68:1-3 [2-4 HB])

■ **1 [2 HB]** May God <u>arise</u>, may his enemies be <u>scattered</u>, may his foes <u>flee</u> before him (emphasis added). An ancient Israelite would have recognized this allusion to Num 10:35 as well as the poet's modification of it. The ancient rubric given to Moses when the ark of the covenant set out leading Israel on their journey was: "Rise up, LORD! May your enemies be scattered; may your foes flee before you." A corresponding pronouncement was spoken when the ark returned to its place: "Return, LORD, to the countless thousands of Israel" (v 36).

Only here in Ps 68:1 [2 HB] and in Num 10 do these three verbs appear, and in this order: arise . . . scatter . . . flee. It would appear the reader/worshipper is expected to relate the Ps 68 poem to the procession of the ark of the covenant. Thus the suggestion that David's movement of the ark to the city of David may be in the background here.

The NIV and most English versions, following the LXX, translate the opening verbs as imperatives or wishes, **<u>May</u> God arise, <u>may</u> his enemies be scattered**, and so on, reminiscent of the Numbers passage. The MT, however, has a simple "indicative" form, affirming either what Yahweh is doing or will do. An early reader would also have noted this change from the traditional imperative to the psalmist's affirmation: "God will arise, His enemies shall be scattered, His foes shall flee before Him" (NJPS), so Kidner (1973, 238-39); Hossfeld (2005, 158); compare Goldingay (2007, 313-14).

The ark itself was thought to be God's portable throne, the most striking image associated with this God who had no image. All of the verbs in the opening three verses should probably be taken as affirmations that introduce the themes of God's royal victory on behalf of his people. Movement from these affirmations to the following petitions may signal a transition in the poem.

Just what the worshipper should expect is not clear. Some uses of the rubric of the ark assume it rises to go to battle and to return victoriously. Recollection of historic battles may prompt faith in God's presence now. Or perhaps Yahweh simply rises. He simply stands by his throne. At the sight of him the enemies scatter.

■ **2 [3 HB]** The first two cola divide their reference. Referring back, v 2*a* describes the manner in which God's enemies are scattered. Emphasis falls on the fragility of the foes and on the ease with which Yahweh dispatches them.

Verse 2*b* anticipates 2*c*. The perishing of the wicked is as predictable as the melting of wax by the fire.

■ **3 [4 HB]** In contrast to the demise of the wicked, the righteous thrive, rejoicing and exulting before God. This good news the poet underscores by packing this colon with "s" and "ts" sounds. This contrasting of the wicked and the righteous (*rěšāʿîm* and *ṣědāqîm*) reaches back to Ps 1 and the introduction of this major theme of the Psalter of contrasting destinies.

2. Praise the Rider on the Clouds (68:4-6 [5-7 HB])

■ **4 [5 HB]** The transition to a call to praise God marks a transition to another unit. Four verbs emphasize this invitation: **Sing . . . sing . . . extol . . . rejoice.** The second verb designates singing to accompaniment or the accompaniment itself; Hossfeld translates "Play for his name" (2005, 258). He gets "play" from the verb ZMR that usually assumes song with a stringed instrument. The third verb, **extol**, translates a word not often used as a musical term, more often for *piling up* material. Here, metaphorically, the call is perhaps to *heap up praise* to God's name.

Extol him who rides on the clouds. As the marginal note in the NIV informs us, this could be translated **prepare the way for him who rides through the deserts.** Since the discovery of the Ugaritic materials where the storm god Baal is "the one who rides on the clouds," that would no longer be the best rendering. We can appreciate the theological move made by the psalmist. By appropriating Baal's title he proclaims Yahweh—not Baal—lord of the storm and fertility. In the process he expels the Canaanite Baal. (See Gordon UT 19.2331 and KTU 1.4.iii.11, 18 for Ugaritic texts extoling Baal as the One who Rides on the Clouds.)

■ **5 [6 HB]** Not until v 24 [25 HB] is Yahweh explicitly identified as king in this poem. But implicitly his kingship has been acknowledged by reference to the ark, his mobile throne. Now the poet attributes to him the traditional tasks of kings: **A father to the fatherless, a defender of widows, is God.**

Centuries before our poet, the great Hammurabi boasted in the epilogue to his famous stele, that he had become "the beneficent shepherd whose scepter is righteous," sheltering the people of Sumer and Akkad in his wisdom, in order "that justice might be dealt the orphan (and) the widow" in Babylon (*ANET*, 178). Note these concerns brought together in 94:6; 109:9; and in a full list in 146:9, including the sojourner and the poor. In our verse the **defender** has in mind defense in legal judgments. This may be why this transpires in Yahweh's **holy dwelling,** that is, the temple.

■ **6 [7 HB] The lonely in families.** The Hebrew word that often singles a person out as an especially beloved one, as in the case of Isaac (Gen 22:2), can also mean a **lonely** one, as here. **Families** translates the common word that usually means ***house***. Here it carries the meaning ***household*** or "family." (See *HALOT*, 125.)

With singing translates a hapax legomenon (a word only occurring once) of uncertain meaning. It could mean ***prosperity*** or ***skilled*** related to music or midwifery. See Tate's informative note for a more technical discussion (1990, 163).

3. The March to Yahweh's Land (68:7-10 [8-11 HB])

■ **7 [8 HB]** Content and form signal a new unit whose first and last word is God/*ĕlôhîm*. The paragraph traces the ancient journey from Sinai to Canaan with deft references to key aspects of it. Extensive allusions to the Song of Deborah (Judg 5:4 ff.) rework its classic lines to suit the poet's purpose here. The opening bicolon locates the reader in the departure from Egypt.

■ **8 [9 HB]** The quaking **earth**, and dripping **heavens** signal a theophany and recall God's provision. These signs took place **before God, the One of Sinai, before God, the God of Israel**. These lines are verbatim from Judg 5:5, including the unusual *zeh Sînay*, **the One of Sinai**, and the exchange of Judges' Yahweh for Elohim in our Elohistic psalm.

■ **9-10 [10-11 HB]** God's provision of rain and showers for his weary inheritance replaces the historical notes in the Song of Deborah. Emphasis here is on God's sustaining goodness for the poor.

4. Yahweh Scattered the Kings (68:11-14 [12-15 HB])

■ **11 [12 HB]** The general message in this strophe is reasonably clear. Yahweh goes to battle victorious over the kings (presumably) of Canaan. Beyond that, certainty eludes us. A command by the Lord launches the action. Adonai/*ădônāy* here has its strong sense, which Hossfeld captures in translating "The Lord of all gave the word" (2005, 158). One of the aspects of the Song of Deborah echoed here is the prominence of women in the action. Here it is a great host of **women who proclaim** the Lord's **word**.

■ **12 [13 HB] Kings and armies flee in haste** uses a slight emendation rather than the MT's "kings of armies." **Flee in haste** emends the MT, which here reads two preformative verbs: *"They flee, they flee!"* Interestingly, Judg 5:12 has a similar, fascinating verse: "Wake up, wake up, Deborah! Wake up, wake up, break out in song!" All of these exhibit similar repetitive patterns, though the vocabulary differs. Again women appear, now dividing the spoil. Both their appearance and their roles here remind one of Judg 5. One thinks particularly of Jael and the women in Sisera's family (Judg 5:24-30).

■ **13 [14 HB]** The appearance in both texts of unusual words like ***sheep fold*** (compare Judg 5:16) pressed to different ends argues for a connection between the two texts and for considerable liberty by our psalmist in his use of the old text/tradition.

The wings of my dove are sheathed with silver, its feathers with shining gold. What these lines mean remains a mystery. The doves have been taken as "bejeweled doves" that "fly up and symbolically spread the news of victory" (Hossfeld 2005, 165), as part of the booty (J. Gray 1977, 2-26, cited by Tate 1990, 164), or to the women "peacocking around" in their finery (Kidner 1973, 241), or to messenger doves released after a victorious battle (Tate 1990, 179), to sample but a few of the many proposals. What seems clear is our lack of clarity about these birds.

■ **14 [15 HB]** The Almighty's scattering of **the kings in the land** could be a description of Israel's victories in the conquest, though this language has not been used thus far for that purpose. The word conventionally translated as **Almighty** should probably be taken not as an adjective but as an ancient divine name, ***Shaddai***, "The One of the Mountain" (Cross 1973, 52-60).

If an actual mountain is in mind here, Djebel Druze near Shechem is known from Judg 9:48 and could be a viable candidate. Tall enough to get snow in the winter, the basalt, volcanic stone of the region could account for its name, "Black Mountain." The snowfall should probably be taken as a sign of divine participation in the routing of the kings. It also introduces the mountain theme prominent in the next strophe.

5. The Ascent to God's Dwelling (68:15-18 [16-19 HB])

■ **15-16 [16-17 HB]** Mount Bashan, majestic mountain, Mount Bashan, rugged mountain, why... The ambiguity in this text appears in the development of the NIV editions. In the 2011 edition the poet addresses Mount Bashan directly, calling for an answer to a question, "why?" The nouns are taken as singulars, under the influence of the so-called divine superlative, even though some of these lines could call for plurals. In earlier editions the NIV rendered as narrative, construing the references as plurals: "The mountains of Bashan are majestic mountains; rugged are the mountains of Bashan."

Either is possible grammatically. The more recent rendering provides a better introduction to the question being asked. The **Mountains of Bashan** would probably refer to the rugged, volcanic peaks east, northeast of the Sea of Galilee. The topographic details of Mount Bashan serve in the end to heighten by contrast the majesty of the mountain God has chosen for his dwelling. Rugged as they are, they look to God's mount with envy.

■ **17 [18 HB] Thousands of thousands** catches the MT's emphasis on the gigantic army (chariotry) led by the Lord, even though chariotry was not a significant part of Israel's taking of the land. The lines link the Sinai tradition of

Israel's journey out of Egypt with the Jerusalem and temple traditions from the other end of the journey. This seems likely, even though the precise meaning of the MT's *šin'ân*, another hapax, remains uncertain. *HALOT* (1596-97) presents four different possible derivations, with the NIV's choice as good as any.

■ **18 [19 HB] You [O *Yahweh God*] took many captives; you received gifts from people.** Yahweh's battle scene continues, now picturing the moment in the conquest when captives are marched past the conqueror and tribute is extracted from the rulers, **even from the rebellious.** These scenes of conquest were well known to the ancients from experience and art, as we know them from Egyptian and Assyrian art depicting them.

That you, LORD God, might dwell there. The climax to the trek from Sinai eventually came in David's conquest of the Jebusite city, Jerusalem (2 Sam 5:6-16).

6. Praise to God the Savior (68:19-23 [20-24 HB])

■ **19-20 [20-21 HB]** God as **Savior** comes now to the fore. Day by day he bears his people's burden and delivers them. To this God the psalmist intones praise. Salvation here has even involved providing an **escape from death.**

■ **21-23 [22-24 HB] Surely God will crush the heads of his enemies.** With classic language now a bit shocking to modern sensibilities, the poet expands on his claim of deliverance from death (v 20 [21 HB])—crushing the heads of the enemies, and washing their feet **in the blood of** their foes (v 23 [24 HB]), providing blood for the victor's **dogs,** returning **from the depths of the sea** (v 22 [23 HB]).

Our text has no Yahweh myth to which it appeals, but the language is known to us from Canaanite (Ugaritic) mythology. In Canaanite storytelling the goddess Anath returns from battle aimed at rescuing Baal. "Anath's liver exults; For she plunges knee-deep in knights' blood, Hip-deep in the gore of heroes. Then, sated with battling in the house . . . Maiden Anath washes her hands . . . she washes her fingers of knights' blood" (KTU 1.3.II.5-40). This is the language world in which our lines are at home.

Stressing that the Lord's help reaches all the land, Mount Bashan, which stands in contrasting parallel to **the depths of the sea,** should probably be taken as *from the heights of Mount Bashan* (v 22 [23 HB]). Hence from the heights and the depths sinners will be brought back for judgment. We should probably follow Bardtke in emending the MT *ymḥṣ* (smite) to *yrḥṣ* (wash) (*BBHS*). The dogs could refer to military canines or simply street dogs (recall Jezebel's demise [2 Kgs 9:36]).

7. God's Procession through the Sanctuary (68:24-27 [25-28 HB])

■ **24 [25 HB]** **Your procession, God, has come into view** has followed the LXX, which is preferred. The worshipping throng marches around and through the sanctuary. See *IBHS* on the preposition **b-** as "through" (196). The procession specifically honors the God of Israel, identified as the personal God and king of the psalmist. The kingship of God as king of Israel has been assumed by the poem, but here for the first time is acknowledged by the psalmist himself.

■ **25 [26 HB]** Our imagination receives some confirmation regarding the sacred processional. Songsters lead the way. After them, those playing stringed instruments, along with maidens playing timbrels. The stringed instruments would be the lyres, strung with a few strings or as many as ten. (See Keel [1997, 35-52] for a rich presentation of music and instruments in ancient Israel.)

■ **26 [27 HB]** Verse 26 puzzles interpreters. In colon a, *maqhēlôt* is taken variously as **the great congregation** (NIV, RSV, LXX?), "in your choirs" (NABRE), "in assemblies" (NJPS), "in groups" (Hossfeld, ad loc.). Then in colon B, *mimmĕqôr* is rendered **the assembly of Israel** or "Israel's fountain" (ESV, LXX, NJPS, RSV), but meaning what? The fount could make sense as Jacob, the nation's fountainhead or the king or Yahweh himself or the temple. As Israel's "assemblies," *māqôr* is redundant from ring "a" of the chiasmic structure (not sure what "a" signifies). It appears that the congregation gathers to bless Yahweh. They do so as those from the fount of Israel, that is, as true Israelites.

■ **27 [28 HB]** Representatives of the tribes of Israel gather to praise. Their tribal names are called out by the psalmist, beginning with Benjamin, whose small size is noted. Princes of Judah, Zebulun, and Naphtali are mentioned. Both south and north tribes have representatives present. Benjamin either leads the procession or, less likely, sleeps (in the sense of being in a trance or an ecstatic state) through the proceedings.

8. Unveiling the Victory of God (68:28-31 [29-32 HB])

■ **28-29 [29-30 HB]** A transition from description of Yahweh's processional to speaking to God in prayer signals a new unit. The psalmist now calls to God to exhibit his strength as at other times of victory or epiphany. What events he has in mind remain unstated. Hints from the preceding verses have conjured up memory of Exodus and Sinai, of the desert trek, of the conquest and early kingdom. By now the temple explicitly figures in the story as the focus of Israel's identity among the kingdoms (1 Kgs 10:23 and earlier context).

■ **30-31 [31-32 HB]** Negatively the psalmist asks God to **rebuke** threats to Israel's welfare. **The beast among the reeds** would be treacherous **Egypt**, perpetually known for her fickle foreign alliances (compare Ezek 29:2-5). **Egypt** and **Cush** are the only parties explicitly named. The others, pictured in metaphors, we cannot identify with confidence, though the practice of presenting persons, especially leaders, as animals is common in Scripture. **The herd of bulls . . . the calves of the nations** recall the "many bulls, . . . strong bulls of Bashan" surrounding the psalmist (22:12-13 [13-14 HB]), Jeremiah's snorting stallions (Jer 8:16), and Amos' "cows of Bashan" (4:1-2).

The catalog of proposed interpretations and attendant emendations seems nearly endless. Consensus may emerge at a few points: (1) That God would demonstrate his power as in the past, because of his temple and Jerusalem. (2) That God would rebuke Egypt, Cush, and all warmongering nations. (3) That Egypt and Cush, bringing tribute, would actually submit to the rule of Israel's God.

9. Sing Praise to the Lord (68:32-35 [33-36 HB])

■ **32-33 [33-34 HB]** Three exhortations call for the worshippers to **sing praise** to God (v 32 [33 HB] [twice] and v 34 [35 HB]). Three phrases tell to whom the praise is to be directed—**to God** (v 32 [33 HB] [twice] and v 34 [35 HB]). One complex sentence gives the content of the praise, particularizing the content of **praise** to matters of strength.

Several versions ancient (LXX, Tg.) and modern (ESV, NABRE, NJPS) follow the MT in prepositioning the direct address of the parties being called to praise. Thus, the colon of v 32*a* [33*a* HB] begins: "O kingdoms of the earth, sing . . ." Accent falls therefore on the universal scope of the call. No kingdom is excluded from response to this "invitation."

<u>Sing</u> [*šîrû*] to God . . . , <u>sing praise</u> [*zammĕrû*] to the Lord (emphasis added) translates two verbs. The first simply means **sing**. The second, *zammĕrû*, is associated with stringed accompaniment, a nuance of the word itself not easily translated. The recipient of the praise is God, defined in the parallel colon as "Lord." This again is *ădônāy* in its strong sense of lordship, not a simple translation convention for the name Yahweh (that is, not LORD).

Much like v 4 [5 HB], v 33 [34 HB] reaches again to classic language borrowed from Canaanite adulation of the storm god Baal. Verse 4 had God as the one who rides on the clouds. Here the God of Israel is the one who **rides** on **the highest of the ancient heavens**. His mighty voice is the rolling thunder of the storm. These moves in naming Yahweh with "loaded" language from Canaanite theology brings that foreign thought under Yahweh's domain. Israel's monotheizing tendency surfaces here.

■ **34 [35 HB]** The theme of the songs we readers are called to sing is the strength and majesty of Israel's God. The worshipper is to attribute strength to God and to acknowledge that God's strength overshadows his people Israel. It amounts to a confession of Israel's need of this Mighty One.

■ **35 [36 HB]** The poem closes with address to **God** himself, declaring God's awesomeness in his sanctuaries. The NJPS follows the LXX in translating the MT "holy places," plural. Not just Jerusalem is in view here then, but all the places where God was worshipped and from which his majesty shows forth. The NJPS also follows the MT in the claim that God is awesome "in" his holy places, not "from his sanctuary" (most English versions). In their worship of this God, he imparts strength, power to his people. Two words conclude the psalm, ***Blessed [be] God.***

FROM THE TEXT

Psalm 68 emphasizes the majesty and glory of God, as well as his compassion for the needy and vulnerable. The writer's use of material already ancient in his own day added an archaic nuance and depth to the song. This is the god of history. The history of deliverance is rehearsed simply by allusion to key words that have been indelibly joined to the signature events of that history.

The NT's major use of Ps 68 is Paul's quotation of v 18. Paul appropriates talk of God's victory over his enemies and his receipt of tribute from his enemies (Eph 4:7-11). Interpreted christologically, the gifts become persons whom Messiah gives to his church.

Psalm 68 repeatedly places the victory of God over against acknowledged enemies. Paul does not reference our psalm at this point, but his instruction to the Ephesians in the letter shows clearly that enemies of the Christ are yet to be finally vanquished. They must be faced by his church and overcome in the armor of the Lord (Eph 6:10-20).

A Prayer from the Mire (69:1-36 [2-37 HB])

BEHIND THE TEXT

This song is already designated a prayer in v 13 [14 HB]. As much as any prayer we encounter in the Psalter, this psalm is so full of metaphor that the actual, historical situation remains mostly hidden. The psalmist prays for deliverance from sundry enemies who falsely accuse him, even mock him for his devotion to Yahweh (vv 4, 7, 9 [5, 8, 10 HB]). The psalm assumes the temple and animal sacrifice (v 29 [30 HB]). It also assumes Zion needs salvation and cities of Judah rebuilding (vv 32-36 [33-37 HB]). Some are yet in exile. Perhaps then we might locate the psalm sometime in the restoration period prior to or early in Nehemiah's ministry.

For more on the SS, see the Introduction, C.1.a, C.1.b, and C.3.f.

IN THE TEXT

1. Prayer from the Miry Pit (69:1-4 [2-5 HB])

■ **1-2 [2-3 HB]** **Save me, O God, for the waters have come up to my neck.** The opening petition is characteristic of this song. A petition addressed to God calls for salvation. The plight from which the psalmist wants deliverance is expressed in metaphoric language. That is, we take it he is not actually in water and mire up to his chin and still sinking. But the poet works the picture as far as he can, even at the expense of contradictory language. He is in "deep waters" (vv 2, 14 [3, 15 HB]), floods engulf him (vv 2, 15 [3, 16 HB]).

■ **3-4 [4-5 HB]** The rigor of his cries for salvation now occupies him. His **throat is parched**, his **eyes fail** from looking long for God to arrive. These lines do not carry the tone of complaint for God's lack of help. Instead they narrate fervent, prolonged prayer for rescue.

Enemies represent one aspect of the deep waters threatening the psalmist. These enemies are numerous—more than **the hairs** on his **head**. These are hateful, lying people, some numbered among his family (v 8 [9 HB]). They have the social wherewithal to force the psalmist, who is not a thief, to suffer the penalties of a thief. He must make restitution apparently for some other person's—the enemy's(?)—thievery.

2. God Knows the Psalmist Thoroughly (69:5-12 [6-13 HB])

■ **5-7 [6-8 HB]** In this world of counterclaims about the psalmist it is important for him to recall God knows him precisely. He does not here set himself up as a moral example. Instead, he implicitly confesses folly and also **guilt** over some unspecified sins (v 5 [6 HB]). (The noun for **guilt** is actually plural, perhaps indicating multiple causes of guilt.) But God's complete knowledge of him appears to support these disclosures.

The psalmist is concerned about the possibility that he may prove an embarrassment or a cause of **shame** to persons who hope in God (v 6 [7 HB]). He packs the B cola of these lines with names for God, thus bringing God and Israel's history with God into the psalmist's present moment.

■ **8-12 [9-13 HB]** For some reason it is because of his relationship with God that he is under reproach, even with his **own family** (v 8 [9 HB]). He does not explain clearly how this transpires. He does claim that his zeal for the temple, God's **house**, has consumed him and that the reproach of persons who suffer reproach has fallen on him (v 9 [10 HB]). Exactly what this means remains unclear, though his participation in some rituals like fasting brings reproach on him. When he puts on **sackcloth** these people mock him, making a joke of his attempts to worship (v 11 [12 HB]). Respectable citizens in the city **gate** and reprobate **drunkards** alike have made him the brunt of their humor (v 12 [13 HB]).

3. From the Miry Pit Again (69:13-18 [14-19 HB])

■ **13-15 [14-16 HB]** Over against these points of misery, the psalmist again lodges his prayer for deliverance. He looks to the loving-kindness of God and his **favor** as the basis for his hope to be heard. This renewed emphasis on his petitions returns to the vocabulary and pictures of the first few verses of the psalm, almost a refrain.

■ **16-18 [17-19 HB]** Again the psalmist pleads to be heard and grounds his prayer in the character of God. God's loving-kindness and compassion provide the confidence he needs to ask again for rescue.

4. God Knows the Psalmist's Need (69:19-28 [20-29 HB])

■ **19-21 [20-22 HB]** The prepositioned, lead pronoun signals the beginning of a new unit in the psalm, this one focused again on God's intimate knowledge of the psalmist's plight. He is ashamed, embarrassed, always aware of his enemies. **Scorn has broken my heart**, concedes the poet. His will to stay focused on God is challenged. Hope-draining reversals abound. He hopes for a meal of condolence and comfort but finds none (v 20 [21 HB]). Instead he suffers attacks on his person; his enemies feed him tainted food and bitter drinks (v 21 [22 HB]).

■ **22-26 [23-27 HB]** The psalmist prays that his enemies will taste the sort of reversals he has endured. A table set for a meal will prove to be a **snare**, yes, even a **trap** (v 22 [23 HB]. Their **eyes** will fail to see, their loins continually in upheaval (v 23 [24 HB]). He implores God to pour out his **anger** on these enemies of his, leaving their dwellings in shambles (vv 24-25 [25-26 HB]). They have the unmitigated arrogance of persecuting further persons (like the psalmist?) who are already under the chastisement of God (v 26 [27 HB]).

■ **27-28 [28-29 HB]** The psalmist wants God in two ways to use God's thorough knowledge of the psalmist's plight to make his innocence and the enemies' guilt clear to everyone in the community. On the one hand, he calls for God to **charge** these liars with the many crimes of which they are guilty (v 27 [28 HB]). On the other hand, he wants their names **blotted out of the book of life**, and they **not be listed with the righteous** (v 28 [29 HB]). The **book of life** would have been an earthly representation of a heavenly copy (compare Exod 32:32-34), listing those granted life by Yahweh and hence persons legitimately members of the covenant community. This book served a purpose different from the heavenly chronicles that, like royal chronicles, inscribed admirable deeds done by people on behalf of or to be remembered by the king (compare Mal 3:16-17; Esth 6:1-3).

5. All the Earth Will Praise Yahweh (69:29-36 [30-37 HB])

■ **29-31 [30-32 HB]** Once again the psalmist signals a turn in his thinking by bringing the personal pronoun to the head of the sentence. ***As for me, I am poor and in pain***. Turning from his desires for the enemies, he confesses his own need of deliverance. As one of the poor ('*ānî*) he is open to the whole range of physical and social suffering. His prayer is that Yahweh's saving presence would **protect** him (v 29 [30 HB]).

He wants to/promises to **praise** the **name** of Yahweh, that is, praise the person and character of Yahweh (v 30 [31 HB]). In singing/song and in thanksgiving (i.e., with the *tôdâ*) he will praise Yahweh. The Todah quite likely here would be the Todah offering, where the praise itself is the sacrifice. The claim that Yahweh deems this offering more desirable **than an ox** or **a bull** with horn and hoof makes that clear (v 31 [32 HB]).

■ **32-33 [33-34 HB]** The **poor**/*the needy* will rejoice, not simply as people of need but as persons who seek God and whose hearts come alive in this pursuit. To have the heart "come alive" here, one suspects, would mean to be refreshed, revived (v 32 [33 HB]). This blessed reality finds support in Yahweh's identity as the one known to listen to the poor, to attend to those in bondage (v 33 [34 HB]).

■ **34-36 [35-37 HB]** Now the horizon broadens to all creation as the source of Yahweh's praise. As though reading from Gen 1 the poet says **heaven and earth** will **praise** Yahweh, then **the seas** and all the life that moves in them (v 34 [35 HB]).

Then comes *kî* as either **for God will save Zion**, stating the reason for the lavish praise just announced, or ***but* God will save Zion** in contrast to the creation-wide praise here not tied to salvation (v 35 [36 HB]). We follow the LXX and most English versions reading **for**. The restoration of Zion and the cities of Judah is sufficiently momentous as to generate praise from all creation.

A lengthy tricolon (3 + 3 + 3) (vv 35*c*, 36*a*, 36*b* [36*c*, 37*a*, 37*b* HB]) concludes this prayer song. Without prior notice we are taken back to Israel's beginnings and the promises made there. "Possession," "inheritance," and "dwelling" is the language of those historic promises. These words are also the language of Israel's renewal as the nation was being taken captive in exile and at the same time being promised a return to (i.e., repossession of) the land.

FROM THE TEXT

The NT's appropriation of Ps 69 has surprising breadth and variety, running all the way from allusion to verbatim quotation. Following the order of the psalm itself, these appropriations are as follows:

Psalm 69:4 in John 15:25. Jesus quotes this verse to explain the Jewish rejection he and his disciples experience. He cites the psalm as "Torah/law," and sees the Jewish behavior as "fulfillment" of that Torah.

Psalm 69:9 in John 2:17. When Jesus cleared the temple of merchants, the disciples recalled the psalm's text about zeal for God's house consuming the psalmist. After the resurrection, reflecting on Jesus' words about rebuilding the temple, the disciples are said to have "believed" both the Scripture and Jesus' word.

Psalm 69:9 in Rom 15:3. Quoting our passage with the formal citation rubric, "as it is written," Paul uses the psalm to buttress his exhortation to follow Christ in a Christian response to reproach.

Psalm 69:21. The Synoptic Gospel writers do not quote or paraphrase 69:21 in the telling of Jesus being offered strong drink as he suffered on the cross. Informed readers will no doubt see an allusion to the psalmist's words. See Matt 27:34, 48; Mark 15:23, 36; Luke 23:36.

Although John does not quote or allude to the psalm text (69:21) in John 19:29, it is clear he intends his reader to connect the goings on at the cross regarding wine/vinegar with this passage. In fact, according to John, Jesus did speak and act in certain ways with awareness of his participation in the "fulfillment" of Scripture and for the purpose of accomplishing that fulfillment. This would caution us against seeing the concept of "fulfillment" of Scripture as a causal force somehow independent of the choices of persons involved in those fulfillments.

Psalm 69:22-23 in Rom 11:8-10. In the process of arguing for the faithfulness of God, Paul quotes the psalmist's lines about providential reversals—a table becoming a snare, eyes unable to see. The psalmist intends these to be judgment, retribution for the wicked. Paul redirects these lines and uses them to warn Jews and Gentiles against misunderstanding the nature of divine election and of their participation in it.

Psalm 69:25 in Acts 1:20. Luke has Peter quoting our psalm to explain (note the "for . . .") the unfortunate fate of Judas and Ps 109:8 to endorse the church's action to fill his office now deserted (Acts 1:23-26). Though Peter quotes both Ps. 69:25*a* and 25*b*, it is only v 25*a* that applies. See Craig Keener's extensive discussion of this text and issues surrounding it (2012, 765-68).

Psalm 69:28. Referring to the Book of Life, the psalmist taps into a tradition that endures to the present. The Jewish and Christian communities both spoke of God maintaining a book in which the names of all bona fide members of their respective groups were written. As our psalmist had it, to have one's name in the book meant to "be listed with the righteous." He assumes God has the right both to inscribe one's name in the book and also to blot it out, presumably terminating one's place in the community.

Christians brought the concept directly into their use. A chief development is that now the Son also has the prerogative of inscribing and also of expunging names from the book (Rev 3:5). Persons who worshipped the beast would not be in the book (Rev 13:8; 17:8). At the great white throne judgment, one's place or lack of it in the book will determine everlasting fate (Rev 20:11-15). As a matter of fact, so significant is the role of the Lamb in all of these proceedings that it finally becomes the Lamb's Book of Life (Rev 21:27).

Hebrew Scriptures also know of a book or set of books separate from the Book of Life. More than a list of names, these books were thought to be analogous to the Royal Chronicles or Annals that contained record of the king's exploits. The Chronicles also recorded deeds of royal subjects that were thought to be of particular interest to the crown (Esth 6:1-2). The record for remembrance in Mal 3:16 could have been such a chronicle.

A Prayer of Petitions (70:1-5 [2-6 HB])

BEHIND THE TEXT

Psalm 70 is an almost exact duplicate of Ps 40:13-17 [14-18 HB]. The compositional relationship between the two is debated. Zenger is probably correct in arguing that the elegance of the chiastic structure of Ps 70 supports its composition as a discrete work. This artistry is more likely to have stood on its own than to have been extracted from a larger piece that did not as a whole exhibit the same complexity (Hossfeld and Zenger 2005, 187-88). See the treatment of this issue also at Ps 40.

IN THE TEXT

The chiastic structure referred to above does not exhibit a meticulously balanced passage. It does have sufficient precision as to put the two halves of the psalm in clear conversation with each other. Verses 1-3 [2-4 HB] speak mainly to the behaviors and destiny of the wicked. Verses 4-5 [5-6 HB] speak primarily regarding the petitioner and his community. Vocabulary, form, and syntax are all involved simultaneously in the chiasm as follows:

Imperative "hasten" (vv 1*a*, 5*b* [2*a*, 6*b* HB])

My "help" (vv 1*b*, 5*c* [2*b*, 6*c* HB])

"Ones who seek" (vv 2*b*, 4*b* [3*b*, 5*b* HB]), "who desire" (v 2*d* [3*d* HB]), and "who love" (v 4*d* [5*d* HB]), in ptcs.

"Shame" vocabulary (vv 2, 4 [3, 5 HB]; no "shame" in v 4 [5 HB]) versus "joy/gladness" vocabulary (v 4 [5 HB])

"Fall back," "delay" (vv 2*c*, 5*d* [3*c*, 6*d* HB])

"Say" (vv 3*b*, 4*c* [4*b*, 5*c* HB]

Jussives (vv 2*a*, 2*c*, 3*c*, 4*a*, 4*c*, 5*d* [3*a*, 3*c*, 4*c*, 5*a*, 5*c*, 6*d* HB])

We have refrained from using more technical lenses in analyzing the chiastic structure of this brief passage. Limitations of space do not allow even this sort of analysis, abbreviated as it may be, on every verse of the Psalter. Nevertheless, this is enough to remind us of the complex, multifaceted nature of poetic parallelism in Hebrew, with several different aspects of the language engaged in heightening the impact of the petitions and praises of these poems.

■ **1-3 [2-4 HB]** In Yahweh the psalmist finds his much-needed help, rescue from persons who wish him ill. His prayer primarily for their humiliation involves, of course, his own vindication.

■ **4-5 [5-6 HB]** Over against the mockery of those set against him stands an affirmation of God's greatness. This orientation clearly confesses the psalmist's need, while at the same time expressing his confidence in Yahweh as his help.

See the comments on Ps 40:13-17 for more interpretive treatment of this passage.

FROM THE TEXT

Psalm 70 could be a template for the standard prayer song. At key points—the specific plight threatening the psalmist, the particular deliverance desired, the identity of the psalmist and his company and that of his enemies—we have general, place-holding language, so-called stock vocabulary and phrases. This allows the worshippers to fill the generalizations with content from their own lives. Interestingly, the more general the poem, the more specific the appropriation is possible. When space is provided, readers make the psalm their own.

The template also instructs as to the agendas that need to be included in such a prayer. The problem(s) confronting the petitioner, the identity of the petitioner and the petitioner's community, the identity of the one to whom petition is made, the grounds on which the petitions stand, and the consequences at stake—these are all appropriate for inclusion in a prayer psalm. They remain agendas for Christian prayer as well.

A Prayer for Approaching Old Age (71:1-24)

BEHIND THE TEXT

Treating Ps 70 we noted the language shared with Ps 71. Psalm 71 actually shares language with several other preceding psalms as follows:

persons who seek (ptc.)	71:13, 24; 70:3, 5 [4, 6 HB]; 69:7 [8 HB]; 40:15, 17 [16, 18 HB]; 38:13 [14 HB]; 35:4
shame, disgrace	71:13, 24; 70:3 [4 HB]; 69:7 [8 HB], 19, 20 [20, 21 HB]; 40:15 [16 HB]; 38:4 [5 HB]; 35:4, 26
continually	71:3, 6, 14; 70:5 [6 HB]; 69:23 [24 HB]; 38:13 [14 HB]
righteousness	71:2, 15, 16, 19, 24; 69:17 [18 HB]; 36:2, 6 [3, 7 HB]; 31:1 [2 HB]

In addition, note shared language between Ps 71:5-6, 17 and Ps 22:9-10 [10-11 HB]; Ps 71:12a and Ps 22:1, 11, 19 [2, 12, 20 HB]; Ps 71:18 and Ps 22:30-31 [31-32 HB] (following Tate 1990, 204-5, 211-13, for the preceding references). It proves easier to observe these similarities and their proximity to the close of Books I and II than it is to discern the significance. The references to psalms immediately preceding the ends of Books I and II, that is, those in Pss 38 and 40 along with Pss 69, 70, and 71 invite reflection.

Packed as Ps 71 is with repeated language, some have suggested that the piece is simply a repository of stock language. Most interpreters have thought the poem shows more movement and purpose than that. It exhibits the marks of a prayer designed not necessarily for use in the midst of a crisis but in anticipation of such times. Its abundant affirmation of anticipated salvation gives the psalm as a whole a hopeful air.

IN THE TEXT

1. Concerns of One Growing Old (71:1-8)

■ **1-4** The psalmist affirms his trust in Yahweh, a trust lived out in his taking refuge in him. The language of having **taken refuge** in Yahweh brings the reader all the way back to 2:12 and places the psalmist on the side of those approved and blessed by God (71:1a). Note also his identification of Yahweh as his **refuge** (v 7).

These prayers call Yahweh to snatch him [from danger] (v 1), make an escape for him (v 1), make a deliberate effort to listen to him (v 1b), and save him (v 2).

On the basis of his declared stance, he petitions God. These he grounds in part in who and what God actually represents to him. God constitutes his solid rock, his *cleft in a rock*, his **fortress** (v 3). Although these images overlap, still they evoke different pictures of God's rescue of him. As **rock** God presents solid ground on which he can stand in the torrents of life. As a cleft in the rock, Yahweh is the split in the cliff that allows him *a cranny* to which to cling, out of the reach of others. The **fortress** assumes attack and stands as protection against those assaults. A tricolon in v 3 underscores these realities.

His opening petition was that, because of his refuge in Yahweh, he would **never be put to shame** (v 1). This implies adversaries that he proceeds to name.

These are the **wicked** (v 4), *perverse and oppressive persons* (evil and cruel), people who *post a guard against [his] life* (v 10), *constant accusers* (v 13), *persons who seek ill for [him]* (v 13). He is shamed, put under reproach when these persons have their destructive way. Verses 13 and 24 bracket the last half of the psalm with identical descriptors of his foes—**those who want[ed] to harm me**—linked with their being **put to shame**.

Judging from the talk of these adversaries, converse in which they seem to speak as Yahweh followers, these adversaries may well be competing sectors of the community. They may be foes inside the community, not adversaries outside the temple or the city. Or perhaps Mowinckel was correct in locating the communities involved in this psalm in groups of faithful Israelites not centered in Jerusalem or the temple. These circumstances could suggest a setting in the unsettled and disappointing years of the early postexile (as summarized in Tate 1990, 212-13).

His petitions flow from the character of God, hence he prays, **In your righteousness, rescue me** (v 2). This poem's interest in the concept of Yahweh's righteousness begins here. At times Yahweh's righteousness as tantamount to his righteous deliverance comes to the fore (vv 15, 16, 19). Elsewhere **righteousness** as a character trait itself of Israel's God is more to the point (vv 2, 24).

■ **5-8** All of these preceding affirmations and petitions the psalmist supports by the fact that Yahweh is his hope. This is not just his present claim. He has trusted Yahweh since his **youth** and before, leaned on him from his **mother's womb**. Yahweh has been his strength/protector (with the LXX for the MT 'ôzî) from his infancy.

We have here then not simply the prayer of a naive worshipper, precious as that would have been. Instead we have the prayer and affirmations of one approaching old age. He has considerable experience and still looks upon his life as continual **praise** to Yahweh (v 6). So significant has been Yahweh's work in his life that our supplicant has become something of a **sign to many** around him, because of his reliance upon Yahweh as his **strong refuge** (v 7). Since the term

sign is usually associated with judgments, perhaps his rescue has been a warning to his foes, or, perhaps the occasion of the adversities revealed at the outset.

The concluding line of this paragraph finds him full of **praise**, all the time (v 8). This note of praise found also in v 6 gives the prayer a buoyant note.

2. Prayer for Protection against Antagonists (71:9-13)

■ **9-13** His petition not to be **cast . . . away** responds to the taunt of his adversaries (vv 9, 11). Together they claim Yahweh actually has forsaken him. Some adversity or difficulty has apparently convinced them our psalmist no longer has Yahweh's favor. So they incite others to take advantage of his perceived isolation. ***Chase him! Seize him!*** they urge (v 11).

He wants Yahweh to attend to him during the dwindling strength of old age. These will be days of increased vulnerability. Against his enemies' predictions, he begs God to rush to his rescue, to be dramatically present—not apparently absent! Mays reminds us that old age has also served as a metaphor describing a community in decline (1994b, 235).

3. A Foundation in Yahweh's Righteousness (71:14-19)

■ **14-15** Shifting now from major attention to his adversaries the psalmist emphatically (by prepositioning the pronoun) declares his hope in the Lord together with his growing praise of Yahweh. He will recount God's "righteousness." Parallel as it is to God's **saving acts**, the term ***righteousness*** in v 15*a* must have in mind God's **saving acts**. This is strengthened by the parallel with "marvelous deeds" in v 17*b*. These marvels he cannot adequately recount.

■ **16** The poet anticipates entry to the place of worship and witness. He will bring to mind Yahweh's righteousness and his **alone**. Here Yahweh's righteous character is no doubt in mind, the one alone whose character gives rise to the deliverance he has experienced and now needs once more.

■ **17-19** Again the psalmist claims his walk with God has spanned his entire life, from **youth** to the present (v 7). From earliest days God has ***instructed*** him. Judging from this psalm, how would God have instructed him? Through the testimony of others who, like him, have recounted the mighty deeds of Yahweh? Through the repertoire of music he himself will imbibe (vv 22-23)?

These affirmations are now matched by his petitions that God never forsake him, even in his old age (v 18). This older saint moves immediately to intergenerational concerns. He himself will declare Yahweh's might to generations coming. Perhaps there is a third topic to which he promises witness—God's righteous deeds whose reputation is as high as the heaven (v 19*a*). Bardtke positions the MT this way (*BBHS*, ad loc.). Quite likely, however, with most English versions we should connect these words with the following lines, with v 19*a* as the first colon in a tricolon.

Where the paragraph break should stand here remains problematic. I am inclined to let the tricolon in v 19 signal the close of a paragraph. The *'ăšer* at the front of v 20 is difficult any way we go here. Bardtke prefers deleting it for metrical reasons. It may simply be the relative pronoun, parallel to the relative clause in v 19 as in the LXX; so most English versions. In this case the two relative clauses, in v 19 and v 20, should be put in the same paragraph. Perhaps it signals a concessive clause. Then we translate, with the NIV and Tate (1990, 210, n. 20a), though I do not find evidence that *'ăšer* functions as a concessive particle. The word is sufficiently intrusive that, for now, I am following Bardtke in deleting it. The clause opens the final paragraph, which includes note of the many adversities through which Yahweh has led the psalmist.

4. Anticipation of Lavish Praise (71:20-24)

■ **20-21** The poet registers the fact that, over the span of his long devotion, Yahweh has led him into hardships many and difficult. To be more precise, he speaks here for the community, if, as we probably should, we read the consonantal text's plural suffixes on the two verbs. **You have made *us* see troubles . . . you will restore *our* life again.**

If the **depths of the earth** is Sheol, then our supplicant has been brought near death.

The *yqtl* verbs signal future here (**will restore; will . . . bring me up; will increase . . . and comfort me**) and as such they locate the psalmist. He is even now in one of the difficulties of which he just spoke. But he is confident of Yahweh's saving grace.

■ **22** Whereas he has just affirmed his confidence in Yahweh's deliverance, he pledges also his own **praise** to Yahweh. With delightfully accompanied song he will play and sing Yahweh's liberating integrity. It is possible that the praise exalts not simply Yahweh's integrity, his truthfulness. The word in question (*'ĕmet*) can also name Yahweh's faithfulness to his covenant promise and to all his oaths to the fathers (as in Mic 7:20).

■ **23-24** An emphatic particle (*gam*) brackets like a package the psalmist's enthusiastic anticipation of his praise of Yahweh. He will be fully engaged—his **lips** (v 23), his soul (v 23), his **tongue** (v 24) joining in praise. As anticipated in Ps 1:2, this righteous man spends his time pondering Yahweh's righteousness, mulling over it. He is reciting, singing to himself and others (the **tongue** is engaged! [v 24]). The vocabulary of **righteousness** makes the final entry in a theme begun in v 2. **Those who wanted to harm me** brackets v 24 with v 13, tying off the last half of the poem, while the **shame** vocabulary takes us back to v 1 with evidence Yahweh has heard that prayer never to be put to shame.

FROM THE TEXT

As we have seen, Ps 71 shares sentences and motifs with Pss 22 and 31, among others. With them Ps 71 has been associated with Jesus' passion and the services of Holy Week. In the common lectionary, Ps 71 is set for Tuesday of Holy Week (Mays 1994b, 234). The psalmist's talk of singing to accompaniment of harp and lyre (v 22) likely places him among the musicians of a temple guild. He is in the business of writing worship materials for others.

At the same time, however, repeatedly throughout the psalm he prays for himself. Moreover he confesses feeling he was a portent to the community, most likely thought to be a sign of God's displeasure, posing something of a conundrum, because of his faithfulness to God. When the psalm is related to Jesus during Holy Week it also calls for response. Following Jesus we are all portents for someone (Mays 1994b, 235-36).

A Song for the King (72:1-20)

BEHIND THE TEXT

Whether *By Solomon* or *For Solomon* or *About Solomon* the SS invites readers to connect this poem with Israel's most famous king. The NIV's **Of Solomon** conveys the openness toward the question of Solomon's actual relationship to the poem. *Selâh*. Only Ps 127 has a similar attribution. The later one goes in the period of the formation of the Psalter, the more extensive the information included in the SSs becomes. Thus the Targum to this psalm has it by the hand of Solomon, a prophecy concerning the Messiah. There is no reason why the song could not have been written either by or for Solomon on the occasion of his coronation (Kidner 1973, 253-55). Evidence does not permit confidence on these questions and other possible settings could be proposed.

Israel crafted her understanding of kingship in part from her surrounding neighbors, that is, especially from Egypt, Canaan, and Mesopotamian influences. It has been compared especially to later Neo-Assyrian royal compositions; this may be true but not necessarily so. Already David's kingdom and especially Solomon's was heavily indebted to Egypt for concepts of kingship and administrative structures for governing the kingdom. The use made of these neighboring traditions often posed a critique of foreign monarchs, especially the Neo-Assyrian tyrants.

The prayers regarding the king's longevity paralleling or exceeding that of the sun is significant in view of two realities. First the vigorous engagement of the divine Sun with kingship in Egypt (Re) and Mesopotamia (Shamash) makes the lack of that engagement in Ps 72 worth reflection. Second, the solarization of Yahweh during some periods especially of the kingdom of Judah makes the lack of interaction between the sun and the king telling and suggests a polemic stance against Yahweh as sun (compare 2 Kgs 23:11; and Ezek 8).

Closing Book II of the Psalter as it does, Ps 72 carries an ironic celebration of Kingship. The colophon following the psalm itself announces the conclusion of the prayers of David son of Jesse, Israel's first great king (v 20). The editors of the Psalter have placed this work in tandem with Ps 89, the conclusion of Book III or the Psalter. This editorial move prompts reflection on the nature and promise of kingship, since Ps 89 carries a strident examination of the Davidic kingship, fractured by the defeat of Judah and the apparent betrayal of the Davidic covenant.

IN THE TEXT

I. The Promise of the King (72:1-4)

■ **1-2 Endow the king with your justice, O God.** The psalm begins with this direct petition, the only such petition in the entire poem, except for the repetition of the prayer assumed in the ellipsis in v 1*b*: *And with righteousness [endow] the king's son*. This foundational prayer is followed in the psalm by a series of verbs open with few exceptions to being translated either by simple futures, **He will judge your people**, or by jussives expressing a wish or a request, **May he judge**. Which is to be preferred is a moot question, even when the form is explicitly future as it is in v 2, *yādîn*.

Goldingay takes the form as evidence that the series of verbs through at least the first section (vv 1-8) should be taken as simple futures (2007, 383). The NIV 1984 edition, for example, translates v 2, "He will judge your people," with the jussive **May he** placed in a footnote. But the 2011 NIV reads **May he judge**, with no note; similarly the RSV and others. The REB takes v 2 as a purpose clause, as does the LXX, "That he may govern" (REB, perhaps LXX). I am inclined to follow the MT futures through the first four verses, and with the LXX to read vv 3 and 4 as purpose clauses subordinate to the first two lines. At v 5 jussive readings seem more appropriate.

Set aside as it is by form and syntax, v 1 makes the foundational petition that God grant the king God's own **justice** and **righteousness**. It is a prayer that the God who installed him in his place of governance will also equip him with character to rule God's people with equity. In so doing the poet taps into the widespread conviction in the ancient world that fair governance, especially of the poor and downtrodden, was the peculiar duty of the king.

■ **3** Within the first three verses three chief aspects of ideal kingship surface: Yahweh's justice (*mišpāṭ*), Yahweh's righteousness (*sĕdāqâh*), and pervasive well-being (*šālôm*). The picture of the mountains carrying or bearing well-being for the people is not immediately transparent. Perhaps the fruit of the king's governance in righteousness and justice is that the hills are covered with *shalom* as they would be with trees and crops and herds. Creation itself responds to congruence in the moral order.

■ **4** Particularly important was the king's responsibility to stand against those in the community prone to abuse their power, especially in court. He must deliver legal judgments protecting the poor and marginalized, persons so easily sold out with bribes and backroom deals buying off the wealthy (compare Amos 2:6-8; Mic 2:1-5).

In these opening petitions for Yahweh to intervene in the life of the king on behalf of his people we encounter a point of critical difference between kingship in Israel and that among her neighbors (Zenger in Hossfeld and Zenger 2005, 210-11). In Egypt, for example, as in Israel the gods, especially the sun god Re, were involved in the establishing of kingship but were little engaged in the life of the king beyond that. The king was the gods' delegated representative and responsible for ruling in their behalf.

Here, in contrast, Yahweh is asked to enter the king's life for the sake of the realm, especially the poor. The petitions in v 4 are underscored by a tricolon, and the first four lines bracketed by another tricolon in v 1 (mentioned again in vv 12-14).

2. The Longevity of the King (72:5-7)

■ **5** The MT's *They will/may they fear you* (v 5*a*) seems out of place and *before the moon* (v 5*b*) makes little sense. A slight emendation following the LXX prays for the king to endure as long as the sun. Most versions simply ignore the preposition *before* and render **as long as the moon** [endures] or the like.

■ **6** The renewing of the land that attends the king's rule is likened to the refreshment of **rain** on mown grass, like **showers** soaking the land. That fertility may attend his rule is the prayer.

■ **7** In his days may **righteousness** flourish *like fresh sprouting plants, with abundant well-being until* the moon is no more. Though the images are cryptic, the overall picture is reasonably clear. The prayer is for fresh and enduring well-being and righteousness in this king's reign, with an emphasis on the endless days of the king. The endless rule of the king is one of the points where Israel's talk of kingship engaged in hyperbole common among her neighbors.

3. The Realm of the King (72:8-11)

■ **8** When Yahweh answers this prayer the king will rule from the Mediterranean to the Dead Sea, from the Euphrates down to the Brook of Egypt. He will, in effect, govern the territory promised to Abraham's offspring (Gen 15:18-20). Solomon already briefly held most of this land (1 Kgs 4:21).

▪ **9-11** Verses 9-11 unpack the general vision of v 8, detailing key protocols that will attend this rule. Thus **desert tribes** would **bow before him, . . . his enemies *licking* the dust**. Dramatic portrayal of this sort of subservience comes to us on Shalmaneser III's black obelisk, where Jehu king of Israel is portrayed bowing before the Assyrian monarch (*ANEP*, 120-22). Often the subjects' bowing prostrate before the Great King accompanied the giving of state gifts or, with a different political message, tribute imposed upon the "donor." Art from Egypt repeatedly brings these themes together and puts modern readers "on location" for these ceremonies (v 9). (See Keel 1997, 304-6.)

Throughout these verses kings from all points of the compass, near and far, are represented in the mention of those bringing gifts. Note the rhyme between vv 9*a* and 10*a*, between **desert tribes/***ṣiyyîm* and ***distant Western Isles/*** *'iyyîm*. Arabian nations north and south on the peninsula also play with sounds: *Šĕbā'* and *Sĕbā'* (v 10). Then bursting the boundaries of reality he prays that **all kings . . . and all nations** would bow to him and serve him, hyperbole of place now matching that of character.

4. The Compassion of the King (72:12-17)

▪ **12-14** What we might have observed in the preceding lines the psalmist now prays plainly—that the king may rescue the ends of the earth, the distant rulers and lands. These persons are crying out, but they have no one to hear them, none **to help** (v 12). The king for whom this prayer is prayed manifests a critical point of difference with the great kings of Egypt and Mesopotamia whose literary, conceptual influence has been clear. The lands conquered by Egyptian and Mesopotamian monarchs were drained of their resources—precious metals, aromatic woods, spices. But Israel's king, it is prayed, will act out of compassion and pity for the lands he will conquer (vv 12-16). He will **save** those he conquers, redeeming (i.e., liberating) them (v 13). He will take them from a culture of violence. All of these strange actions will flow from his regard for the "little ones" of the realm (v 14).

▪ **15** The supplicant prays that generosity of the king will elicit the unending prayers of the royal subjects, blessing themselves daily. We are reminded of the promise to Abram that all the earth's families would bless themselves in Abram's name (Gen 12:3).

▪ **16** The poet begins a recapitulation of the prayer, turning again to the fertility and fruitfulness that attends this king's rule. The key verb in v 16*a* is a hapax legomenon of uncertain meaning. The derivations proposed from either Egyptian or Ugaritic sources seem reasonable (compare *HALOT*, 947). In v

16b the MT's *mē'îr* is also troublesome. Parsing it as an H ptc. of *'wr* would yield **awakening** in the sense of sprouting, prospering, thus **may it come alive like the grass of the ground.**

◼ 17 The psalmist returns to the theme of the longevity of the king's reign. **May his name endure forever; may it continue as long as the sun.** Zenger calls attention to an Egyptian ceremony in which the new king adopts a throne name. More than a simple name, the "throne name" is actually a program for governance adopted for the king's rule. Here in Ps 72 and elsewhere, the king is closely associated with symbols of a fruitful and "eternal" reign (2005, 217). The Egyptian ceremony and our psalm of course cannot be identified without remainder. But it does seem likely that reference to the king's name in our psalm is probably more nuanced and potent than simply the king's personal identity. The character of his rule is at issue and that of his offspring. The king as the chosen instrument of Yahweh's blessing of all the world surfaces one more time. Again the parallel with the blessing of Abraham is significant.

5. Colophon to Book II and the Prayers of David Son of Jesse (72:18-20)

◼ 18 By virtue of their role as colophon to Book II of the Psalter these lines are not tied structurally to Ps 72 alone. They are to be read in light of all the material that precedes and also follows them. Verses 18 and 19 praise the God of Israel in the language of blessing. They focus on Yahweh's unique capacity to act in behalf of the needy among his people.

◼ 19 Verse 19 praises Yahweh's **glorious name** in the form of a blessing and in the desire that all the **earth be filled** with God's radiance, taking **glory** in the sense of radiance known from Isa 6:1-4. The two lines in Ps 72:18-19 parallel closely the blessing in 41:13 [14 HB] that concludes Book I, leading us to think we have here the scribal note ending Book II.

◼ 20 The note that **This concludes the prayers of David son of Jesse** applies most likely to the whole of Books I and II. In these selections all but a few carry the attribution "Of David" (1, 2, 10, 33, 43, 71, and 72), with the number of Davidic psalms reduced significantly in Books III-V. The scribal note thus closes these two books as a single anthology and opens the way for the corpuses of Asaph (Pss 73—83) and of the Sons of Korah (Pss 84, 85, 87, 88) in Book III.

FROM THE TEXT

The NT writers use lines from Ps 72 in treating both "ends" of the incarnation. On the one hand, Zechariah, John the Baptist's father, quotes 72:18 to open his song celebrating the God of Israel's redemptive intervention in the births of John and Jesus (Luke 1:68). On the other hand, John the Revelator finds lines in Ps 72:10-11 eminently suitable to describe the flow into the new Jerusalem of the glory and honor of the nations in the consummation of all history (Rev 21:26).

Perhaps the most significant NT development of the themes of Ps 72 has to do with the so-called royal hyperboles encountered in this psalm, exaggerated statements concerning the chronological length and the geophysical and political breadth sought for the king in this prayer. "May he endure as long as the sun, . . . through all generations" goes the prayer (v 5). "May he rule from sea to sea . . . to the ends of the earth" (v 8). That all kings would stream to his throne with tribute in hand is the dream (vv 11, 14). These are prayerful hopes for a king never yet seen.

In the NT these hyperboles have become realities. The unending reign of the Son of God, Israel's Messiah, has begun. That it will never end is the promise of God to all who believe. Having conquered sin and death, he now sits at the right hand of the Father. What once was hyperbole has become saving reality in Jesus of Nazareth.

www.ingramcontent.com/pod-product-compliance
Lightning Source LLC
Chambersburg PA
CBHW070300240426
43661CB00057B/2603